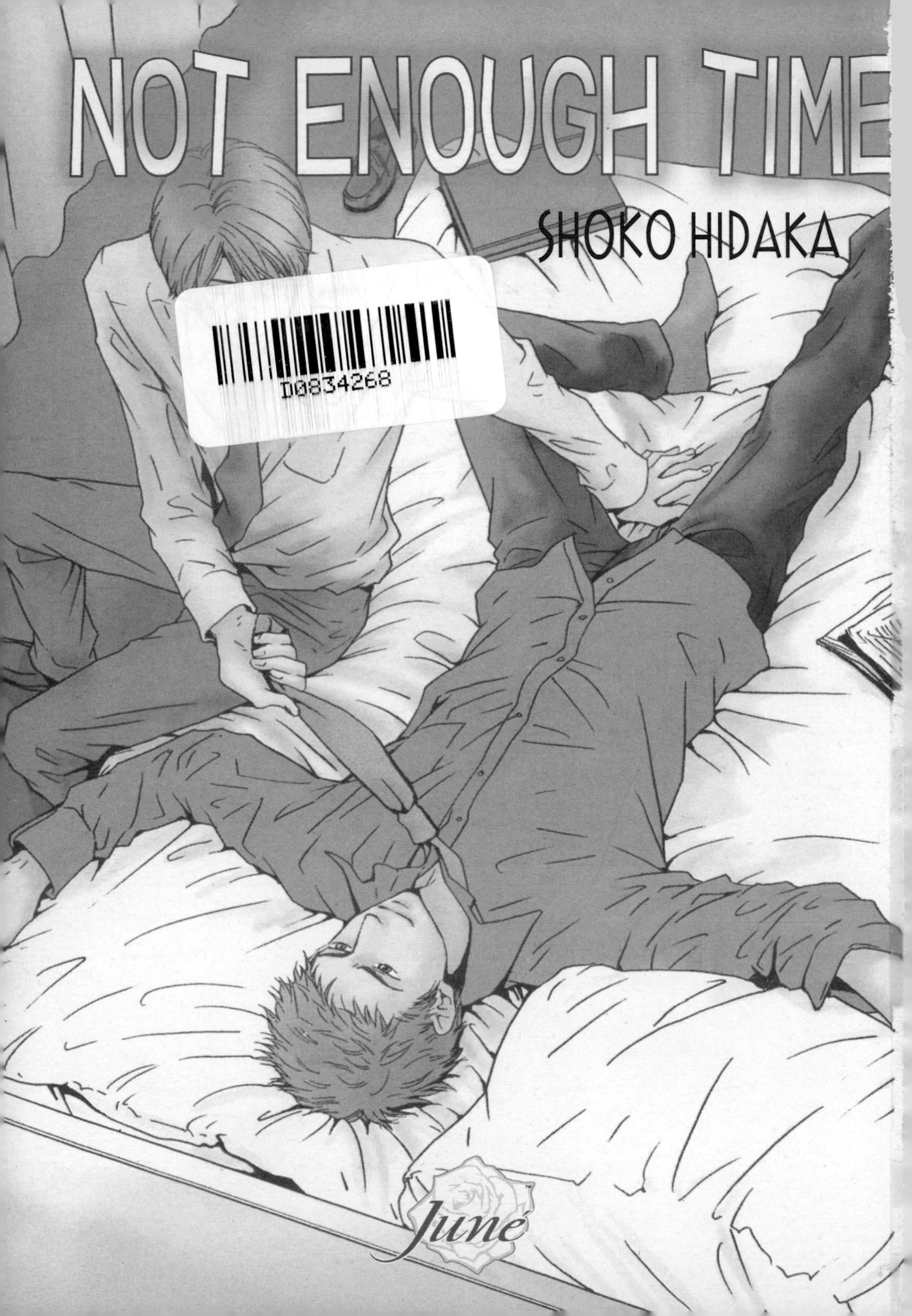
NOT ENOUGH TIME
SHOKO HIDAKA
D0834268
Juné

NOT ENOUGH TIME

TRANSLATION	EMILY OHNO
LETTERING	SAIF EBRAHIM
GRAPHIC DESIGN/LAYOUT	WENDY LEE/FRED LUI
SCRIPTING	WENDY LEE
EDITOR IN CHIEF	FRED LUI
PUBLISHER	HIKARU SASAHARA

ENGLISH EDITION PUBLISHED BY
DIGITAL MANGA PUBLISHING
A DIVISION OF DIGITAL MANGA, INC.
1487 W 178TH STREET, SUITE 300
GARDENA, CA 90248

WWW.DMPBOOKS.COM

FIRST EDITION: JULY 2007
ISBN-10: 1-56970-817-7
ISBN-13: 978-1-56970-817-0

1 3 5 7 9 10 8 6 4 2

PRINTED IN CHINA

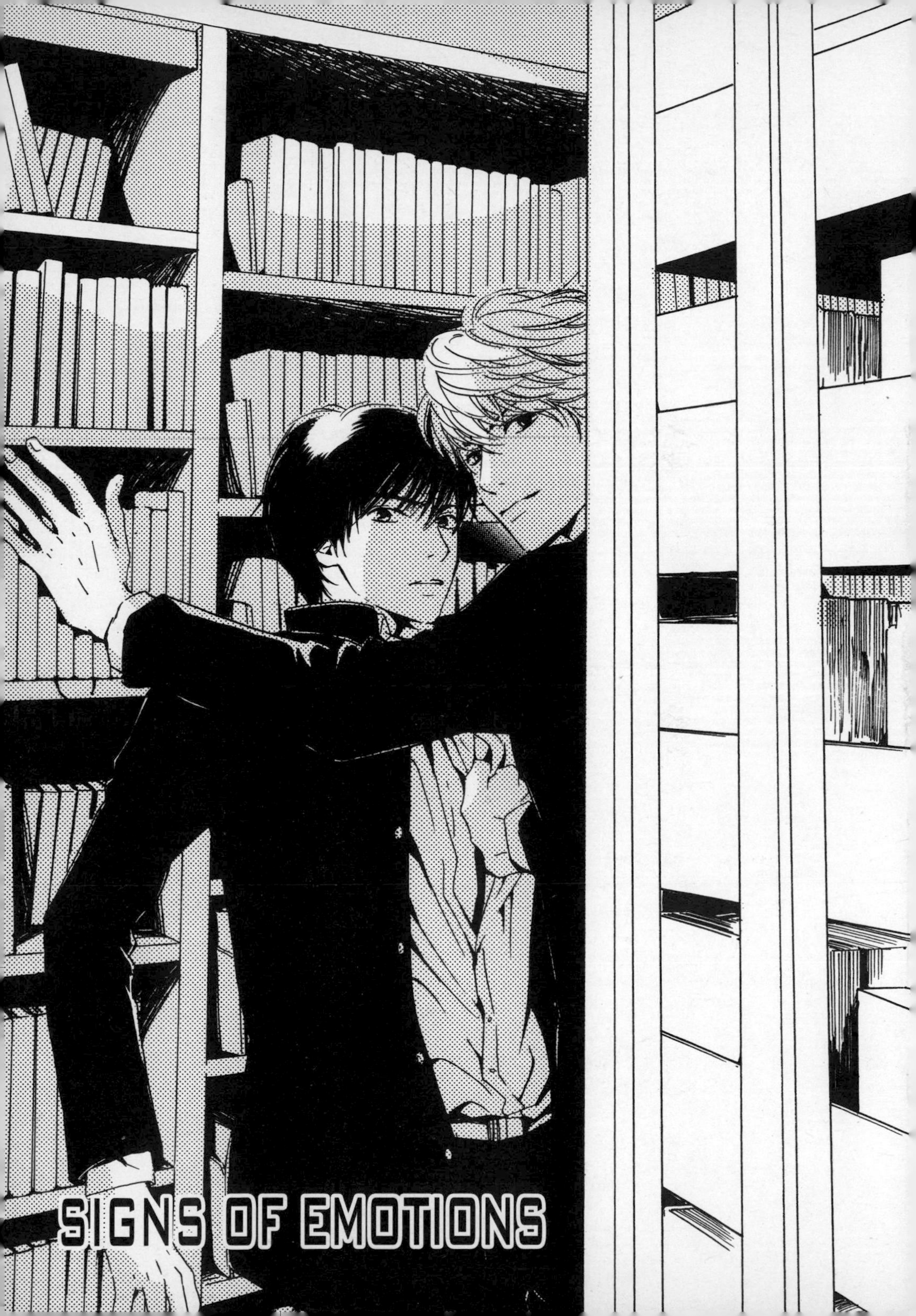
SIGNS OF EMOTIONS

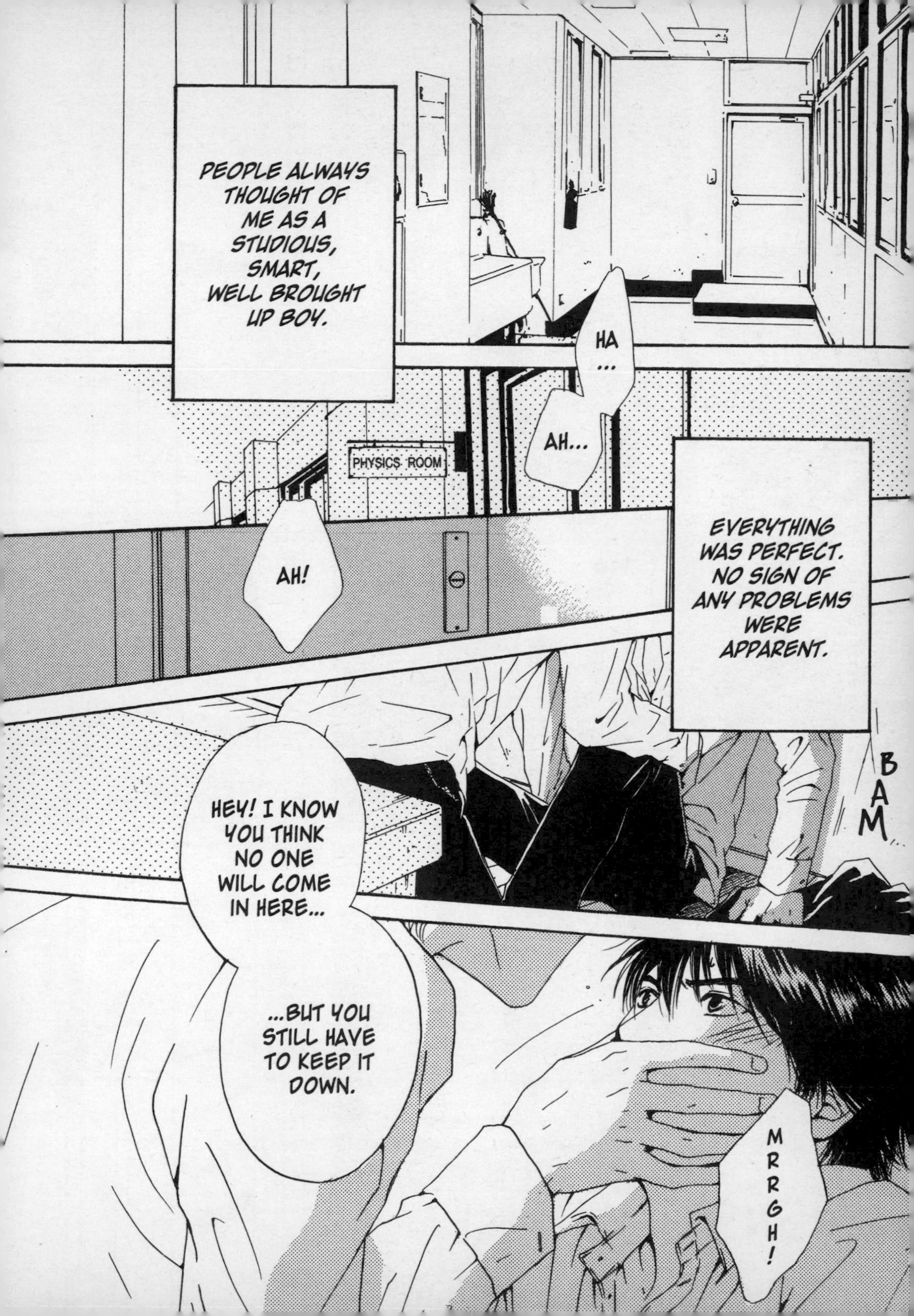
PEOPLE ALWAYS THOUGHT OF ME AS A STUDIOUS, SMART, WELL BROUGHT UP BOY.
HA...
AH...
PHYSICS ROOM
AH!
EVERYTHING WAS PERFECT. NO SIGN OF ANY PROBLEMS WERE APPARENT.
BAM...
HEY! I KNOW YOU THINK NO ONE WILL COME IN HERE...
...BUT YOU STILL HAVE TO KEEP IT DOWN.
MRRGH!

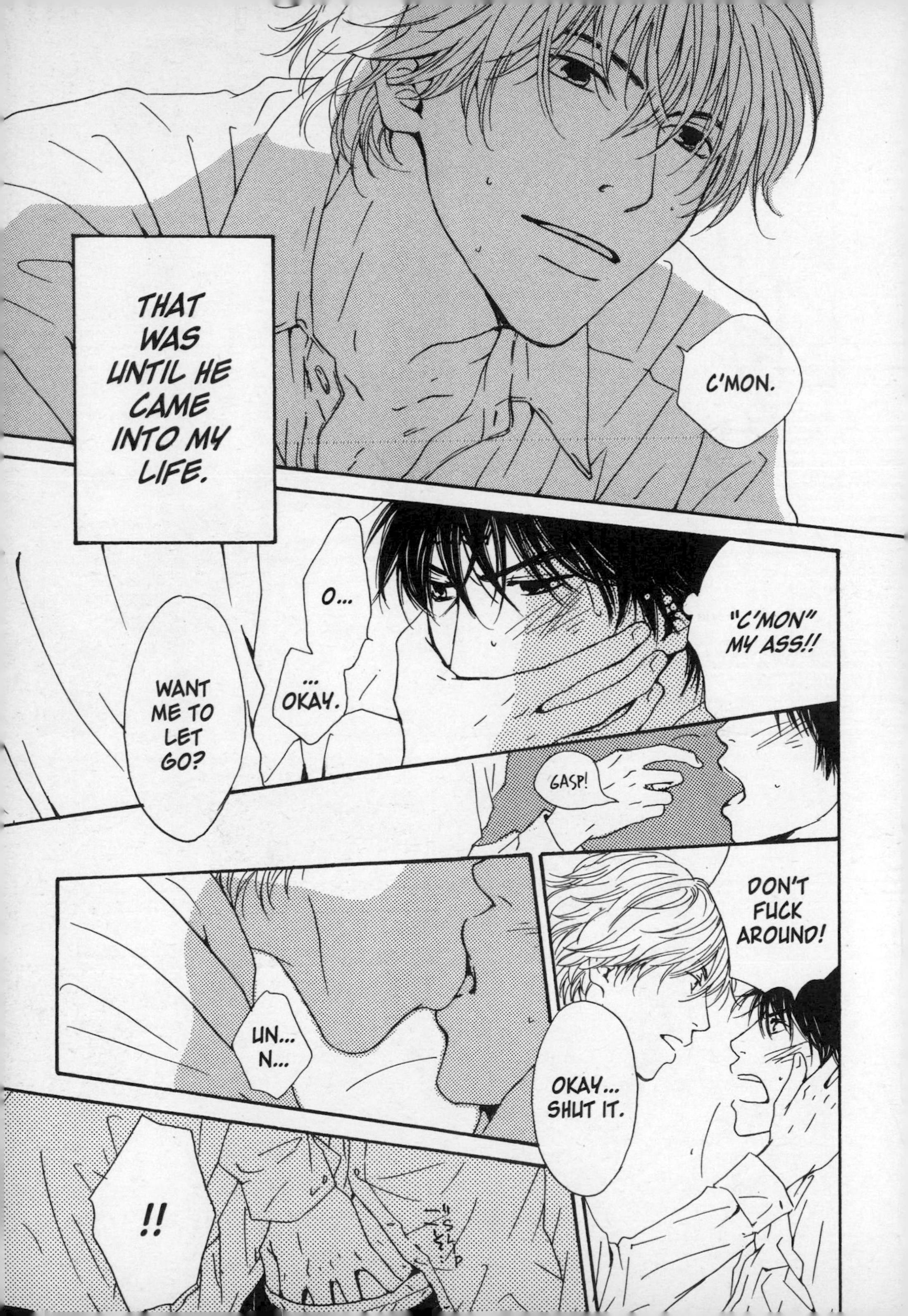
THAT WAS UNTIL HE CAME INTO MY LIFE.
C'MON.
"C'MON" MY ASS!!
O...
... OKAY.
WANT ME TO LET GO?
GASP!
DON'T FUCK AROUND!
OKAY... SHUT IT.
UN... N...
!!

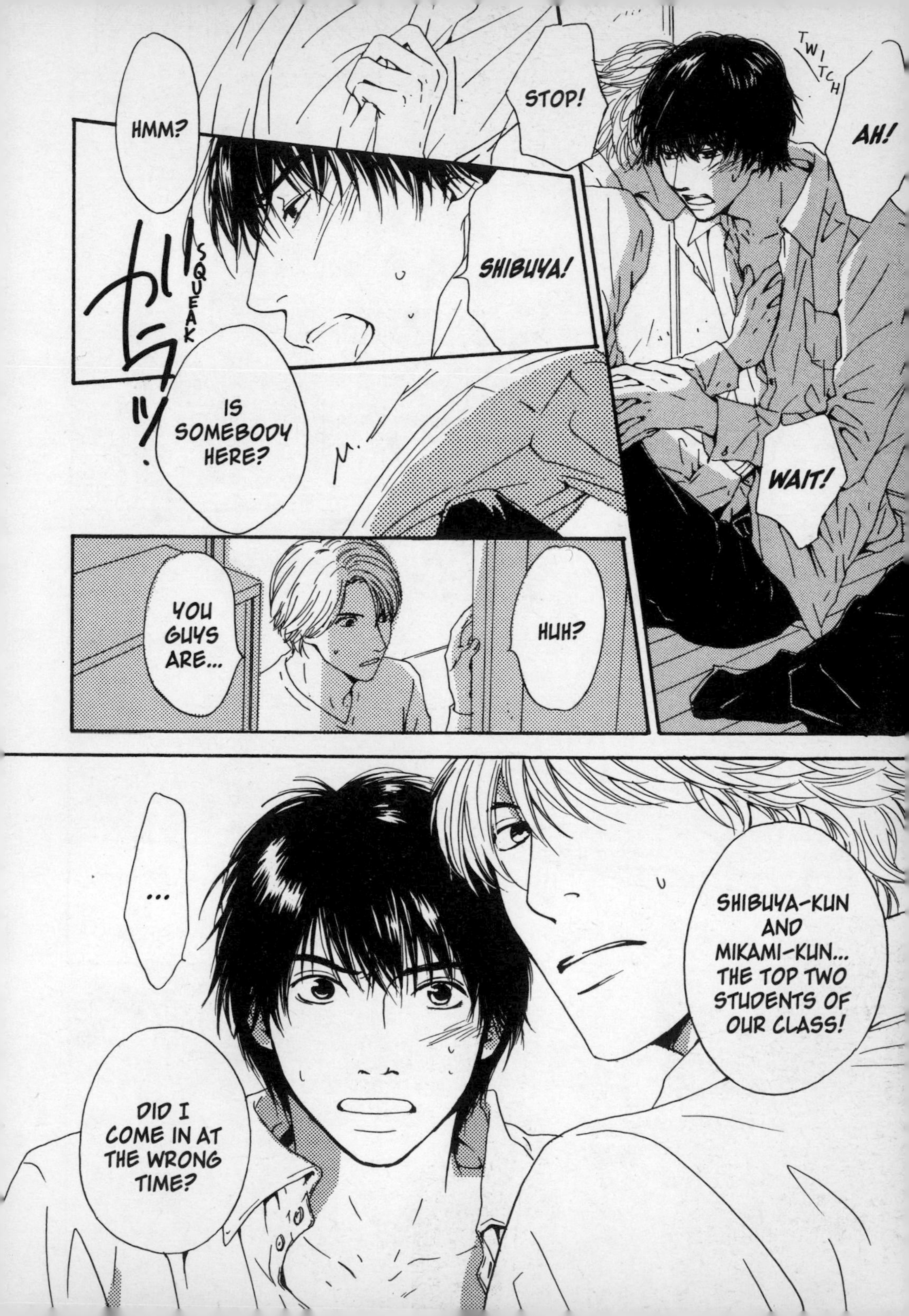
TWITCH
AH!
STOP!
WAIT!
HMM?
SHIBUYA!
SQUEAK
IS SOMEBODY HERE?
HUH?
YOU GUYS ARE...
SHIBUYA-KUN AND MIKAMI-KUN... THE TOP TWO STUDENTS OF OUR CLASS!
...
DID I COME IN AT THE WRONG TIME?

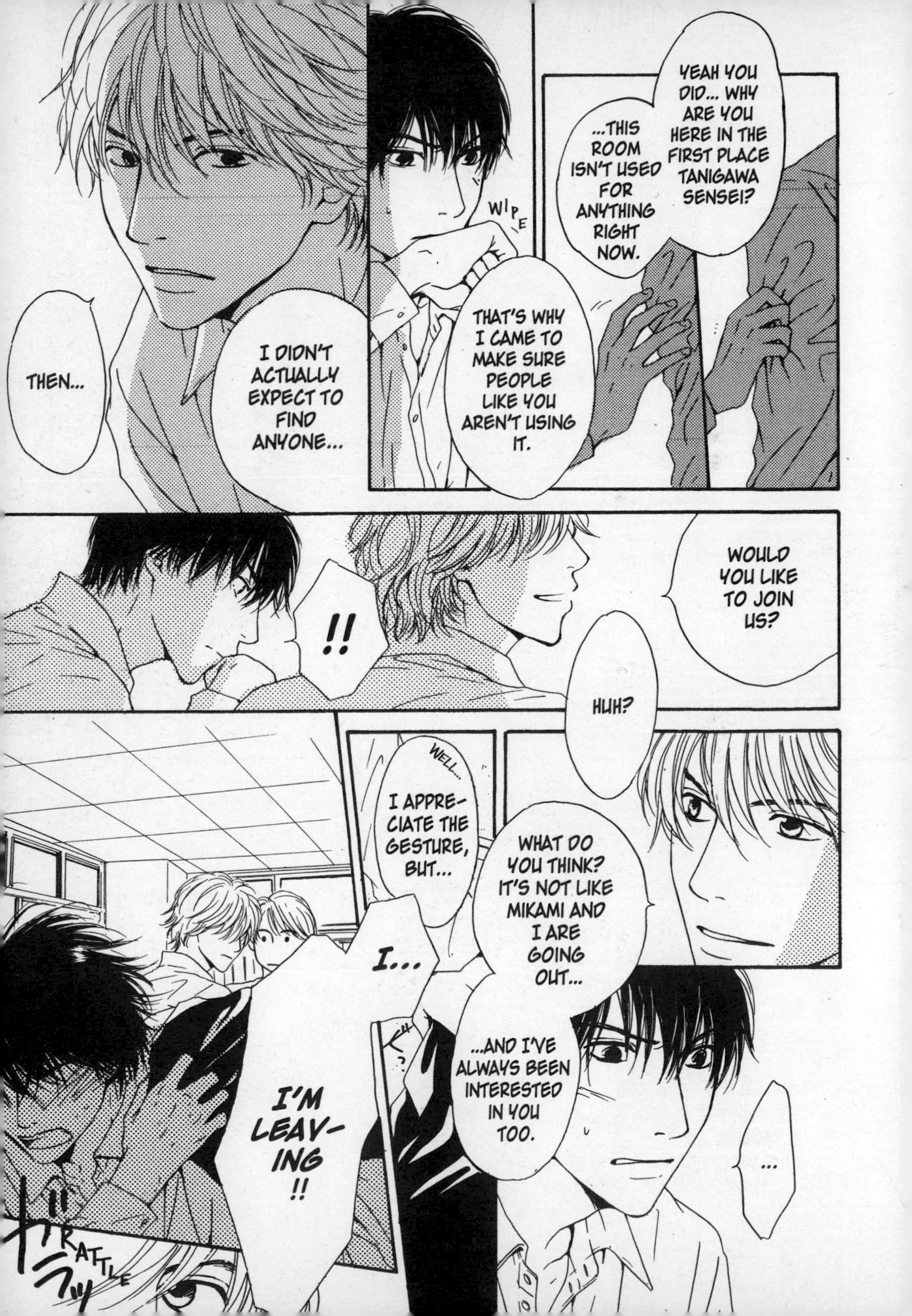
YEAH YOU DID... WHY ARE YOU HERE IN THE FIRST PLACE TANIGAWA SENSEI?
...THIS ROOM ISN'T USED FOR ANYTHING RIGHT NOW.
WIPE
THAT'S WHY I CAME TO MAKE SURE PEOPLE LIKE YOU AREN'T USING IT.
I DIDN'T ACTUALLY EXPECT TO FIND ANYONE...
THEN...
WOULD YOU LIKE TO JOIN US?
!!
HUH?
WHAT DO YOU THINK? IT'S NOT LIKE MIKAMI AND I ARE GOING OUT...
...AND I'VE ALWAYS BEEN INTERESTED IN YOU TOO.
...
WELL...
I APPRECIATE THE GESTURE, BUT...
I...
I'M LEAVING!!
RATTLE

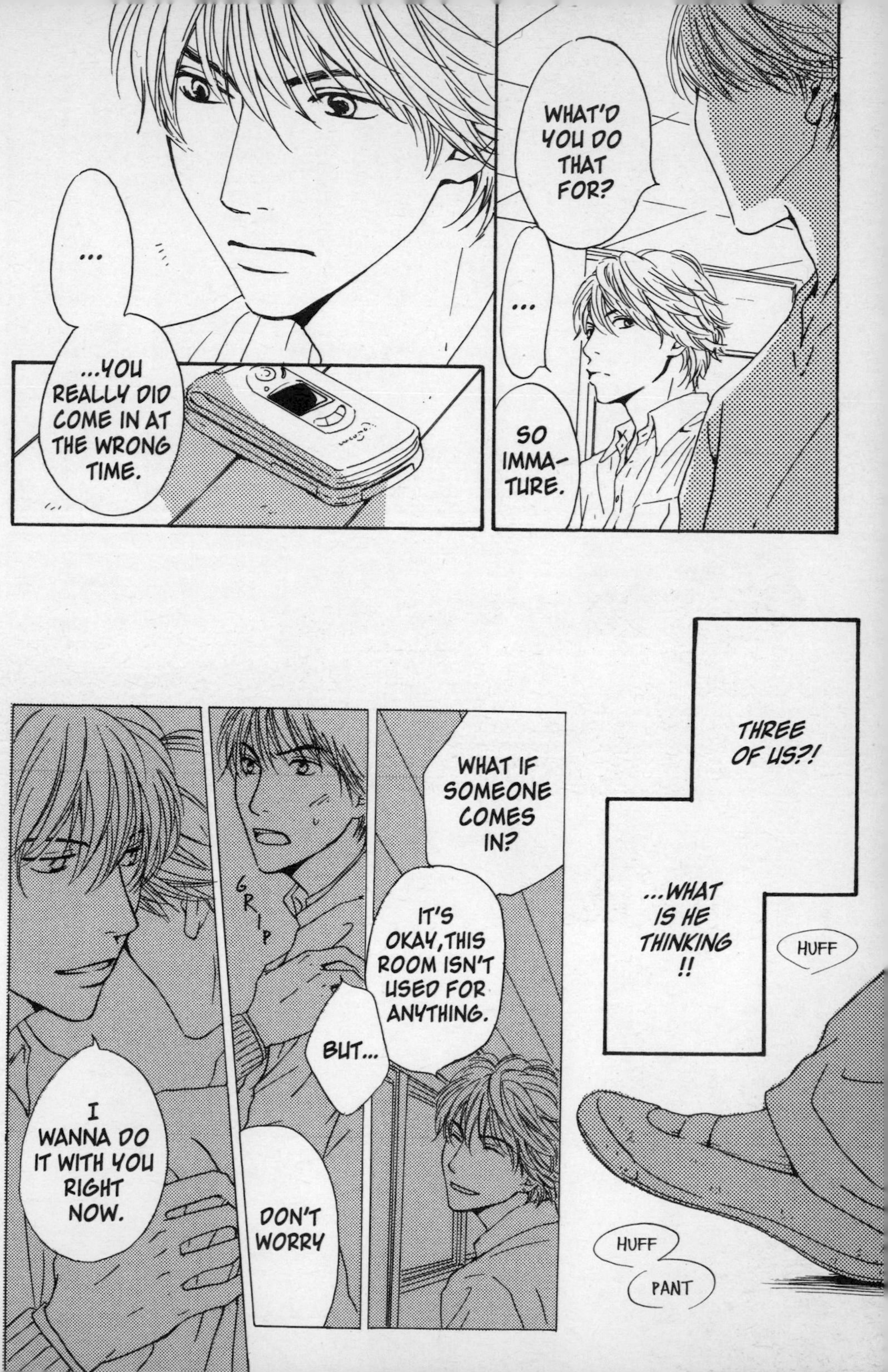
WHAT'D YOU DO THAT FOR?
...
SO IMMATURE.
...
...YOU REALLY DID COME IN AT THE WRONG TIME.
THREE OF US?!
...WHAT IS HE THINKING!!
HUFF
HUFF
PANT
WHAT IF SOMEONE COMES IN?
IT'S OKAY, THIS ROOM ISN'T USED FOR ANYTHING.
GRIP
BUT...
DON'T WORRY
I WANNA DO IT WITH YOU RIGHT NOW.

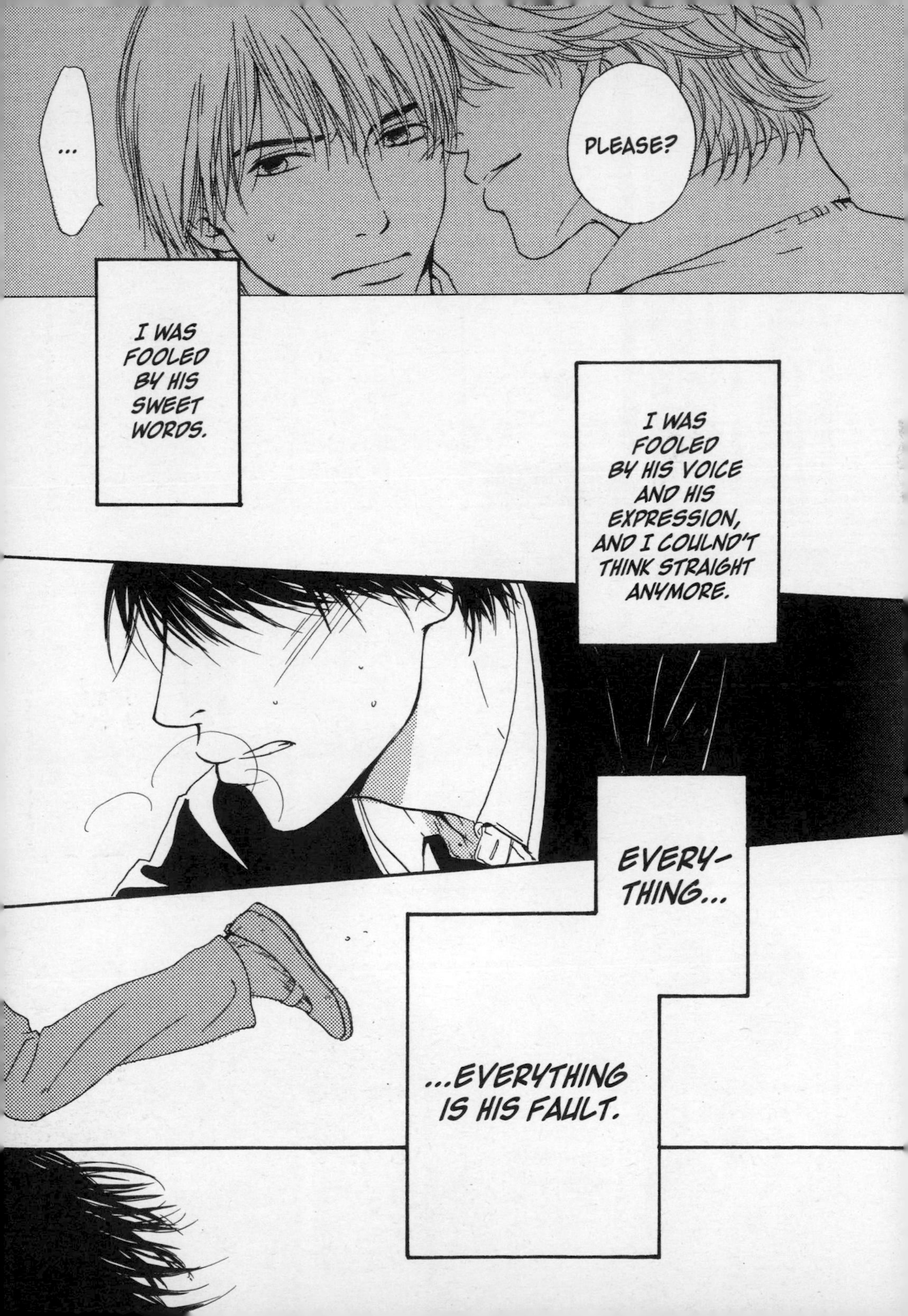
PLEASE?
...
I WAS FOOLED BY HIS SWEET WORDS.
I WAS FOOLED BY HIS VOICE AND HIS EXPRESSION, AND I COULND'T THINK STRAIGHT ANYMORE.
EVERY-THING...
...EVERYTHING IS HIS FAULT.

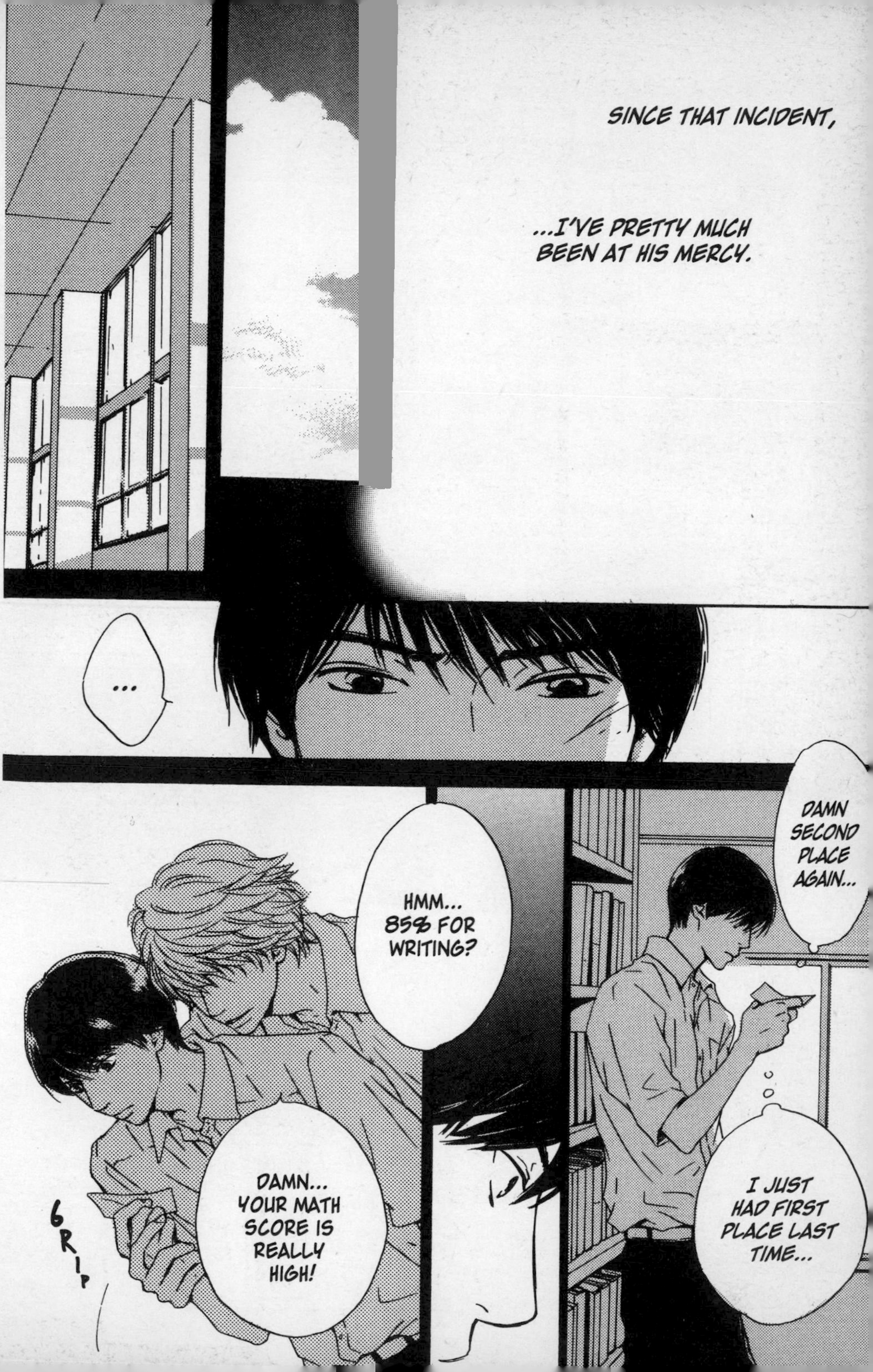
SINCE THAT INCIDENT,
...I'VE PRETTY MUCH BEEN AT HIS MERCY.
...
DAMN SECOND PLACE AGAIN...
I JUST HAD FIRST PLACE LAST TIME...
HMM... 85% FOR WRITING?
DAMN... YOUR MATH SCORE IS REALLY HIGH!
GRIP

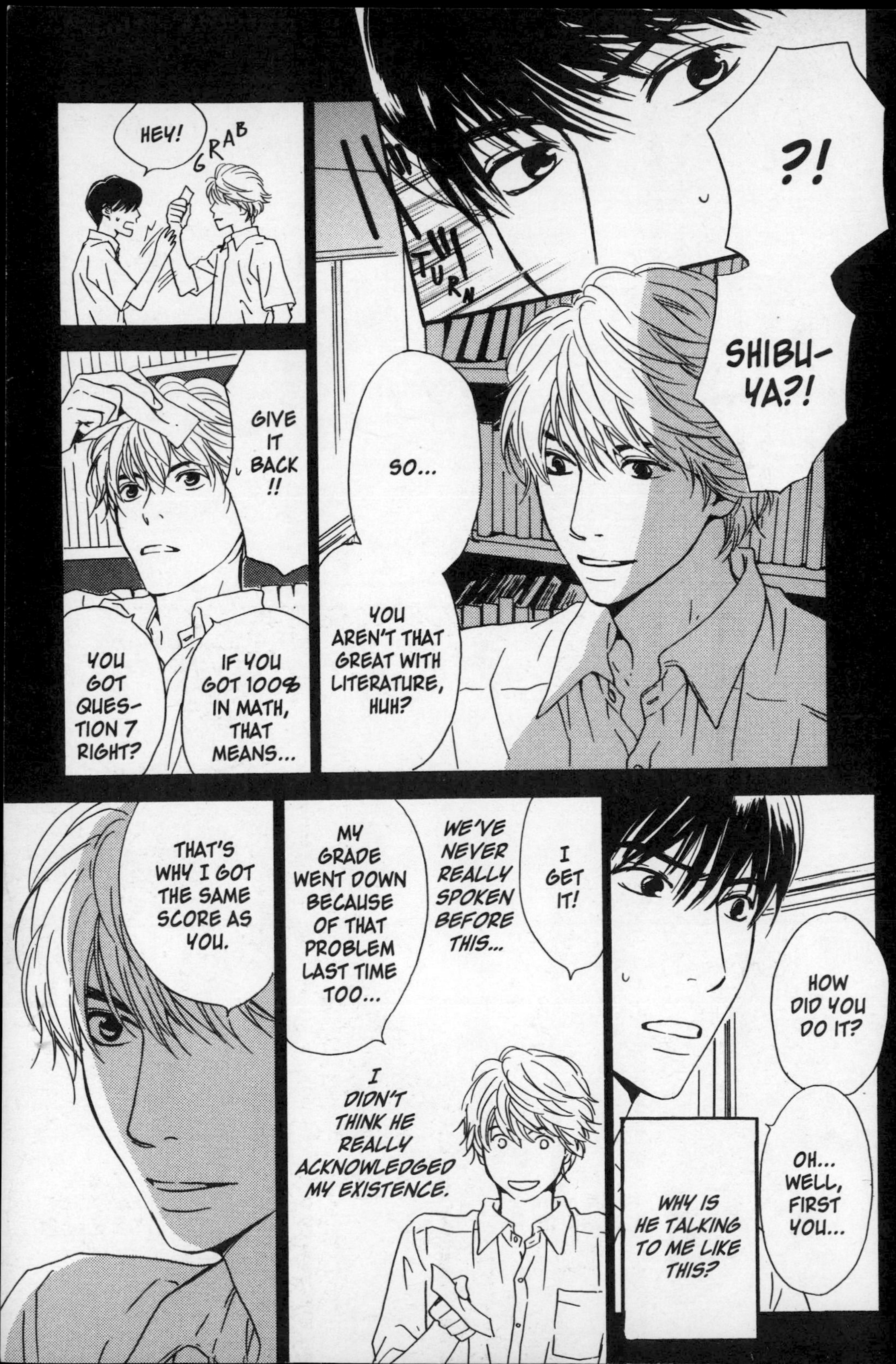
?!
SHIBU-YA?!
TURN
SO...
YOU AREN'T THAT GREAT WITH LITERATURE, HUH?
HEY!
GRAB
GIVE IT BACK !!
IF YOU GOT 100% IN MATH, THAT MEANS...
YOU GOT QUES-TION 7 RIGHT?
HOW DID YOU DO IT?
OH... WELL, FIRST YOU...
WHY IS HE TALKING TO ME LIKE THIS?
I GET IT!
WE'VE NEVER REALLY SPOKEN BEFORE THIS...
MY GRADE WENT DOWN BECAUSE OF THAT PROBLEM LAST TIME TOO...
I DIDN'T THINK HE REALLY ACKNOWLEDGED MY EXISTENCE.
THAT'S WHY I GOT THE SAME SCORE AS YOU.

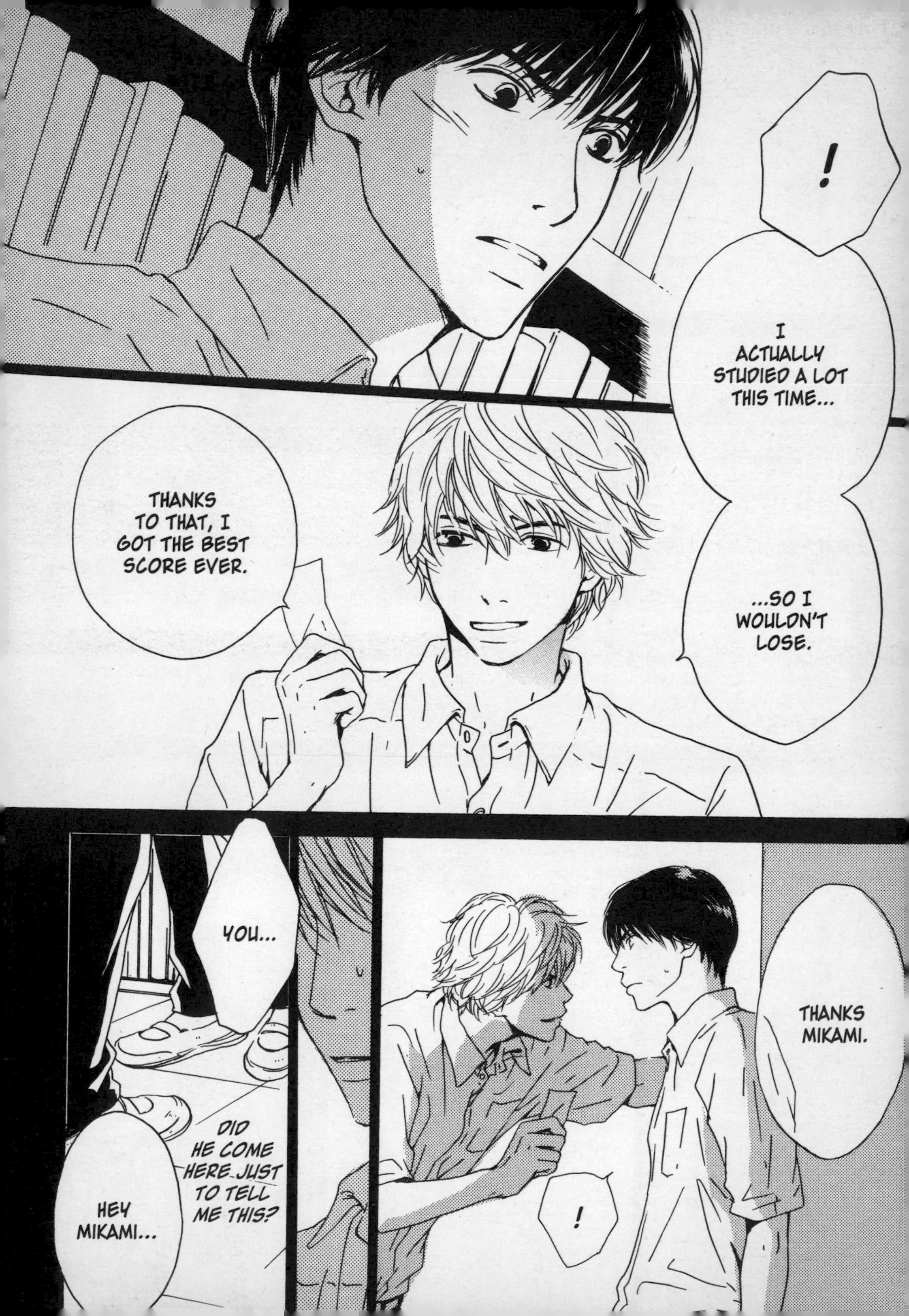
!
I ACTUALLY STUDIED A LOT THIS TIME...
...SO I WOULDN'T LOSE.
THANKS TO THAT, I GOT THE BEST SCORE EVER.
THANKS MIKAMI.
!
YOU...
DID HE COME HERE JUST TO TELL ME THIS?
HEY MIKAMI...

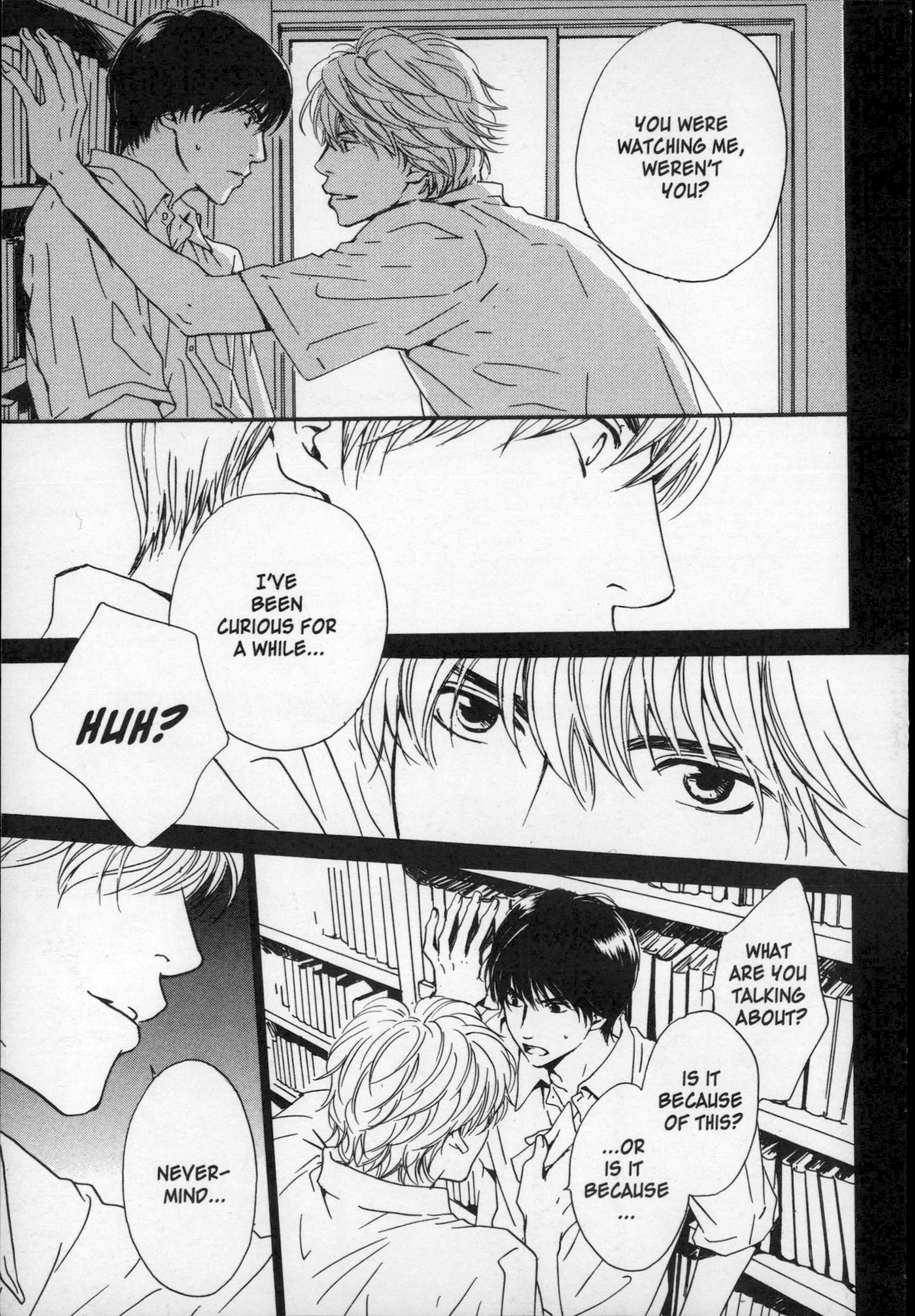
YOU WERE WATCHING ME, WEREN'T YOU?
I'VE BEEN CURIOUS FOR A WHILE...
HUH?
WHAT ARE YOU TALKING ABOUT?
IS IT BECAUSE OF THIS?
...OR IS IT BECAUSE ...
NEVER-MIND...

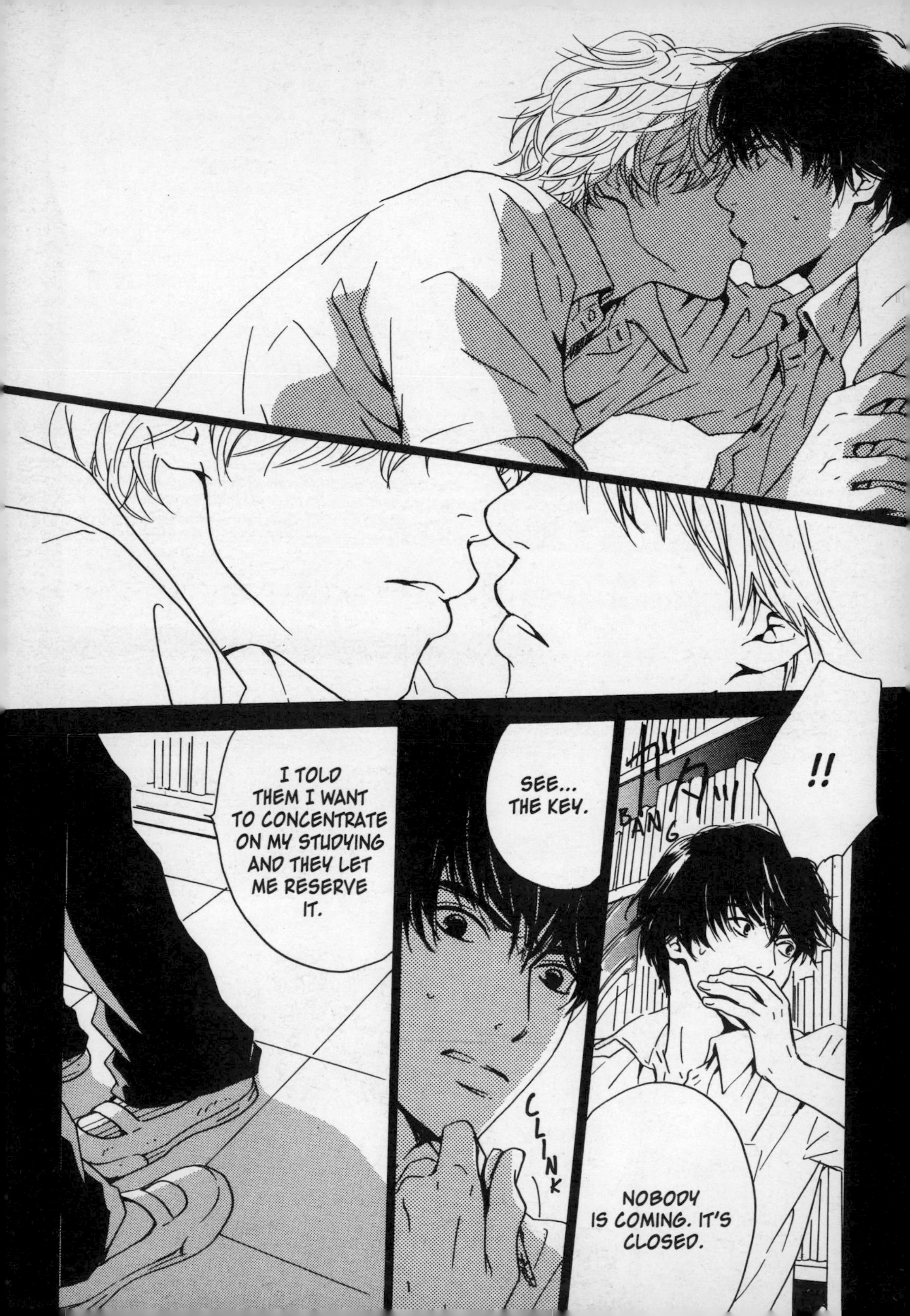
!!
BANG
NOBODY IS COMING. IT'S CLOSED.
SEE... THE KEY.
CLINK
I TOLD THEM I WANT TO CONCENTRATE ON MY STUDYING AND THEY LET ME RESERVE IT.

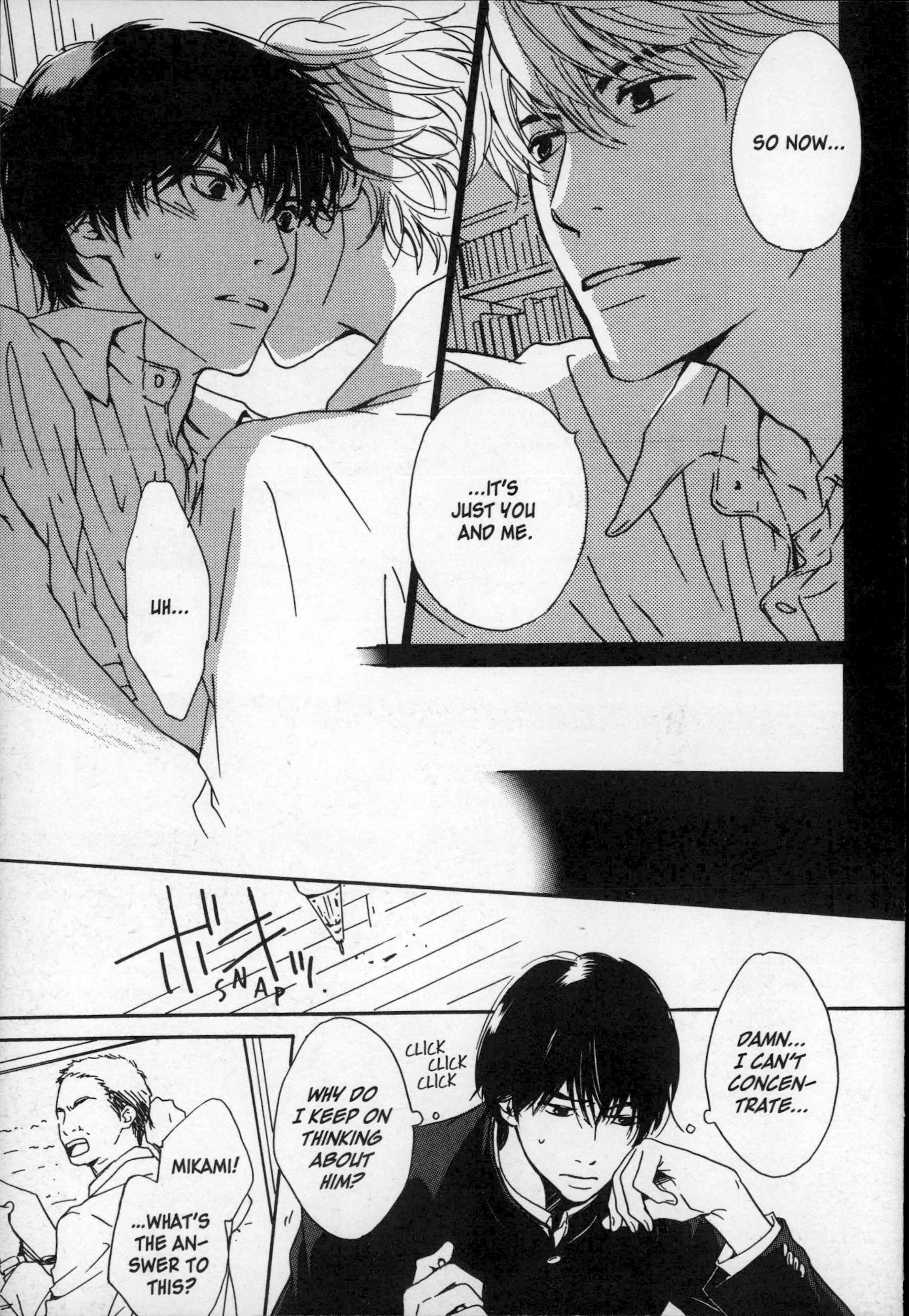
SO NOW...
...IT'S JUST YOU AND ME.
UH...
SNAP
DAMN... I CAN'T CONCEN-TRATE...
CLICK CLICK CLICK
WHY DO I KEEP ON THINKING ABOUT HIM?
MIKAMI!
...WHAT'S THE AN-SWER TO THIS?

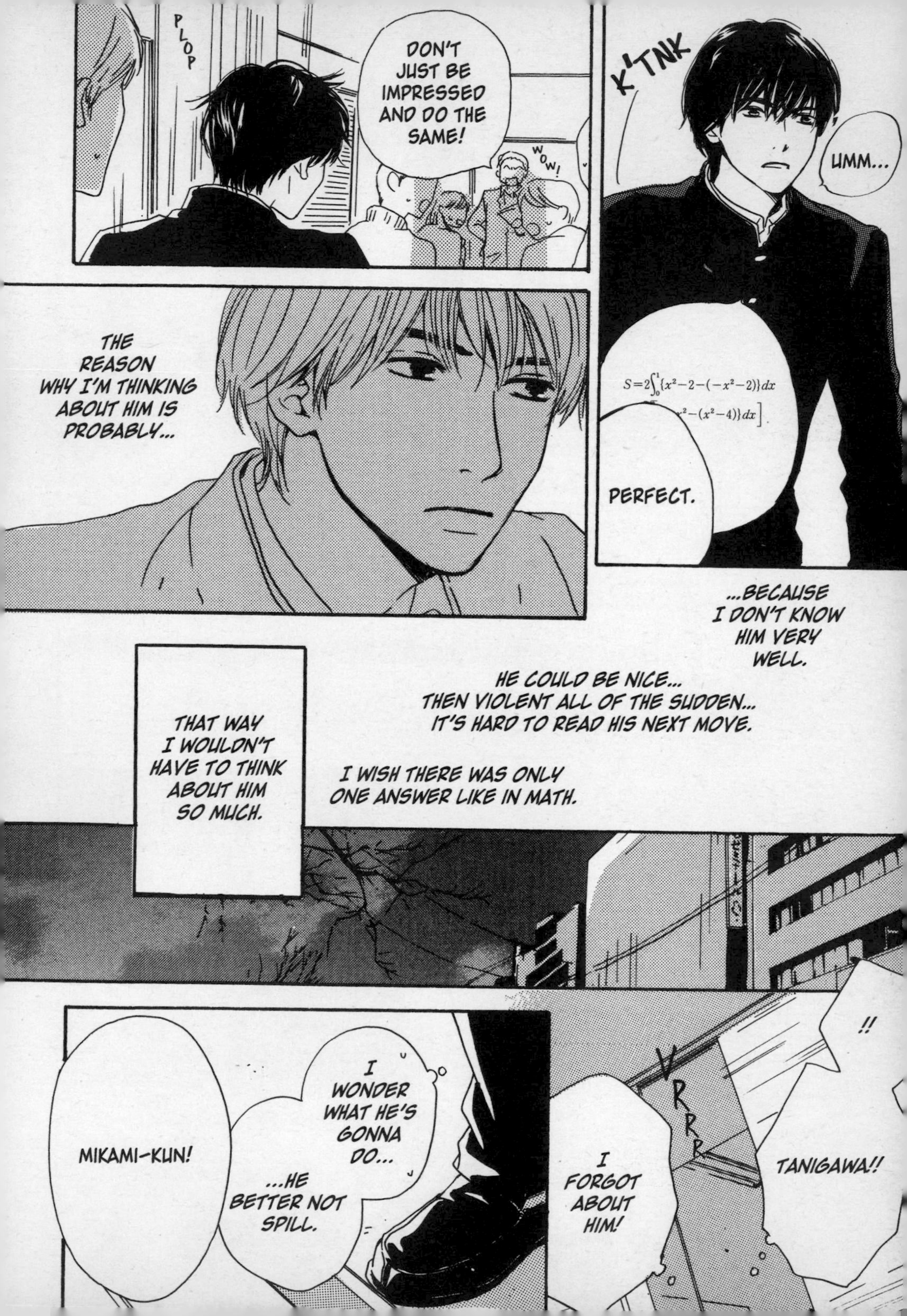
K'TNK
UMM...
$S=2\int_0^1\{x^2-2-(-x^2-2)\}dx$
$x^2-(x^2-4)\}dx\Big]$
PERFECT.
PLOP
DON'T JUST BE IMPRESSED AND DO THE SAME!
WOW!
THE REASON WHY I'M THINKING ABOUT HIM IS PROBABLY...
...BECAUSE I DON'T KNOW HIM VERY WELL.
HE COULD BE NICE... THEN VIOLENT ALL OF THE SUDDEN... IT'S HARD TO READ HIS NEXT MOVE.
I WISH THERE WAS ONLY ONE ANSWER LIKE IN MATH.
THAT WAY I WOULDN'T HAVE TO THINK ABOUT HIM SO MUCH.
!!
VRRR
TANIGAWA!!
I FORGOT ABOUT HIM!
I WONDER WHAT HE'S GONNA DO...
...HE BETTER NOT SPILL.
MIKAMI-KUN!

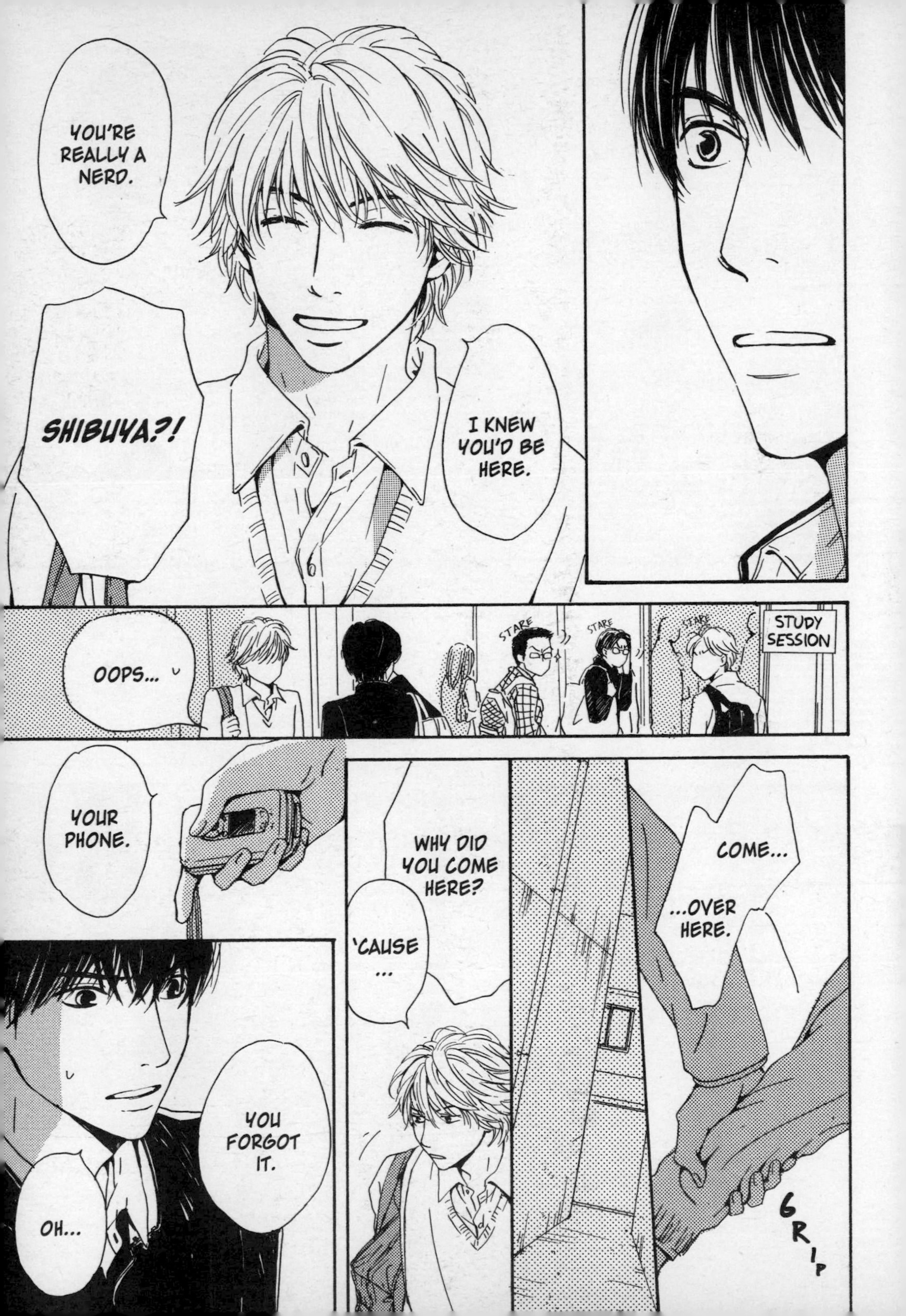
SHIBUYA?!
I KNEW YOU'D BE HERE.
YOU'RE REALLY A NERD.
STUDY SESSION
STARE
STARE
STARE
OOPS...
COME...
...OVER HERE.
GRIP
WHY DID YOU COME HERE?
'CAUSE ...
YOUR PHONE.
YOU FORGOT IT.
OH...

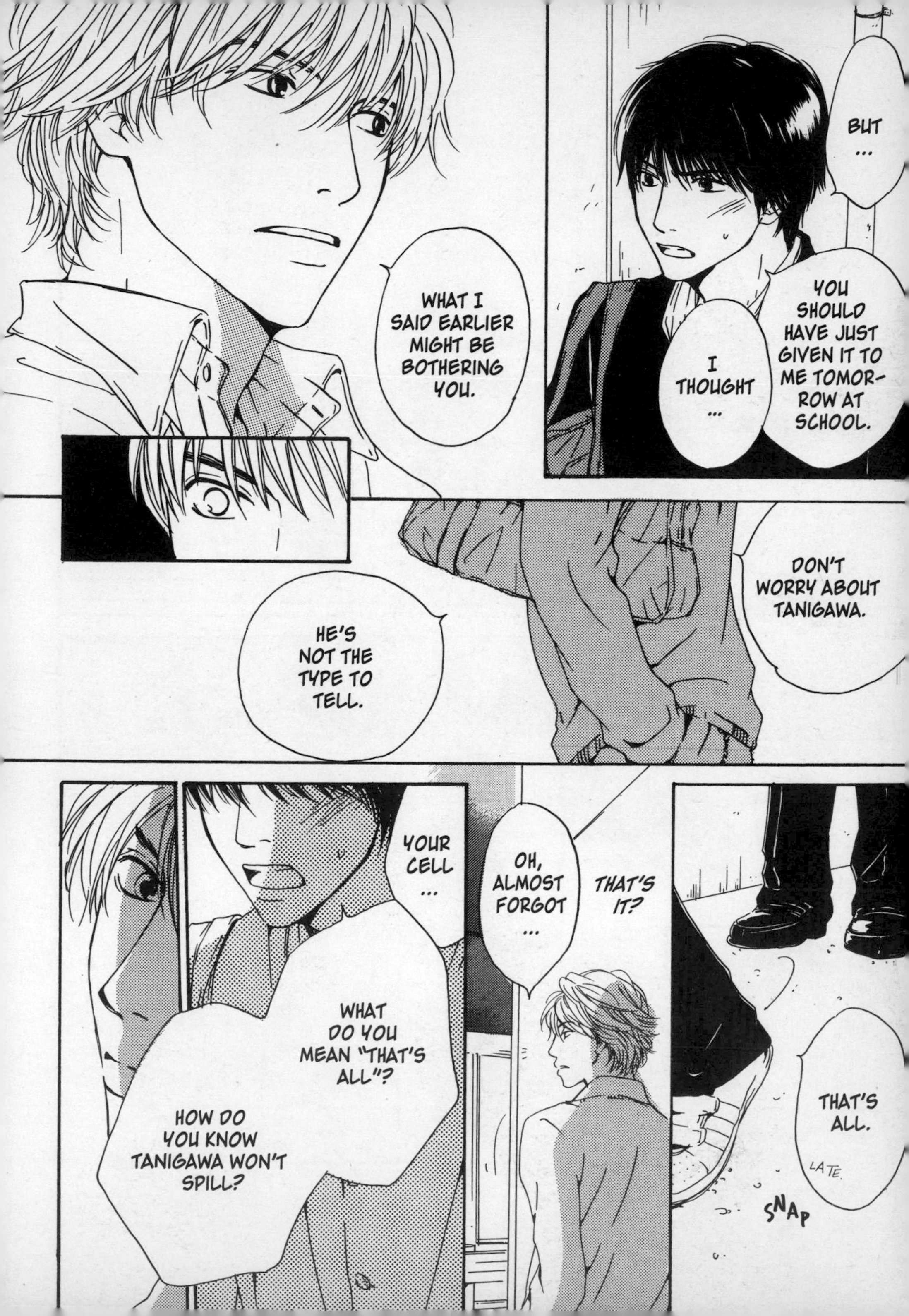
BUT ...
YOU SHOULD HAVE JUST GIVEN IT TO ME TOMORROW AT SCHOOL.
I THOUGHT ...
WHAT I SAID EARLIER MIGHT BE BOTHERING YOU.
DON'T WORRY ABOUT TANIGAWA.
HE'S NOT THE TYPE TO TELL.
THAT'S ALL.
LATE
SNAP
THAT'S IT?
OH, ALMOST FORGOT ...
YOUR CELL ...
WHAT DO YOU MEAN "THAT'S ALL"?
HOW DO YOU KNOW TANIGAWA WON'T SPILL?

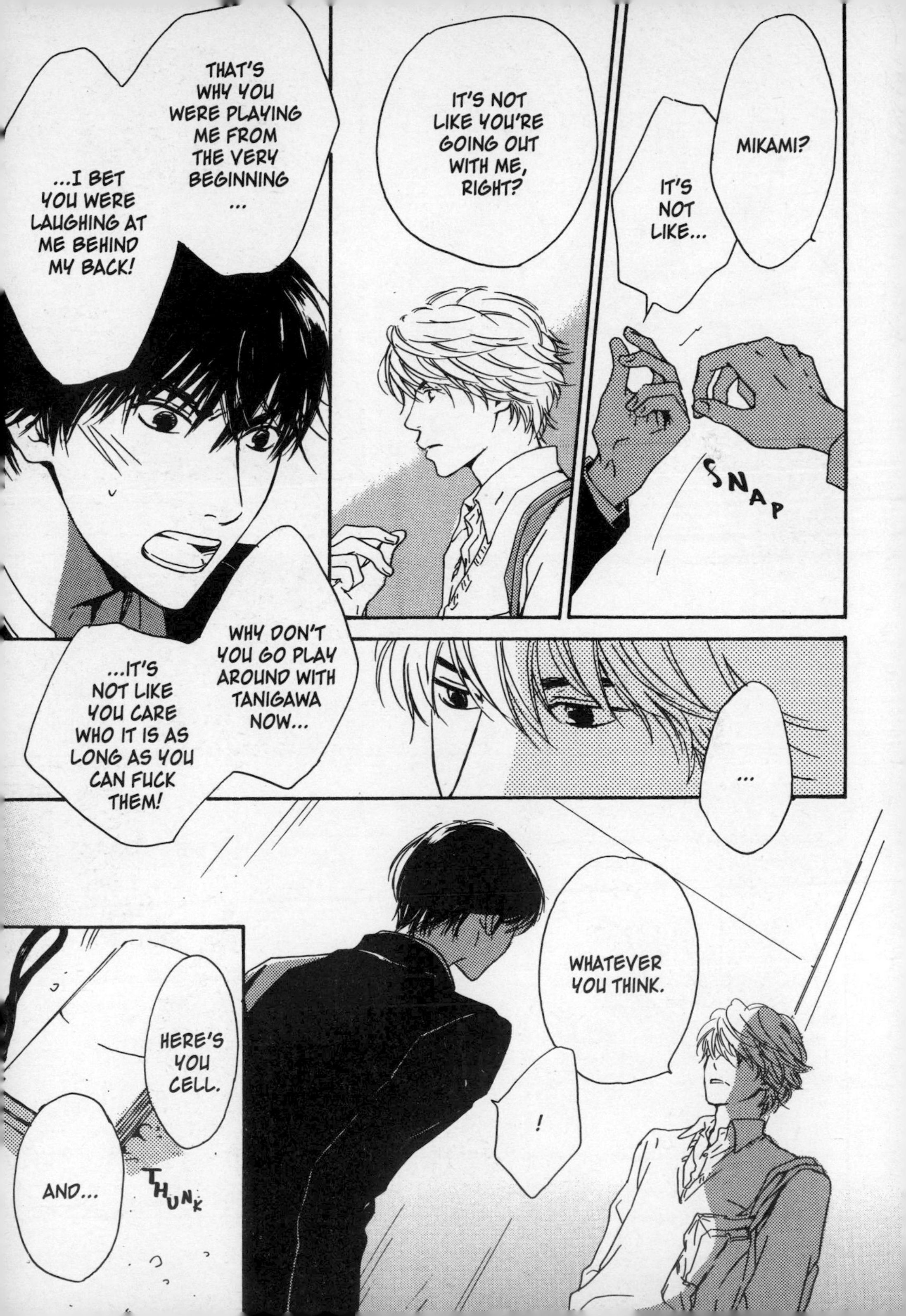
MIKAMI?
IT'S NOT LIKE...
SNAP
IT'S NOT LIKE YOU'RE GOING OUT WITH ME, RIGHT?
THAT'S WHY YOU WERE PLAYING ME FROM THE VERY BEGINNING...
...I BET YOU WERE LAUGHING AT ME BEHIND MY BACK!
...
WHY DON'T YOU GO PLAY AROUND WITH TANIGAWA NOW...
...IT'S NOT LIKE YOU CARE WHO IT IS AS LONG AS YOU CAN FUCK THEM!
WHATEVER YOU THINK.
!
HERE'S YOU CELL.
AND...
THUNK

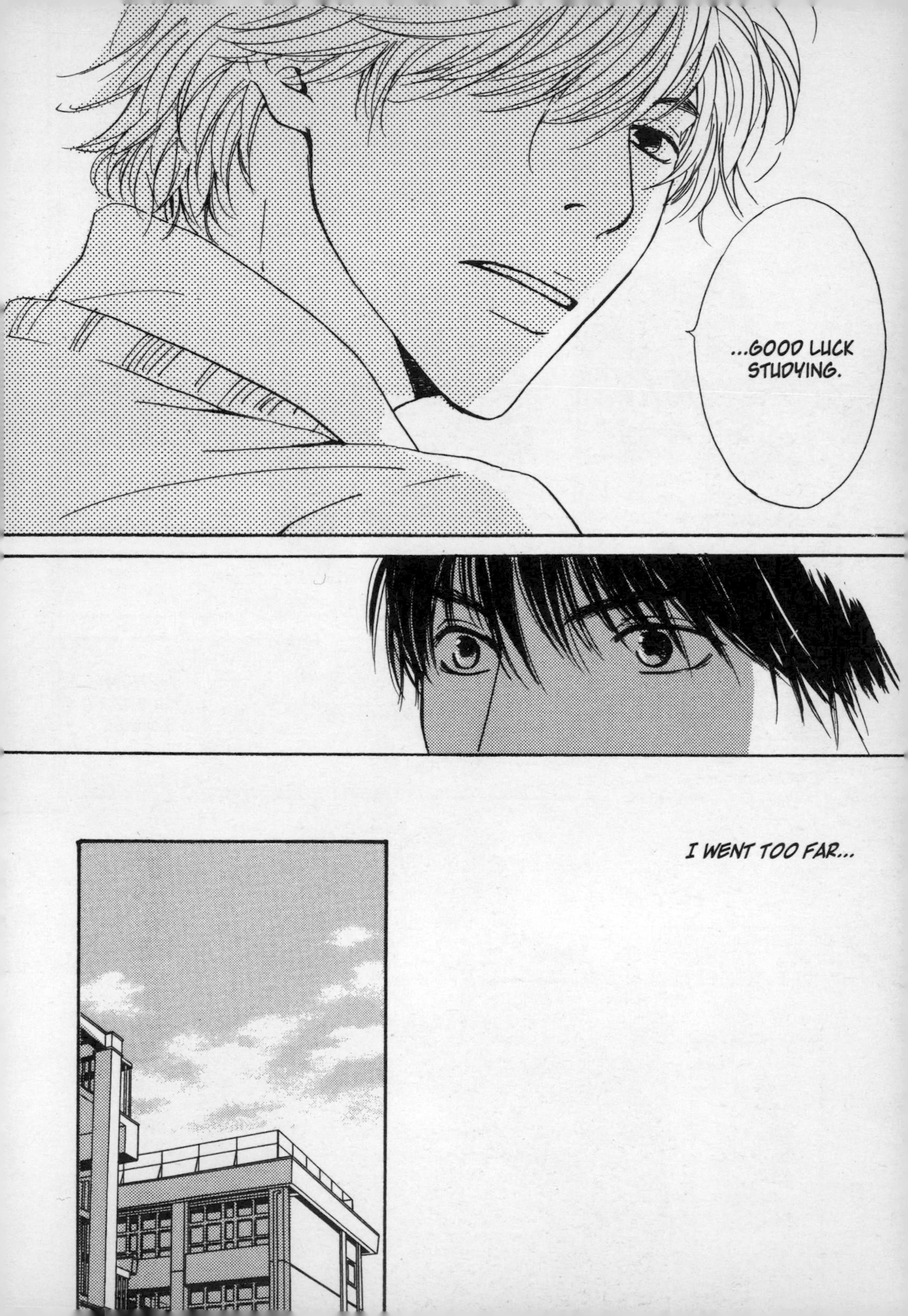
...GOOD LUCK STUDYING.
I WENT TOO FAR...

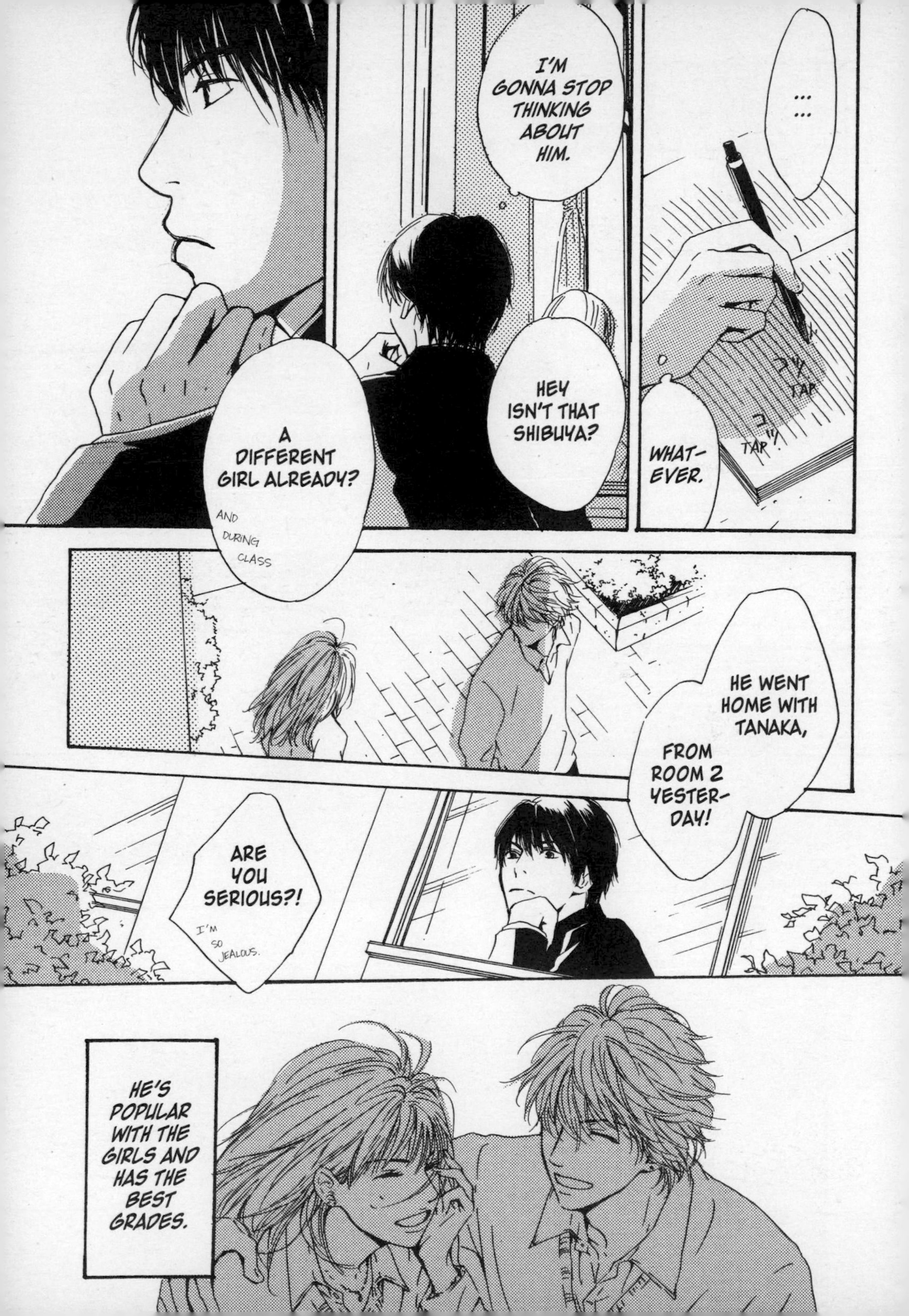
……
……
WHAT-EVER.
TAP
TAP
I'M GONNA STOP THINKING ABOUT HIM.
HEY ISN'T THAT SHIBUYA?
A DIFFERENT GIRL ALREADY?
AND DURING CLASS
HE WENT HOME WITH TANAKA,
FROM ROOM 2 YESTER-DAY!
ARE YOU SERIOUS?!
I'M SO JEALOUS.
HE'S POPULAR WITH THE GIRLS AND HAS THE BEST GRADES.

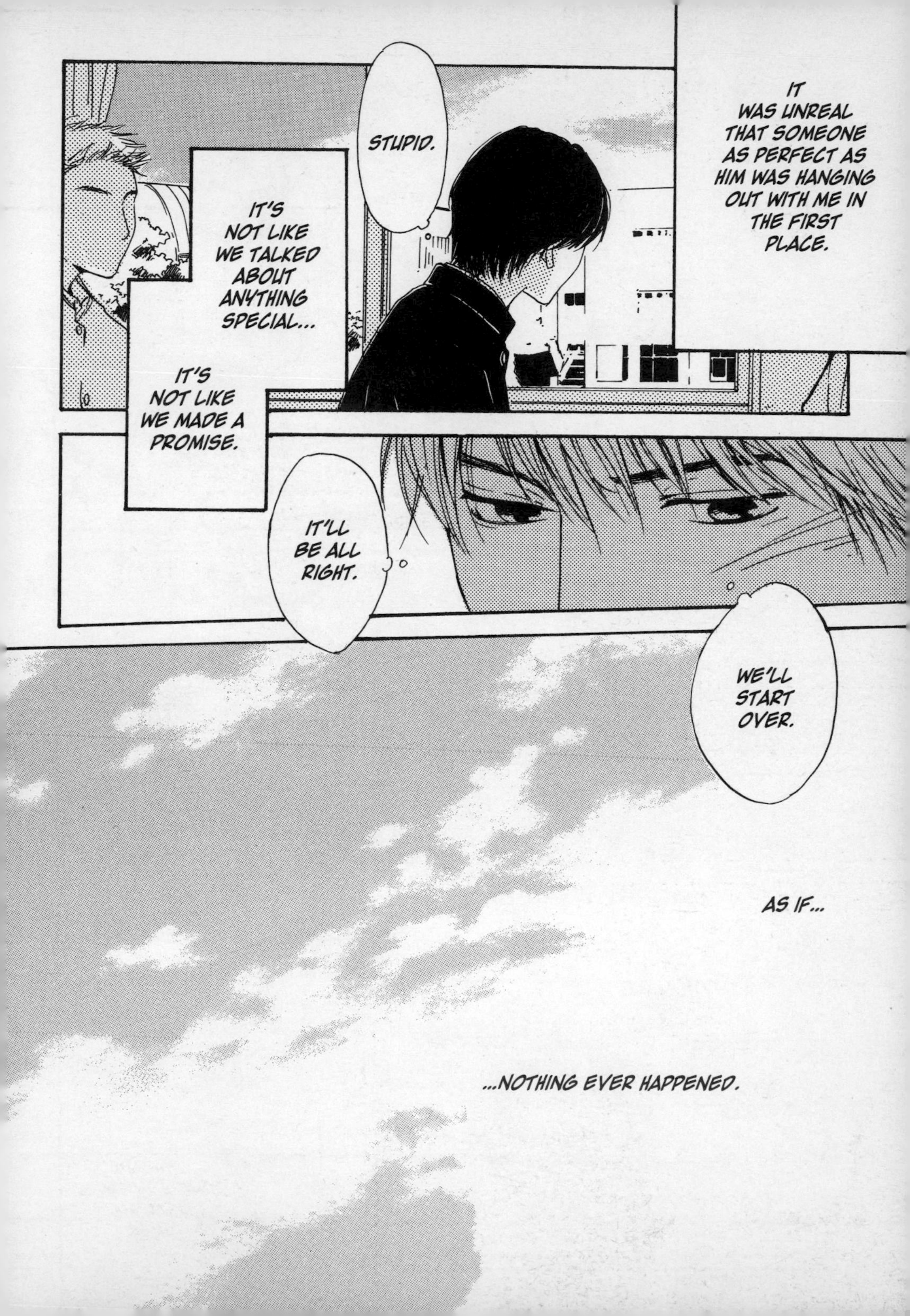
IT WAS UNREAL THAT SOMEONE AS PERFECT AS HIM WAS HANGING OUT WITH ME IN THE FIRST PLACE.
STUPID.
IT'S NOT LIKE WE TALKED ABOUT ANYTHING SPECIAL...
IT'S NOT LIKE WE MADE A PROMISE.
IT'LL BE ALL RIGHT.
WE'LL START OVER.
AS IF...
...NOTHING EVER HAPPENED.

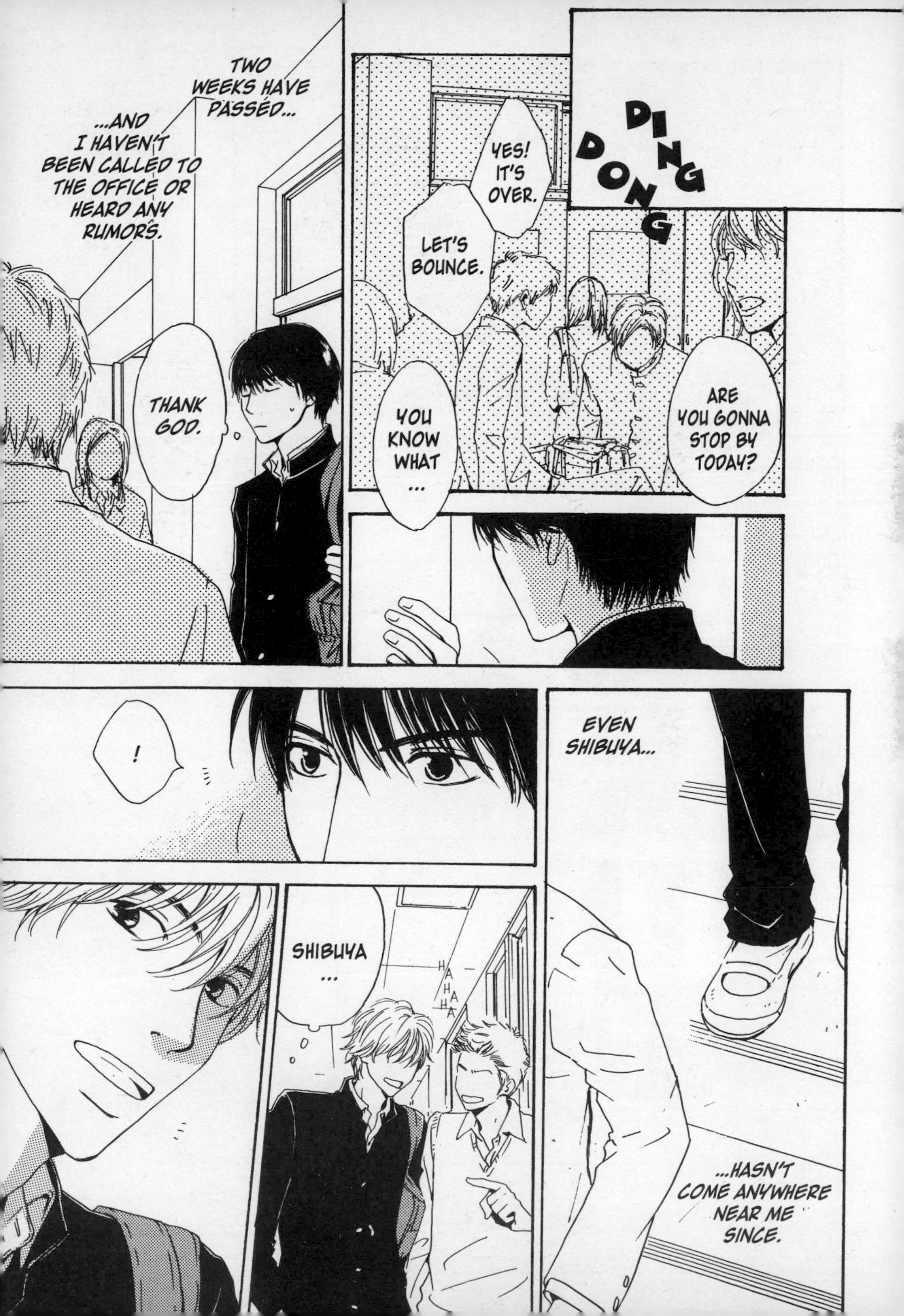
DING DONG
YES! IT'S OVER.
LET'S BOUNCE.
ARE YOU GONNA STOP BY TODAY?
YOU KNOW WHAT...
TWO WEEKS HAVE PASSED...
...AND I HAVEN'T BEEN CALLED TO THE OFFICE OR HEARD ANY RUMORS.
THANK GOD.
EVEN SHIBUYA...
...HASN'T COME ANYWHERE NEAR ME SINCE.
!
SHIBUYA...
HA HA HA

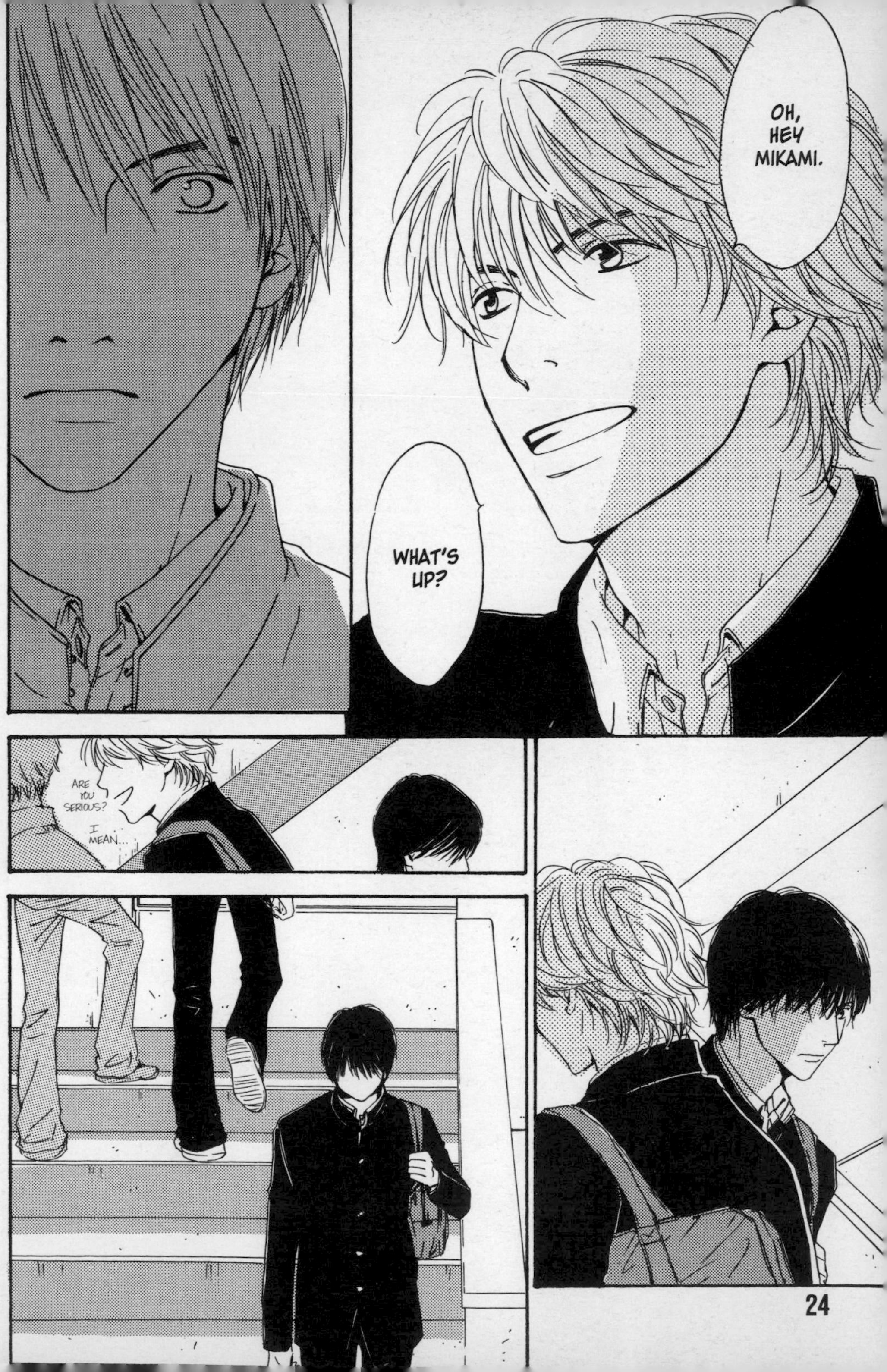

OH, HEY MIKAMI.
WHAT'S UP?
ARE YOU SERIOUS?
I MEAN...

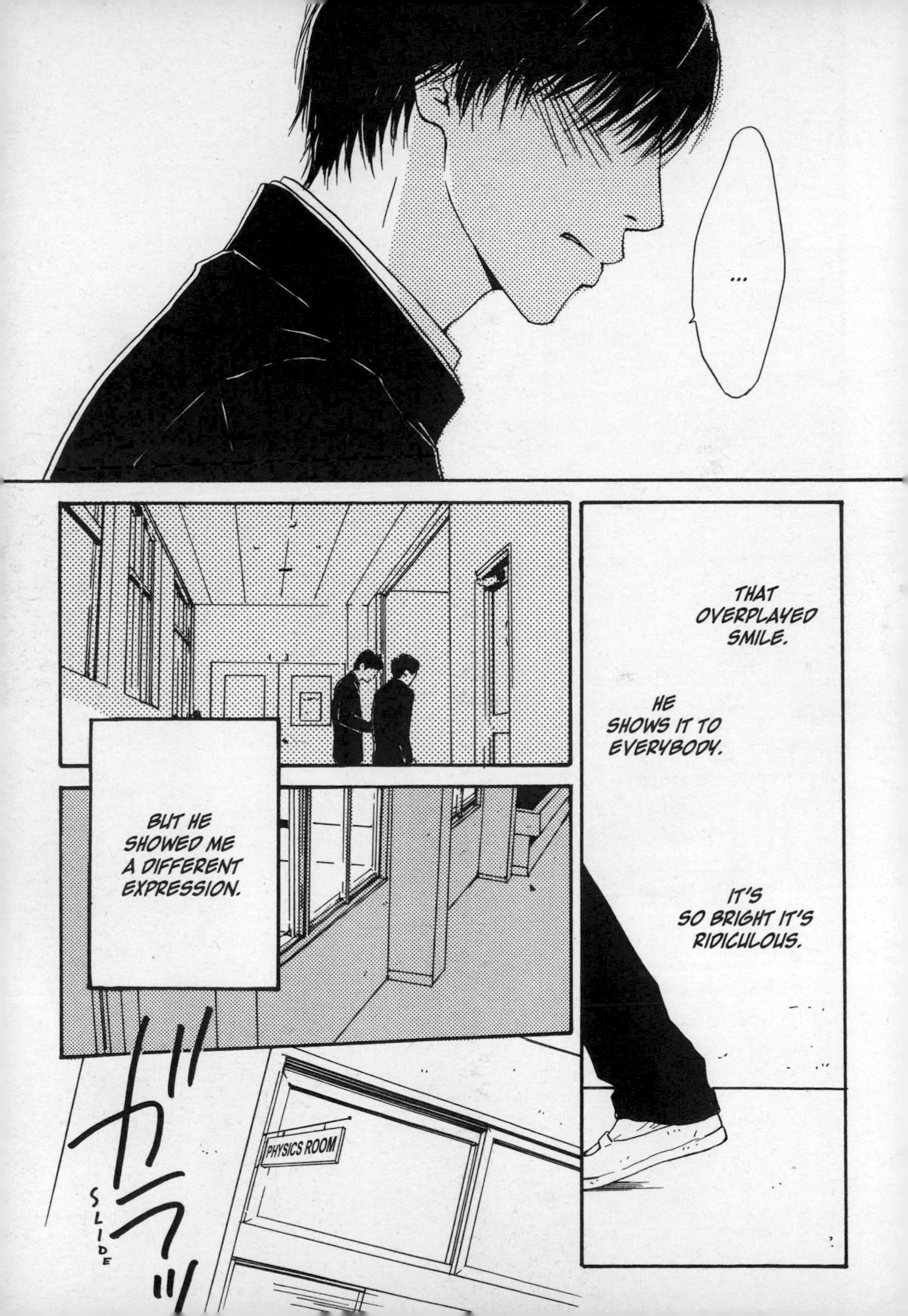
...
THAT OVERPLAYED SMILE.
HE SHOWS IT TO EVERYBODY.
IT'S SO BRIGHT IT'S RIDICULOUS.
BUT HE SHOWED ME A DIFFERENT EXPRESSION.
ガラッ
SLIDE
PHYSICS ROOM

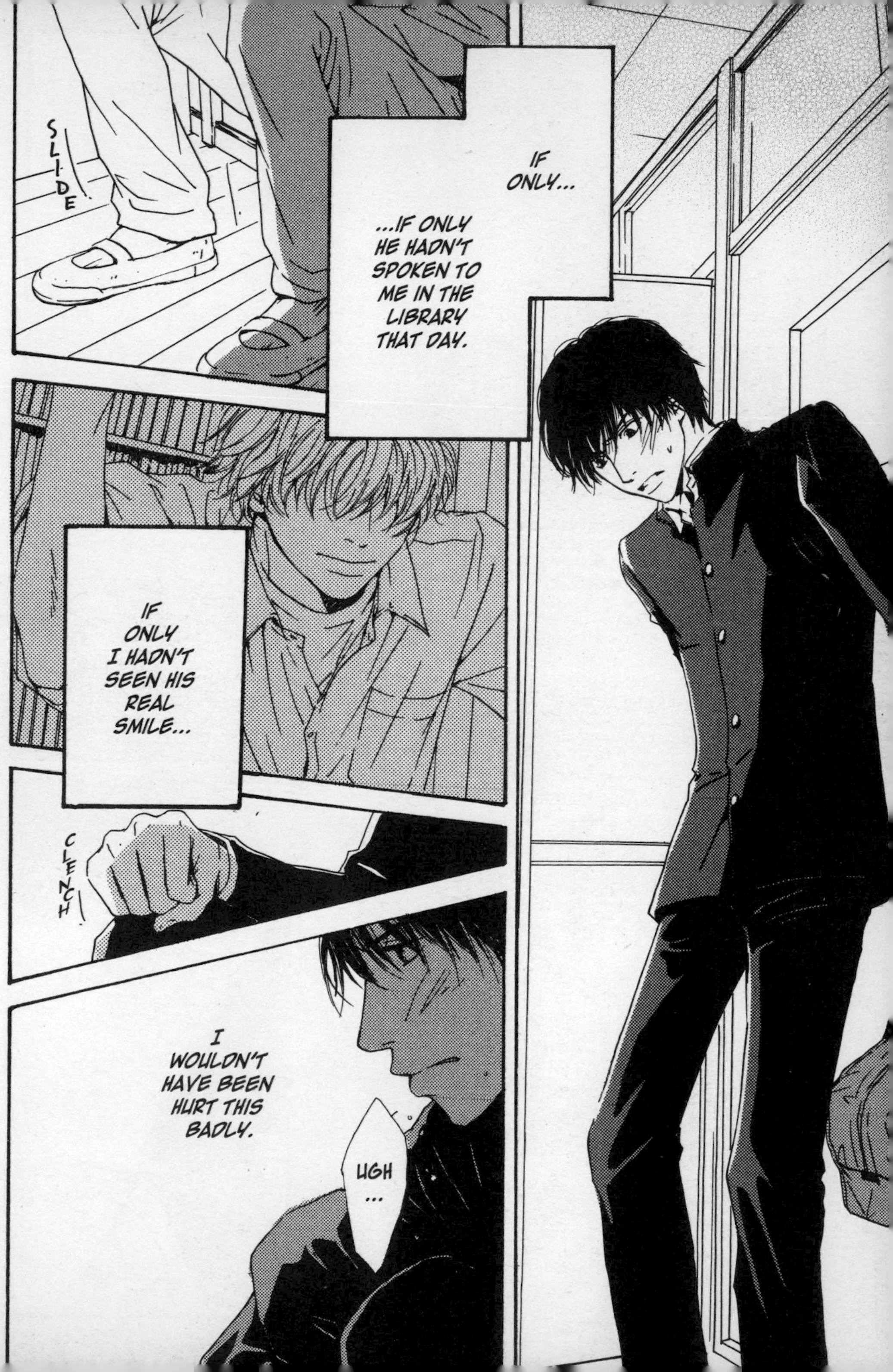
IF ONLY...
...IF ONLY HE HADN'T SPOKEN TO ME IN THE LIBRARY THAT DAY.
SLIDE
IF ONLY I HADN'T SEEN HIS REAL SMILE...
CLENCH
I WOULDN'T HAVE BEEN HURT THIS BADLY.
UGH ...

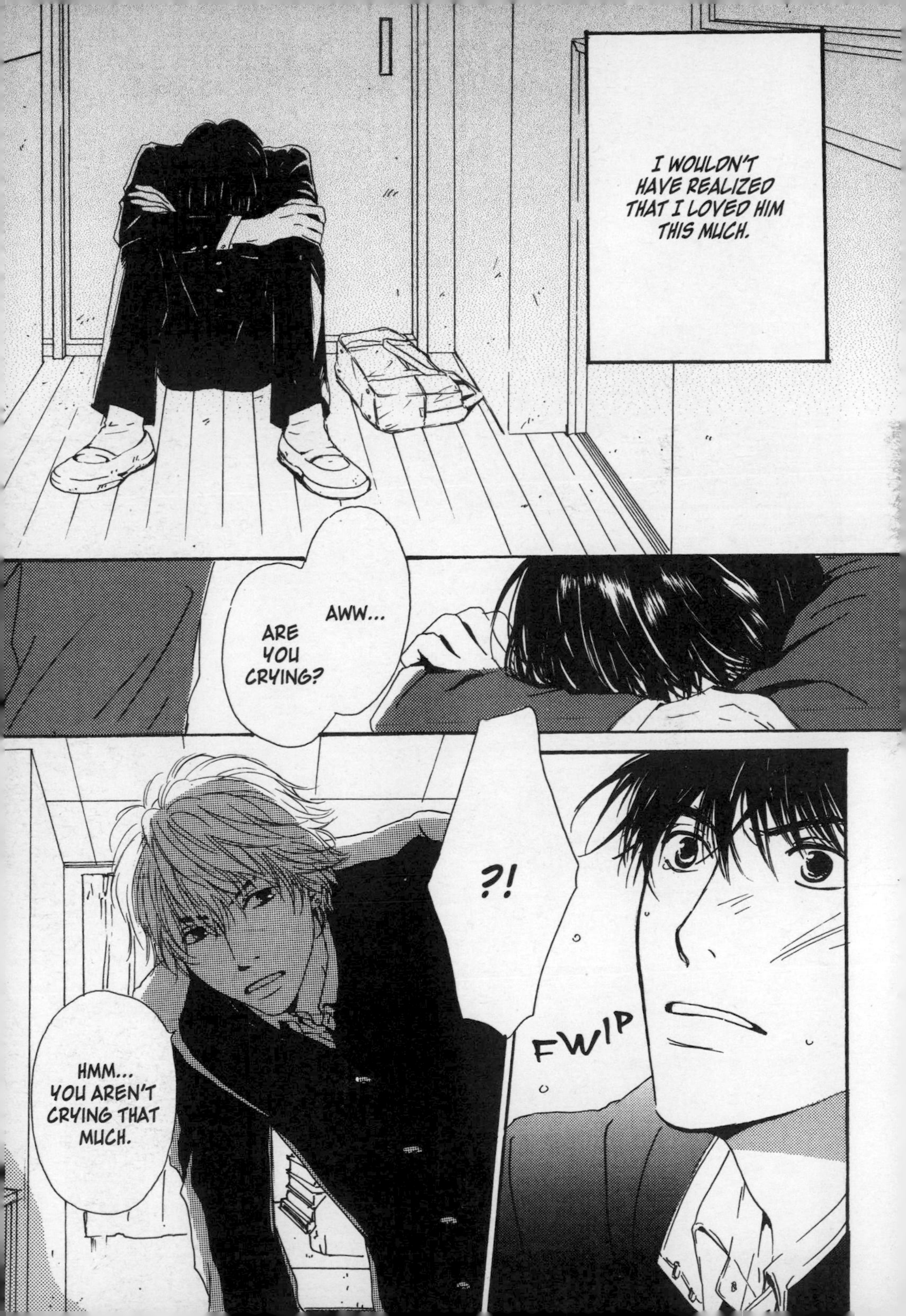
I WOULDN'T HAVE REALIZED THAT I LOVED HIM THIS MUCH.
AWW... ARE YOU CRYING?
?!
FWIP
HMM... YOU AREN'T CRYING THAT MUCH.

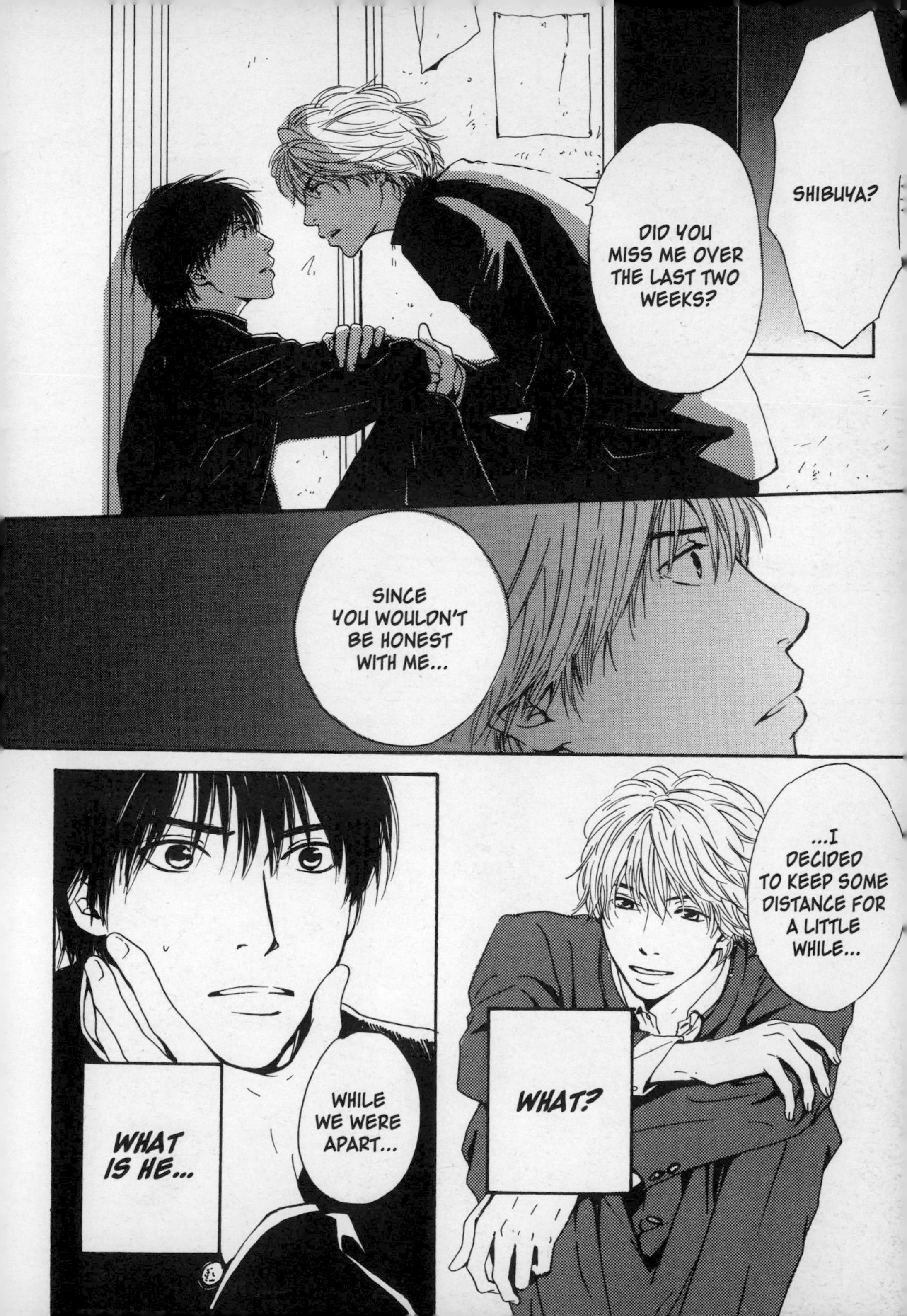
SHIBUYA?
DID YOU MISS ME OVER THE LAST TWO WEEKS?
SINCE YOU WOULDN'T BE HONEST WITH ME...
...I DECIDED TO KEEP SOME DISTANCE FOR A LITTLE WHILE...
WHAT?
WHILE WE WERE APART...
WHAT IS HE...

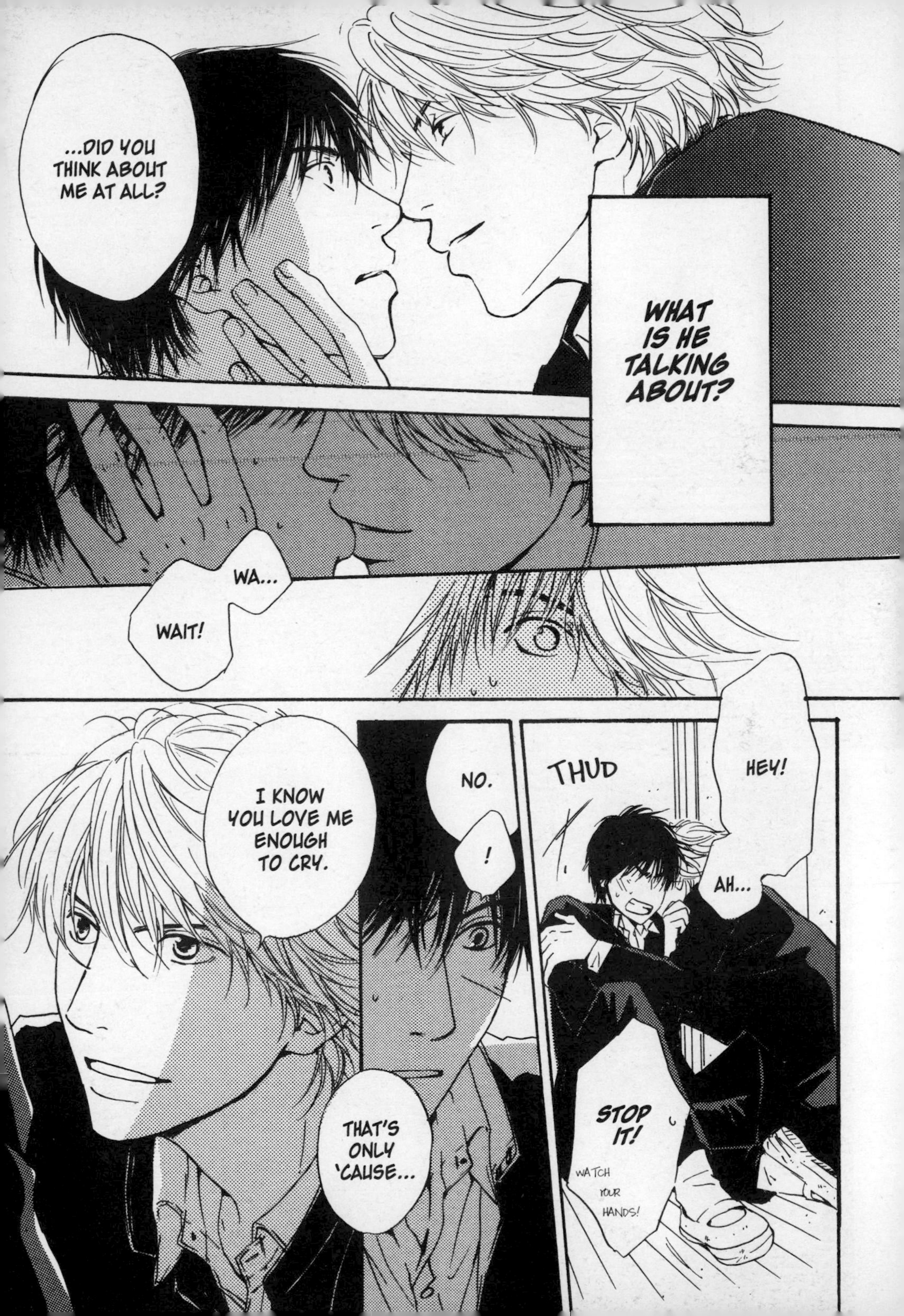
...DID YOU THINK ABOUT ME AT ALL?
WHAT IS HE TALKING ABOUT?
WA...
WAIT!
HEY!
THUD
AH...
STOP IT!
WATCH YOUR HANDS!
NO.
!
THAT'S ONLY 'CAUSE...
I KNOW YOU LOVE ME ENOUGH TO CRY.

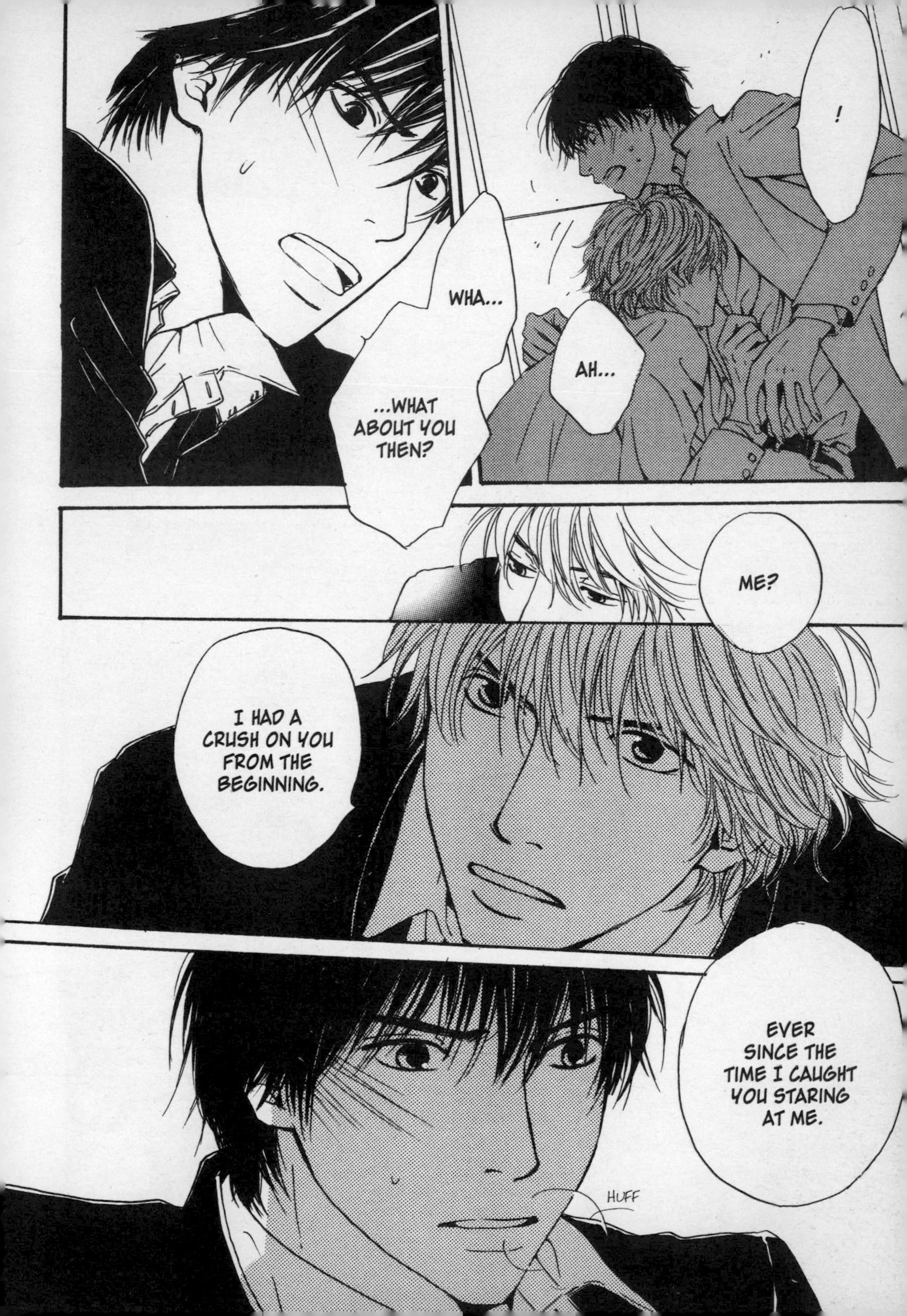
!
AH...
WHA...
...WHAT ABOUT YOU THEN?
ME?
I HAD A CRUSH ON YOU FROM THE BEGINNING.
EVER SINCE THE TIME I CAUGHT YOU STARING AT ME.
HUFF

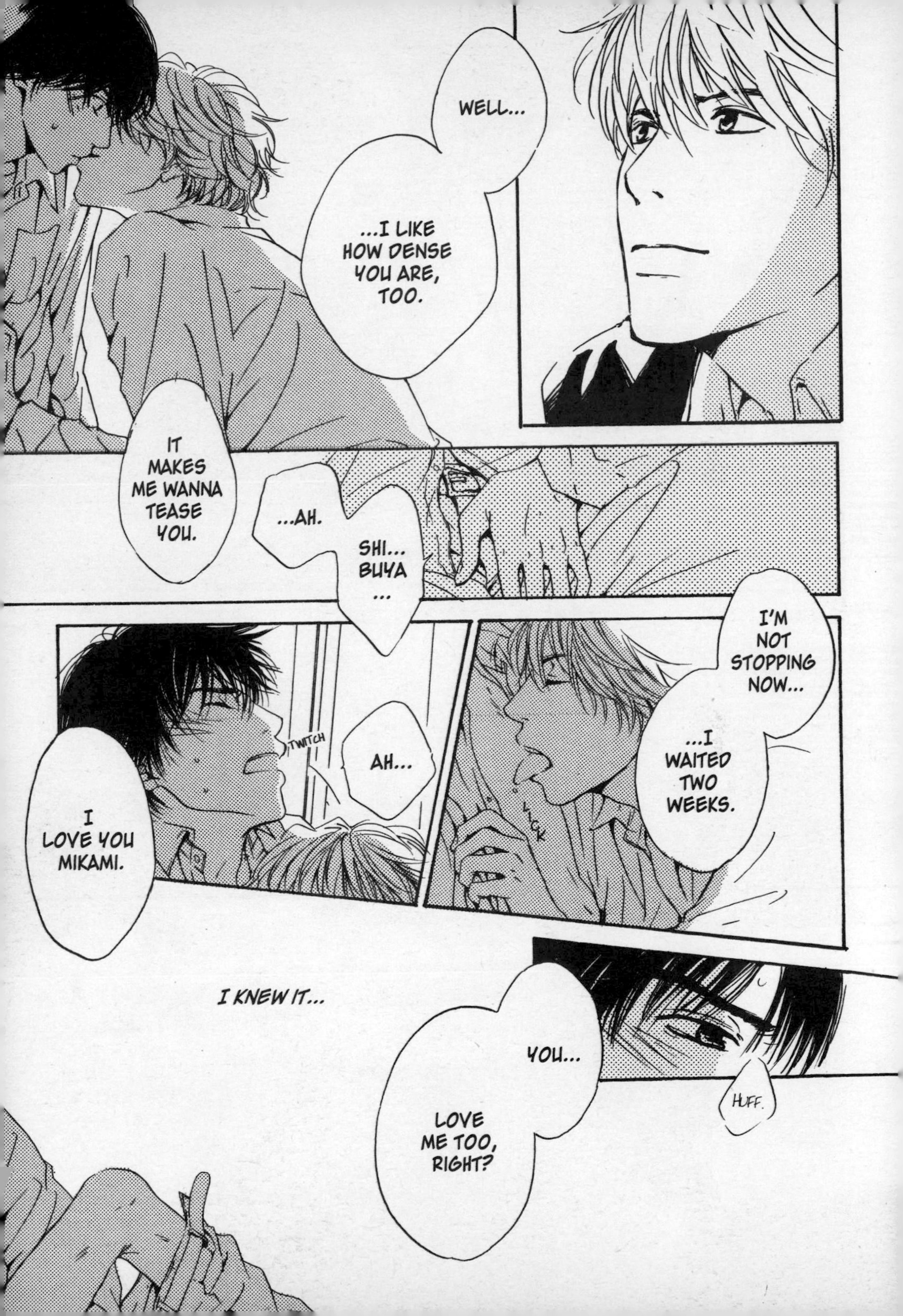
WELL...
...I LIKE HOW DENSE YOU ARE, TOO.
IT MAKES ME WANNA TEASE YOU.
...AH.
SHI... BUYA ...
I'M NOT STOPPING NOW...
...I WAITED TWO WEEKS.
LICK
TWITCH
AH...
I LOVE YOU MIKAMI.
I KNEW IT...
YOU...
LOVE ME TOO, RIGHT?
HUFF.

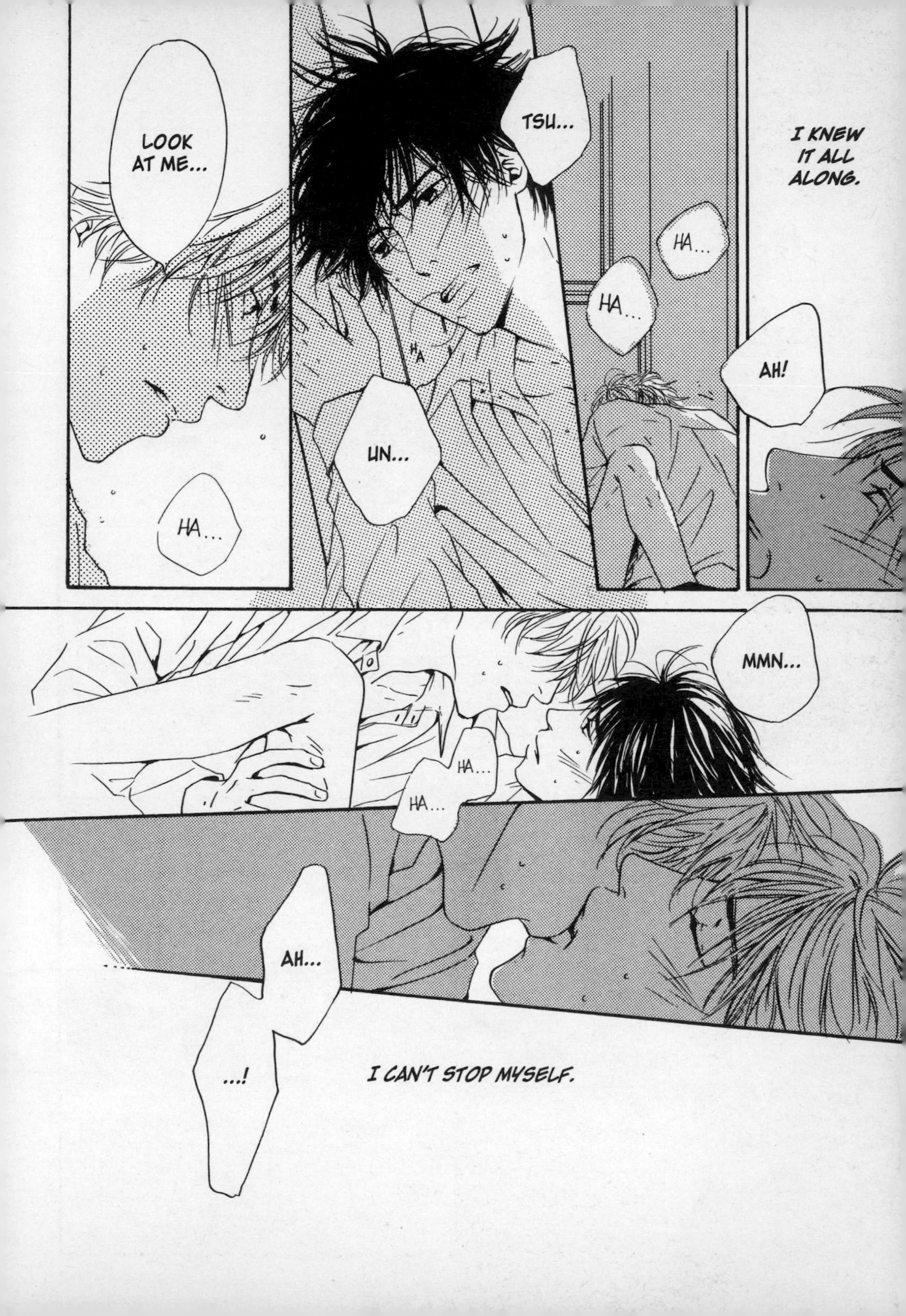
I KNEW IT ALL ALONG.
AH!
HA...
HA...
TSU...
HA
UN...
LOOK AT ME...
HA...
MMN...
HA...
HA...
AH...
...!
I CAN'T STOP MYSELF.

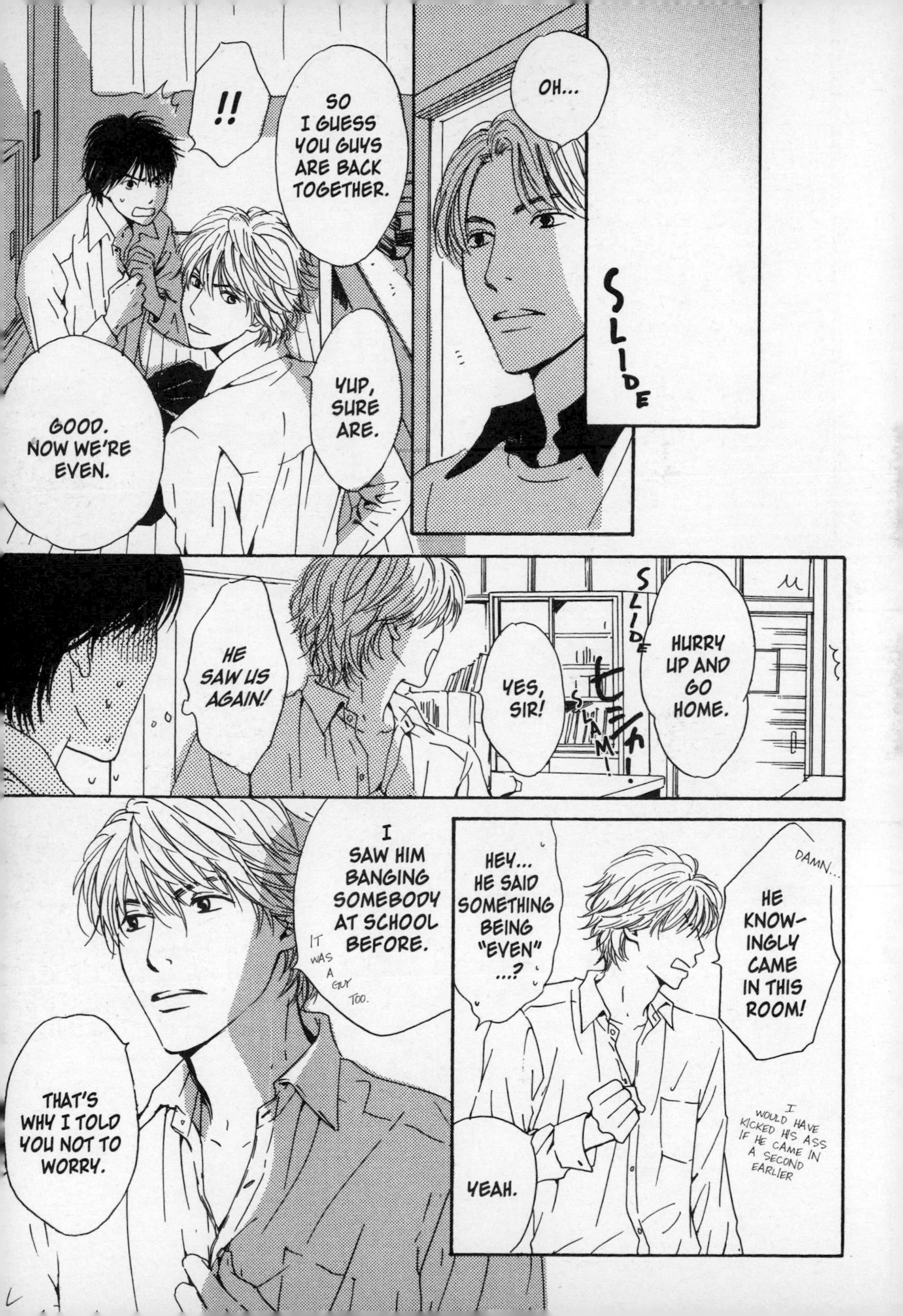
OH...
SLIDE
SO I GUESS YOU GUYS ARE BACK TOGETHER.
!!
YUP, SURE ARE.
GOOD. NOW WE'RE EVEN.
HURRY UP AND GO HOME.
SLIDE
YES, SIR!
SLAM!
HE SAW US AGAIN!
DAMN...
HE KNOW-INGLY CAME IN THIS ROOM!
HEY... HE SAID SOMETHING BEING "EVEN" ...?
I WOULD HAVE KICKED HIS ASS IF HE CAME IN A SECOND EARLIER
YEAH.
I SAW HIM BANGING SOMEBODY AT SCHOOL BEFORE.
IT WAS A GUY TOO.
THAT'S WHY I TOLD YOU NOT TO WORRY.

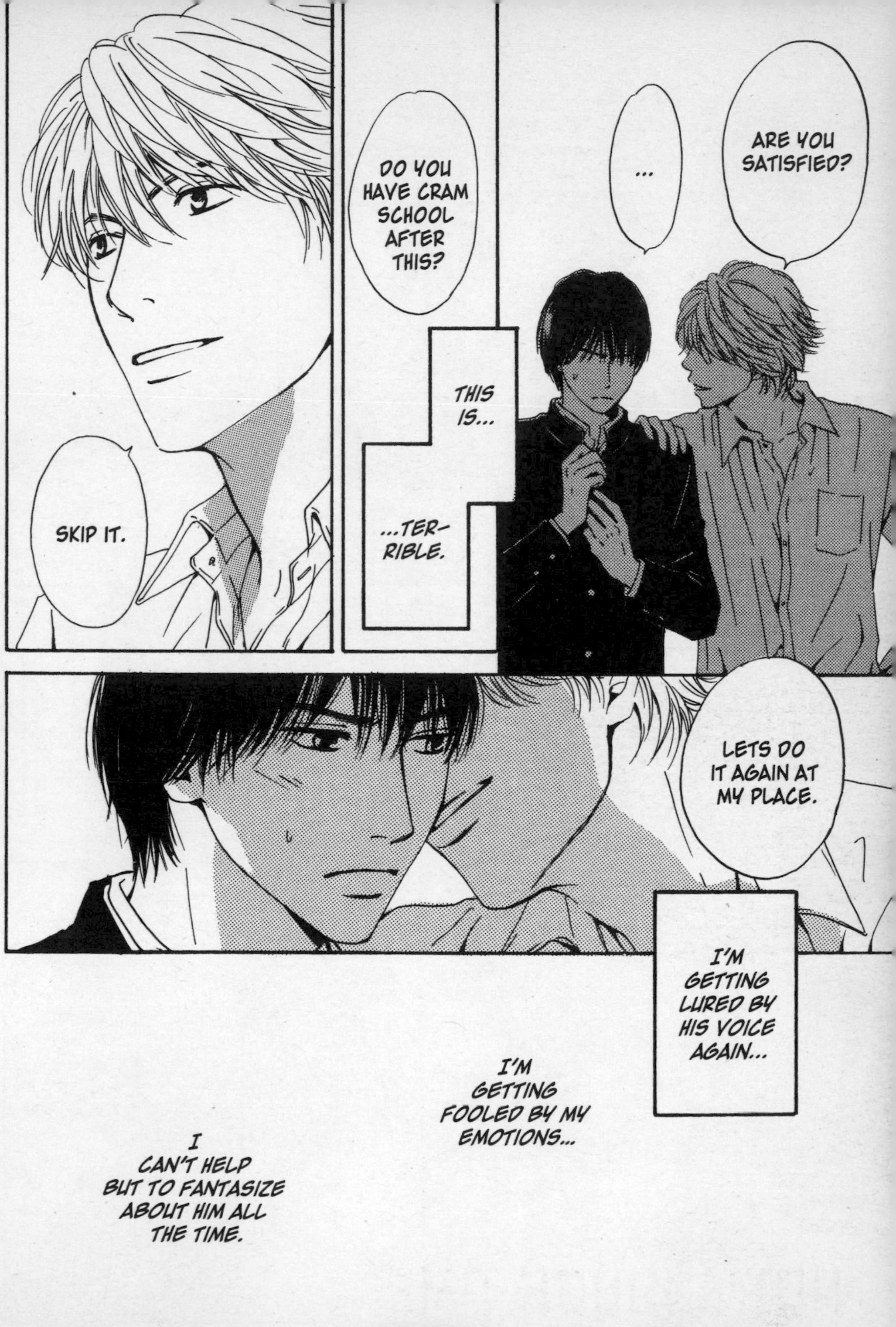
ARE YOU SATISFIED?
...
THIS IS...
...TER-RIBLE.
DO YOU HAVE CRAM SCHOOL AFTER THIS?
SKIP IT.
LETS DO IT AGAIN AT MY PLACE.
I'M GETTING LURED BY HIS VOICE AGAIN...
I'M GETTING FOOLED BY MY EMOTIONS...
I CAN'T HELP BUT TO FANTASIZE ABOUT HIM ALL THE TIME.

END

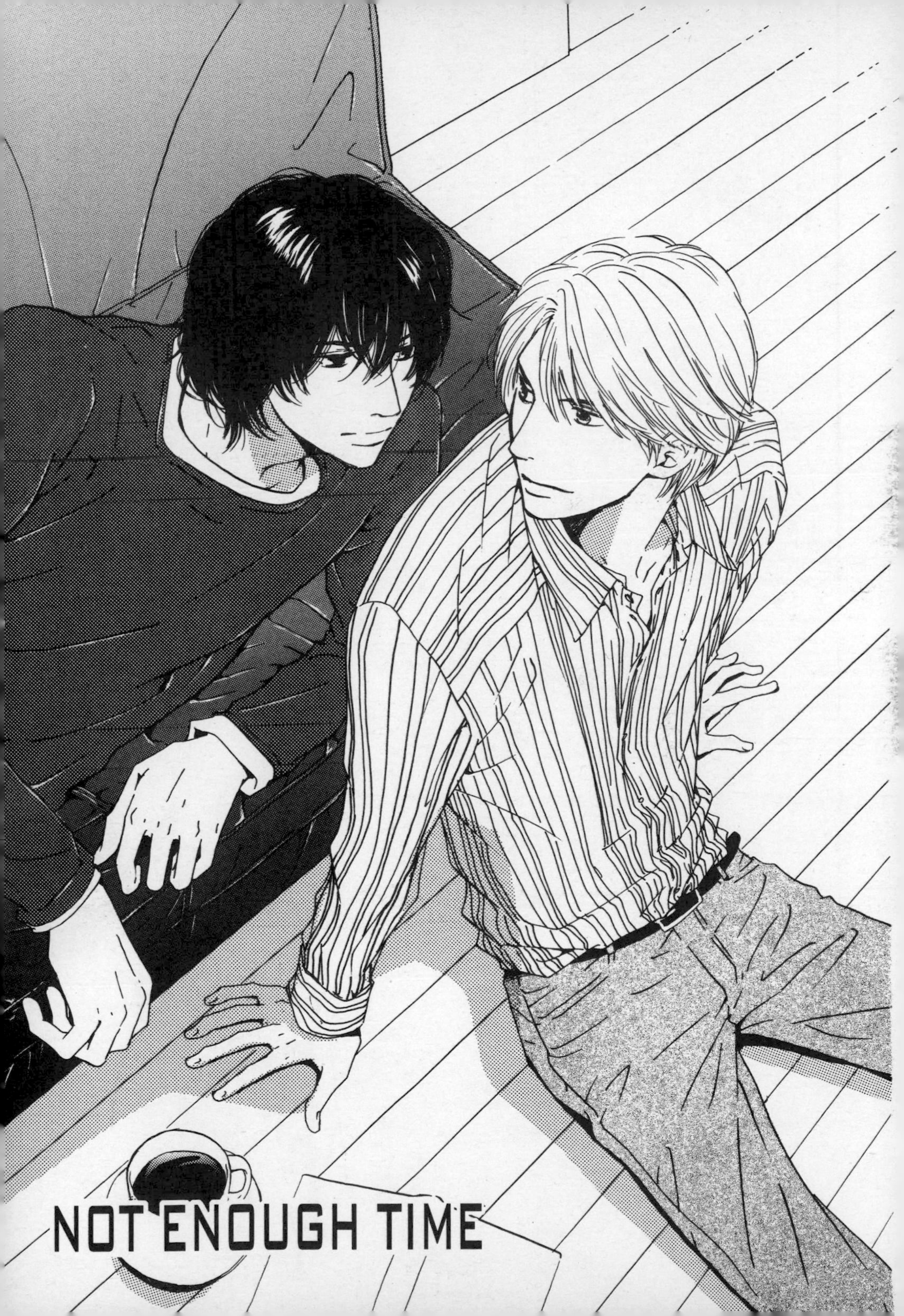
NOT ENOUGH TIME

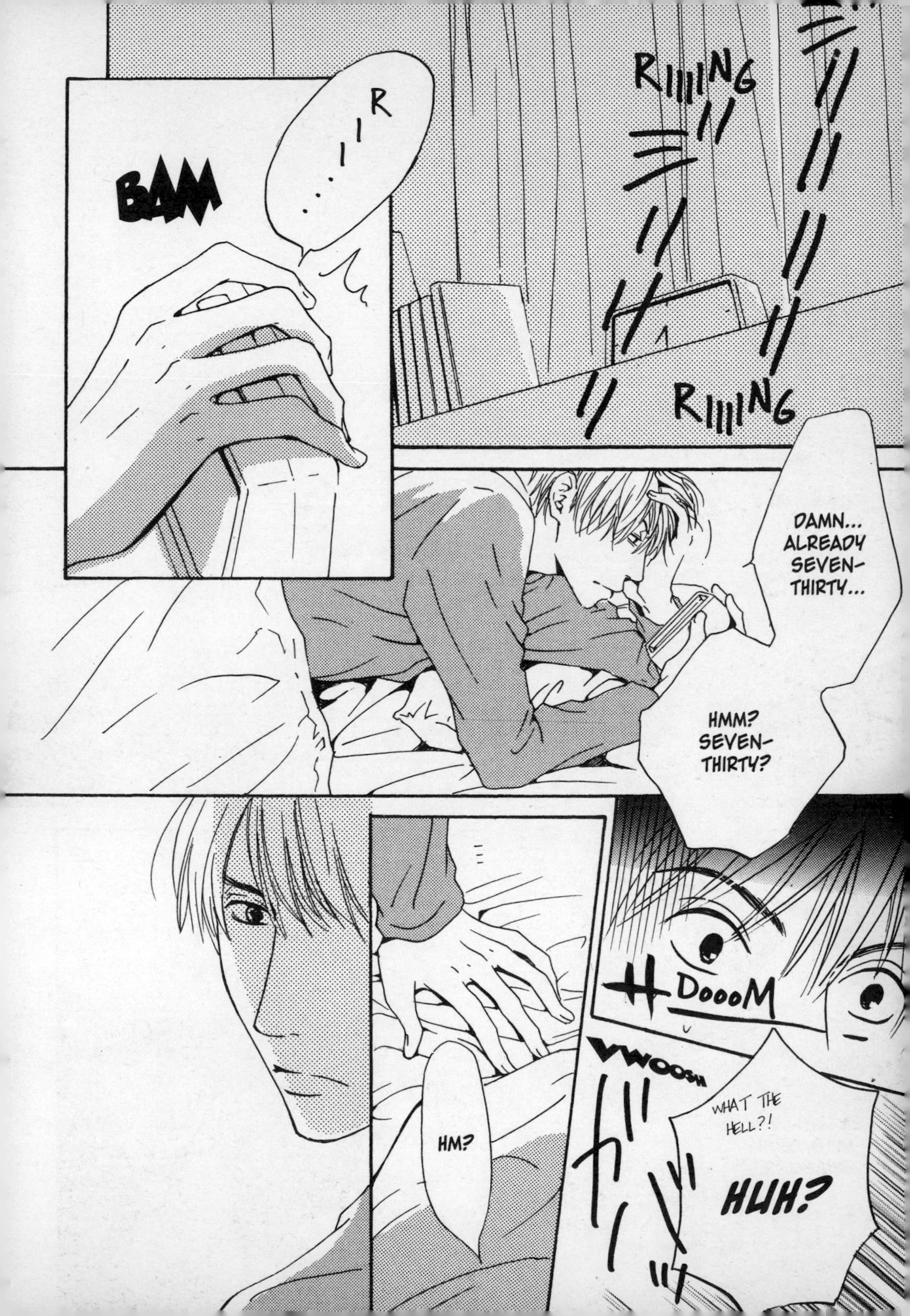

RIIIING
RIIIING
BAM
R
DAMN... ALREADY SEVEN-THIRTY...
HMM? SEVEN-THIRTY?
DoooM
VWOOSH
WHAT THE HELL?!
HUH?
HM?

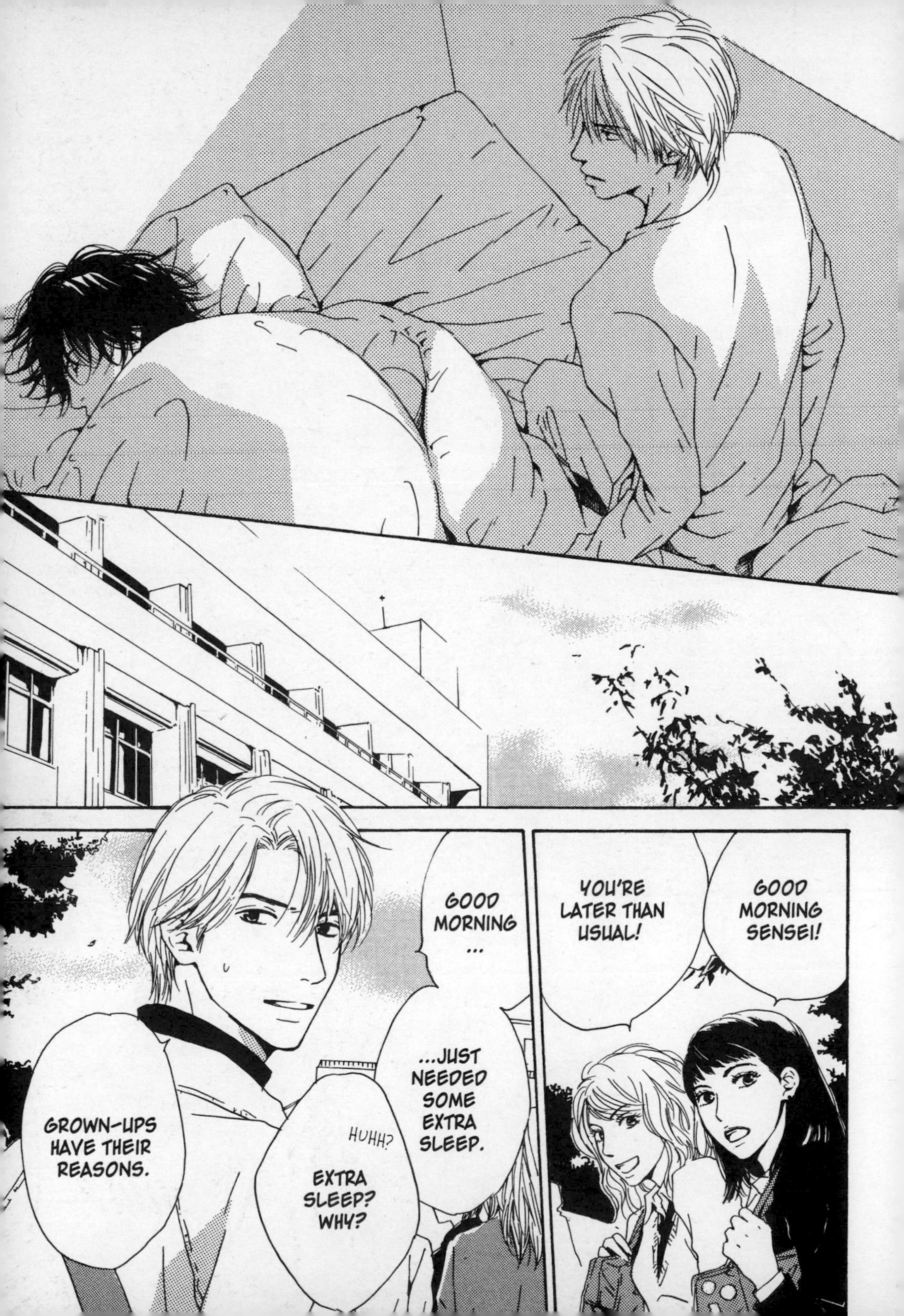
GOOD MORNING SENSEI!
YOU'RE LATER THAN USUAL!
GOOD MORNING ...
...JUST NEEDED SOME EXTRA SLEEP.
HUHH?
EXTRA SLEEP? WHY?
GROWN-UPS HAVE THEIR REASONS.

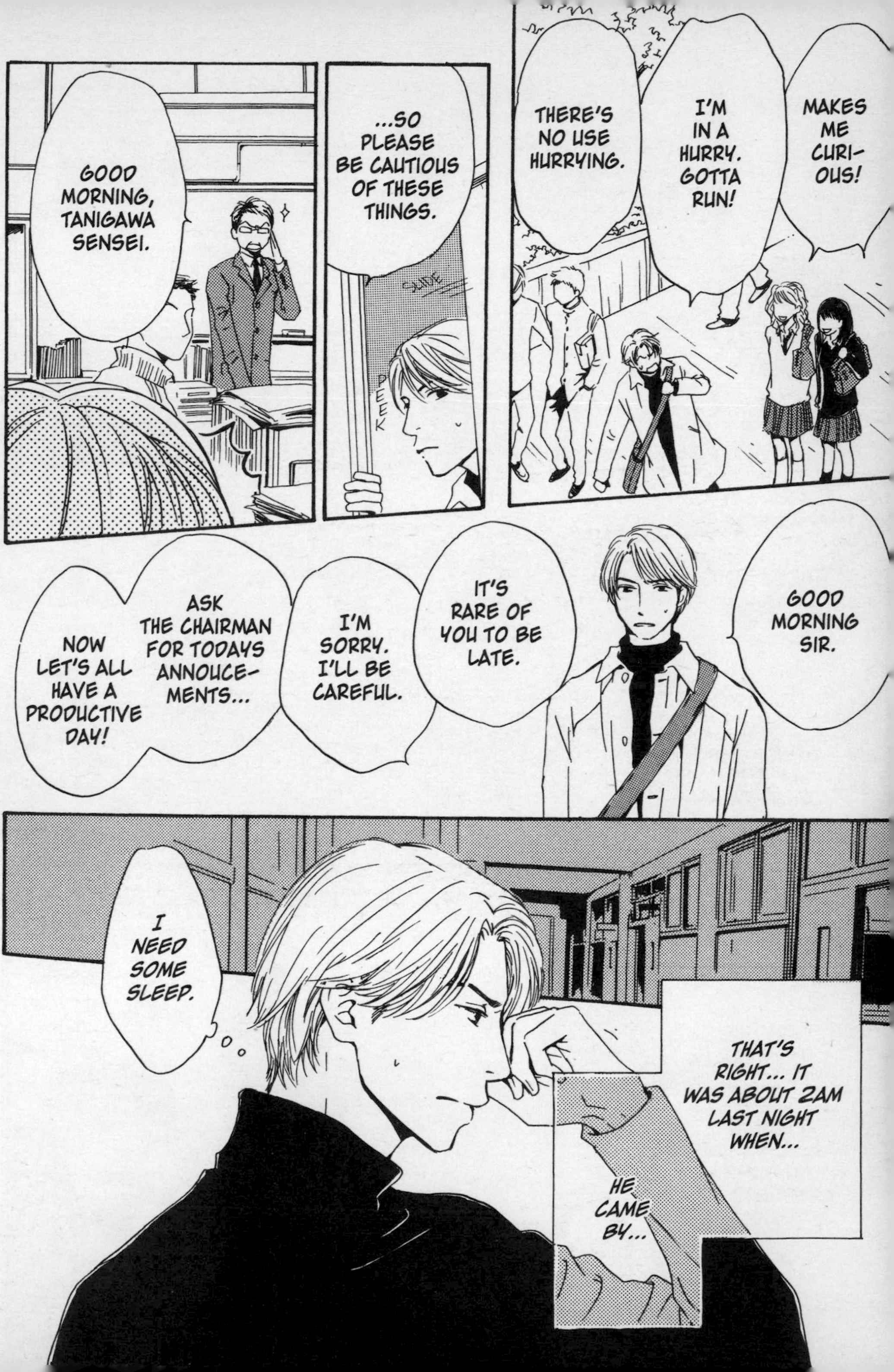
MAKES ME CURI-OUS!
I'M IN A HURRY. GOTTA RUN!
THERE'S NO USE HURRYING.
SLIDE
...SO PLEASE BE CAUTIOUS OF THESE THINGS.
PEEK
GOOD MORNING, TANIGAWA SENSEI.
GOOD MORNING SIR.
IT'S RARE OF YOU TO BE LATE.
I'M SORRY. I'LL BE CAREFUL.
ASK THE CHAIRMAN FOR TODAYS ANNOUCE-MENTS...
NOW LET'S ALL HAVE A PRODUCTIVE DAY!
THAT'S RIGHT... IT WAS ABOUT 2AM LAST NIGHT WHEN...
HE CAME BY...
I NEED SOME SLEEP.

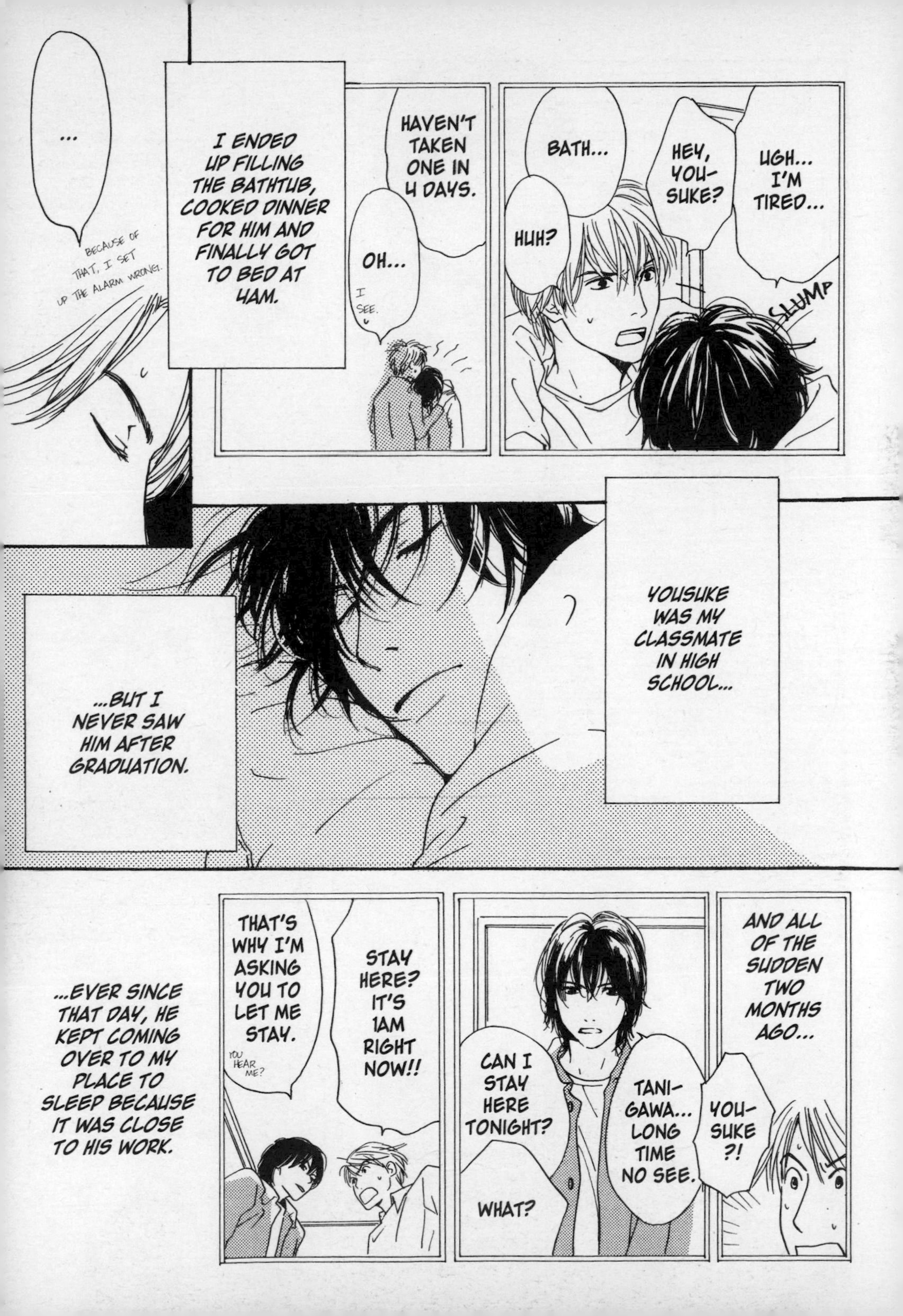
UGH... I'M TIRED...
SLUMP
HEY, YOU-SUKE?
BATH...
HUH?
HAVEN'T TAKEN ONE IN 4 DAYS.
OH...
I SEE.
I ENDED UP FILLING THE BATHTUB, COOKED DINNER FOR HIM AND FINALLY GOT TO BED AT 4AM.
...
BECAUSE OF THAT, I SET UP THE ALARM WRONG.
YOUSUKE WAS MY CLASSMATE IN HIGH SCHOOL...
...BUT I NEVER SAW HIM AFTER GRADUATION.
AND ALL OF THE SUDDEN TWO MONTHS AGO...
YOU-SUKE ?!
TANI-GAWA... LONG TIME NO SEE.
CAN I STAY HERE TONIGHT?
WHAT?
STAY HERE? IT'S 1AM RIGHT NOW!!
THAT'S WHY I'M ASKING YOU TO LET ME STAY.
YOU HEAR ME?
...EVER SINCE THAT DAY, HE KEPT COMING OVER TO MY PLACE TO SLEEP BECAUSE IT WAS CLOSE TO HIS WORK.

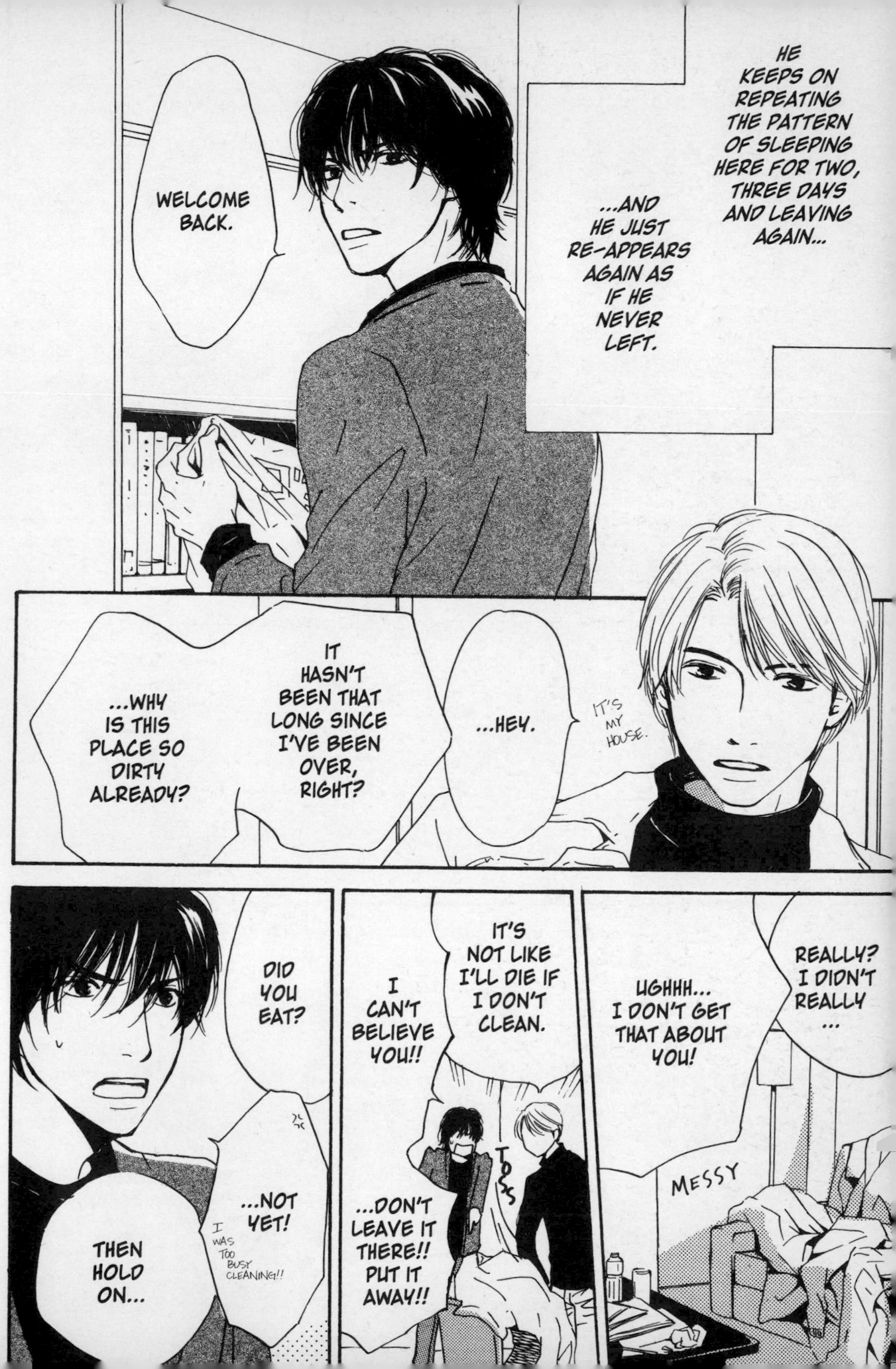
HE KEEPS ON REPEATING THE PATTERN OF SLEEPING HERE FOR TWO, THREE DAYS AND LEAVING AGAIN...
...AND HE JUST RE-APPEARS AGAIN AS IF HE NEVER LEFT.
WELCOME BACK.
IT'S MY HOUSE.
...HEY.
IT HASN'T BEEN THAT LONG SINCE I'VE BEEN OVER, RIGHT?
...WHY IS THIS PLACE SO DIRTY ALREADY?
REALLY? I DIDN'T REALLY ...
UGHHH... I DON'T GET THAT ABOUT YOU!
MESSY
IT'S NOT LIKE I'LL DIE IF I DON'T CLEAN.
I CAN'T BELIEVE YOU!!
TOSS
...DON'T LEAVE IT THERE!! PUT IT AWAY!!
DID YOU EAT?
...NOT YET!
I WAS TOO BUSY CLEANING!!
THEN HOLD ON...

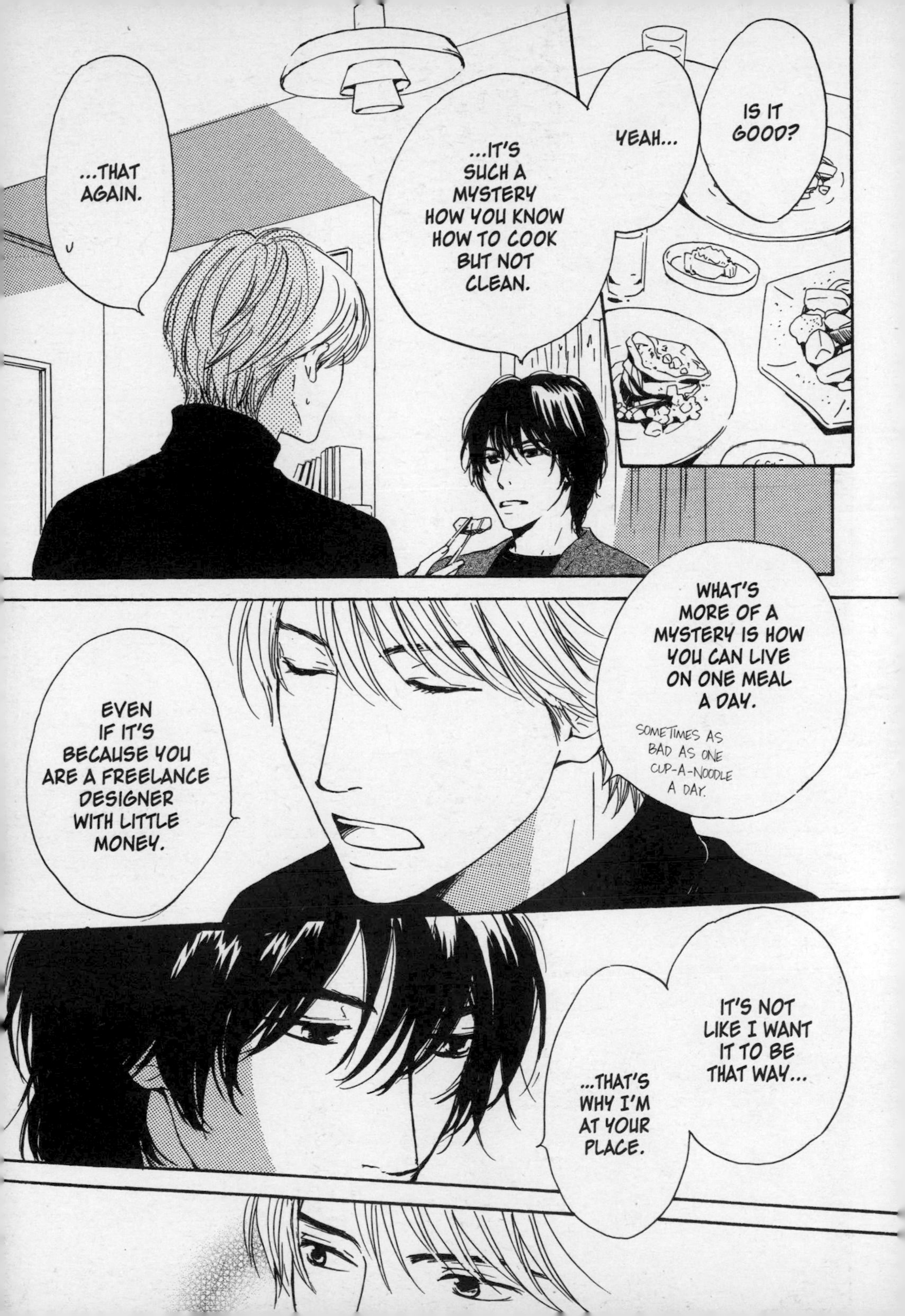
IS IT GOOD?
YEAH...
...IT'S SUCH A MYSTERY HOW YOU KNOW HOW TO COOK BUT NOT CLEAN.
...THAT AGAIN.
WHAT'S MORE OF A MYSTERY IS HOW YOU CAN LIVE ON ONE MEAL A DAY.
SOMETIMES AS BAD AS ONE CUP-A-NOODLE A DAY.
EVEN IF IT'S BECAUSE YOU ARE A FREELANCE DESIGNER WITH LITTLE MONEY.
IT'S NOT LIKE I WANT IT TO BE THAT WAY...
...THAT'S WHY I'M AT YOUR PLACE.

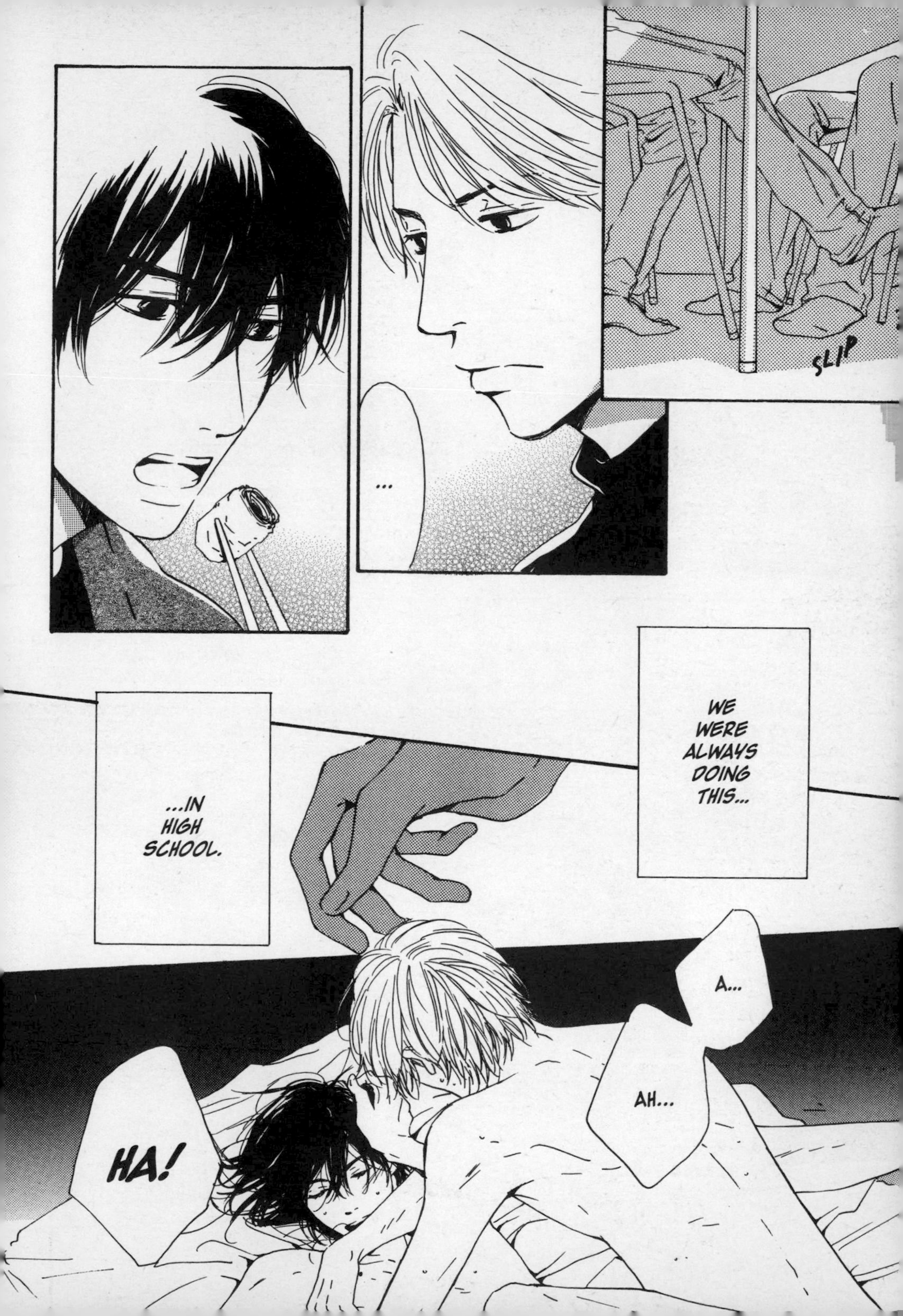
SLIP
...
WE WERE ALWAYS DOING THIS...
...IN HIGH SCHOOL.
A...
AH...
HA!

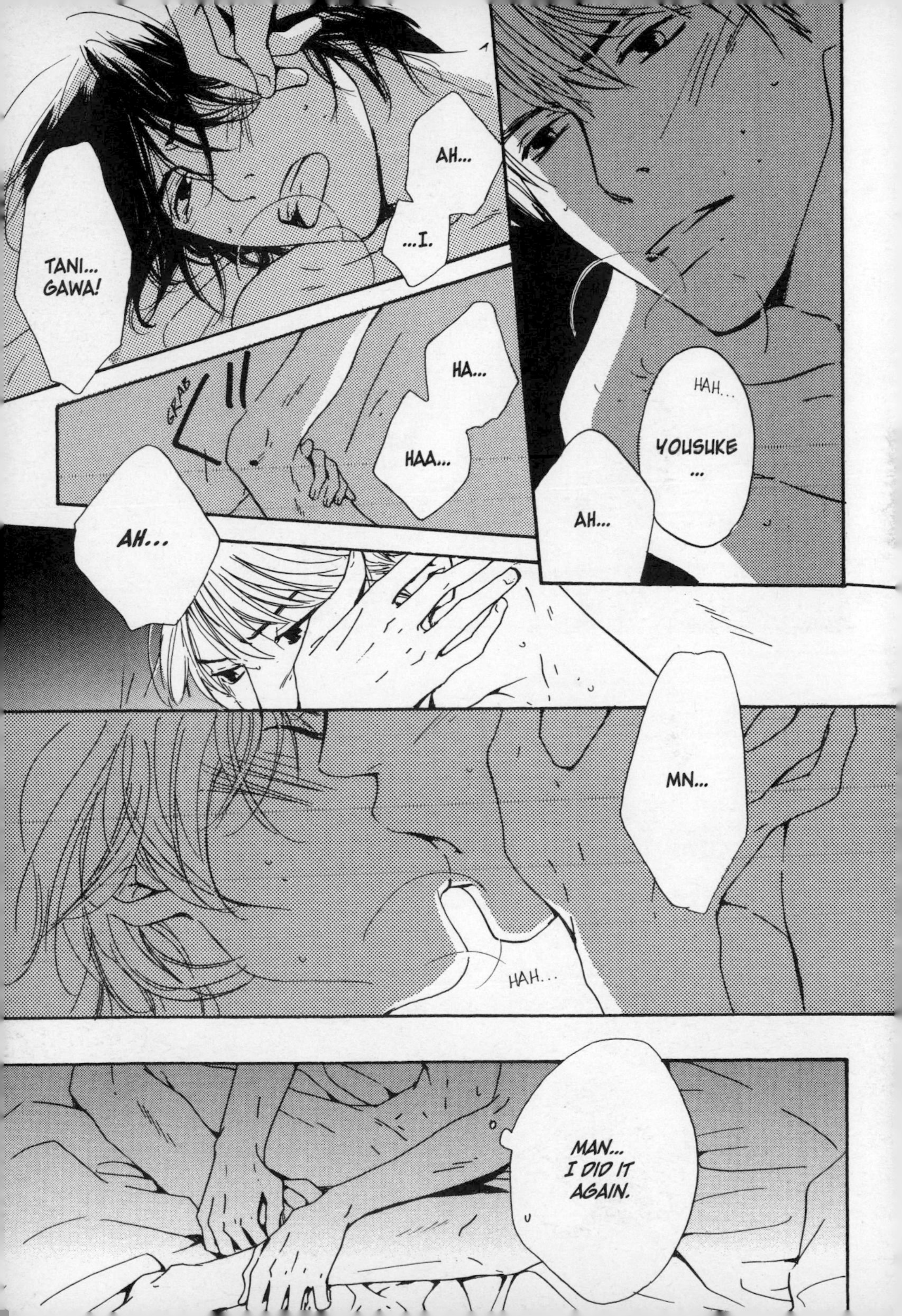
HAH...
YOUSUKE...
AH...
AH...
...I.
TANI... GAWA!
GRAB
HA...
HAA...
AH...
MN...
HAH...
MAN... I DID IT AGAIN.

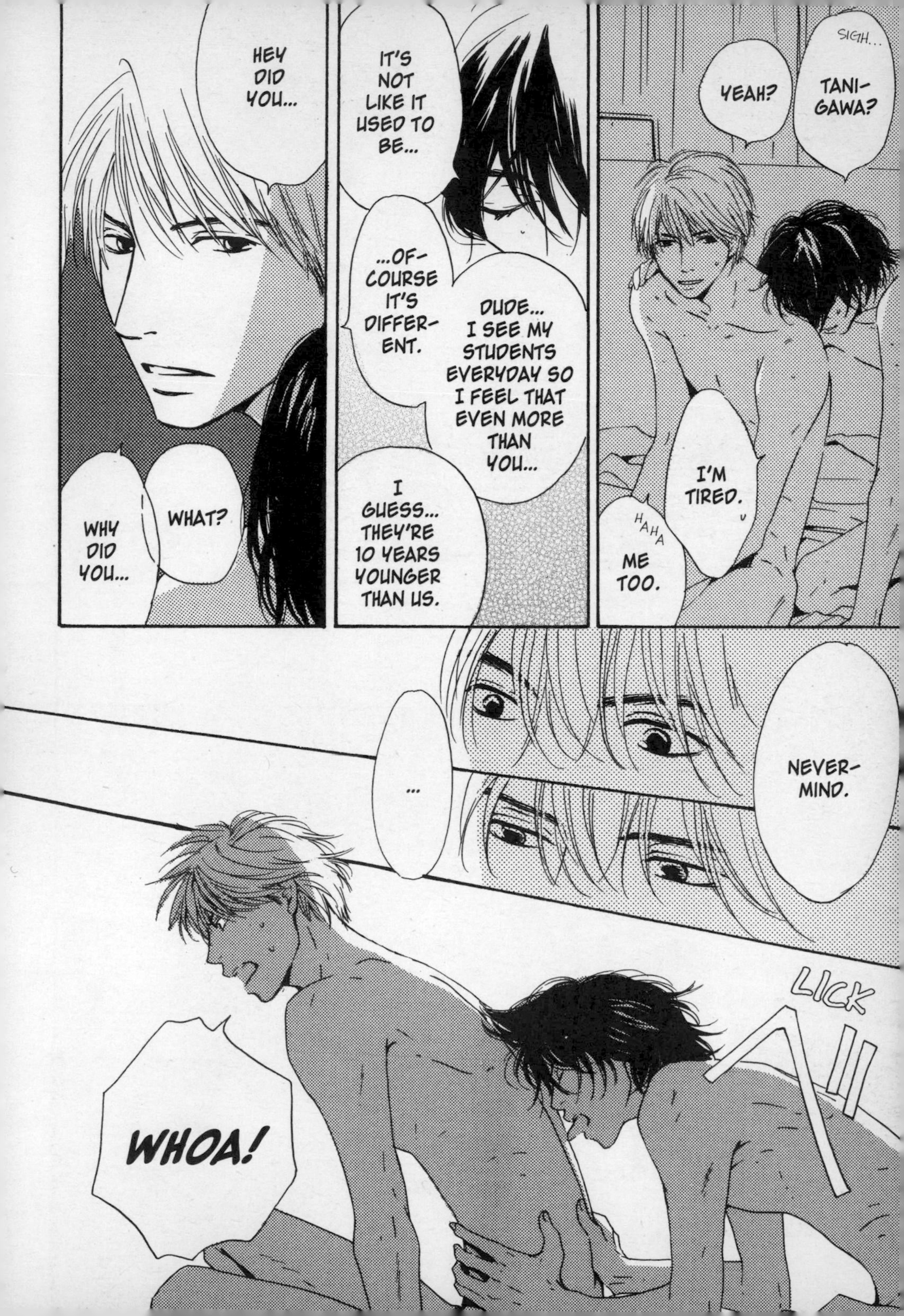
SIGH...
TANI-GAWA?
YEAH?
I'M TIRED.
HAHA
ME TOO.
IT'S NOT LIKE IT USED TO BE...
...OF-COURSE IT'S DIFFER-ENT.
DUDE... I SEE MY STUDENTS EVERYDAY SO I FEEL THAT EVEN MORE THAN YOU...
I GUESS... THEY'RE 10 YEARS YOUNGER THAN US.
HEY DID YOU...
WHAT?
WHY DID YOU...
NEVER-MIND.
...
LICK
WHOA!

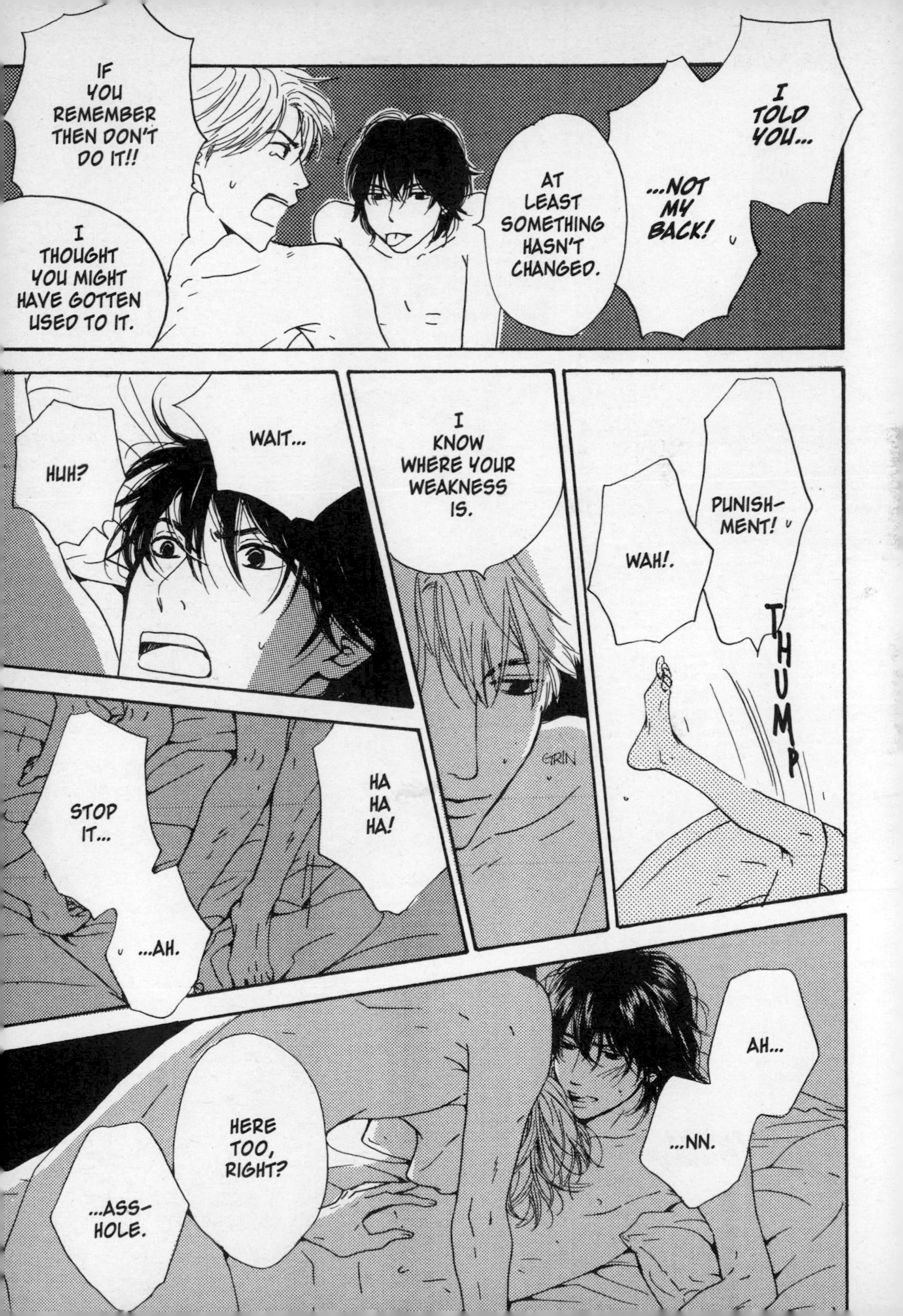
I TOLD YOU...
...NOT MY BACK!
AT LEAST SOMETHING HASN'T CHANGED.
IF YOU REMEMBER THEN DON'T DO IT!!
I THOUGHT YOU MIGHT HAVE GOTTEN USED TO IT.
PUNISH-MENT!
WAH!.
THUMP
I KNOW WHERE YOUR WEAKNESS IS.
GRIN
WAIT...
HUH?
HA HA HA!
STOP IT...
...AH.
AH...
...NN.
HERE TOO, RIGHT?
...ASS-HOLE.

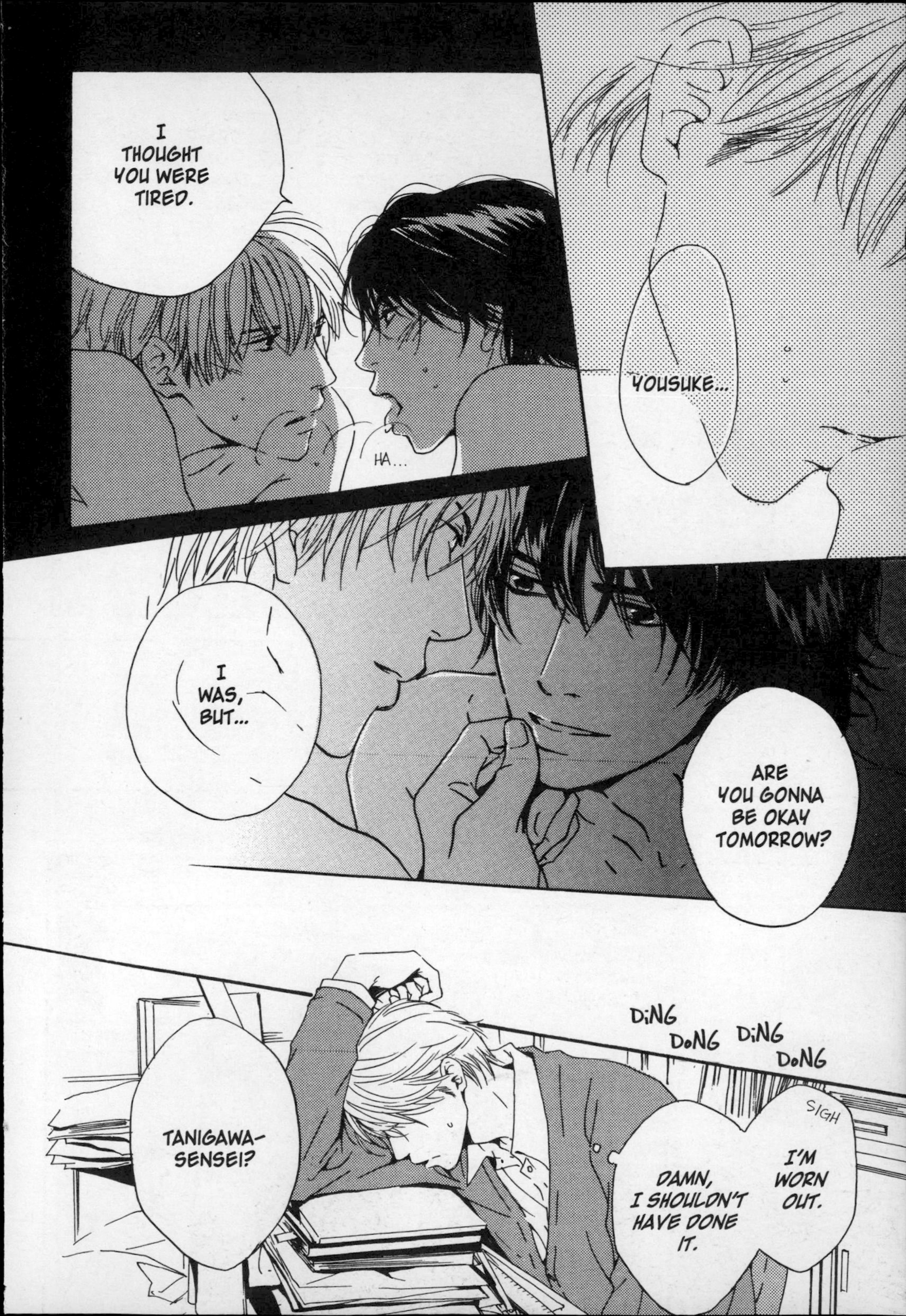
YOUSUKE...
I THOUGHT YOU WERE TIRED.
HA...
ARE YOU GONNA BE OKAY TOMORROW?
I WAS, BUT...
DiNG DoNG DiNG DoNG
SIGH
I'M WORN OUT.
DAMN, I SHOULDN'T HAVE DONE IT.
TANIGAWA-SENSEI?

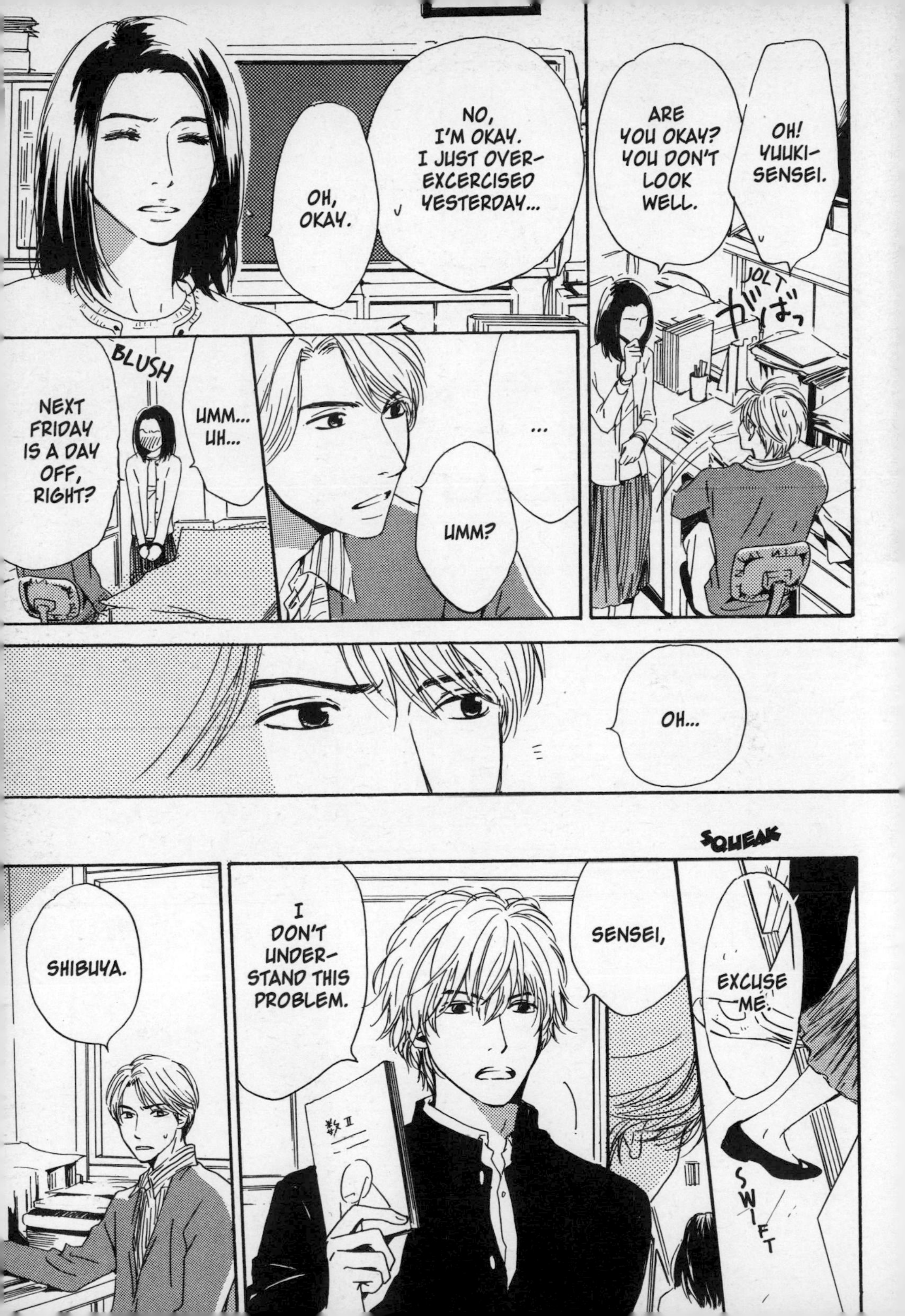
OH! YUUKI-SENSEI.
ARE YOU OKAY? YOU DON'T LOOK WELL.
JOLT
がばっ
NO, I'M OKAY. I JUST OVER-EXCERCISED YESTERDAY...
OH, OKAY.
...
UMM?
UMM... UH...
BLUSH
NEXT FRIDAY IS A DAY OFF, RIGHT?
OH...
SQUEAK
EXCUSE ME.
SWIFT
SENSEI,
I DON'T UNDERSTAND THIS PROBLEM.
数II
SHIBUYA.

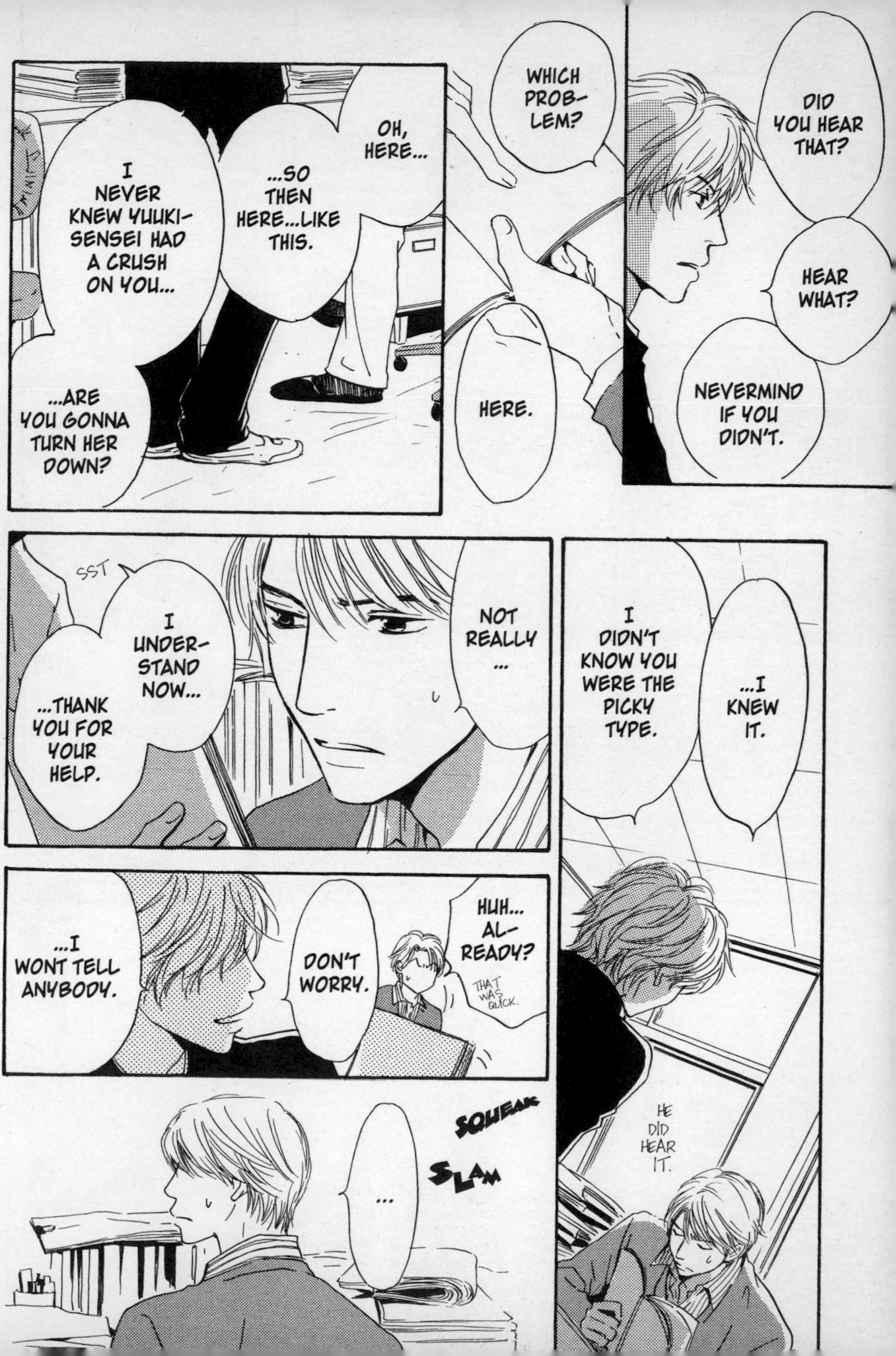
DID YOU HEAR THAT?
HEAR WHAT?
NEVERMIND IF YOU DIDN'T.
WHICH PROB-LEM?
HERE.
OH, HERE...
...SO THEN HERE...LIKE THIS.
I NEVER KNEW YUUKI-SENSEI HAD A CRUSH ON YOU...
...ARE YOU GONNA TURN HER DOWN?
...I KNEW IT.
I DIDN'T KNOW YOU WERE THE PICKY TYPE.
HE DID HEAR IT.
NOT REALLY ...
SST
I UNDER-STAND NOW...
...THANK YOU FOR YOUR HELP.
HUH... AL-READY?
THAT WAS QUICK.
DON'T WORRY.
...I WONT TELL ANYBODY.
SQUEAK
SLAM
...

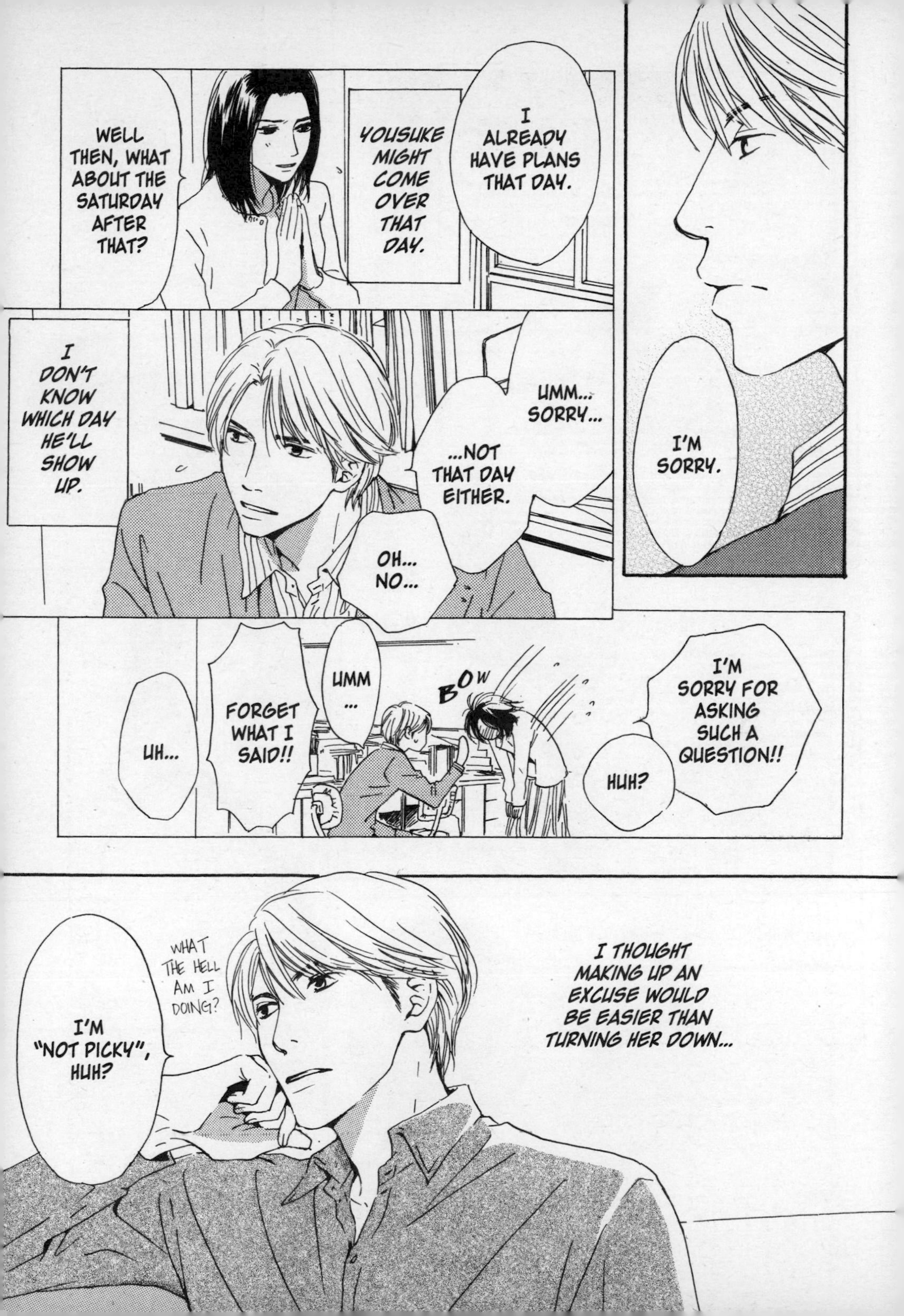
I'M SORRY.
I ALREADY HAVE PLANS THAT DAY.
YOUSUKE MIGHT COME OVER THAT DAY.
WELL THEN, WHAT ABOUT THE SATURDAY AFTER THAT?
UMM... SORRY...
...NOT THAT DAY EITHER.
I DON'T KNOW WHICH DAY HE'LL SHOW UP.
OH... NO...
I'M SORRY FOR ASKING SUCH A QUESTION!!
HUH?
BOW
UMM ...
FORGET WHAT I SAID!!
UH...
I THOUGHT MAKING UP AN EXCUSE WOULD BE EASIER THAN TURNING HER DOWN...
WHAT THE HELL AM I DOING?
I'M "NOT PICKY", HUH?

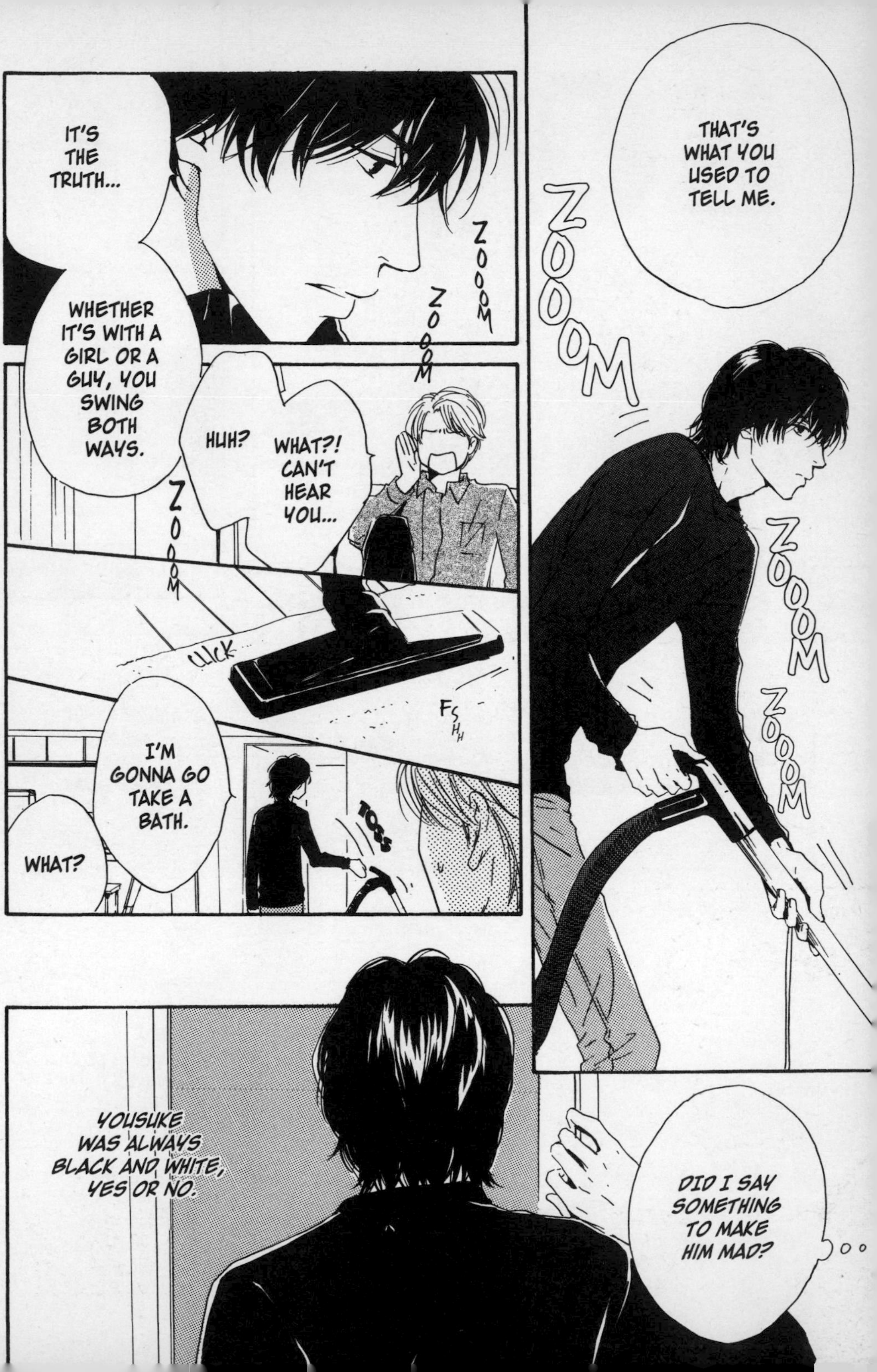
THAT'S WHAT YOU USED TO TELL ME.
ZOOOM
ZOOOM
ZOOOM
IT'S THE TRUTH...
WHETHER IT'S WITH A GIRL OR A GUY, YOU SWING BOTH WAYS.
ZOOOM
ZOOOM
WHAT?! CAN'T HEAR YOU...
HUH?
ZOOOM
CLICK
FSHH
I'M GONNA GO TAKE A BATH.
TOSS
WHAT?
DID I SAY SOMETHING TO MAKE HIM MAD?
YOUSUKE WAS ALWAYS BLACK AND WHITE, YES OR NO.

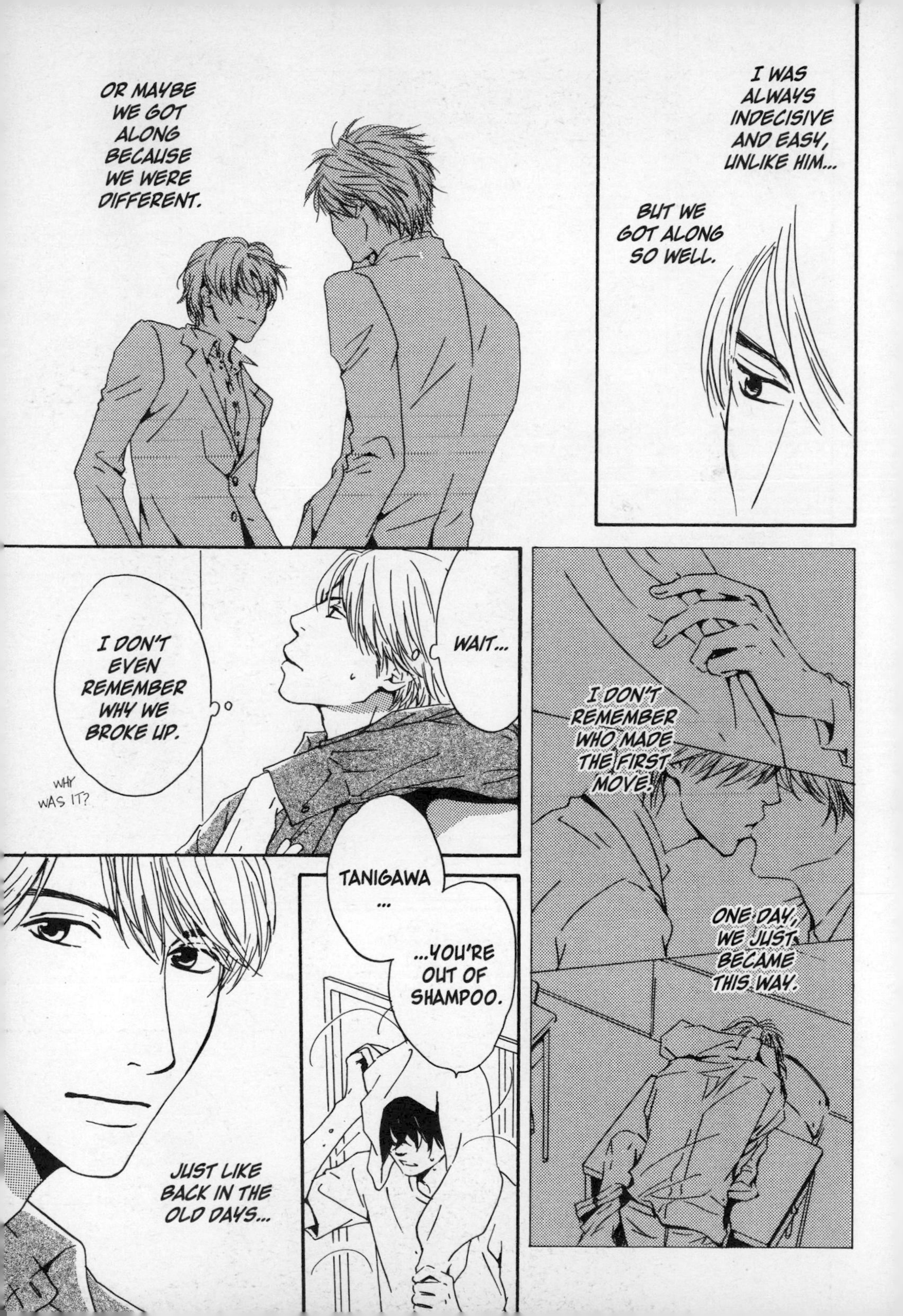
I WAS ALWAYS INDECISIVE AND EASY, UNLIKE HIM...
BUT WE GOT ALONG SO WELL.
OR MAYBE WE GOT ALONG BECAUSE WE WERE DIFFERENT.
I DON'T REMEMBER WHO MADE THE FIRST MOVE.
ONE DAY, WE JUST BECAME THIS WAY.
WAIT...
I DON'T EVEN REMEMBER WHY WE BROKE UP.
WHY WAS IT?
TANIGAWA ...
...YOU'RE OUT OF SHAMPOO.
JUST LIKE BACK IN THE OLD DAYS...

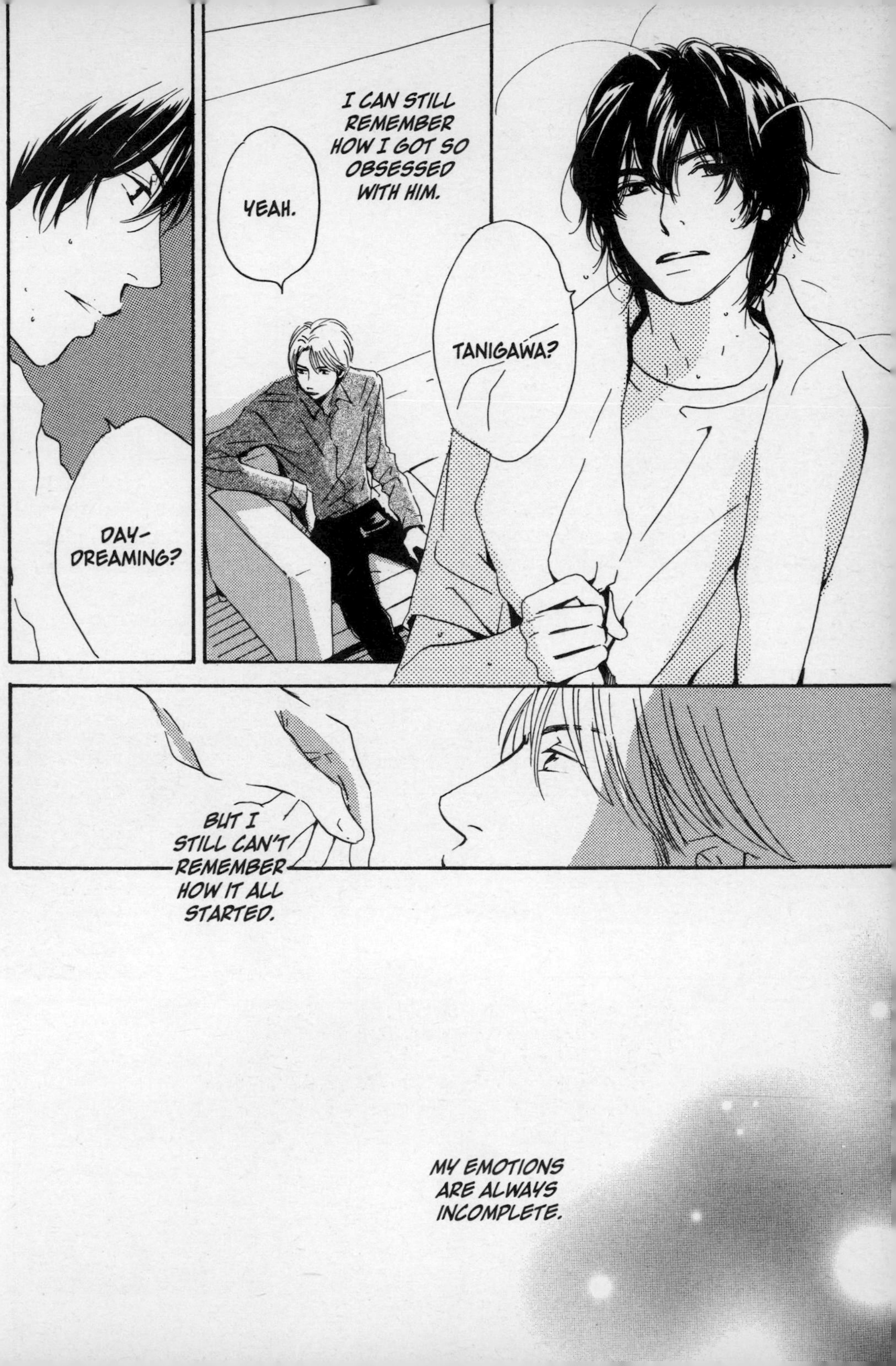
TANIGAWA?
I CAN STILL REMEMBER HOW I GOT SO OBSESSED WITH HIM.
YEAH.
DAY-DREAMING?
BUT I STILL CAN'T REMEMBER HOW IT ALL STARTED.
MY EMOTIONS ARE ALWAYS INCOMPLETE.

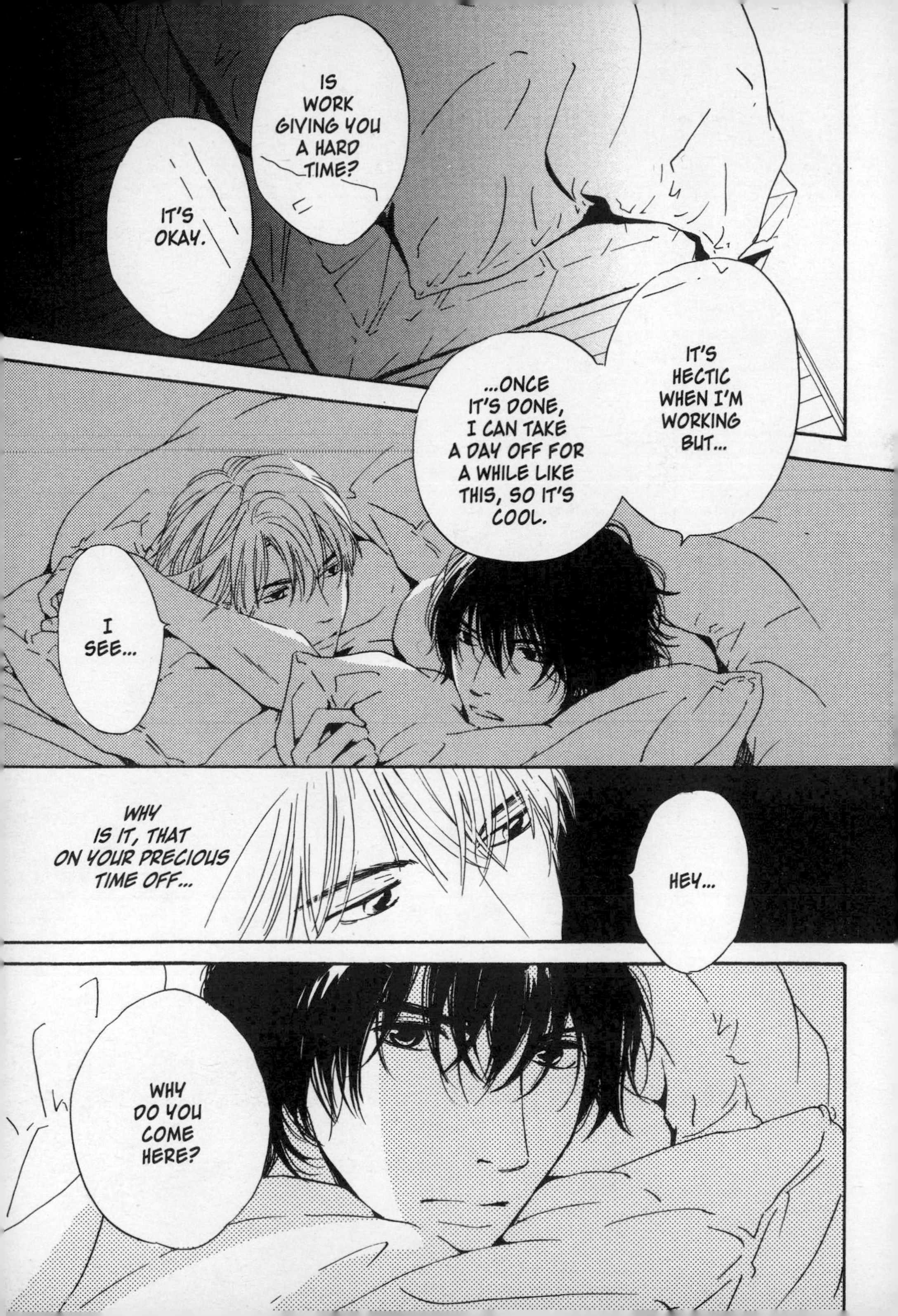
IS WORK GIVING YOU A HARD TIME?
IT'S OKAY.
IT'S HECTIC WHEN I'M WORKING BUT...
...ONCE IT'S DONE, I CAN TAKE A DAY OFF FOR A WHILE LIKE THIS, SO IT'S COOL.
I SEE...
HEY...
WHY IS IT, THAT ON YOUR PRECIOUS TIME OFF...
WHY DO YOU COME HERE?

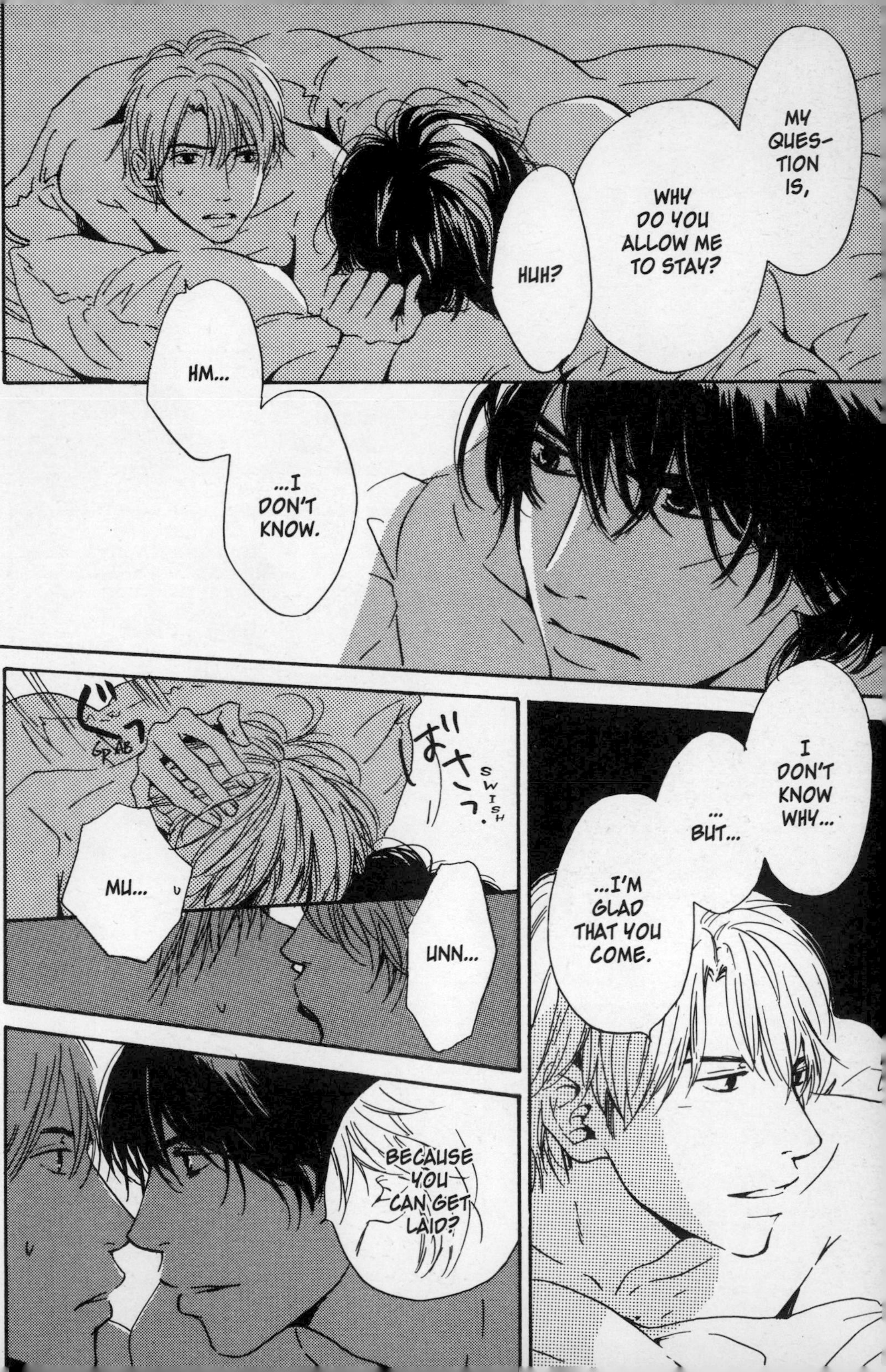
MY QUES-TION IS,
WHY DO YOU ALLOW ME TO STAY?
HUH?
HM...
...I DON'T KNOW.
I DON'T KNOW WHY...
...BUT...
...I'M GLAD THAT YOU COME.
GRAB
SWISH
MU...
UNN...
BECAUSE YOU CAN GET LAID?

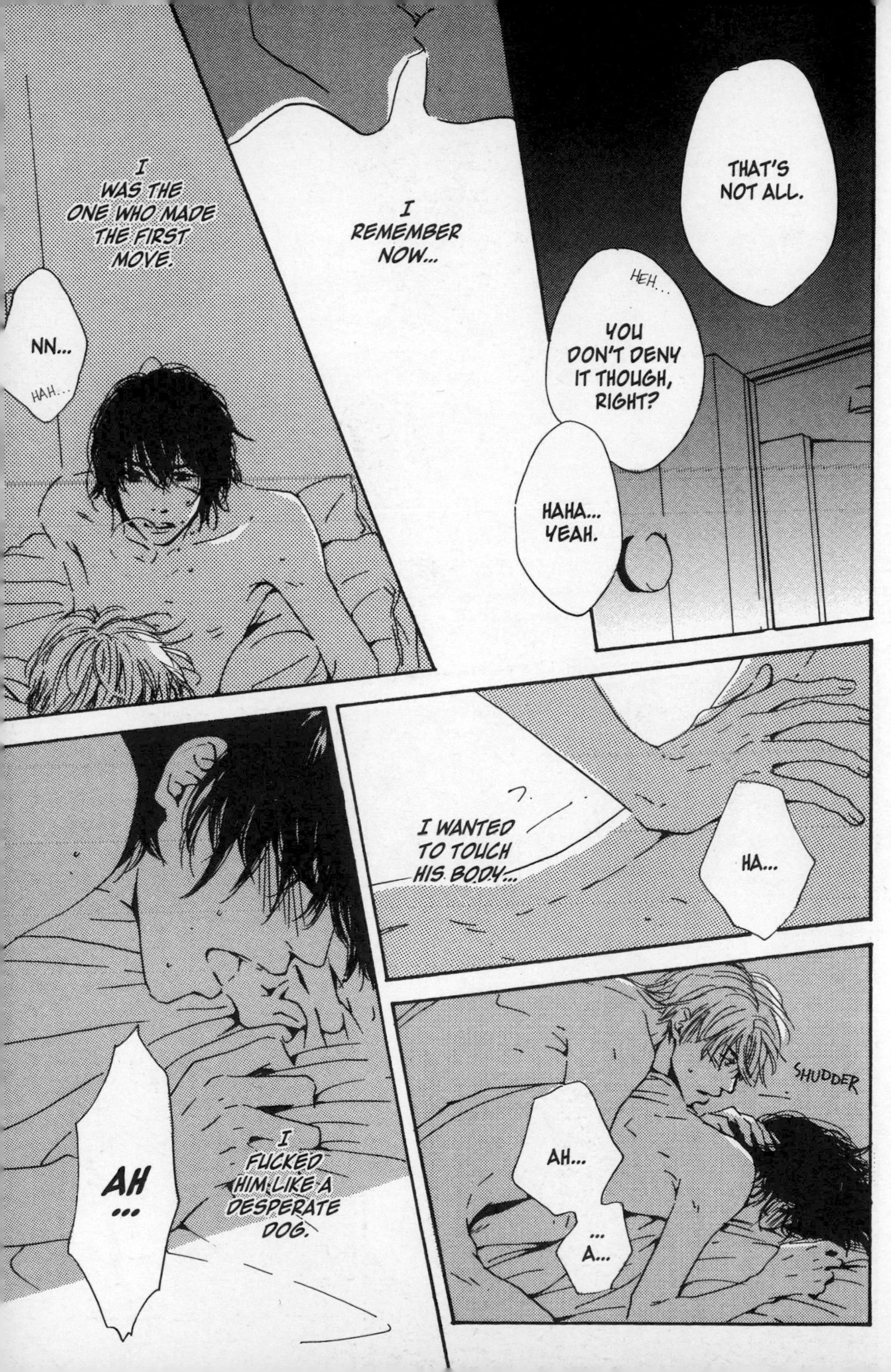
THAT'S NOT ALL.
HEH...
YOU DON'T DENY IT THOUGH, RIGHT?
HAHA... YEAH.
I REMEMBER NOW...
I WAS THE ONE WHO MADE THE FIRST MOVE.
NN...
HAH...
I WANTED TO TOUCH HIS BODY...
HA...
SHUDDER
AH...
... A...
I FUCKED HIM LIKE A DESPERATE DOG.
AH ...

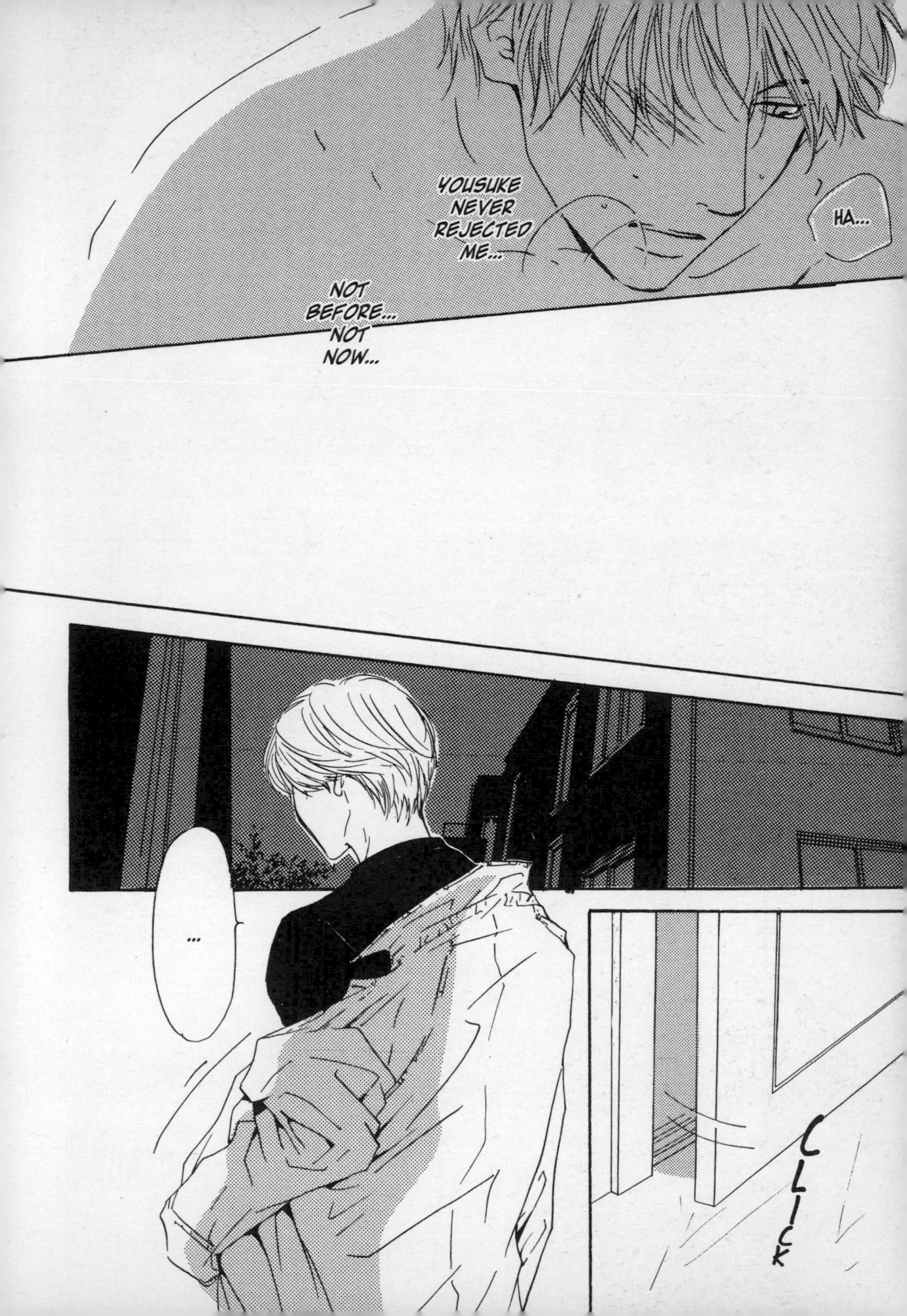
HA...
YOUSUKE NEVER REJECTED ME...
NOT BEFORE... NOT NOW...
CLICK
...

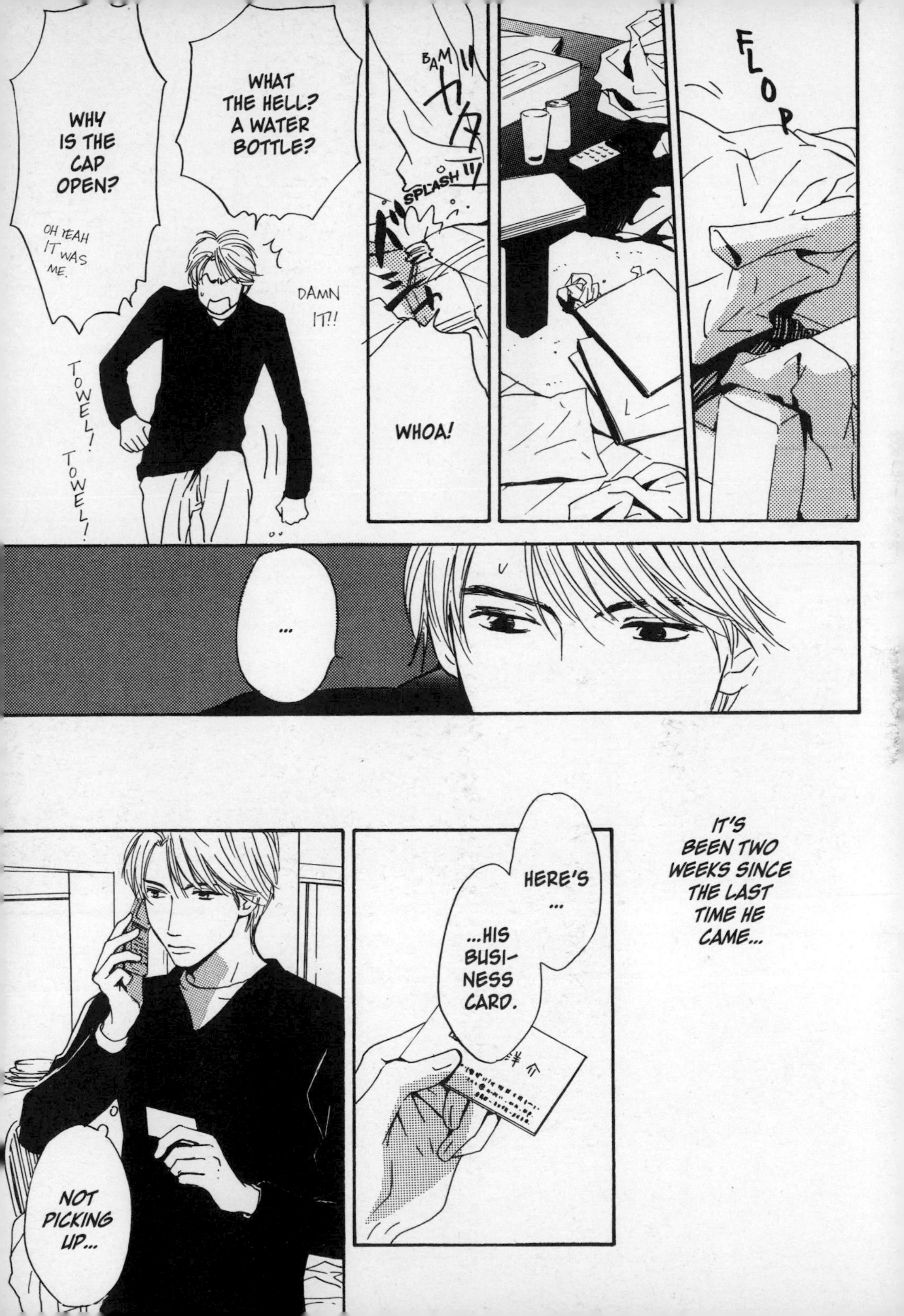
FLOP
BAM
SPLASH
WHOA!
WHAT THE HELL? A WATER BOTTLE?
WHY IS THE CAP OPEN?
OH YEAH IT WAS ME.
DAMN IT!!
TOWEL! TOWEL!
...
IT'S BEEN TWO WEEKS SINCE THE LAST TIME HE CAME...
HERE'S...
...HIS BUSINESS CARD.
NOT PICKING UP...

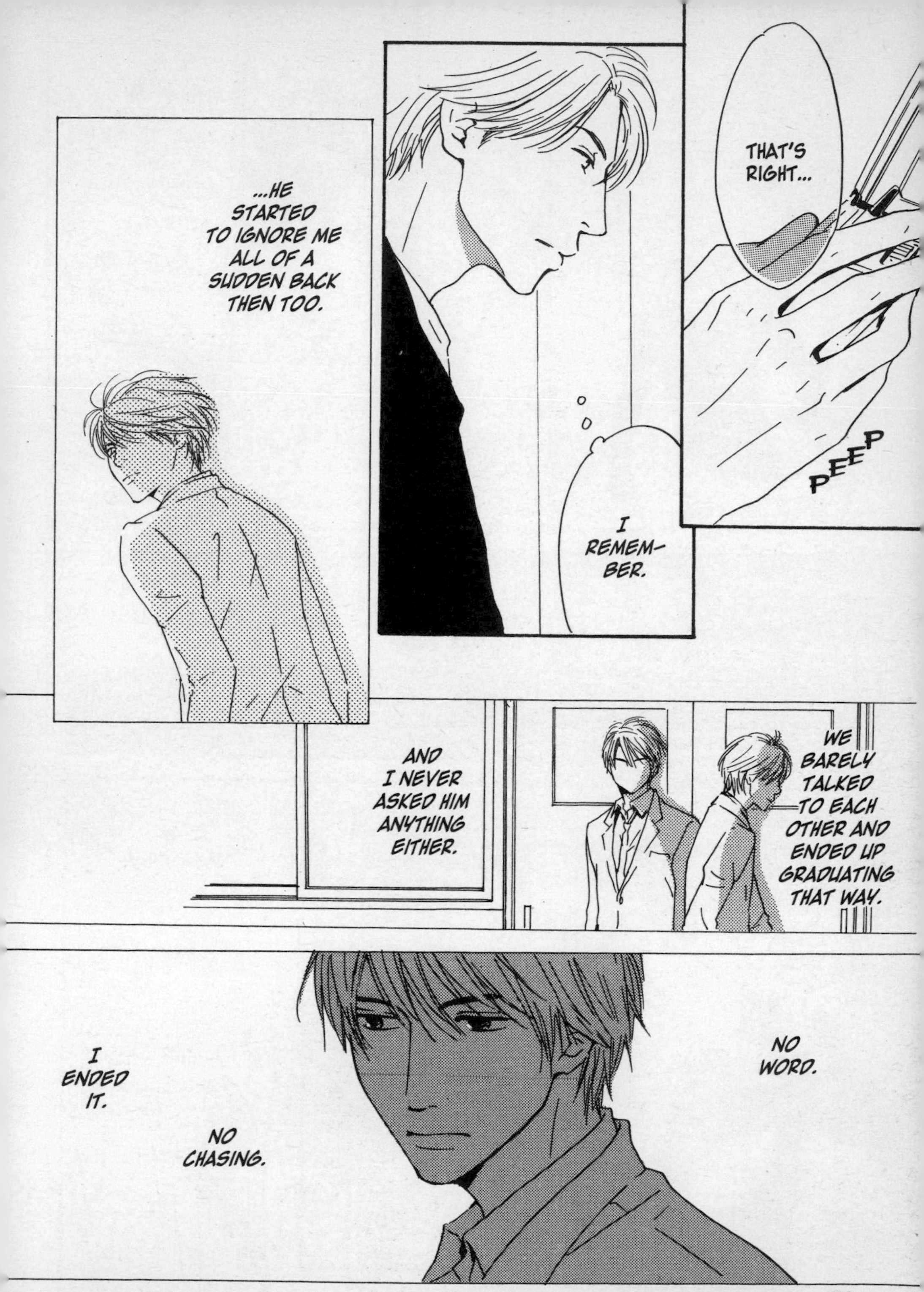
THAT'S RIGHT...
PEEP
I REMEMBER.
...HE STARTED TO IGNORE ME ALL OF A SUDDEN BACK THEN TOO.
WE BARELY TALKED TO EACH OTHER AND ENDED UP GRADUATING THAT WAY.
AND I NEVER ASKED HIM ANYTHING EITHER.
NO WORD.
I ENDED IT.
NO CHASING.

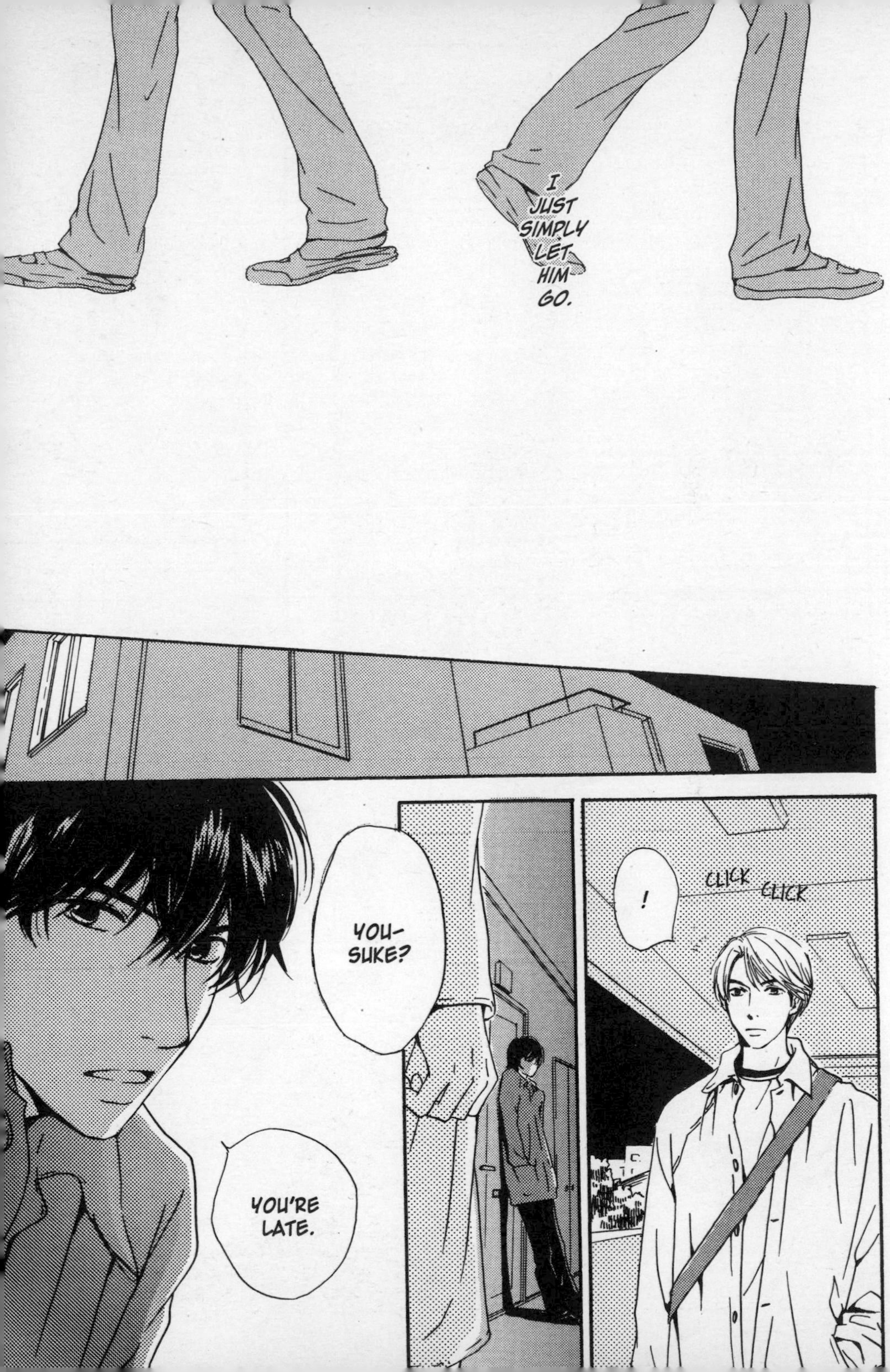
I JUST SIMPLY LET HIM GO.
!
CLICK
CLICK
YOU-SUKE?
YOU'RE LATE.

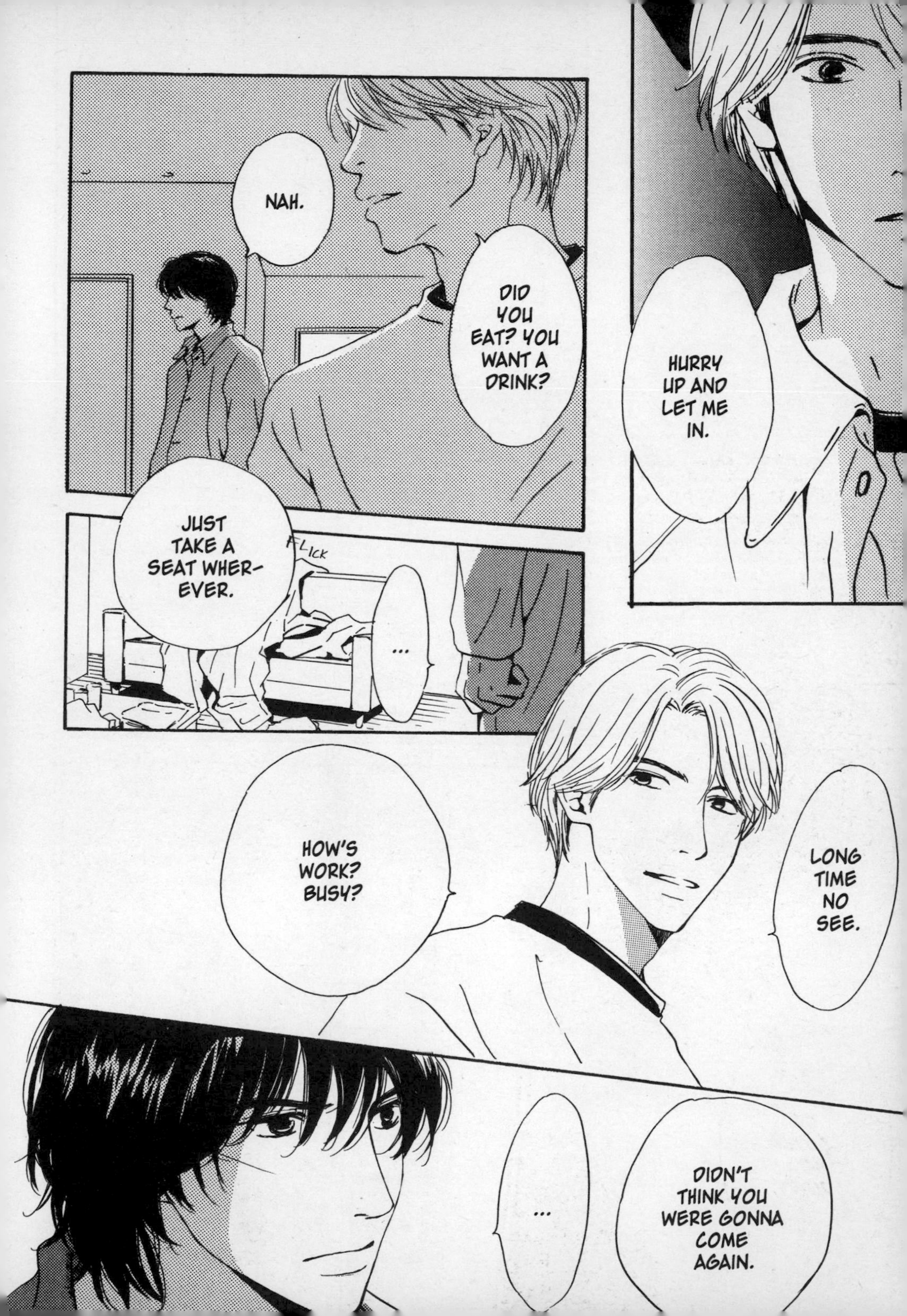
HURRY UP AND LET ME IN.
DID YOU EAT? YOU WANT A DRINK?
NAH.
JUST TAKE A SEAT WHER-EVER.
FLICK
...
LONG TIME NO SEE.
HOW'S WORK? BUSY?
DIDN'T THINK YOU WERE GONNA COME AGAIN.
...

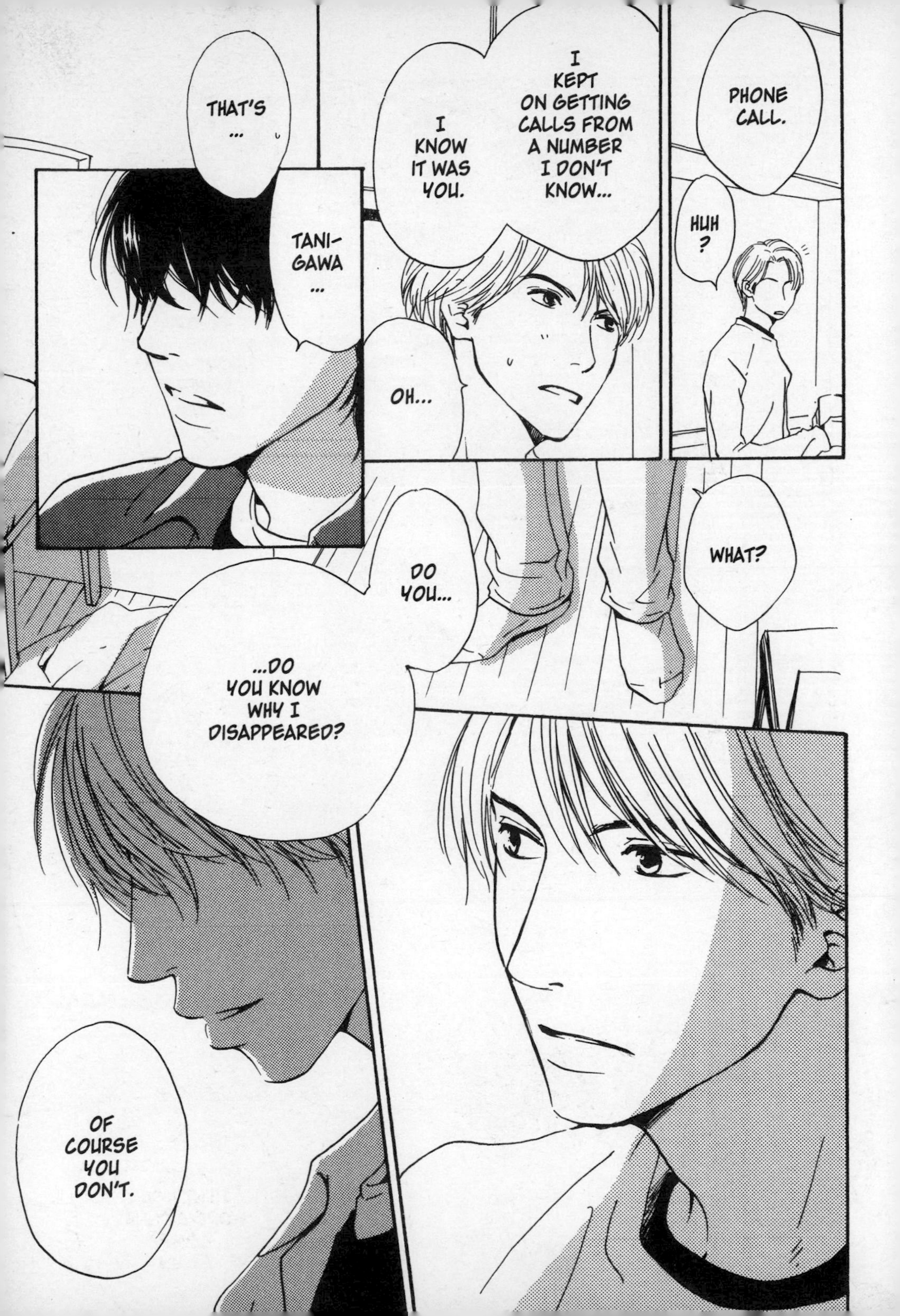
PHONE CALL.
HUH?
I KEPT ON GETTING CALLS FROM A NUMBER I DON'T KNOW...
I KNOW IT WAS YOU.
OH...
THAT'S ...
TANI-GAWA ...
WHAT?
DO YOU...
...DO YOU KNOW WHY I DISAPPEARED?
OF COURSE YOU DON'T.

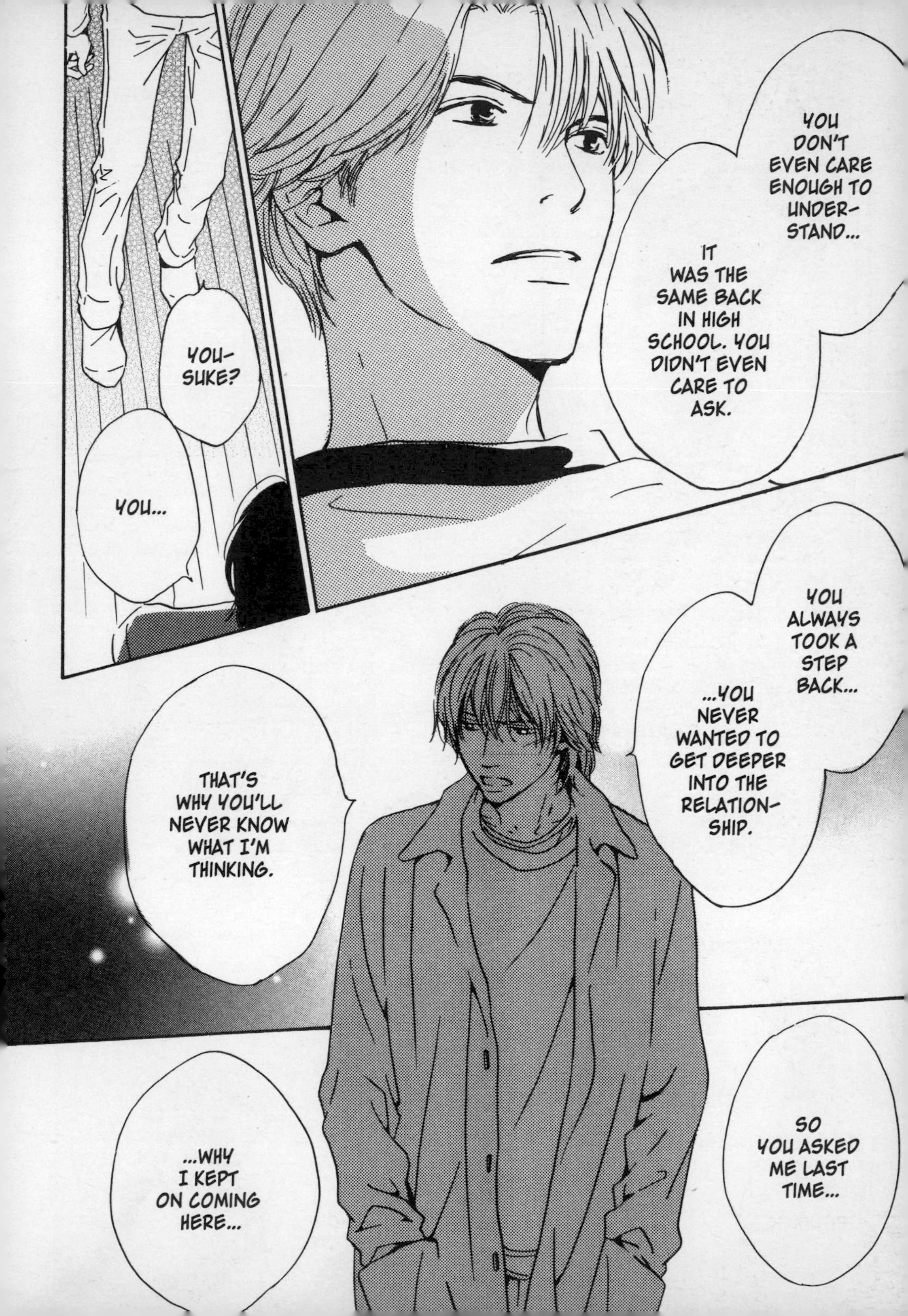
YOU DON'T EVEN CARE ENOUGH TO UNDER-STAND...
IT WAS THE SAME BACK IN HIGH SCHOOL. YOU DIDN'T EVEN CARE TO ASK.
YOU-SUKE?
YOU...
YOU ALWAYS TOOK A STEP BACK...
...YOU NEVER WANTED TO GET DEEPER INTO THE RELATION-SHIP.
THAT'S WHY YOU'LL NEVER KNOW WHAT I'M THINKING.
SO YOU ASKED ME LAST TIME...
...WHY I KEPT ON COMING HERE...

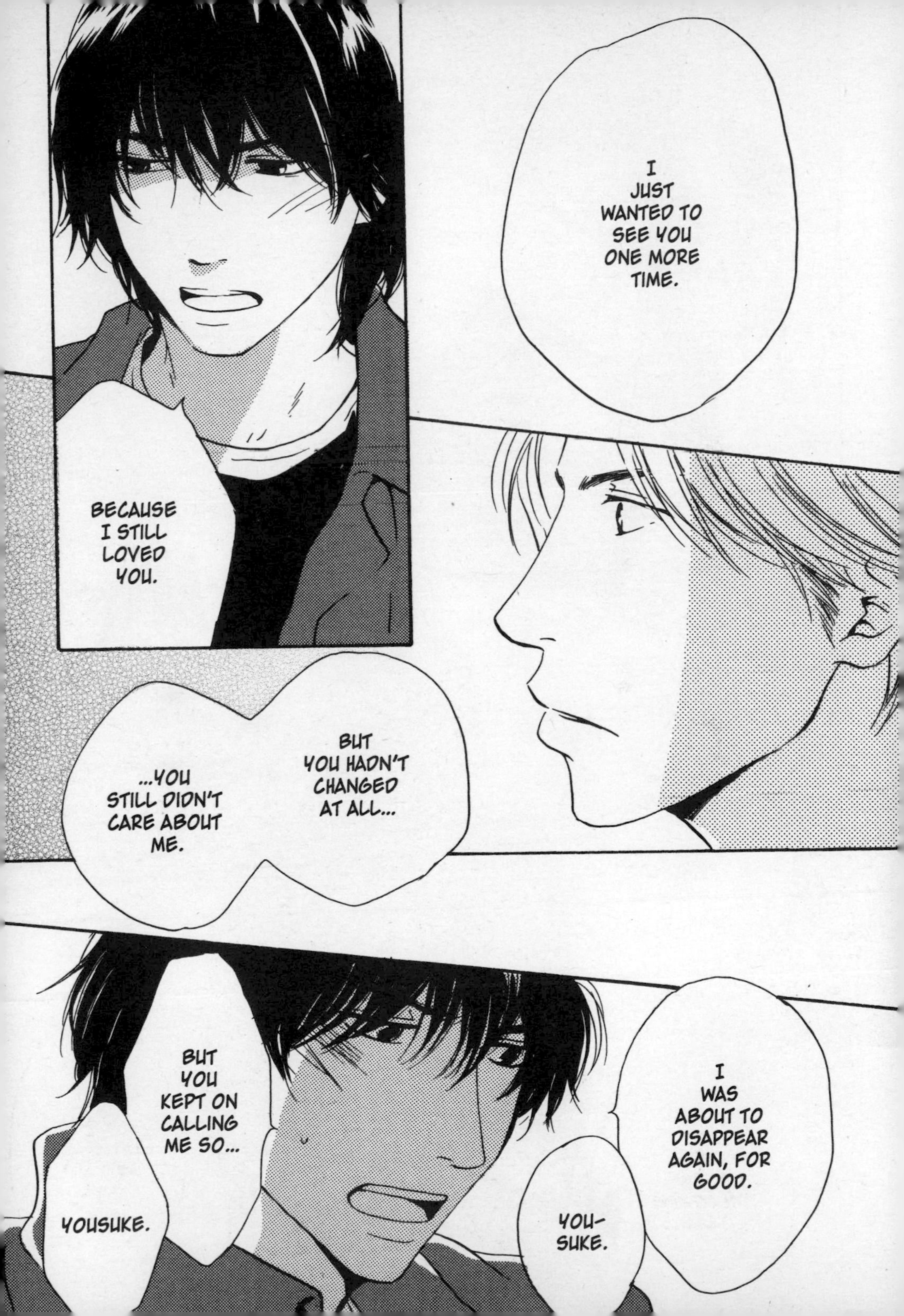
I JUST WANTED TO SEE YOU ONE MORE TIME.
BECAUSE I STILL LOVED YOU.
BUT YOU HADN'T CHANGED AT ALL...
...YOU STILL DIDN'T CARE ABOUT ME.
I WAS ABOUT TO DISAPPEAR AGAIN, FOR GOOD.
YOU-SUKE.
BUT YOU KEPT ON CALLING ME SO...
YOUSUKE.

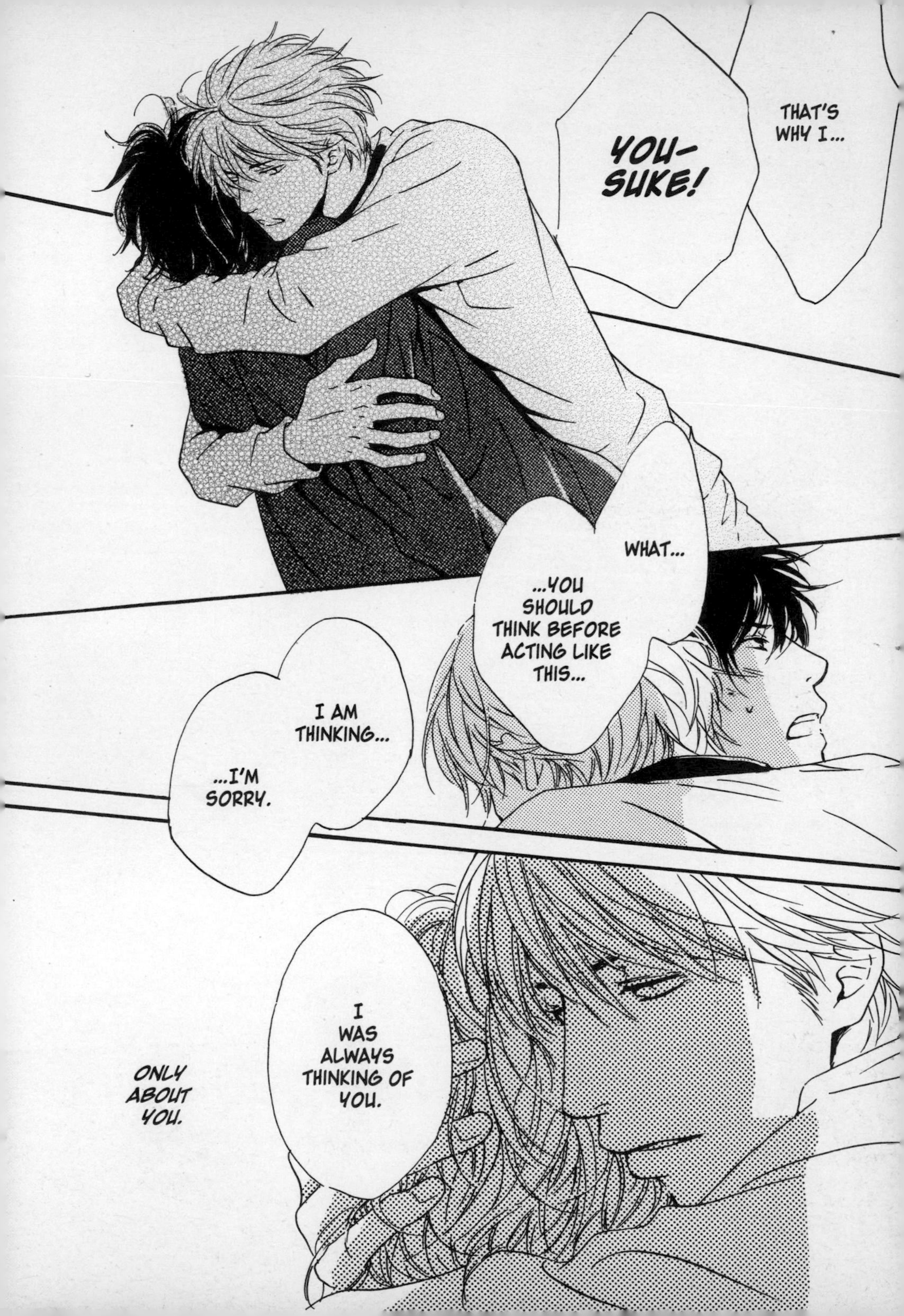
THAT'S WHY I...
YOU-SUKE!
WHAT...
...YOU SHOULD THINK BEFORE ACTING LIKE THIS...
I AM THINKING...
...I'M SORRY.
I WAS ALWAYS THINKING OF YOU.
ONLY ABOUT YOU.

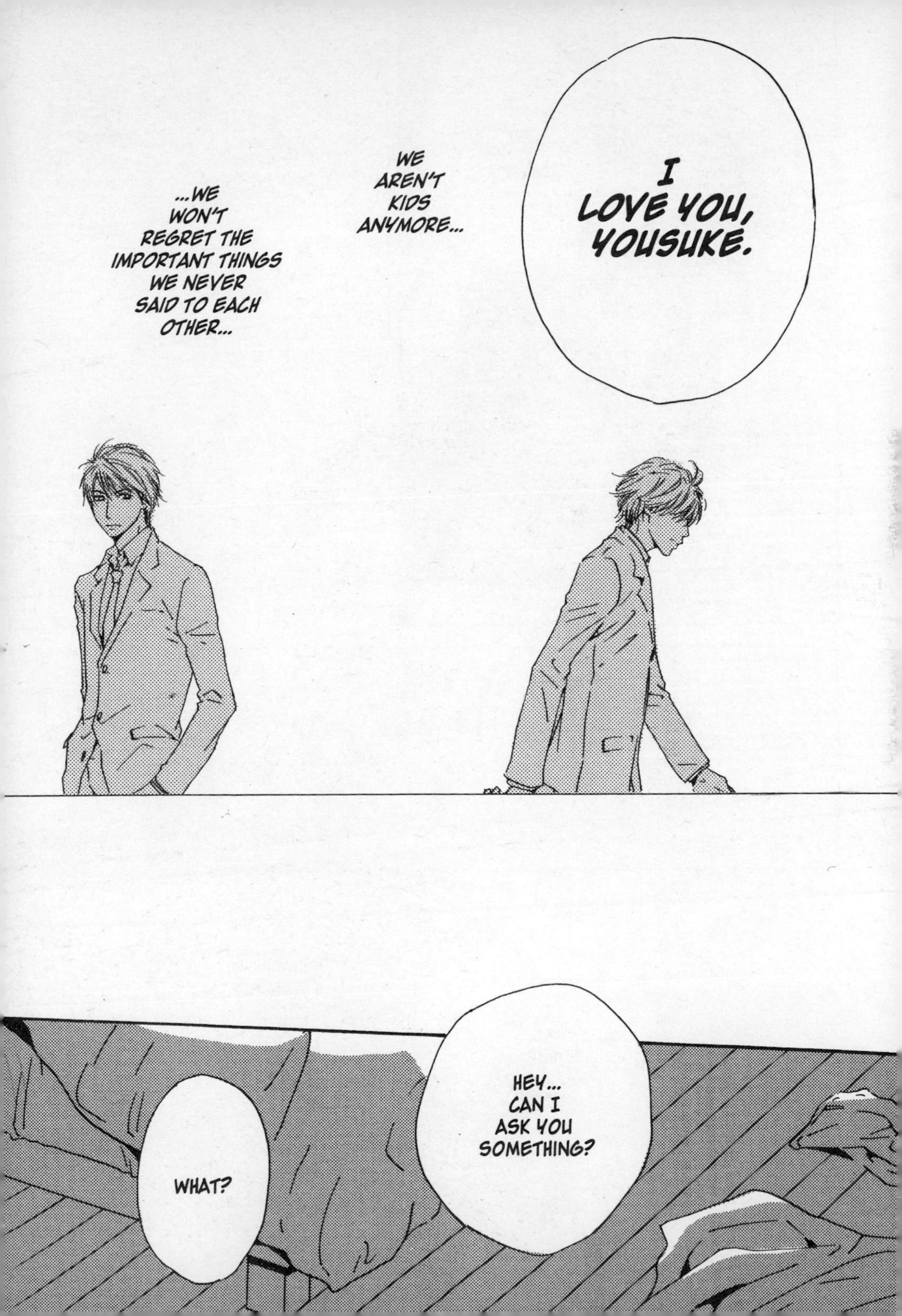
I LOVE YOU, YOUSUKE.
WE AREN'T KIDS ANYMORE...
...WE WON'T REGRET THE IMPORTANT THINGS WE NEVER SAID TO EACH OTHER...
HEY... CAN I ASK YOU SOMETHING?
WHAT?

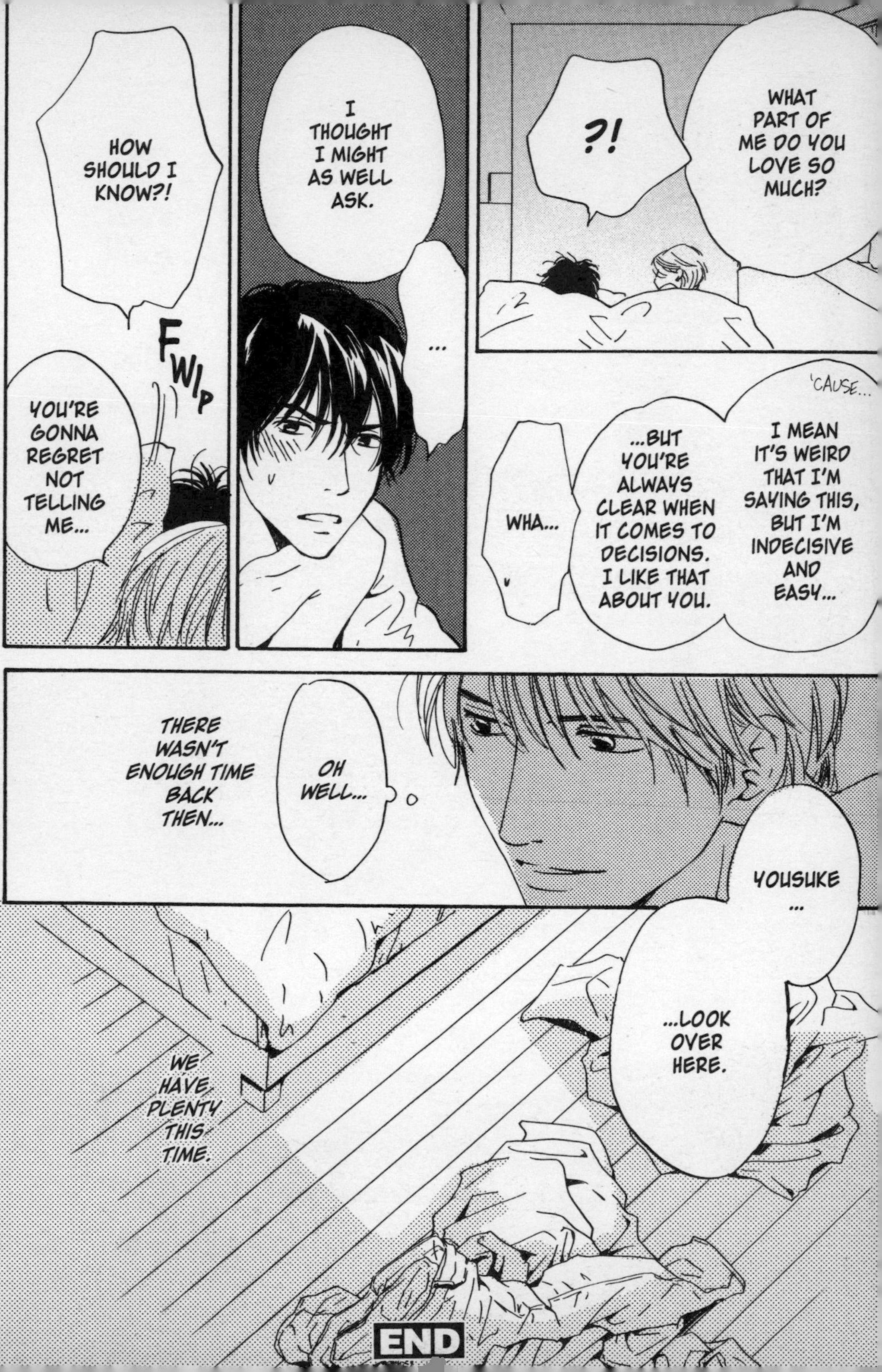
WHAT PART OF ME DO YOU LOVE SO MUCH?
?!
'CAUSE...
I MEAN IT'S WEIRD THAT I'M SAYING THIS, BUT I'M INDECISIVE AND EASY...
...BUT YOU'RE ALWAYS CLEAR WHEN IT COMES TO DECISIONS. I LIKE THAT ABOUT YOU.
WHA...
I THOUGHT I MIGHT AS WELL ASK.
...
HOW SHOULD I KNOW?!
FWIP
YOU'RE GONNA REGRET NOT TELLING ME...
YOUSUKE ...
OH WELL...
THERE WASN'T ENOUGH TIME BACK THEN...
...LOOK OVER HERE.
WE HAVE PLENTY THIS TIME.
END

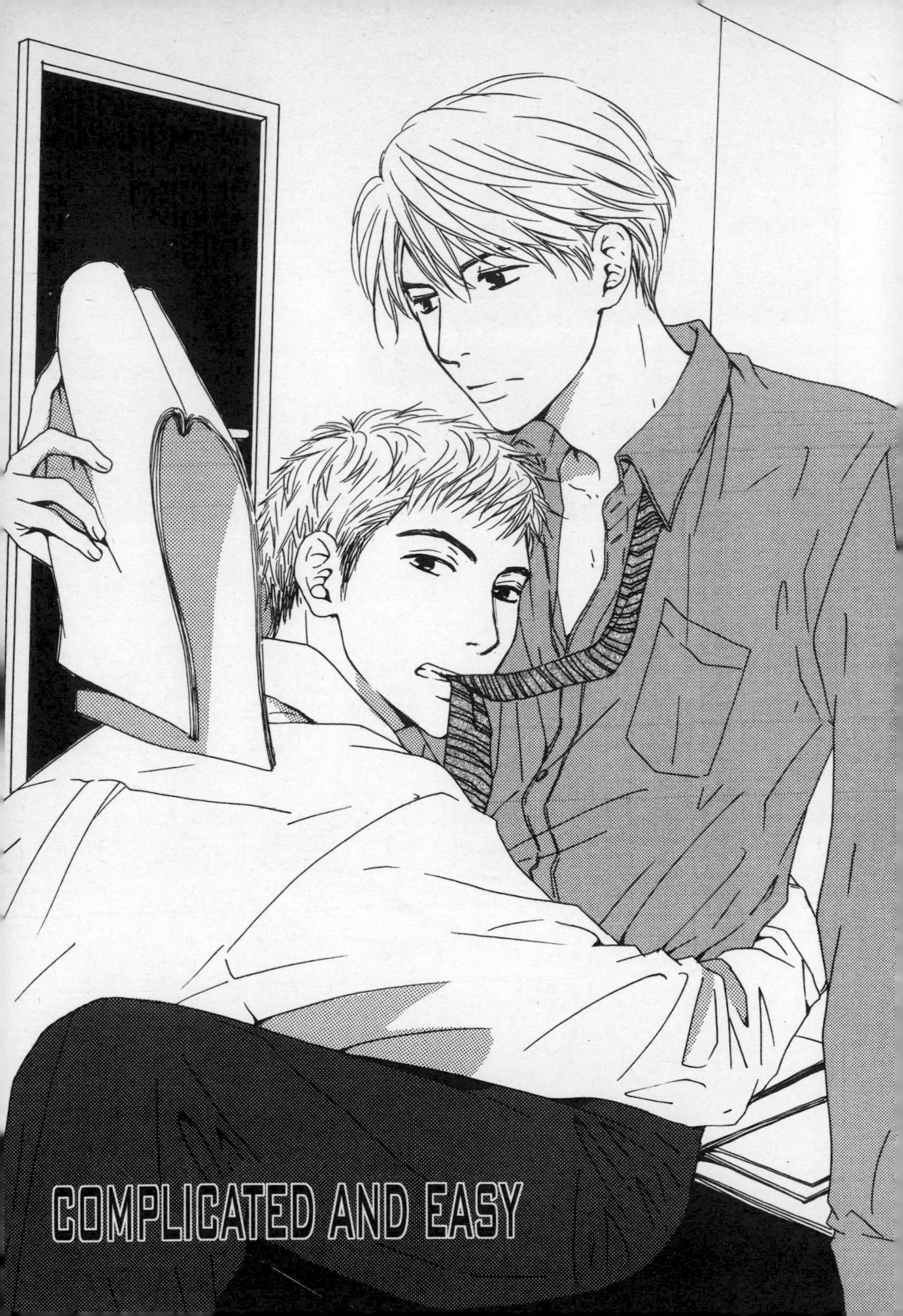
COMPLICATED AND EASY

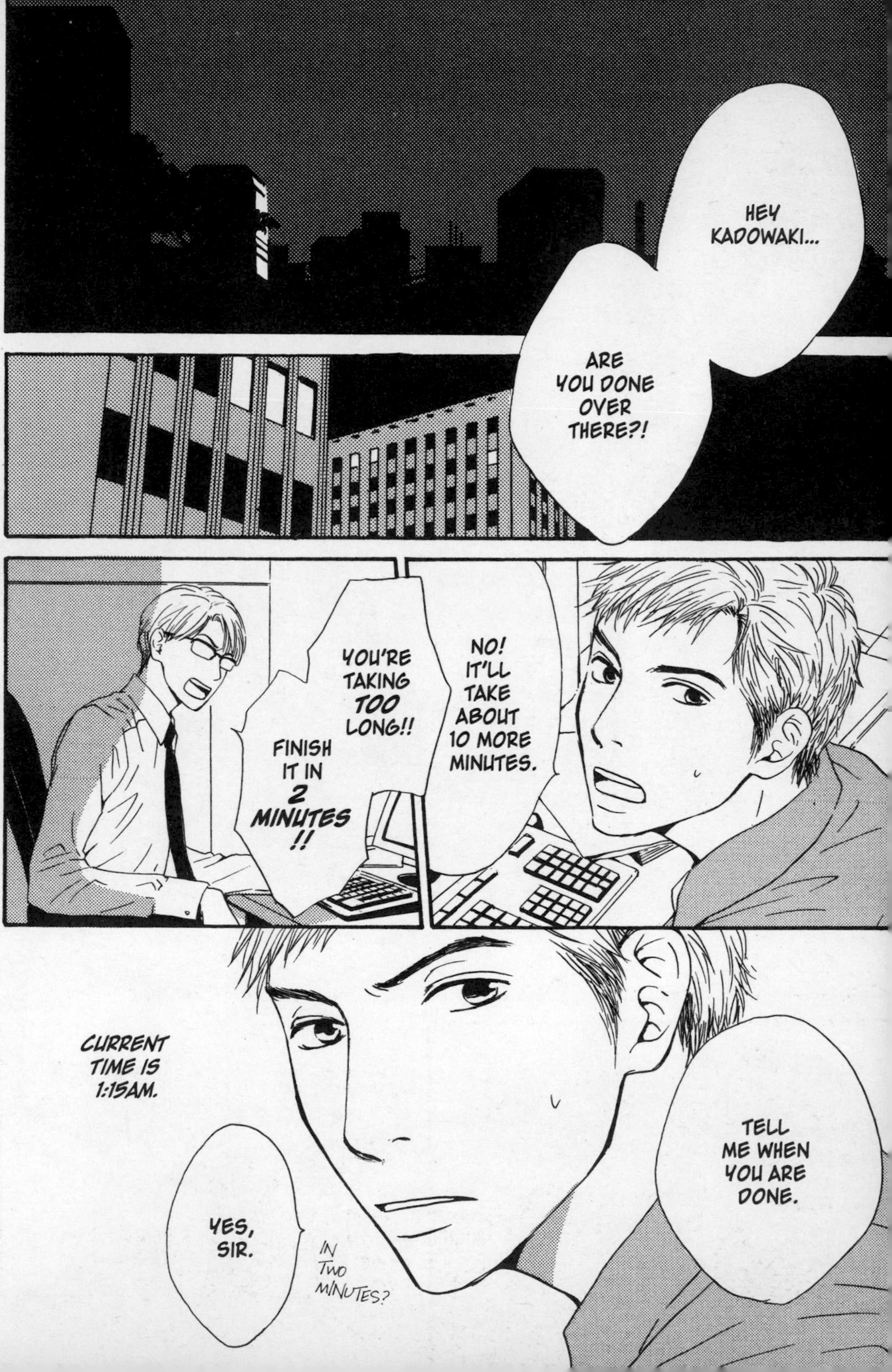
HEY KADOWAKI...
ARE YOU DONE OVER THERE?!
NO! IT'LL TAKE ABOUT 10 MORE MINUTES.
YOU'RE TAKING TOO LONG!!
FINISH IT IN 2 MINUTES!!
TELL ME WHEN YOU ARE DONE.
CURRENT TIME IS 1:15AM.
YES, SIR.
IN TWO MINUTES?

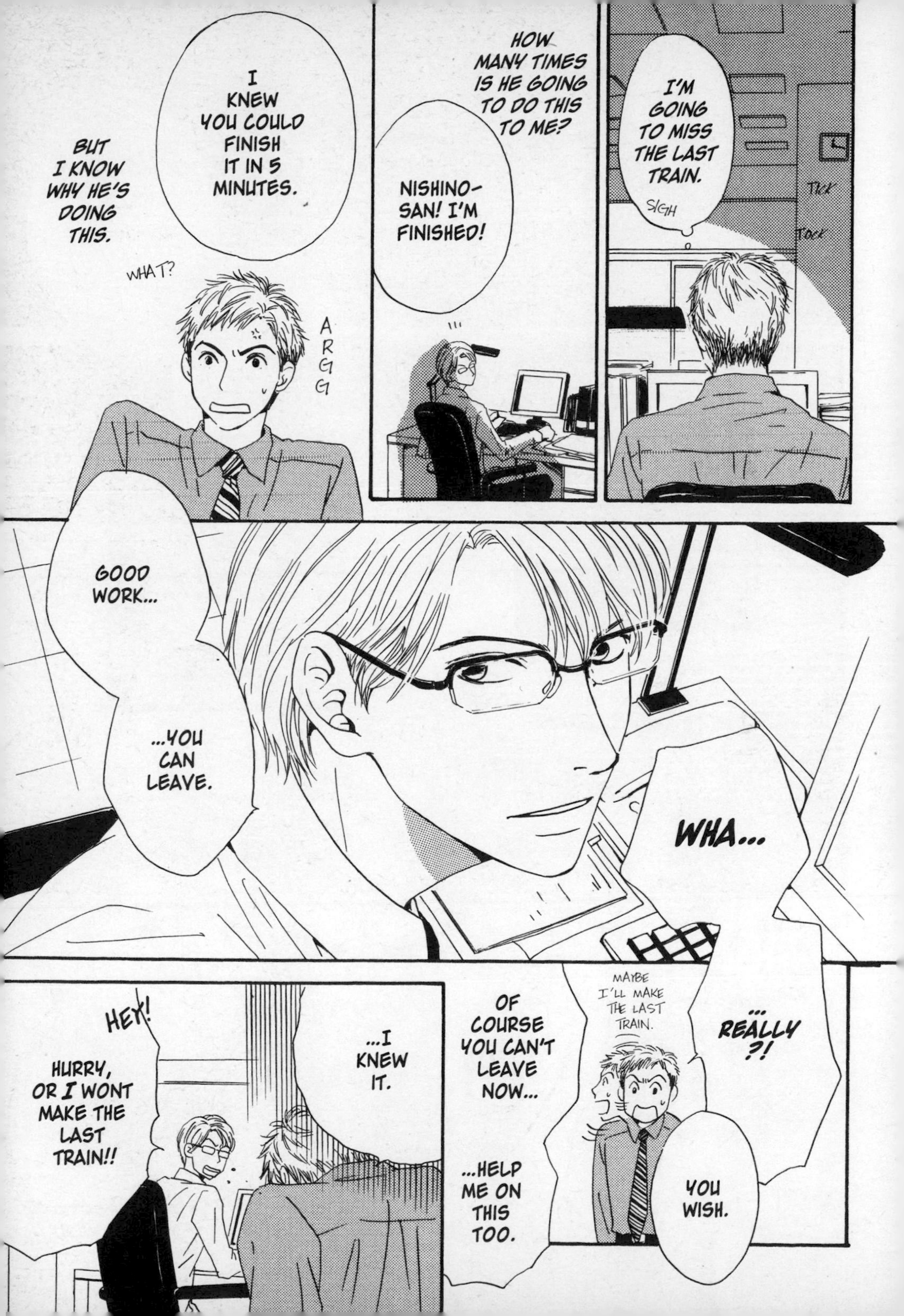
I'M GOING TO MISS THE LAST TRAIN.
SIGH
TICK
TOCK
HOW MANY TIMES IS HE GOING TO DO THIS TO ME?
NISHINO-SAN! I'M FINISHED!
I KNEW YOU COULD FINISH IT IN 5 MINUTES.
BUT I KNOW WHY HE'S DOING THIS.
WHAT?
ARGG
GOOD WORK...
...YOU CAN LEAVE.
WHA...
...REALLY?!
MAYBE I'LL MAKE THE LAST TRAIN.
YOU WISH.
OF COURSE YOU CAN'T LEAVE NOW...
...HELP ME ON THIS TOO.
...I KNEW IT.
HEY!
HURRY, OR I WONT MAKE THE LAST TRAIN!!

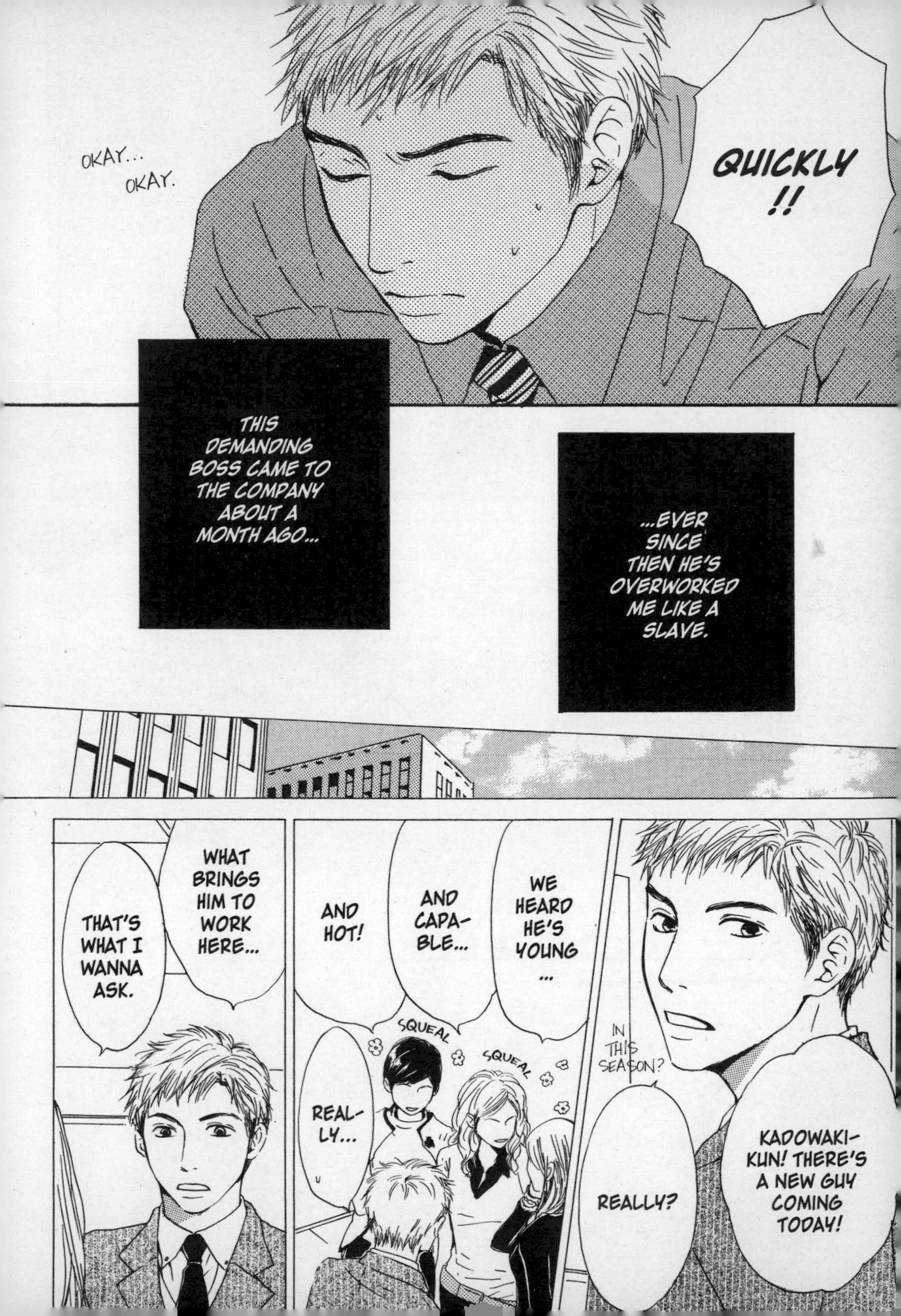
QUICKLY!!
OKAY... OKAY.
THIS DEMANDING BOSS CAME TO THE COMPANY ABOUT A MONTH AGO...
...EVER SINCE THEN HE'S OVERWORKED ME LIKE A SLAVE.
KADOWAKI-KUN! THERE'S A NEW GUY COMING TODAY!
REALLY?
IN THIS SEASON?
WE HEARD HE'S YOUNG...
AND CAPA-BLE...
AND HOT!
SQUEAL
SQUEAL
REAL-LY...
WHAT BRINGS HIM TO WORK HERE...
THAT'S WHAT I WANNA ASK.

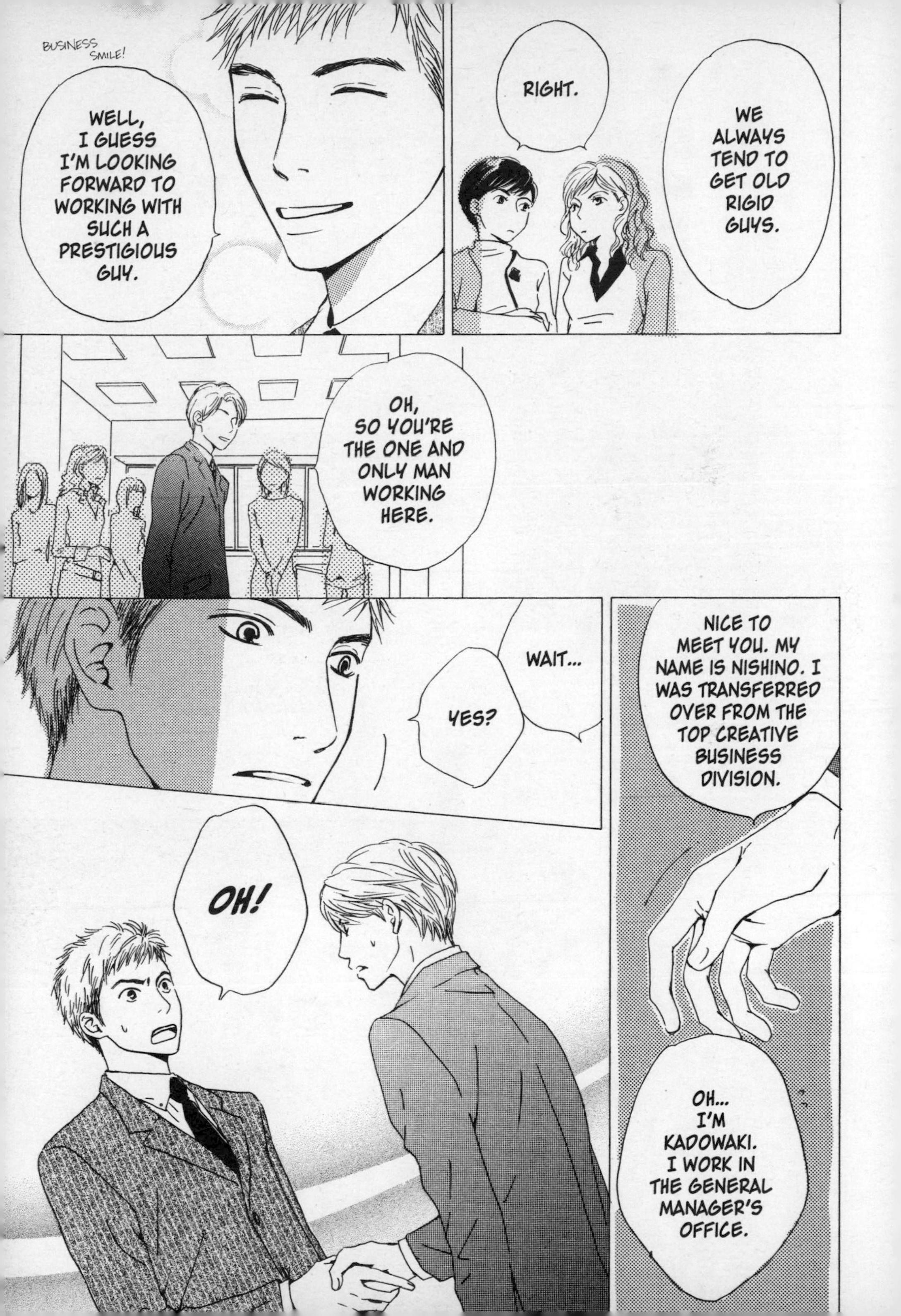
WE ALWAYS TEND TO GET OLD RIGID GUYS.
RIGHT.
BUSINESS SMILE!
WELL, I GUESS I'M LOOKING FORWARD TO WORKING WITH SUCH A PRESTIGIOUS GUY.
OH, SO YOU'RE THE ONE AND ONLY MAN WORKING HERE.
NICE TO MEET YOU. MY NAME IS NISHINO. I WAS TRANSFERRED OVER FROM THE TOP CREATIVE BUSINESS DIVISION.
OH... I'M KADOWAKI. I WORK IN THE GENERAL MANAGER'S OFFICE.
WAIT...
YES?
OH!

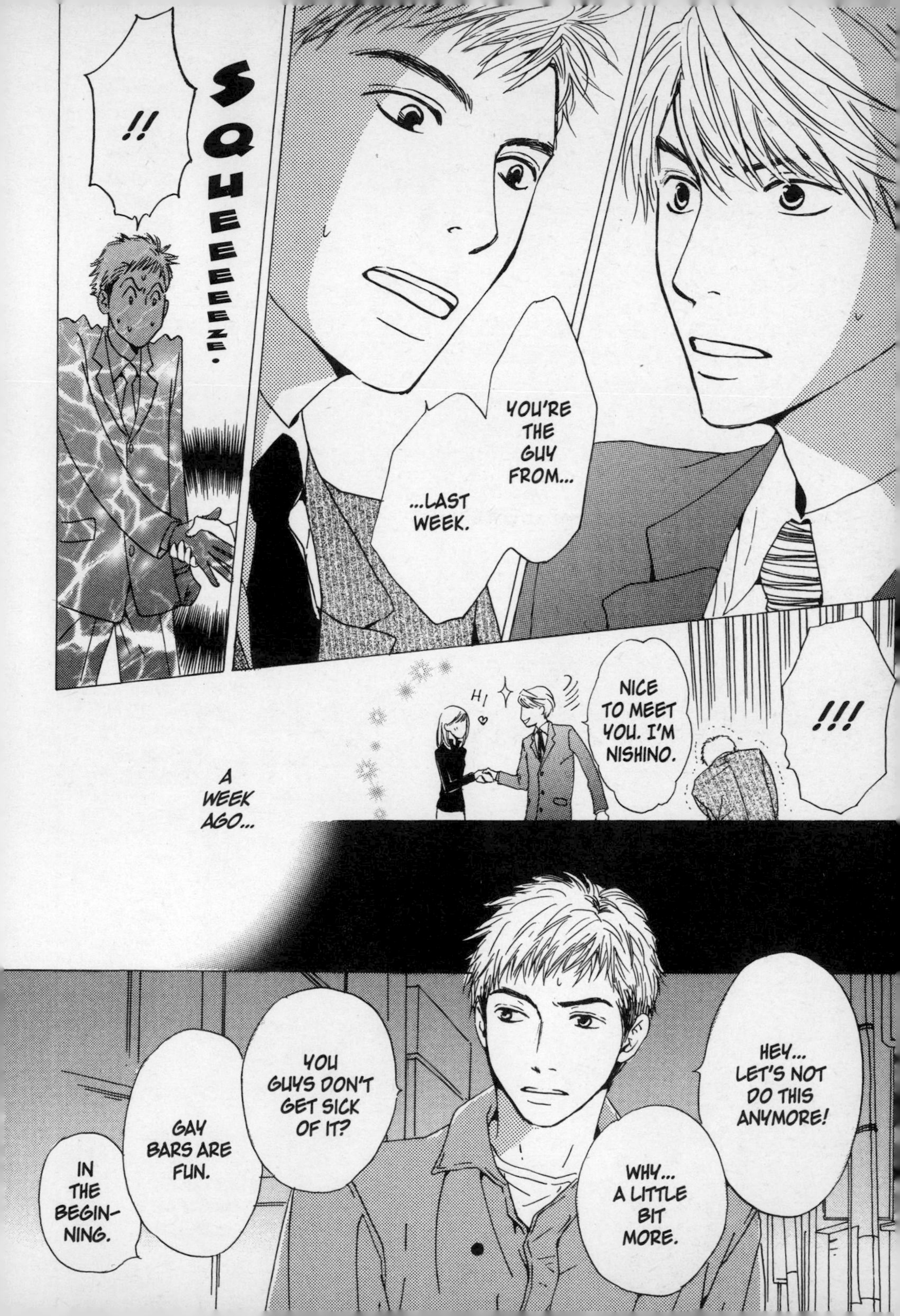

YOU'RE THE GUY FROM...
...LAST WEEK.
!!
SQUEEEEEZE.
!!!
NICE TO MEET YOU. I'M NISHINO.
HI
A WEEK AGO...
HEY... LET'S NOT DO THIS ANYMORE!
WHY... A LITTLE BIT MORE.
YOU GUYS DON'T GET SICK OF IT?
GAY BARS ARE FUN.
IN THE BEGIN-NING.

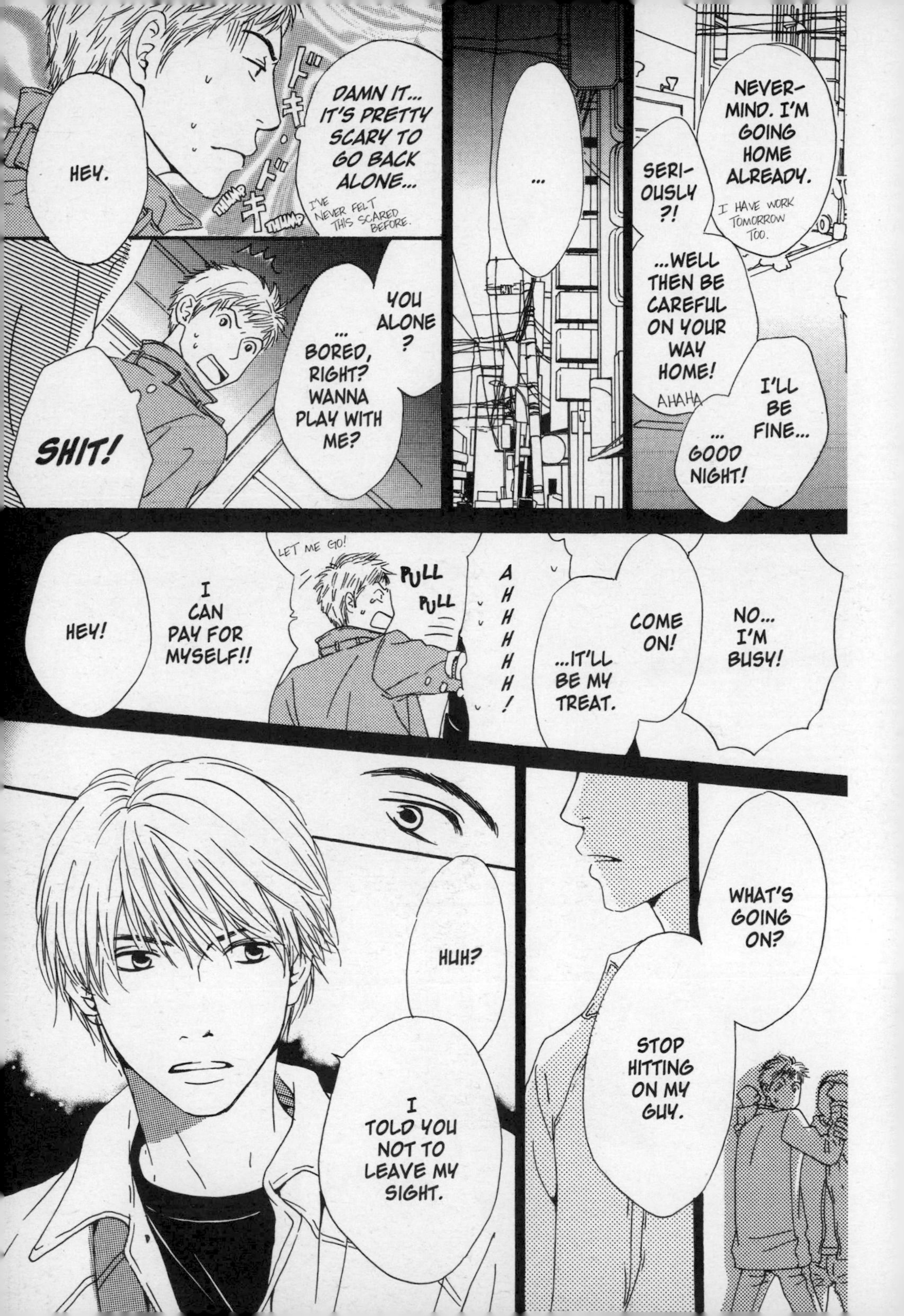

NEVER-MIND. I'M GOING HOME ALREADY.
I HAVE WORK TOMORROW TOO.
SERI-OUSLY?!
...WELL THEN BE CAREFUL ON YOUR WAY HOME!
AHAHA
I'LL BE FINE...
...GOOD NIGHT!
...
DAMN IT... IT'S PRETTY SCARY TO GO BACK ALONE...
I'VE NEVER FELT THIS SCARED BEFORE.
THUMP
THUMP
HEY.
YOU ALONE?
...BORED, RIGHT? WANNA PLAY WITH ME?
SHIT!
NO... I'M BUSY!
COME ON!
...IT'LL BE MY TREAT.
AHHHHHH!
PULL
PULL
LET ME GO!
I CAN PAY FOR MYSELF!!
HEY!
WHAT'S GOING ON?
STOP HITTING ON MY GUY.
HUH?
I TOLD YOU NOT TO LEAVE MY SIGHT.

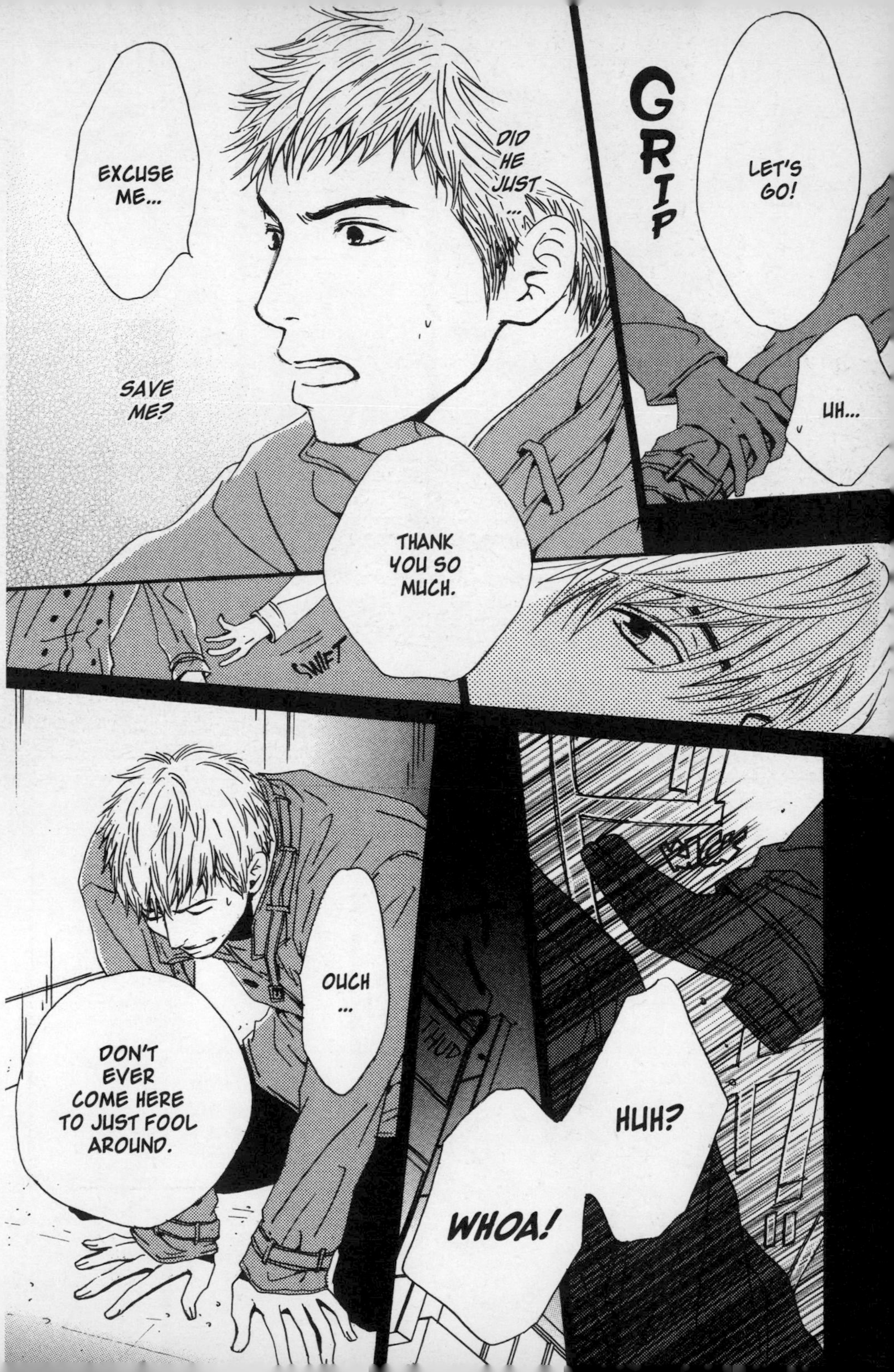
GRIP
LET'S GO!
UH...
DID HE JUST ...
EXCUSE ME...
SAVE ME?
THANK YOU SO MUCH.
SWIFT
HUH?
WHOA!
OUCH ...
THUD
DON'T EVER COME HERE TO JUST FOOL AROUND.

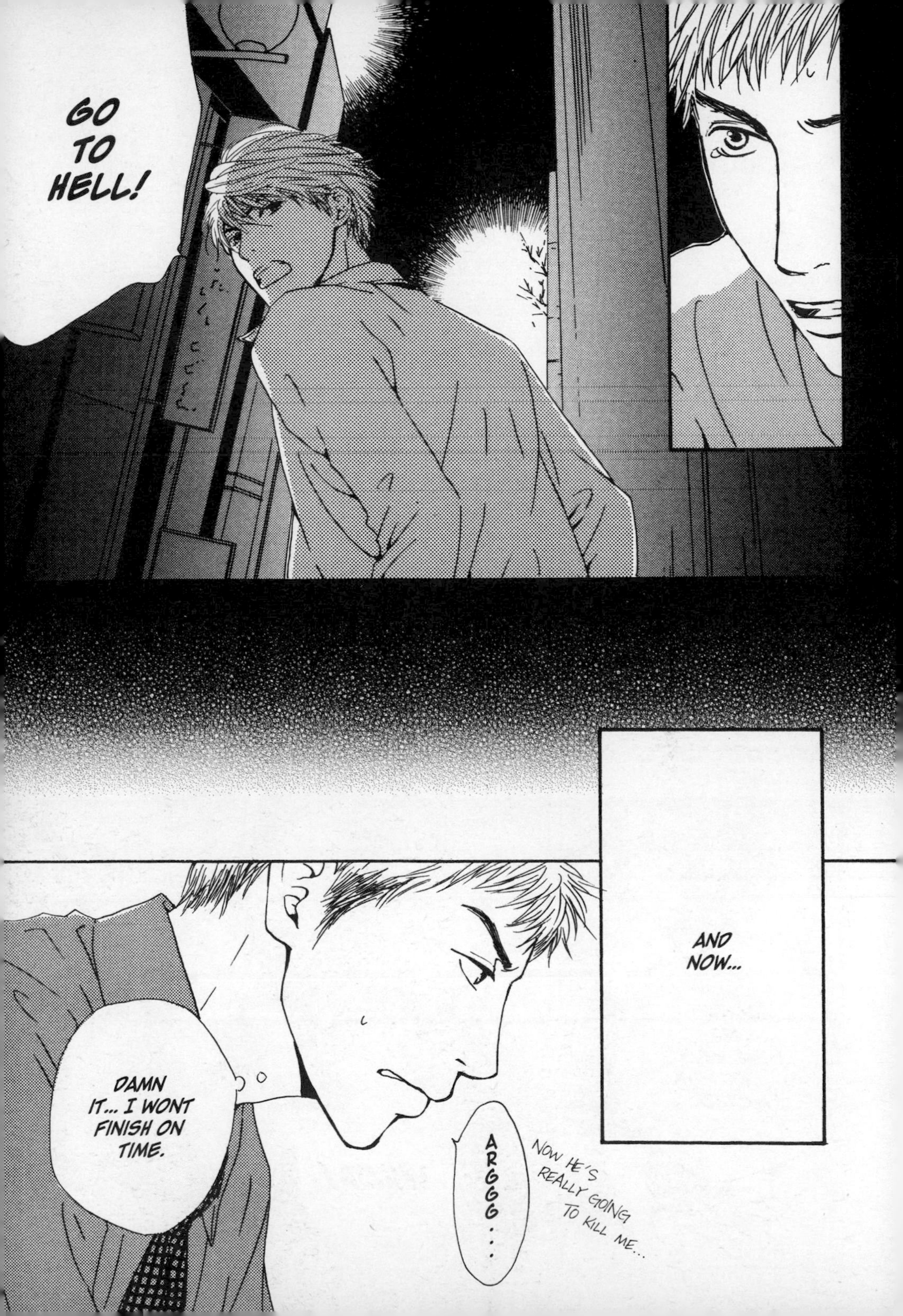
GO TO HELL!
AND NOW...
ARGGG...
NOW HE'S REALLY GOING TO KILL ME...
DAMN IT... I WONT FINISH ON TIME.

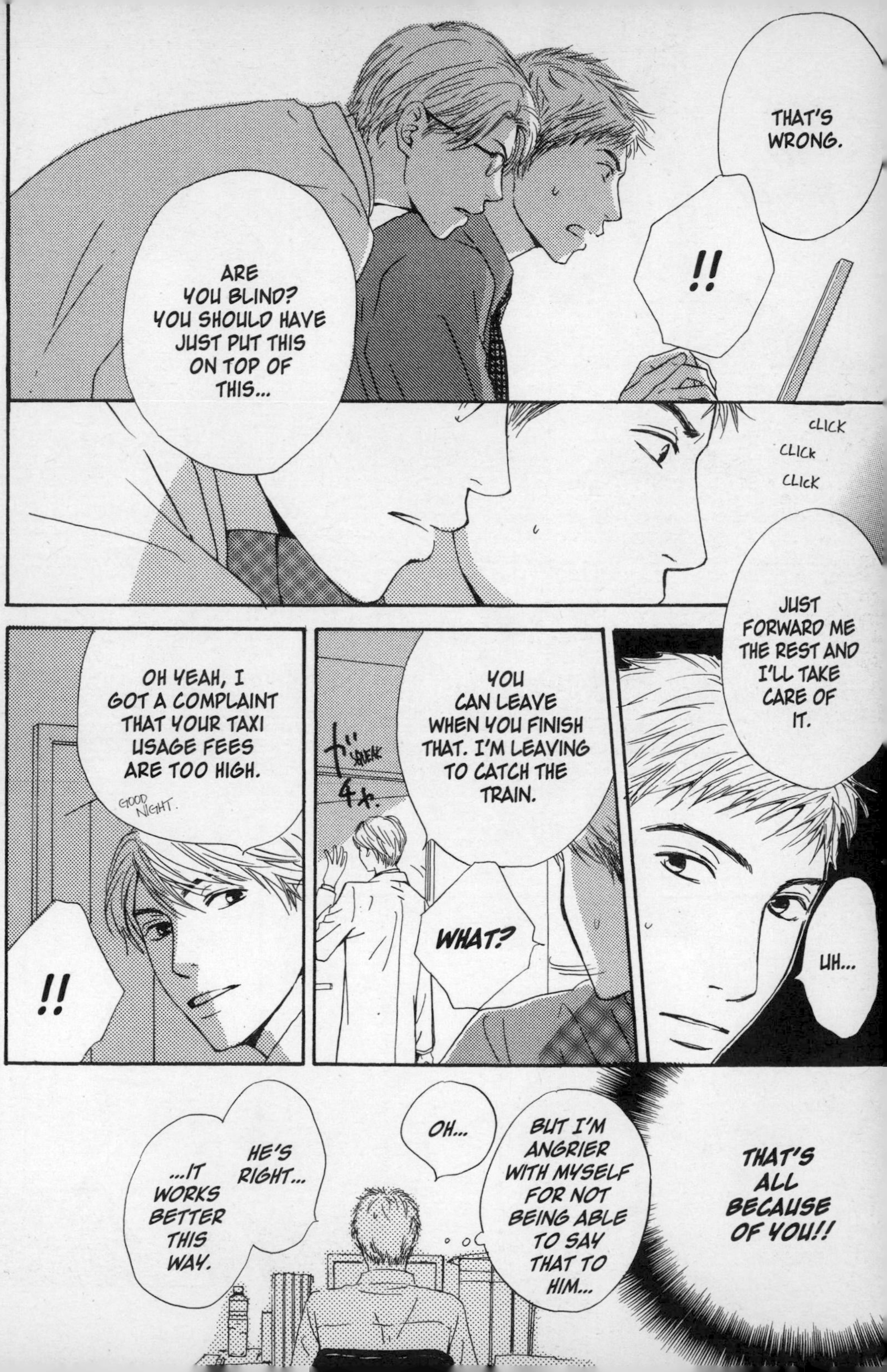
THAT'S WRONG.
!!
ARE YOU BLIND? YOU SHOULD HAVE JUST PUT THIS ON TOP OF THIS...
CLICK
CLICK
CLICK
JUST FORWARD ME THE REST AND I'LL TAKE CARE OF IT.
UH...
YOU CAN LEAVE WHEN YOU FINISH THAT. I'M LEAVING TO CATCH THE TRAIN.
WHAT?
SQUEAK
OH YEAH, I GOT A COMPLAINT THAT YOUR TAXI USAGE FEES ARE TOO HIGH.
GOOD NIGHT.
!!
THAT'S ALL BECAUSE OF YOU!!
BUT I'M ANGRIER WITH MYSELF FOR NOT BEING ABLE TO SAY THAT TO HIM...
OH...
HE'S RIGHT...
...IT WORKS BETTER THIS WAY.

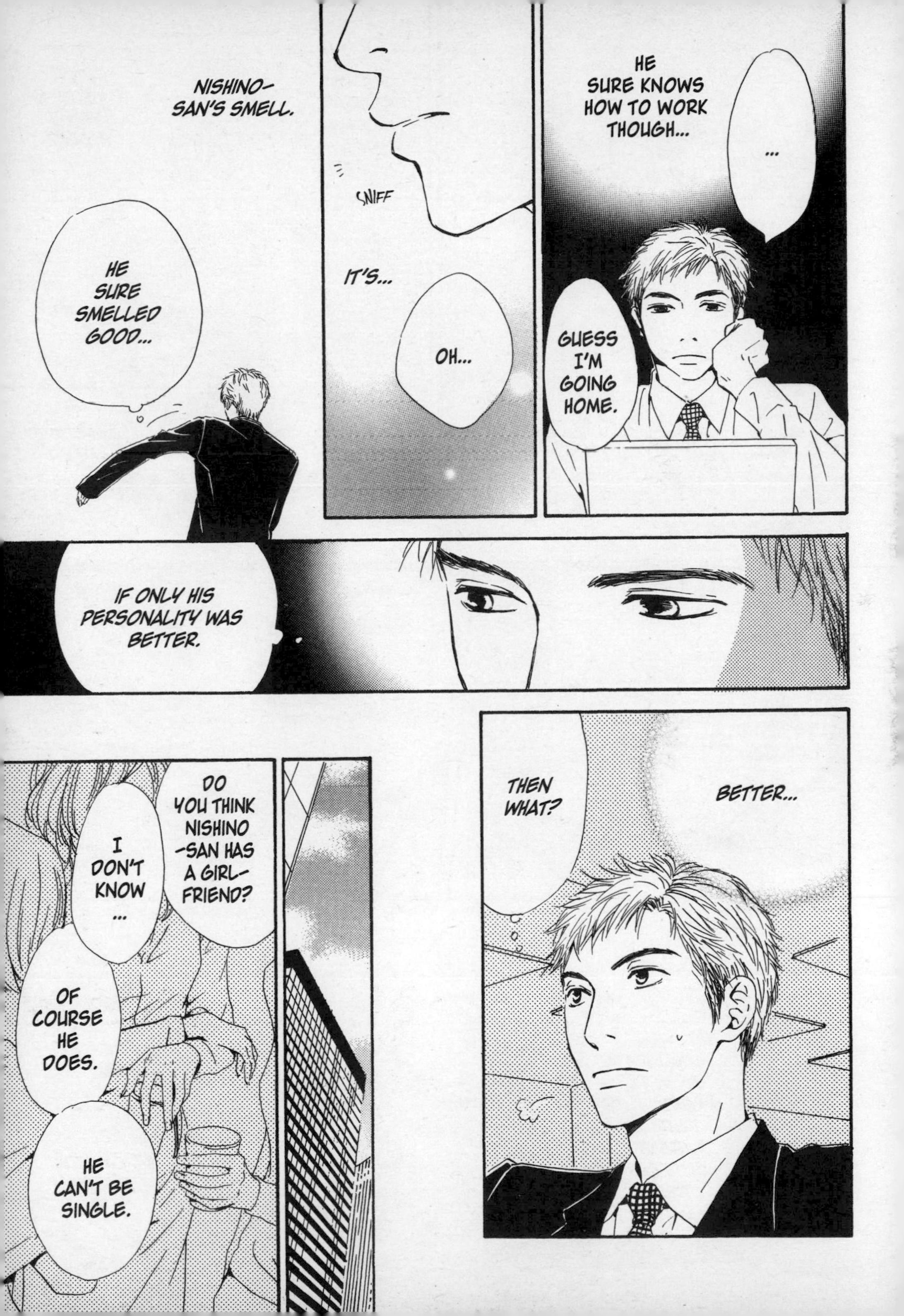
HE SURE KNOWS HOW TO WORK THOUGH...
...
GUESS I'M GOING HOME.
SNIFF
IT'S...
OH...
NISHINO-SAN'S SMELL.
HE SURE SMELLED GOOD...
IF ONLY HIS PERSONALITY WAS BETTER.
BETTER...
THEN WHAT?
DO YOU THINK NISHINO-SAN HAS A GIRLFRIEND?
I DON'T KNOW...
OF COURSE HE DOES.
HE CAN'T BE SINGLE.

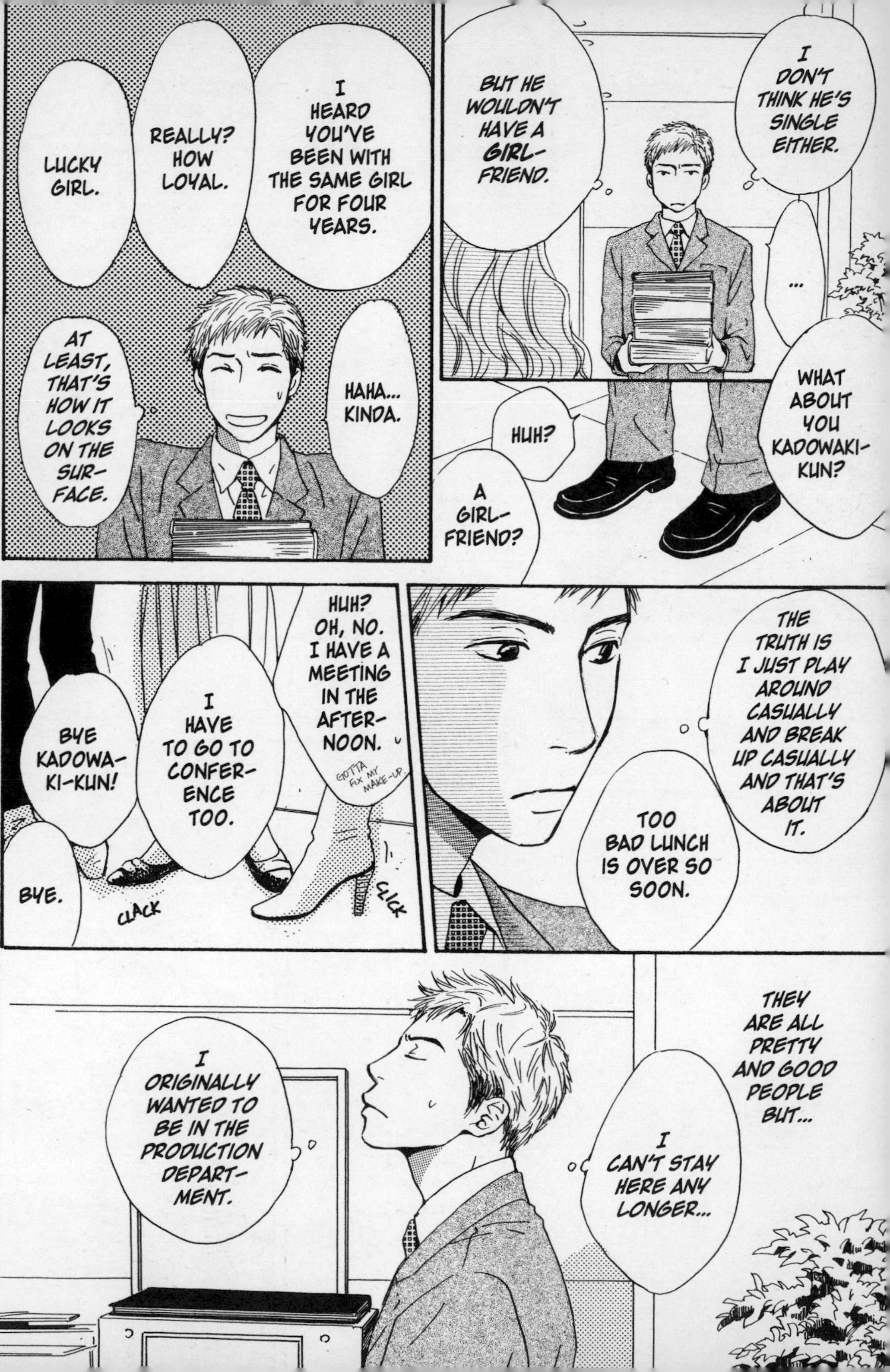
I DON'T THINK HE'S SINGLE EITHER.
BUT HE WOULDN'T HAVE A GIRLFRIEND.
...
WHAT ABOUT YOU KADOWAKI-KUN?
HUH?
A GIRLFRIEND?
I HEARD YOU'VE BEEN WITH THE SAME GIRL FOR FOUR YEARS.
REALLY? HOW LOYAL.
LUCKY GIRL.
HAHA... KINDA.
AT LEAST, THAT'S HOW IT LOOKS ON THE SURFACE.
THE TRUTH IS I JUST PLAY AROUND CASUALLY AND BREAK UP CASUALLY AND THAT'S ABOUT IT.
TOO BAD LUNCH IS OVER SO SOON.
HUH? OH, NO. I HAVE A MEETING IN THE AFTERNOON.
GOTTA FIX MY MAKE-UP.
I HAVE TO GO TO CONFERENCE TOO.
BYE KADOWAKI-KUN!
CLICK
CLACK
BYE.
THEY ARE ALL PRETTY AND GOOD PEOPLE BUT...
I CAN'T STAY HERE ANY LONGER...
I ORIGINALLY WANTED TO BE IN THE PRODUCTION DEPARTMENT.

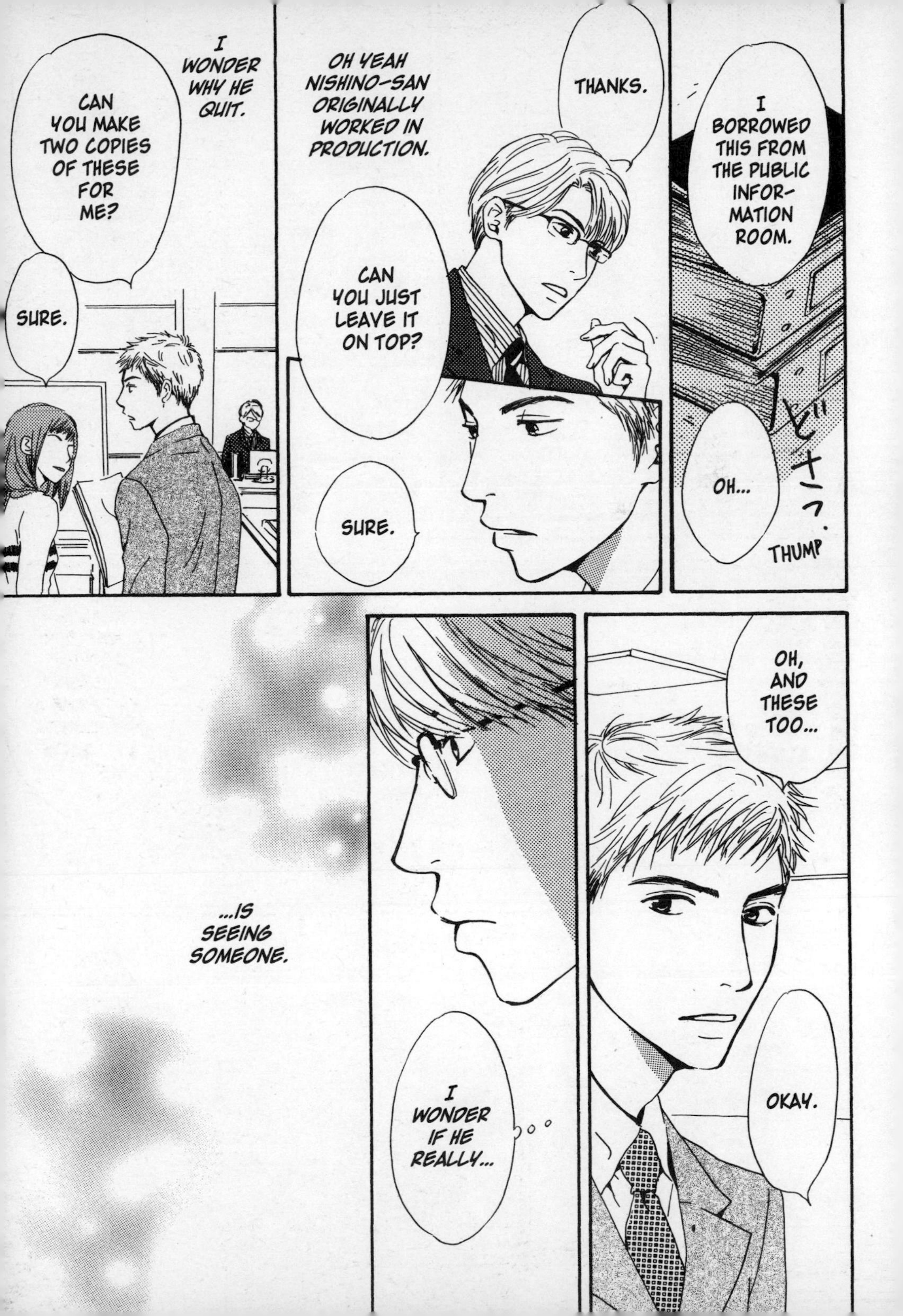
I BORROWED THIS FROM THE PUBLIC INFORMATION ROOM.
OH...
THUMP
THANKS.
OH YEAH NISHINO-SAN ORIGINALLY WORKED IN PRODUCTION.
CAN YOU JUST LEAVE IT ON TOP?
SURE.
I WONDER WHY HE QUIT.
CAN YOU MAKE TWO COPIES OF THESE FOR ME?
SURE.
OH, AND THESE TOO...
OKAY.
I WONDER IF HE REALLY...
...IS SEEING SOMEONE.

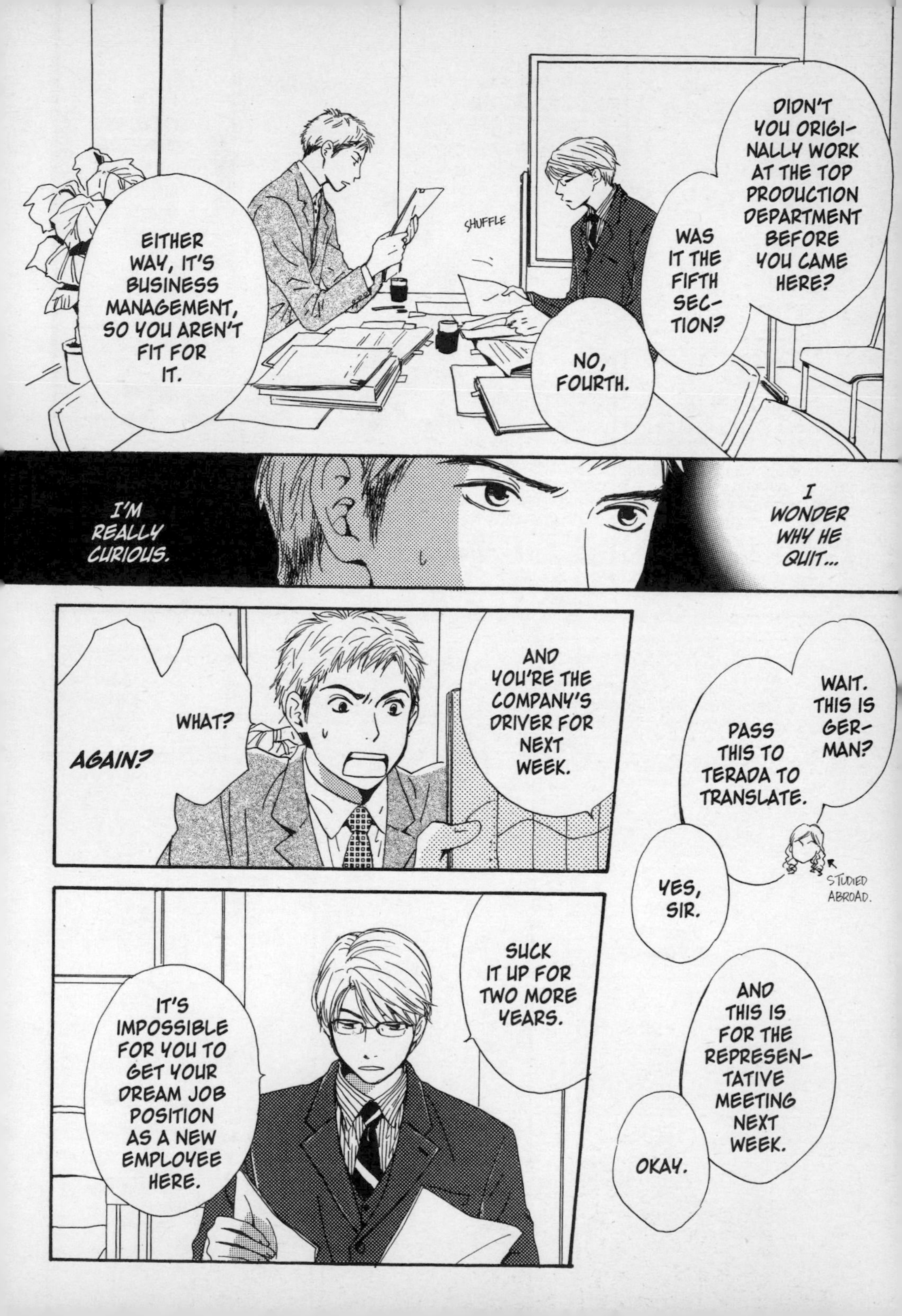
DIDN'T YOU ORIGINALLY WORK AT THE TOP PRODUCTION DEPARTMENT BEFORE YOU CAME HERE?
WAS IT THE FIFTH SECTION?
NO, FOURTH.
SHUFFLE
EITHER WAY, IT'S BUSINESS MANAGEMENT, SO YOU AREN'T FIT FOR IT.
I WONDER WHY HE QUIT...
I'M REALLY CURIOUS.
WAIT. THIS IS GERMAN?
PASS THIS TO TERADA TO TRANSLATE.
STUDIED ABROAD.
YES, SIR.
AND THIS IS FOR THE REPRESENTATIVE MEETING NEXT WEEK.
OKAY.
AND YOU'RE THE COMPANY'S DRIVER FOR NEXT WEEK.
WHAT?
AGAIN?
SUCK IT UP FOR TWO MORE YEARS.
IT'S IMPOSSIBLE FOR YOU TO GET YOUR DREAM JOB POSITION AS A NEW EMPLOYEE HERE.

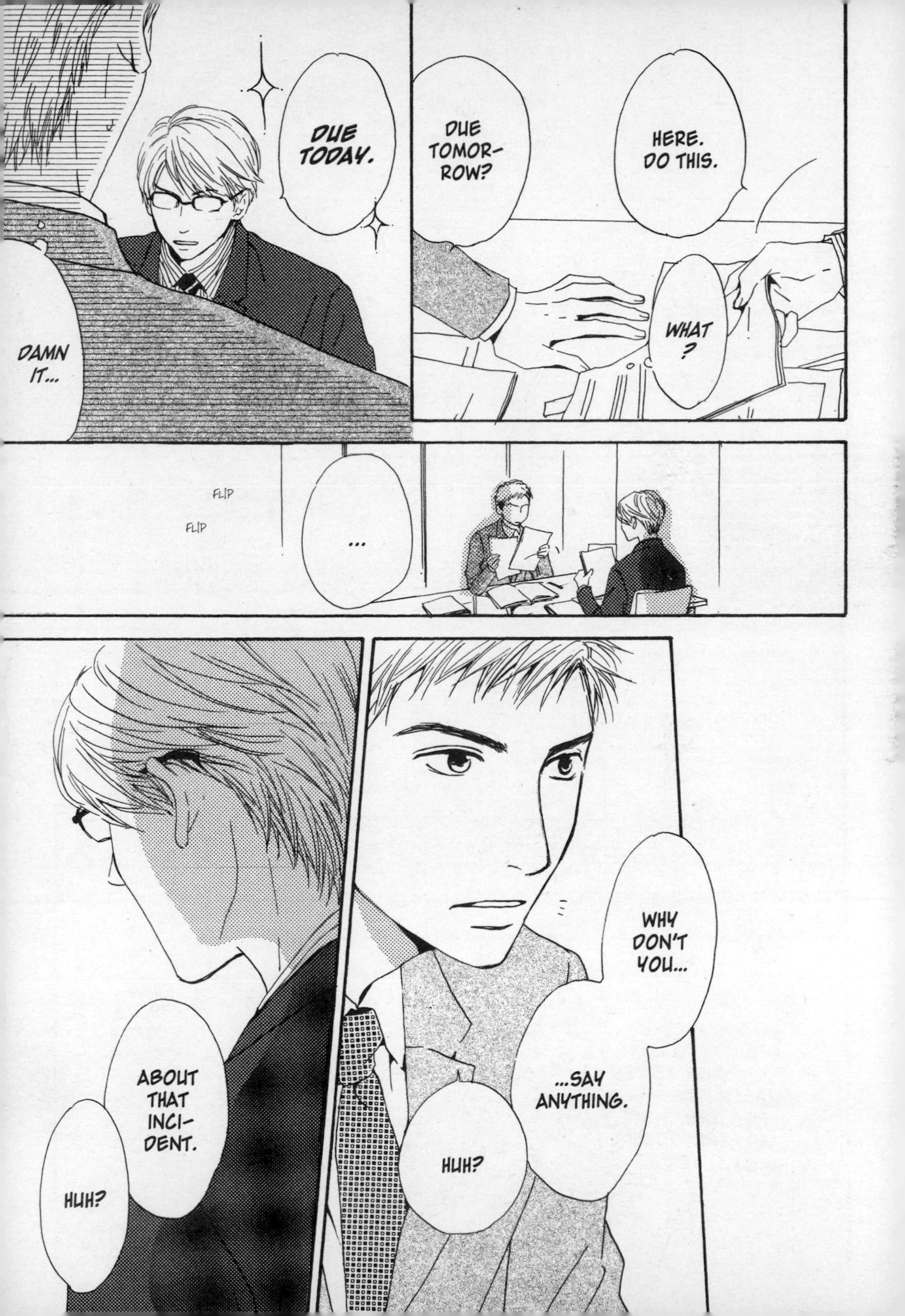
HERE. DO THIS.
DUE TOMOR-ROW?
WHAT?
DUE TODAY.
DAMN IT...
...
FLIP
FLIP
WHY DON'T YOU...
...SAY ANYTHING.
HUH?
ABOUT THAT INCI-DENT.
HUH?

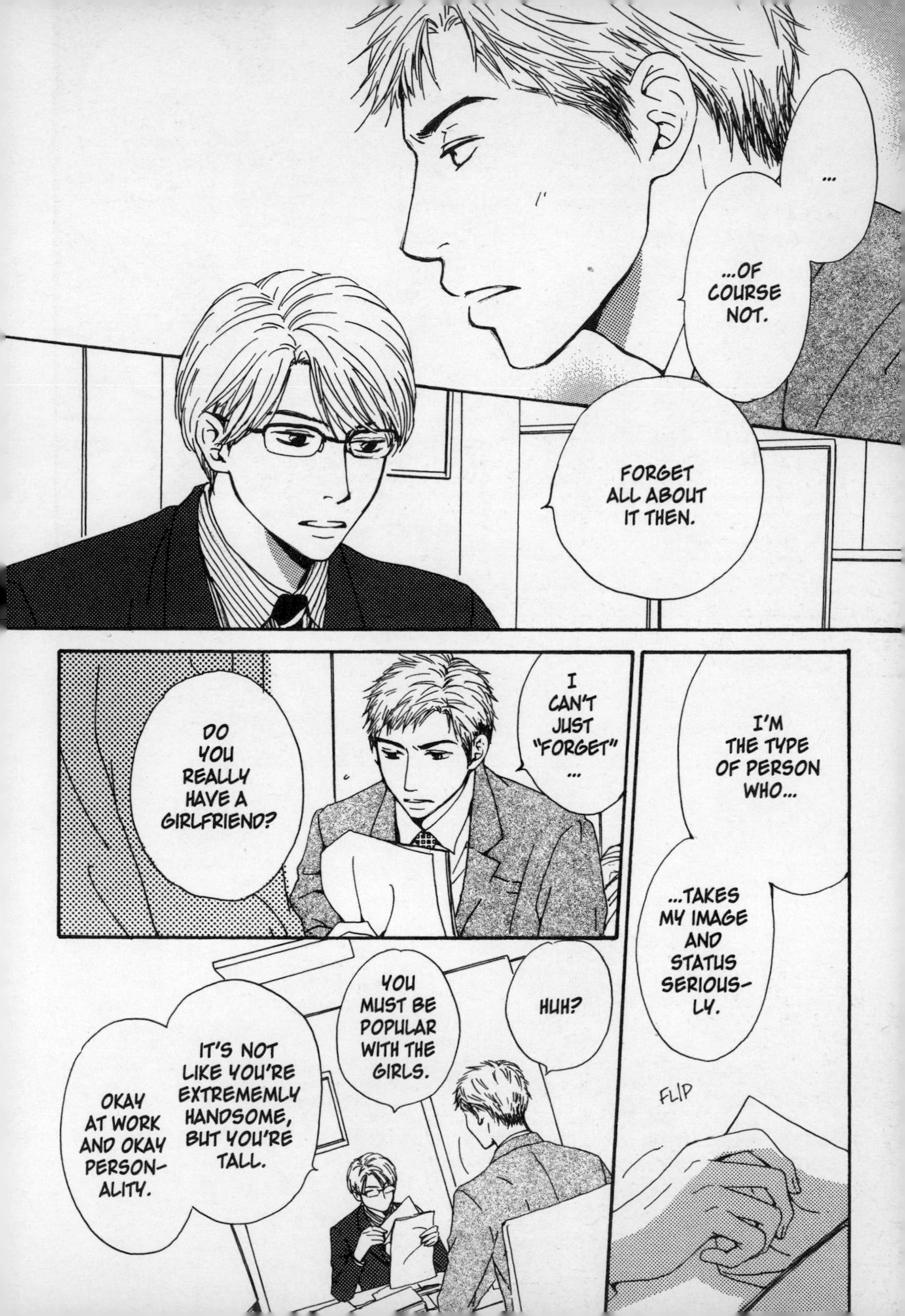
...
...OF COURSE NOT.
FORGET ALL ABOUT IT THEN.
I'M THE TYPE OF PERSON WHO...
...TAKES MY IMAGE AND STATUS SERIOUS-LY.
FLIP
I CAN'T JUST "FORGET"...
DO YOU REALLY HAVE A GIRLFRIEND?
HUH?
YOU MUST BE POPULAR WITH THE GIRLS.
IT'S NOT LIKE YOU'RE EXTREMEMLY HANDSOME, BUT YOU'RE TALL.
OKAY AT WORK AND OKAY PERSON-ALITY.

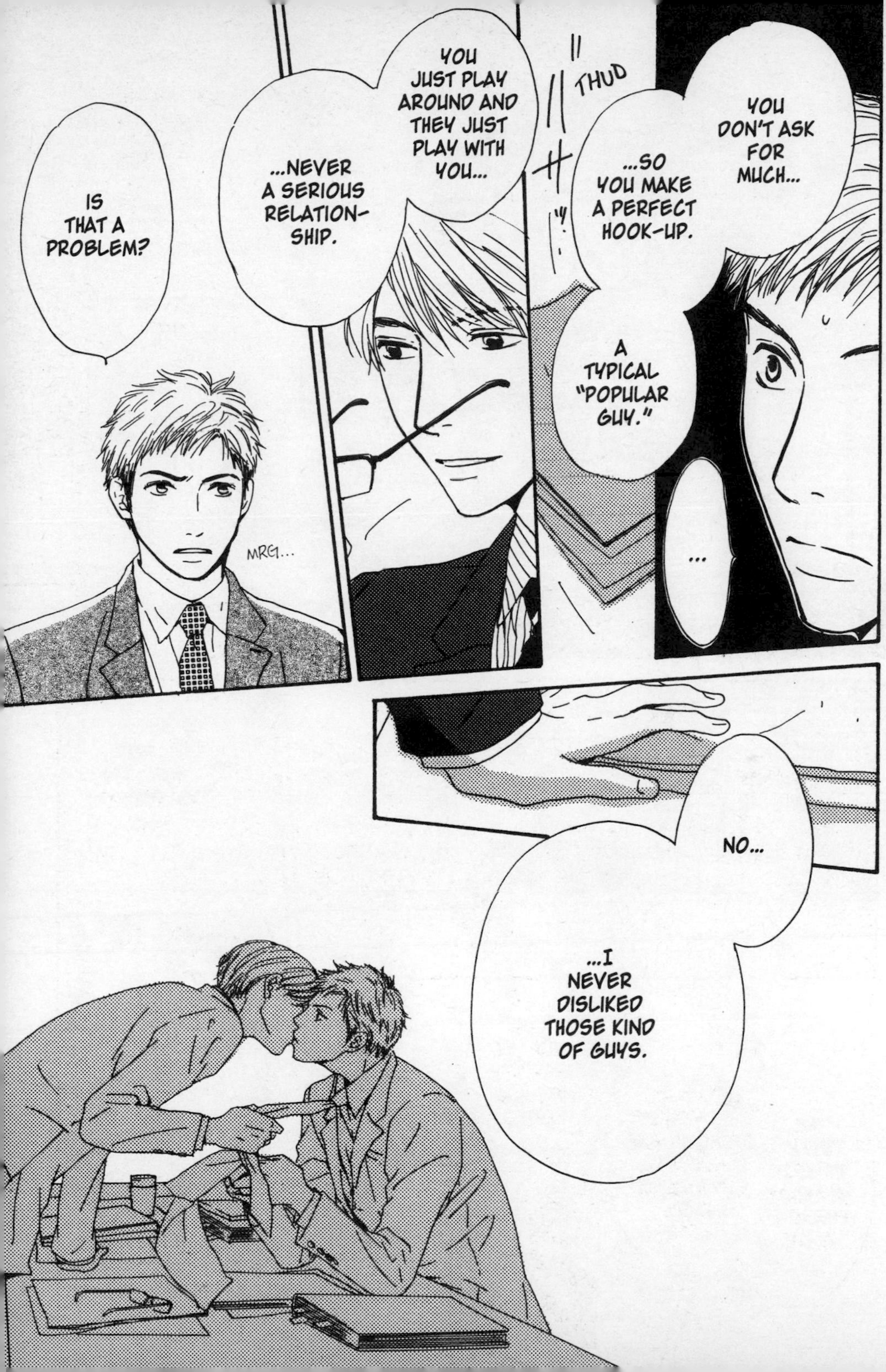
THUD
YOU DON'T ASK FOR MUCH...
...SO YOU MAKE A PERFECT HOOK-UP.
A TYPICAL "POPULAR GUY."
...
YOU JUST PLAY AROUND AND THEY JUST PLAY WITH YOU...
...NEVER A SERIOUS RELATION-SHIP.
IS THAT A PROBLEM?
MRG...
NO...
...I NEVER DISLIKED THOSE KIND OF GUYS.

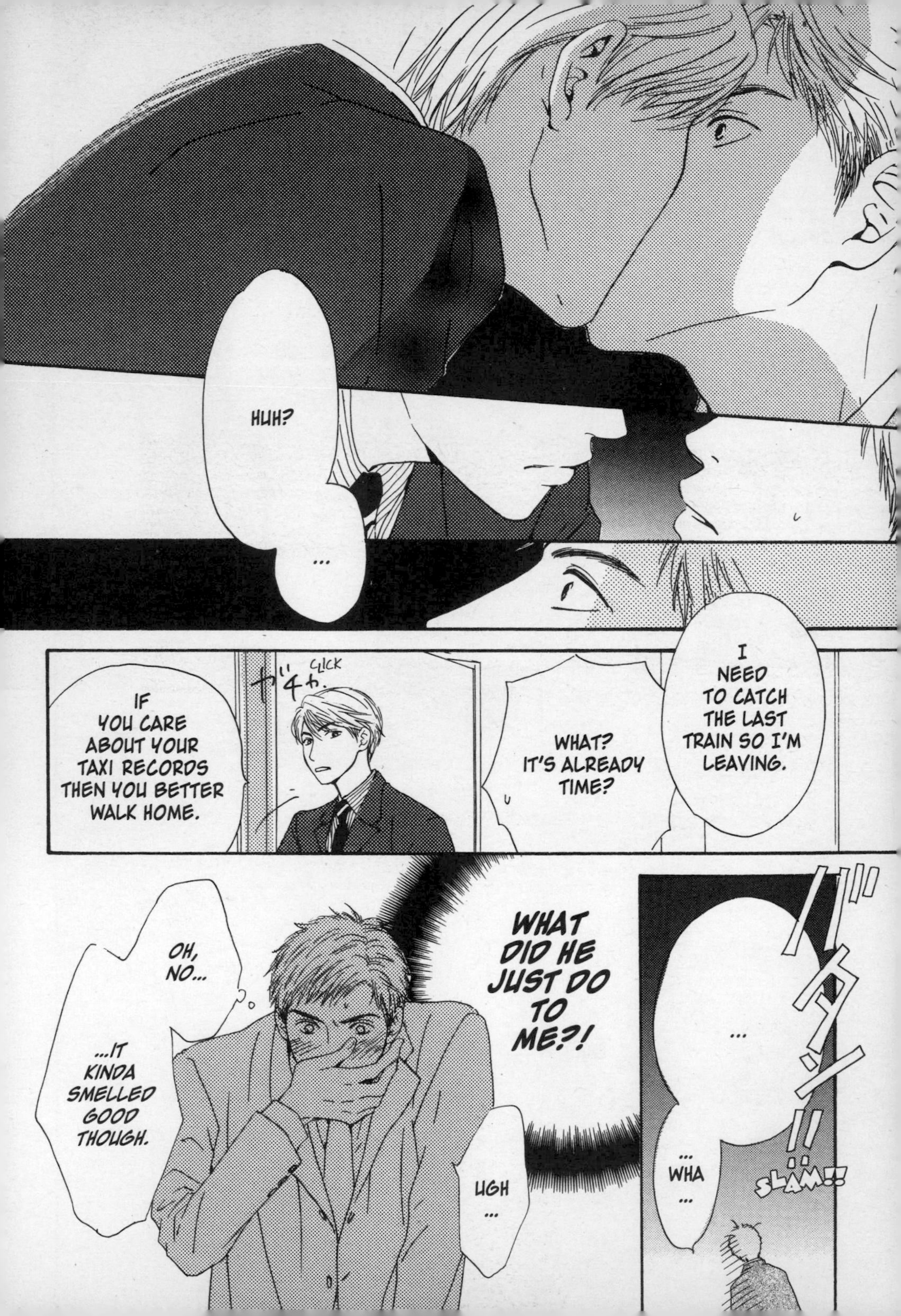
HUH?
...
I NEED TO CATCH THE LAST TRAIN SO I'M LEAVING.
WHAT? IT'S ALREADY TIME?
CLICK
IF YOU CARE ABOUT YOUR TAXI RECORDS THEN YOU BETTER WALK HOME.
...
...WHA...
SLAM!!
WHAT DID HE JUST DO TO ME?!
UGH...
OH, NO...
...IT KINDA SMELLED GOOD THOUGH.

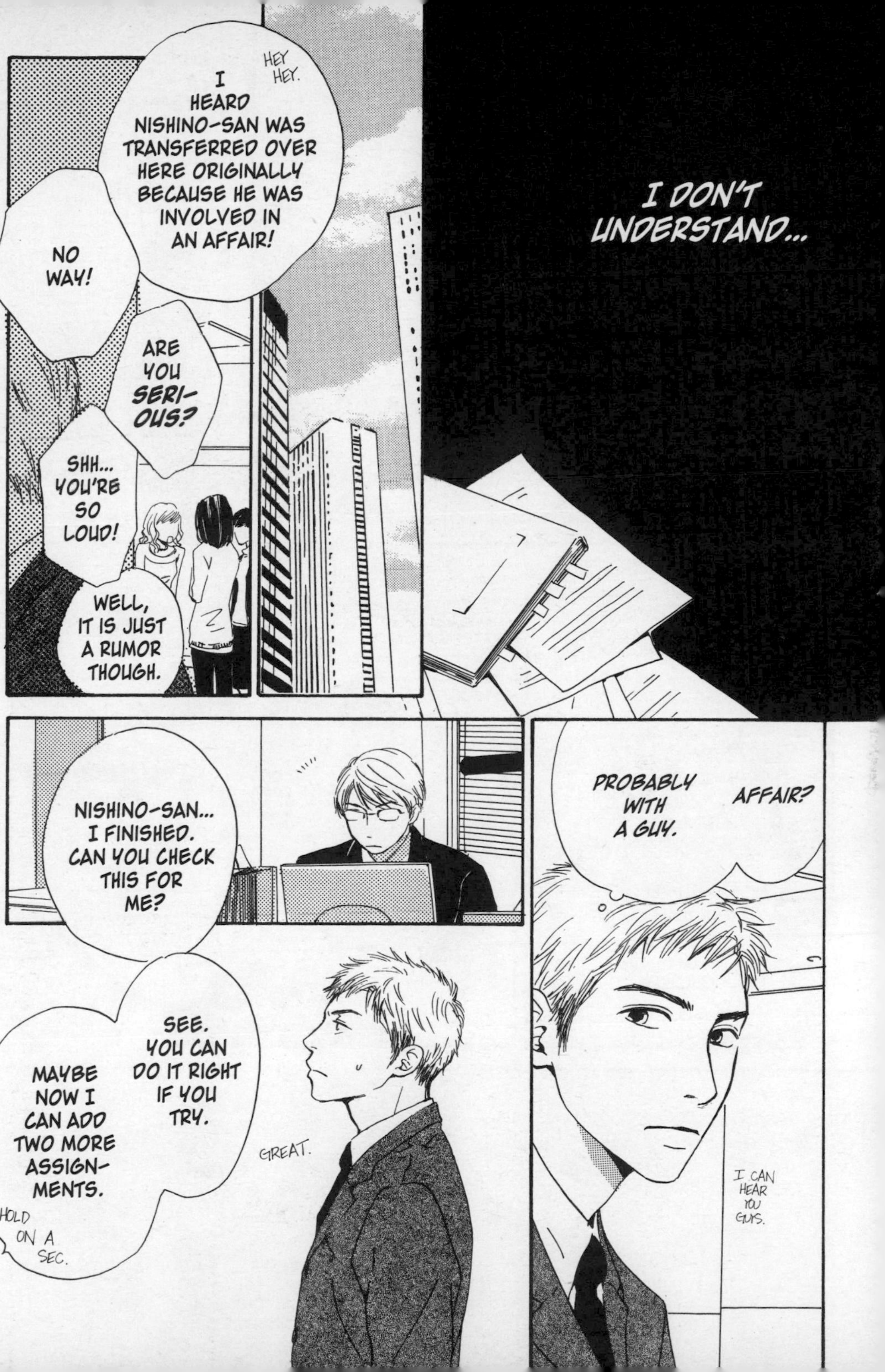
I DON'T UNDERSTAND...
HEY HEY.
I HEARD NISHINO-SAN WAS TRANSFERRED OVER HERE ORIGINALLY BECAUSE HE WAS INVOLVED IN AN AFFAIR!
NO WAY!
ARE YOU *SERI-OUS?*
SHH... YOU'RE SO LOUD!
WELL, IT IS JUST A RUMOR THOUGH.
AFFAIR?
PROBABLY WITH A GUY.
I CAN HEAR YOU GUYS.
NISHINO-SAN... I FINISHED. CAN YOU CHECK THIS FOR ME?
SEE. YOU CAN DO IT RIGHT IF YOU TRY.
GREAT.
MAYBE NOW I CAN ADD TWO MORE ASSIGN-MENTS.
HOLD ON A SEC.

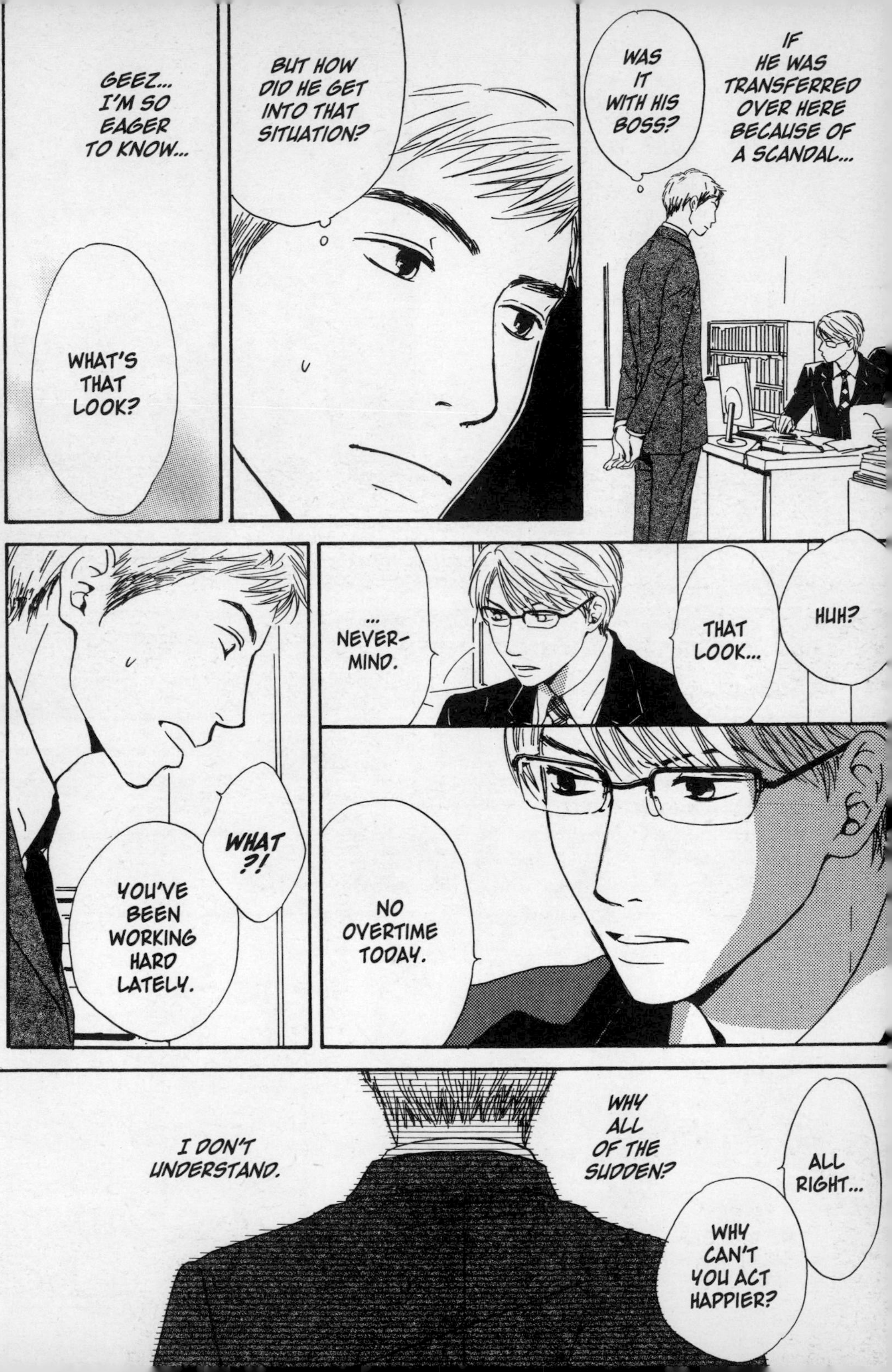
IF HE WAS TRANSFERRED OVER HERE BECAUSE OF A SCANDAL...
WAS IT WITH HIS BOSS?
BUT HOW DID HE GET INTO THAT SITUATION?
GEEZ... I'M SO EAGER TO KNOW...
WHAT'S THAT LOOK?
HUH?
THAT LOOK...
... NEVER-MIND.
NO OVERTIME TODAY.
WHAT?!
YOU'VE BEEN WORKING HARD LATELY.
ALL RIGHT...
WHY CAN'T YOU ACT HAPPIER?
WHY ALL OF THE SUDDEN?
I DON'T UNDERSTAND.

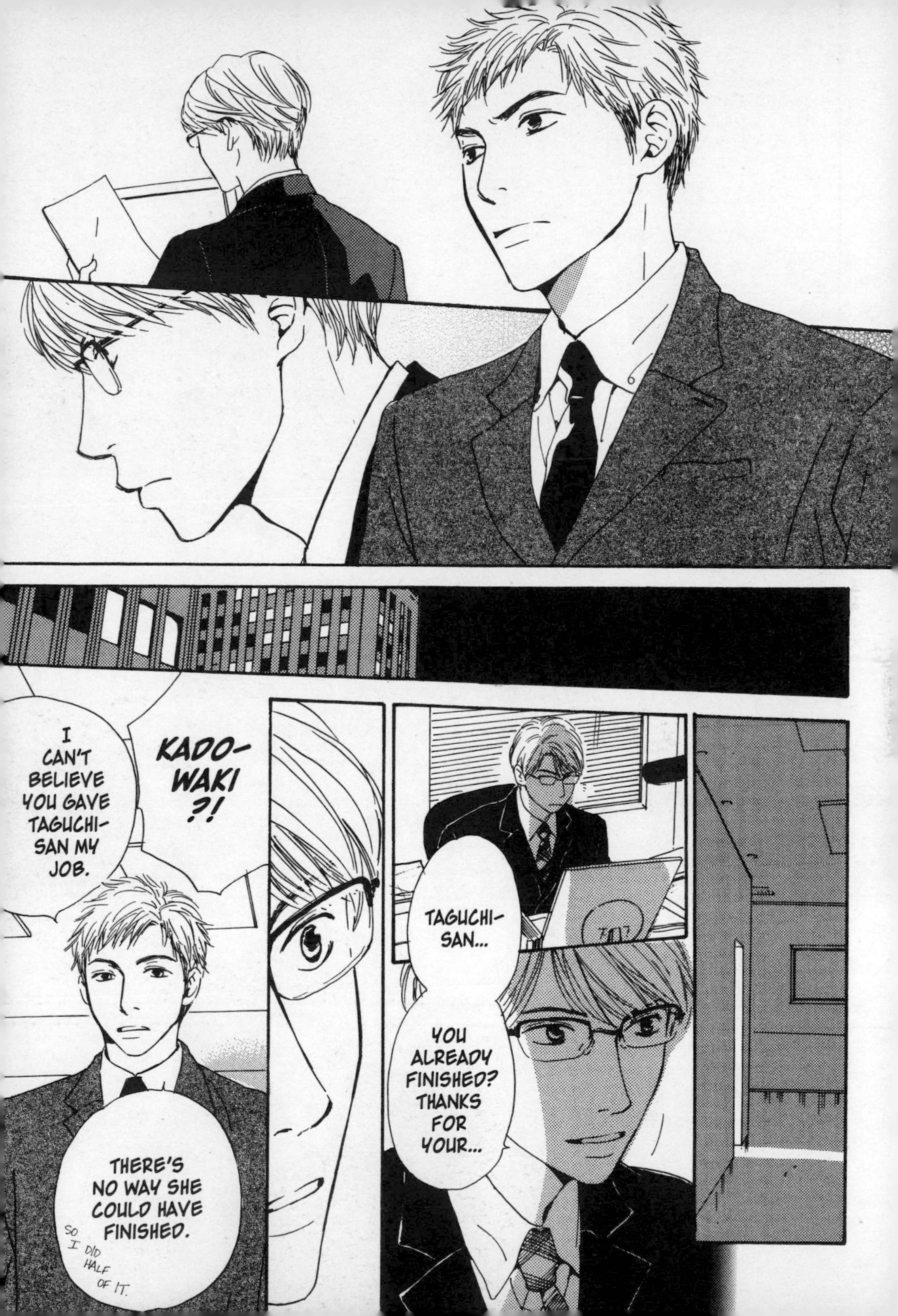
TAGUCHI-SAN...
YOU ALREADY FINISHED? THANKS FOR YOUR...
KADO-WAKI ?!
I CAN'T BELIEVE YOU GAVE TAGUCHI-SAN MY JOB.
THERE'S NO WAY SHE COULD HAVE FINISHED.
SO I DID HALF OF IT.

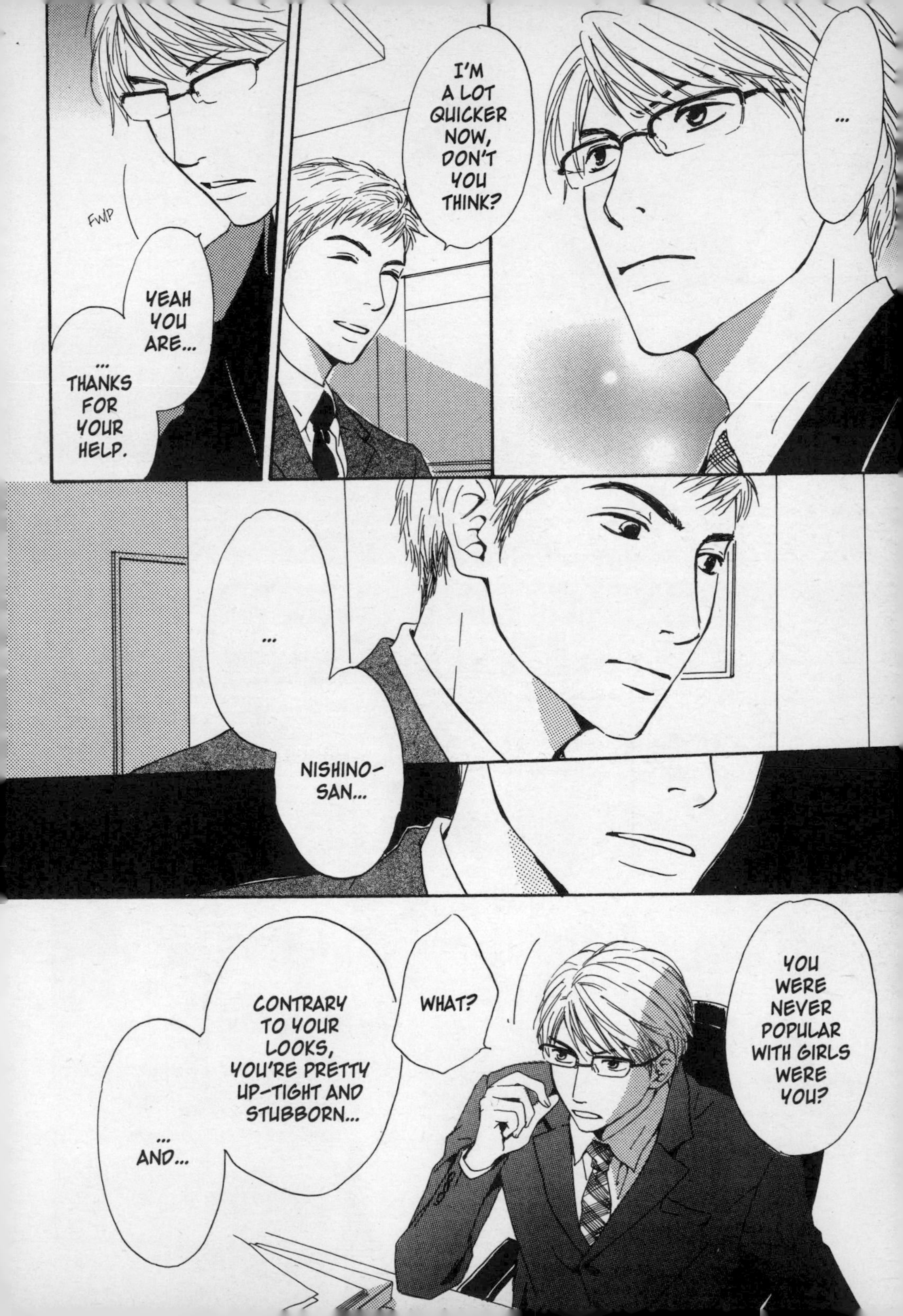
...
I'M A LOT QUICKER NOW, DON'T YOU THINK?
FWIP
YEAH YOU ARE... ... THANKS FOR YOUR HELP.
...
NISHINO-SAN...
YOU WERE NEVER POPULAR WITH GIRLS WERE YOU?
WHAT?
CONTRARY TO YOUR LOOKS, YOU'RE PRETTY UP-TIGHT AND STUBBORN... ... AND...

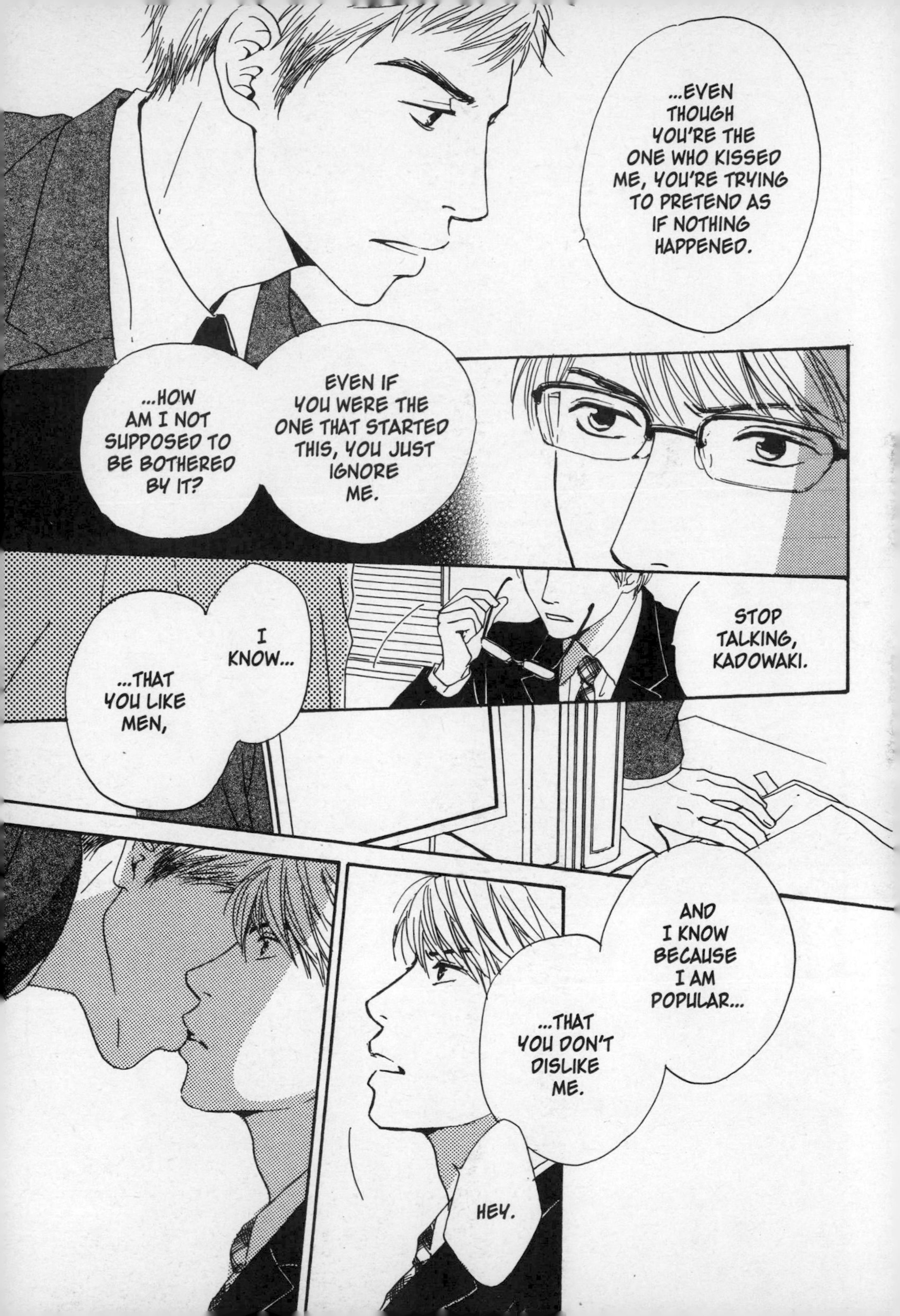
...EVEN THOUGH YOU'RE THE ONE WHO KISSED ME, YOU'RE TRYING TO PRETEND AS IF NOTHING HAPPENED.
EVEN IF YOU WERE THE ONE THAT STARTED THIS, YOU JUST IGNORE ME.
...HOW AM I NOT SUPPOSED TO BE BOTHERED BY IT?
STOP TALKING, KADOWAKI.
I KNOW...
...THAT YOU LIKE MEN,
AND I KNOW BECAUSE I AM POPULAR...
...THAT YOU DON'T DISLIKE ME.
HEY.

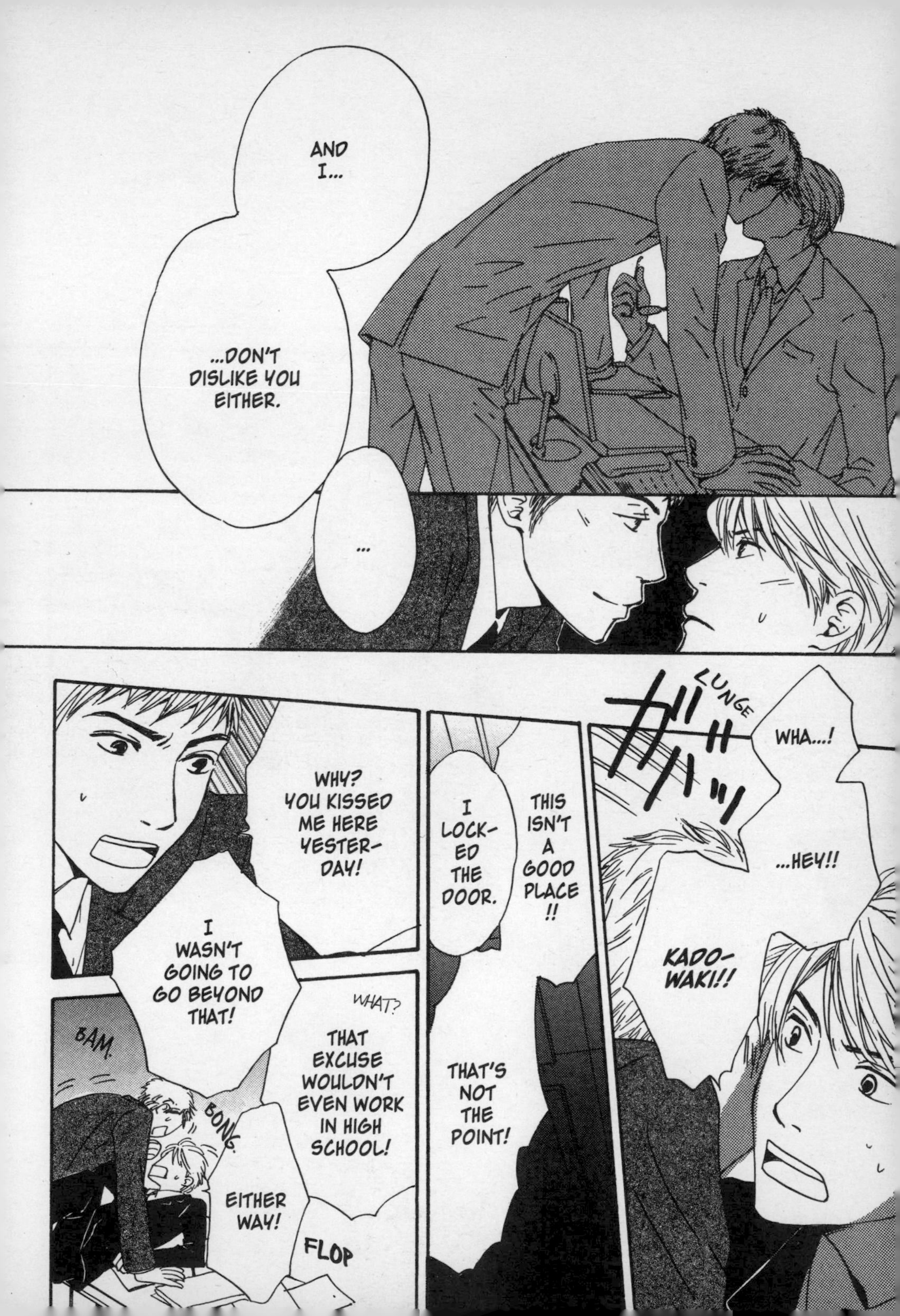
AND I...
...DON'T DISLIKE YOU EITHER.
...
LUNGE
WHA...!
...HEY!!
KADO-WAKI!!
THIS ISN'T A GOOD PLACE!!
I LOCK-ED THE DOOR.
THAT'S NOT THE POINT!
WHY? YOU KISSED ME HERE YESTER-DAY!
I WASN'T GOING TO GO BEYOND THAT!
WHAT?
THAT EXCUSE WOULDN'T EVEN WORK IN HIGH SCHOOL!
BAM
BONG
EITHER WAY!
FLOP

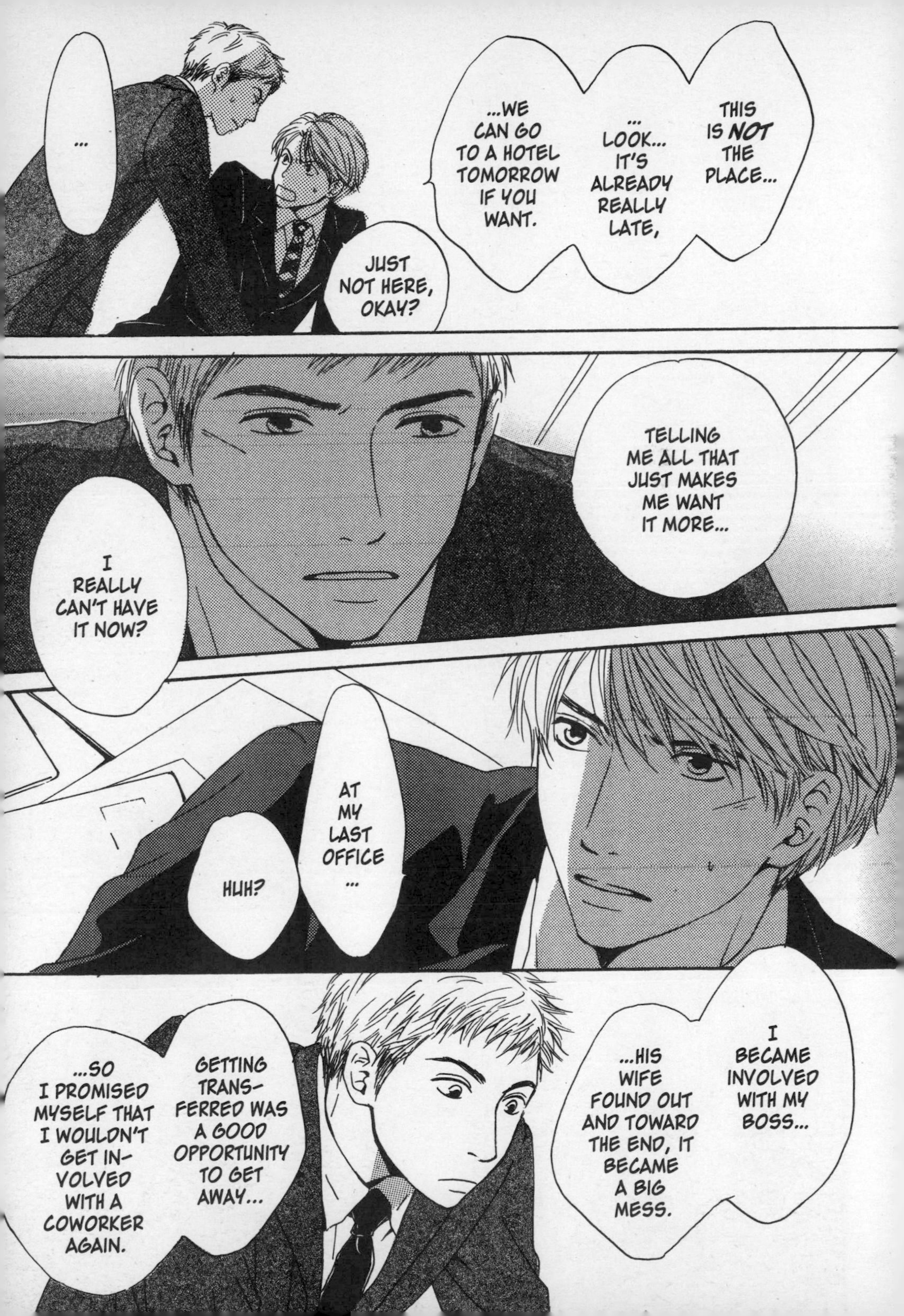
THIS IS **NOT** THE PLACE...
... LOOK... IT'S ALREADY REALLY LATE,
...WE CAN GO TO A HOTEL TOMORROW IF YOU WANT.
JUST NOT HERE, OKAY?
...
TELLING ME ALL THAT JUST MAKES ME WANT IT MORE...
I REALLY CAN'T HAVE IT NOW?
AT MY LAST OFFICE ...
HUH?
I BECAME INVOLVED WITH MY BOSS...
...HIS WIFE FOUND OUT AND TOWARD THE END, IT BECAME A BIG MESS.
GETTING TRANS-FERRED WAS A GOOD OPPORTUNITY TO GET AWAY...
...SO I PROMISED MYSELF THAT I WOULDN'T GET IN-VOLVED WITH A COWORKER AGAIN.

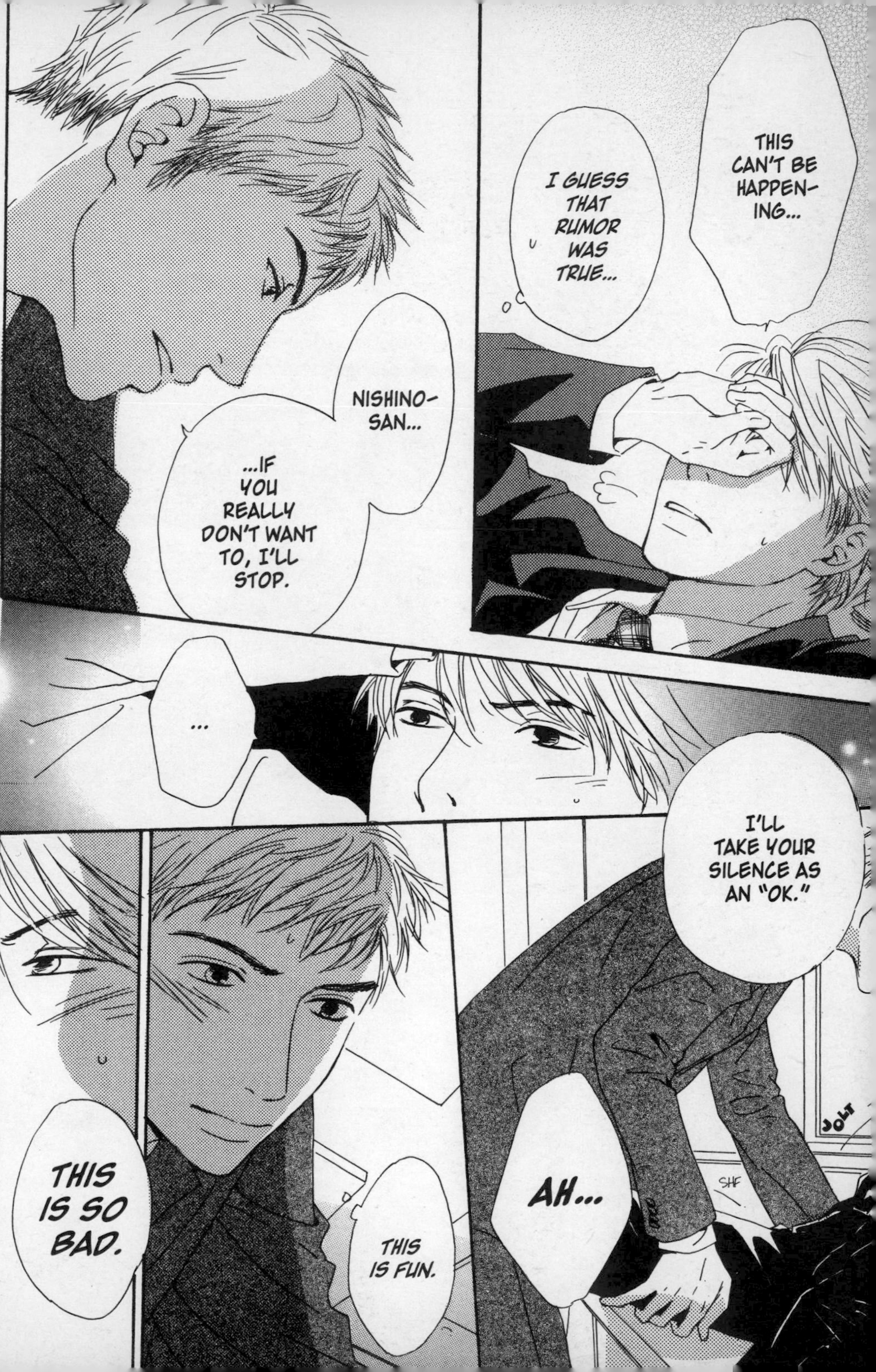
THIS CAN'T BE HAPPENING...
I GUESS THAT RUMOR WAS TRUE...
NISHINO-SAN...
...IF YOU REALLY DON'T WANT TO, I'LL STOP.
...
I'LL TAKE YOUR SILENCE AS AN "OK."
JOLT
SHF
AH...
THIS IS FUN.
THIS IS SO BAD.

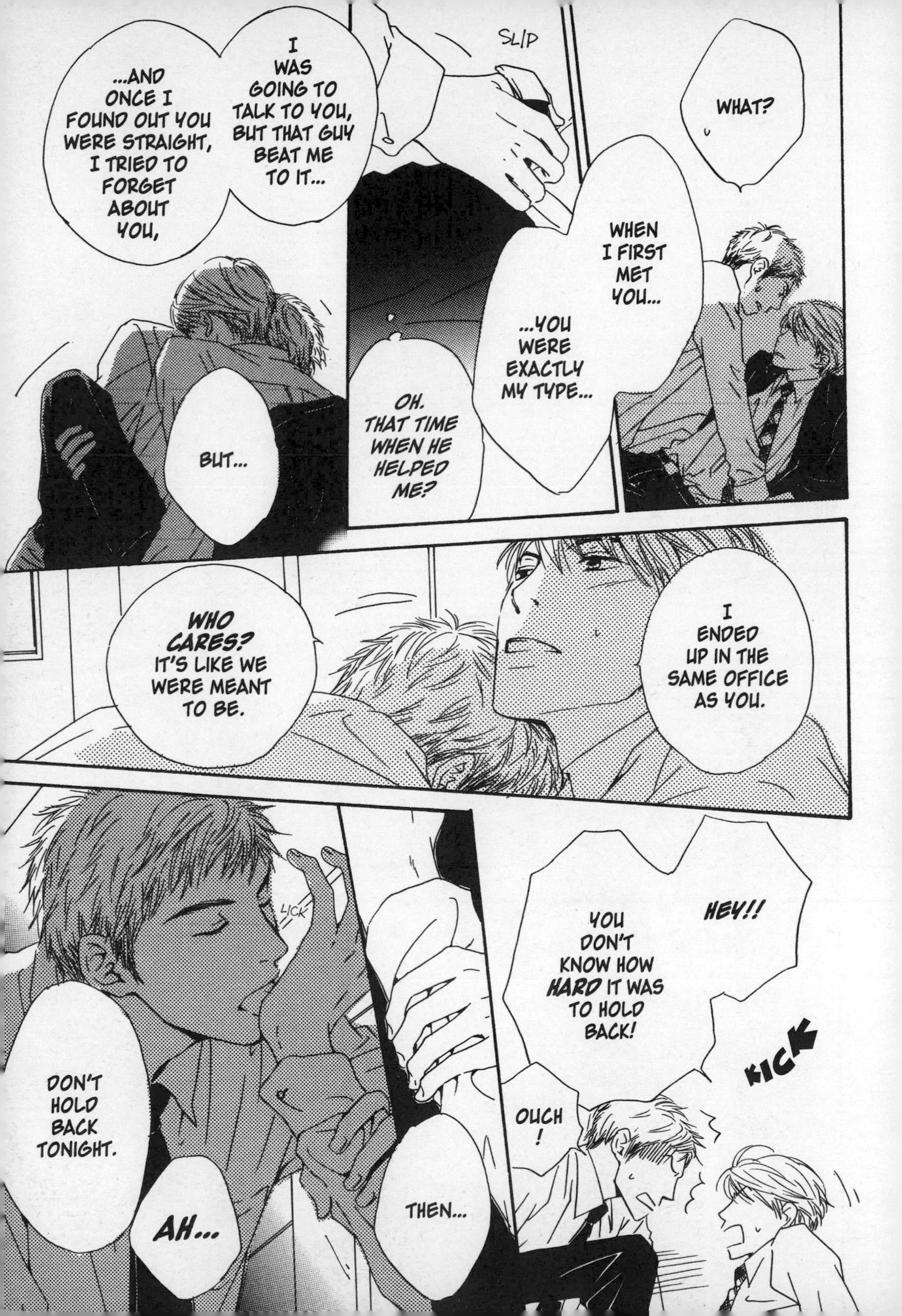
SLIP
WHAT?
WHEN I FIRST MET YOU...
...YOU WERE EXACTLY MY TYPE...
OH. THAT TIME WHEN HE HELPED ME?
I WAS GOING TO TALK TO YOU, BUT THAT GUY BEAT ME TO IT...
...AND ONCE I FOUND OUT YOU WERE STRAIGHT, I TRIED TO FORGET ABOUT YOU,
BUT...
I ENDED UP IN THE SAME OFFICE AS YOU.
WHO CARES? IT'S LIKE WE WERE MEANT TO BE.
HEY!!
YOU DON'T KNOW HOW HARD IT WAS TO HOLD BACK!
KICK
OUCH!
LICK
THEN...
DON'T HOLD BACK TONIGHT.
AH...

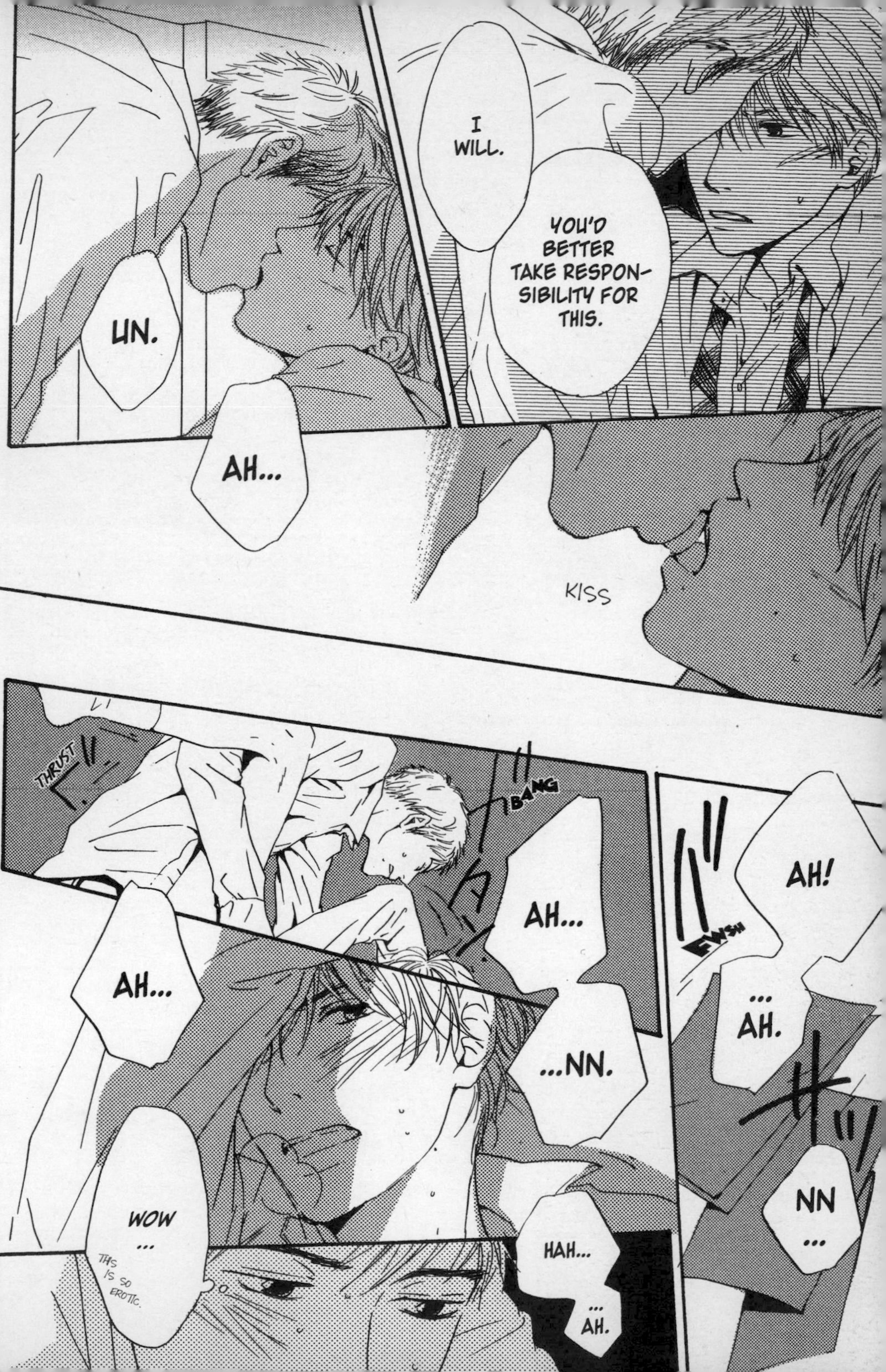
YOU'D BETTER TAKE RESPONSIBILITY FOR THIS.
I WILL.
UN.
AH...
KISS
AH!
FWSH
...AH.
NN ...
THRUST
BANG
AH...
...NN.
AH...
WOW ...
THIS IS SO EROTIC.
HAH...
...AH.

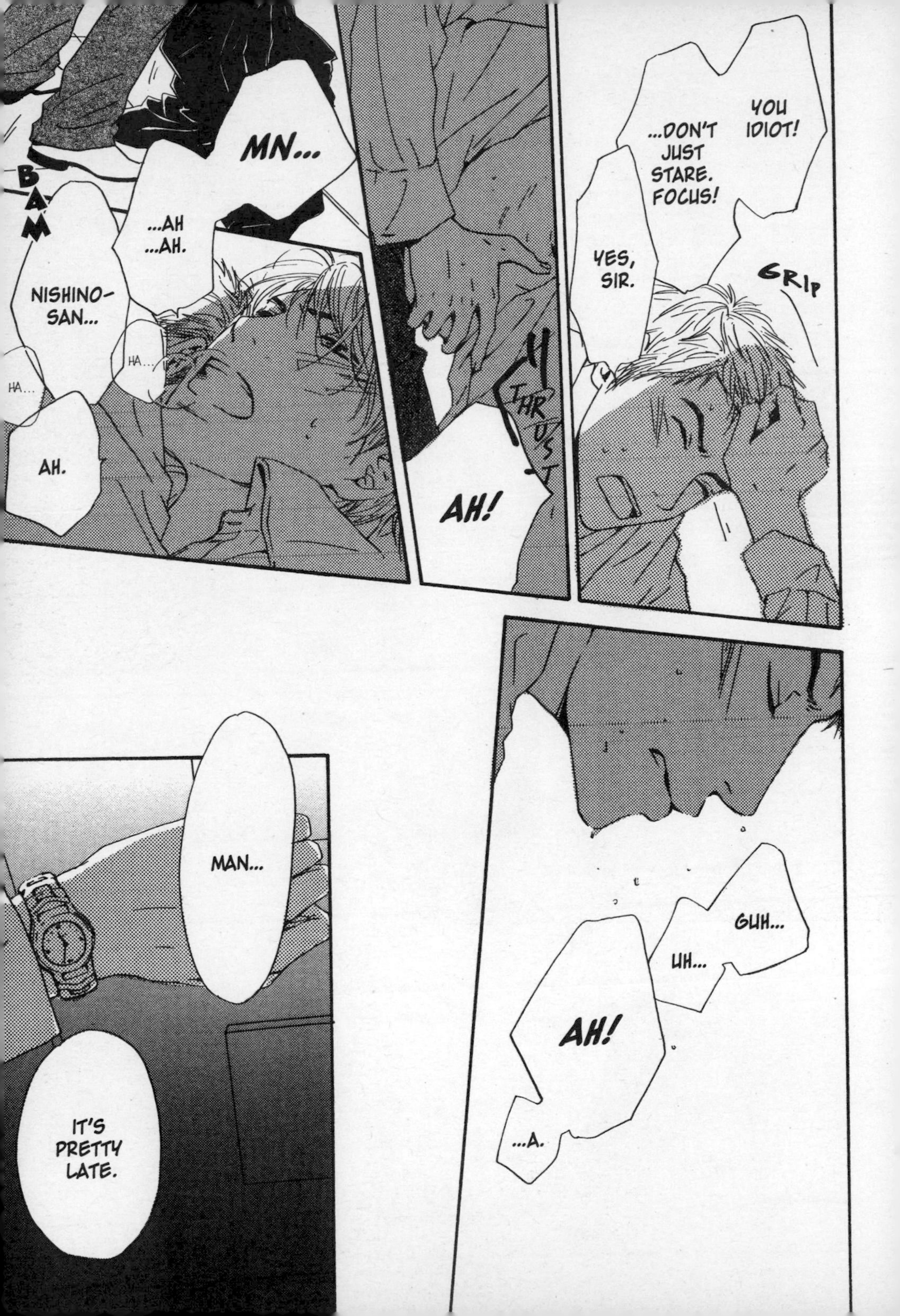
YOU IDIOT!
...DON'T JUST STARE. FOCUS!
YES, SIR.
GRIP
THRUST
AH!
MN...
BAM
...AH ...AH.
NISHINO-SAN...
HA...
HA...
AH.
GUH...
UH...
AH!
...A.
MAN...
IT'S PRETTY LATE.

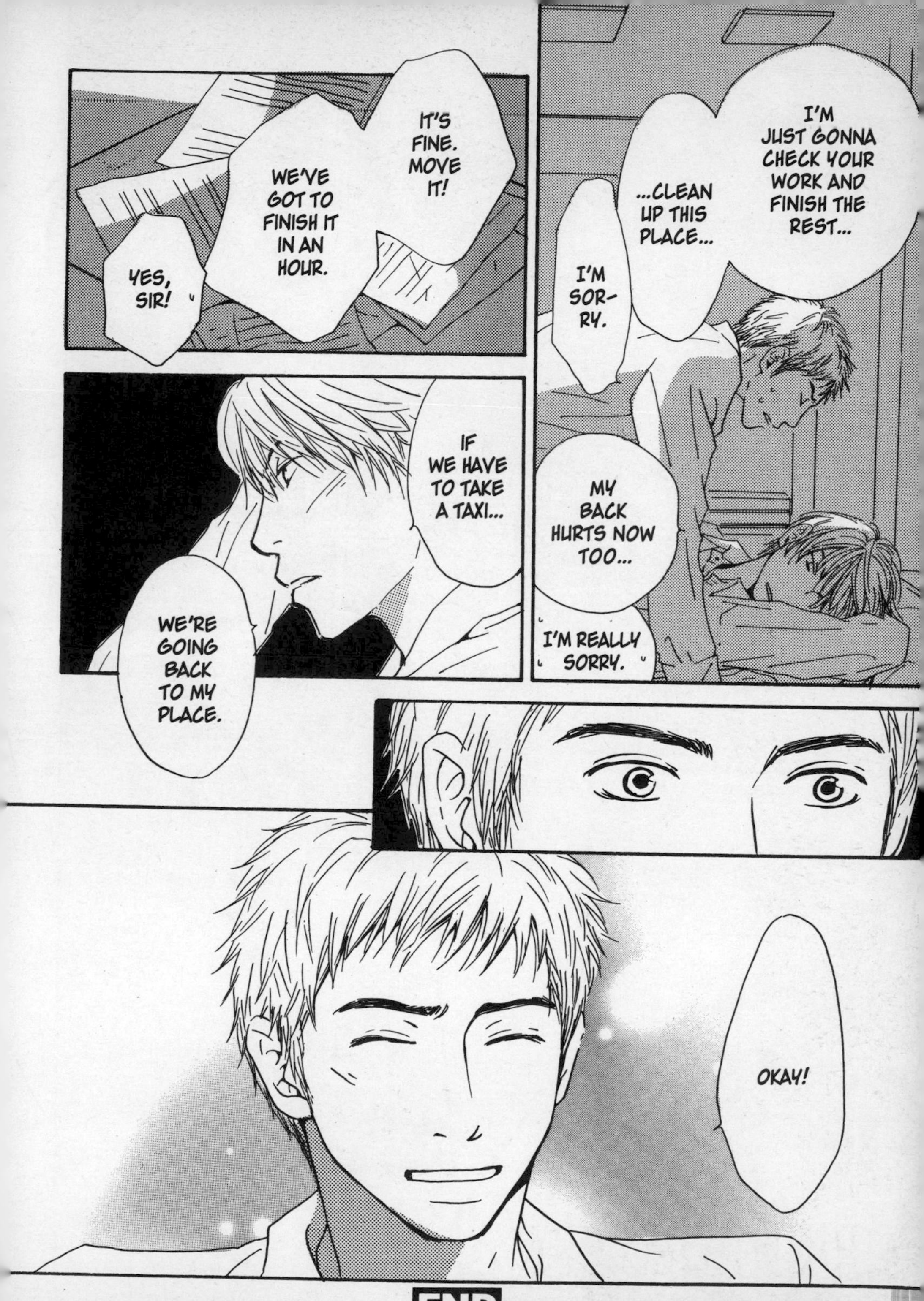
I'M JUST GONNA CHECK YOUR WORK AND FINISH THE REST...
...CLEAN UP THIS PLACE...
I'M SOR-RY.
MY BACK HURTS NOW TOO...
I'M REALLY SORRY.
IT'S FINE. MOVE IT!
WE'VE GOT TO FINISH IT IN AN HOUR.
YES, SIR!
IF WE HAVE TO TAKE A TAXI...
WE'RE GOING BACK TO MY PLACE.
OKAY!

END

RIGHT OR LEFT

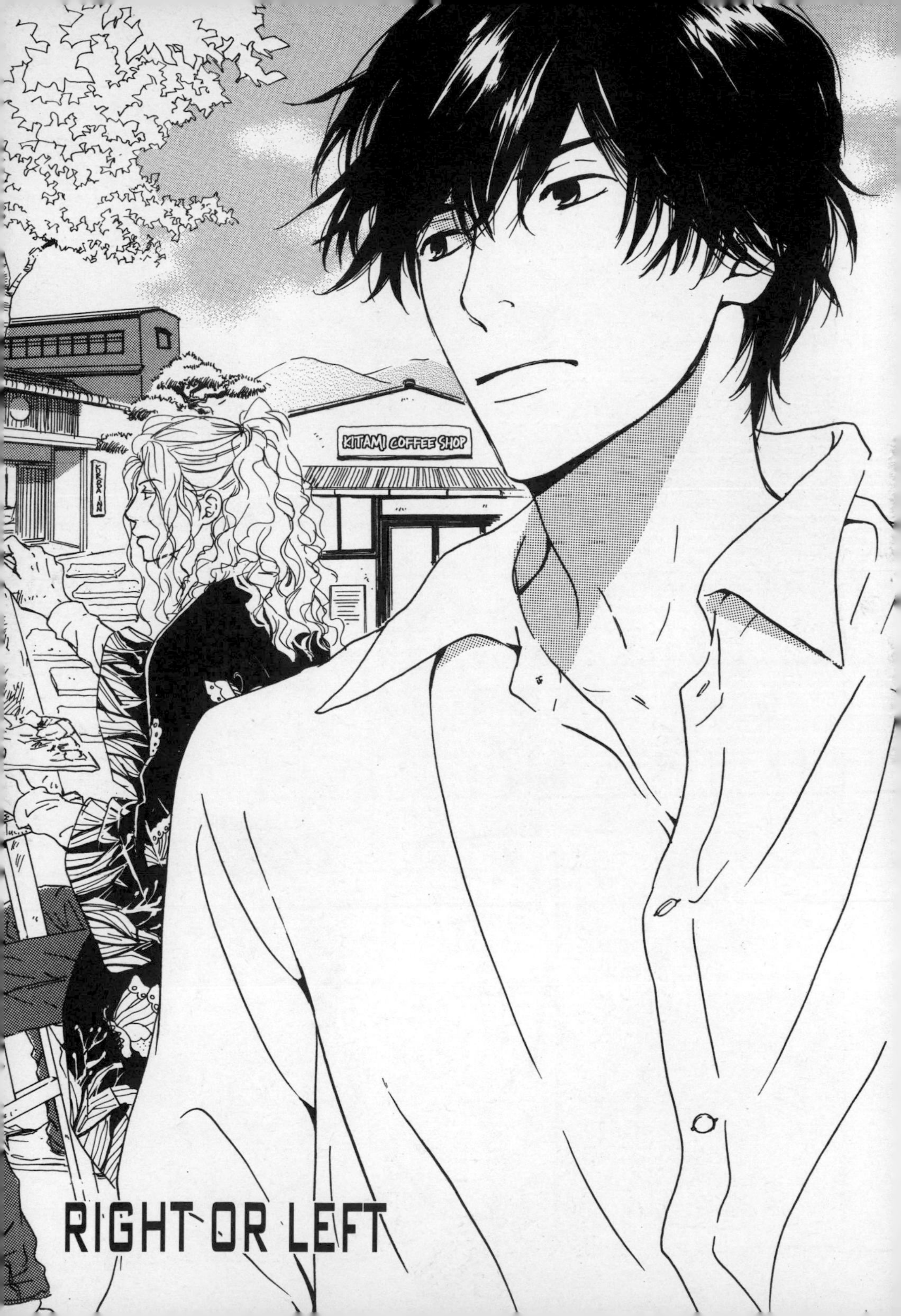
KITAMI COFFEE SHOP

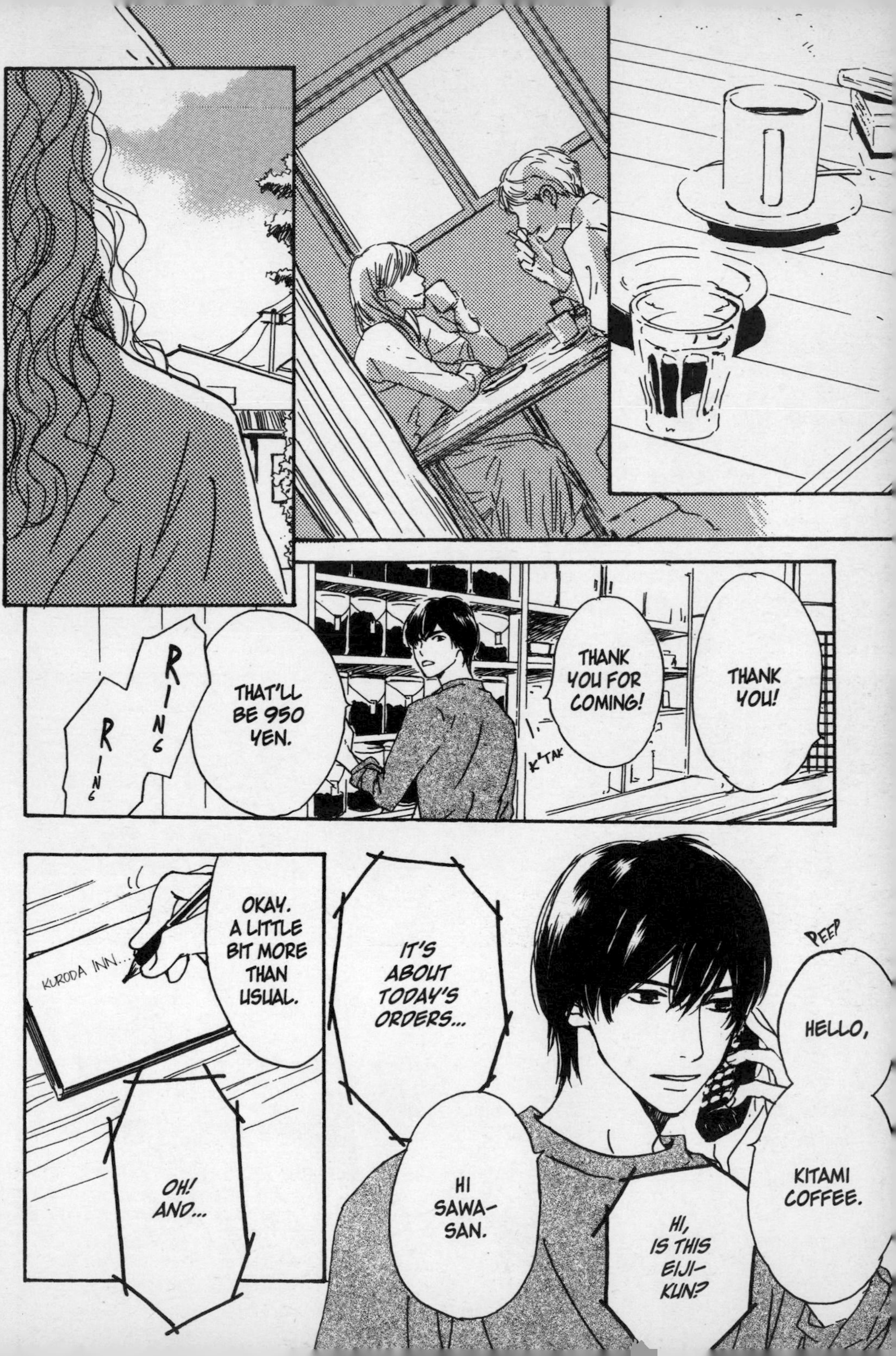
THANK YOU!
THANK YOU FOR COMING!
K'TAK
THAT'LL BE 950 YEN.
RING RING
PEEP
HELLO,
KITAMI COFFEE.
HI, IS THIS EIJI-KUN?
HI SAWA-SAN.
IT'S ABOUT TODAY'S ORDERS...
OKAY. A LITTLE BIT MORE THAN USUAL.
KURODA INN...
OH! AND...

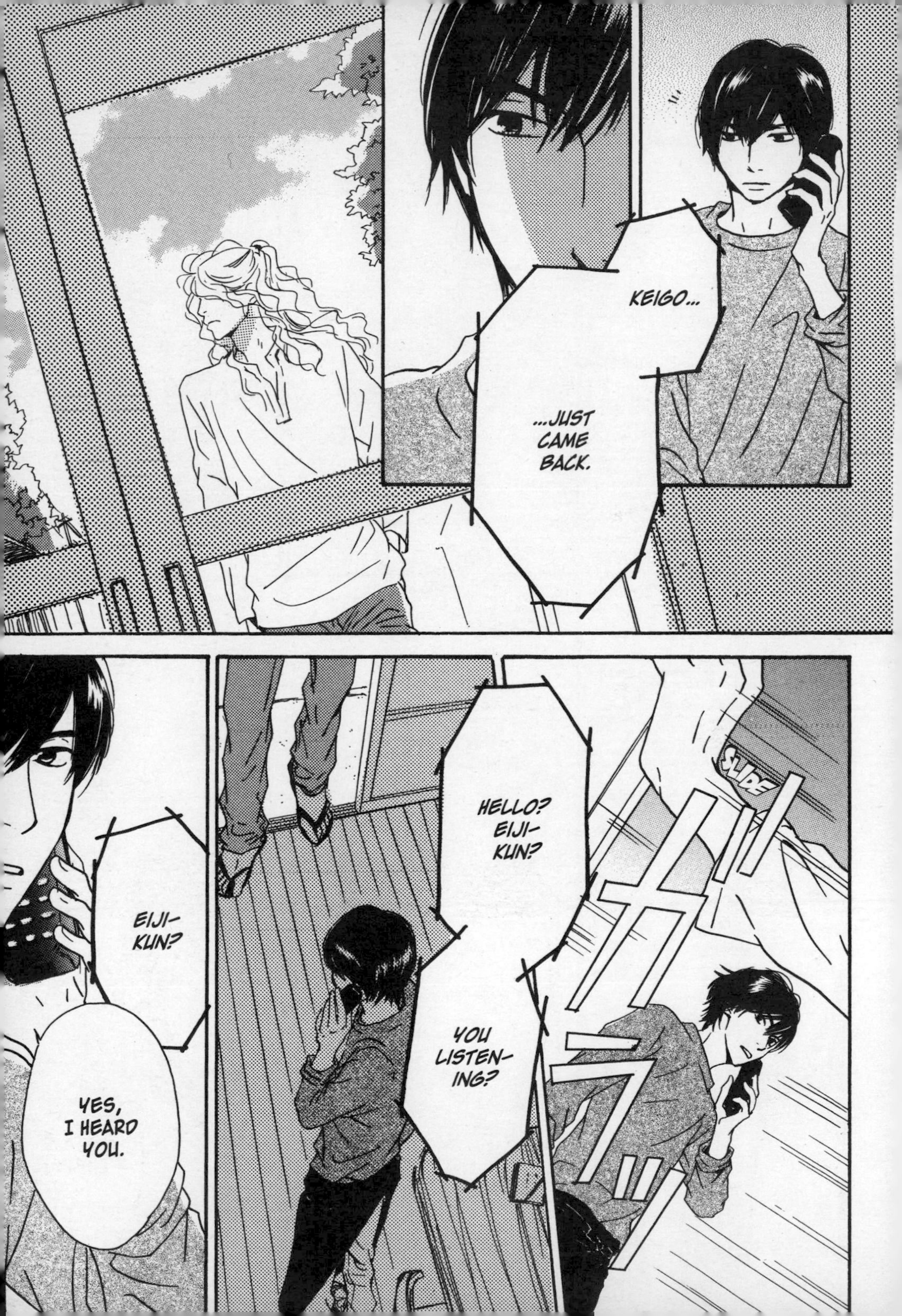
KEIGO...
...JUST CAME BACK.
SLIDE
HELLO? EIJI-KUN?
YOU LISTENING?
EIJI-KUN?
YES, I HEARD YOU.

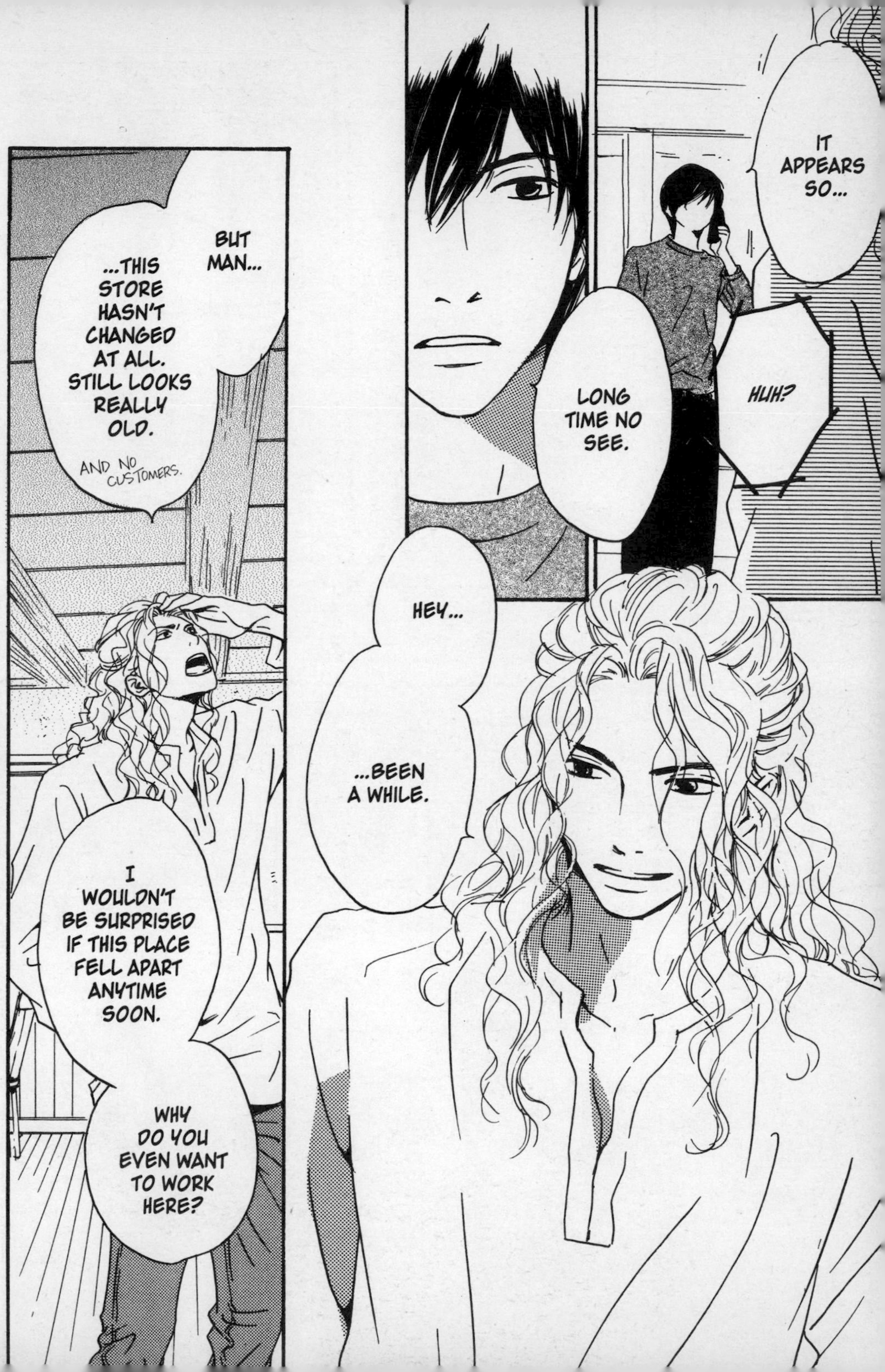
IT APPEARS SO...
HUH?
LONG TIME NO SEE.
HEY...
...BEEN A WHILE.
BUT MAN...
...THIS STORE HASN'T CHANGED AT ALL. STILL LOOKS REALLY OLD.
AND NO CUSTOMERS.
I WOULDN'T BE SURPRISED IF THIS PLACE FELL APART ANYTIME SOON.
WHY DO YOU EVEN WANT TO WORK HERE?

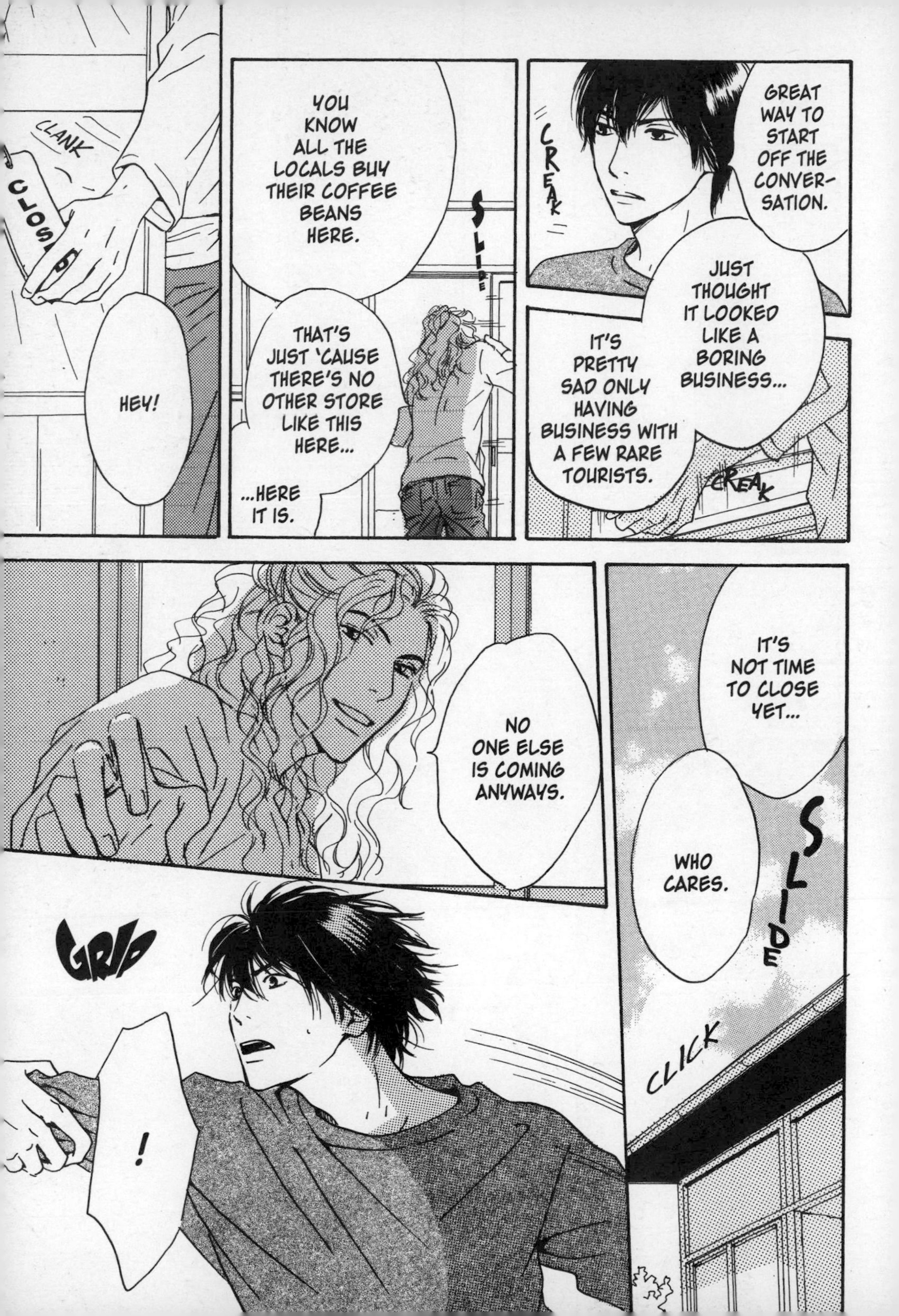
CREAK
GREAT WAY TO START OFF THE CONVER-SATION.
JUST THOUGHT IT LOOKED LIKE A BORING BUSINESS...
IT'S PRETTY SAD ONLY HAVING BUSINESS WITH A FEW RARE TOURISTS.
CREAK
YOU KNOW ALL THE LOCALS BUY THEIR COFFEE BEANS HERE.
SLIDE
THAT'S JUST 'CAUSE THERE'S NO OTHER STORE LIKE THIS HERE...
...HERE IT IS.
CLANK
HEY!
IT'S NOT TIME TO CLOSE YET...
WHO CARES.
SLIDE
CLICK
NO ONE ELSE IS COMING ANYWAYS.
GRIP
!

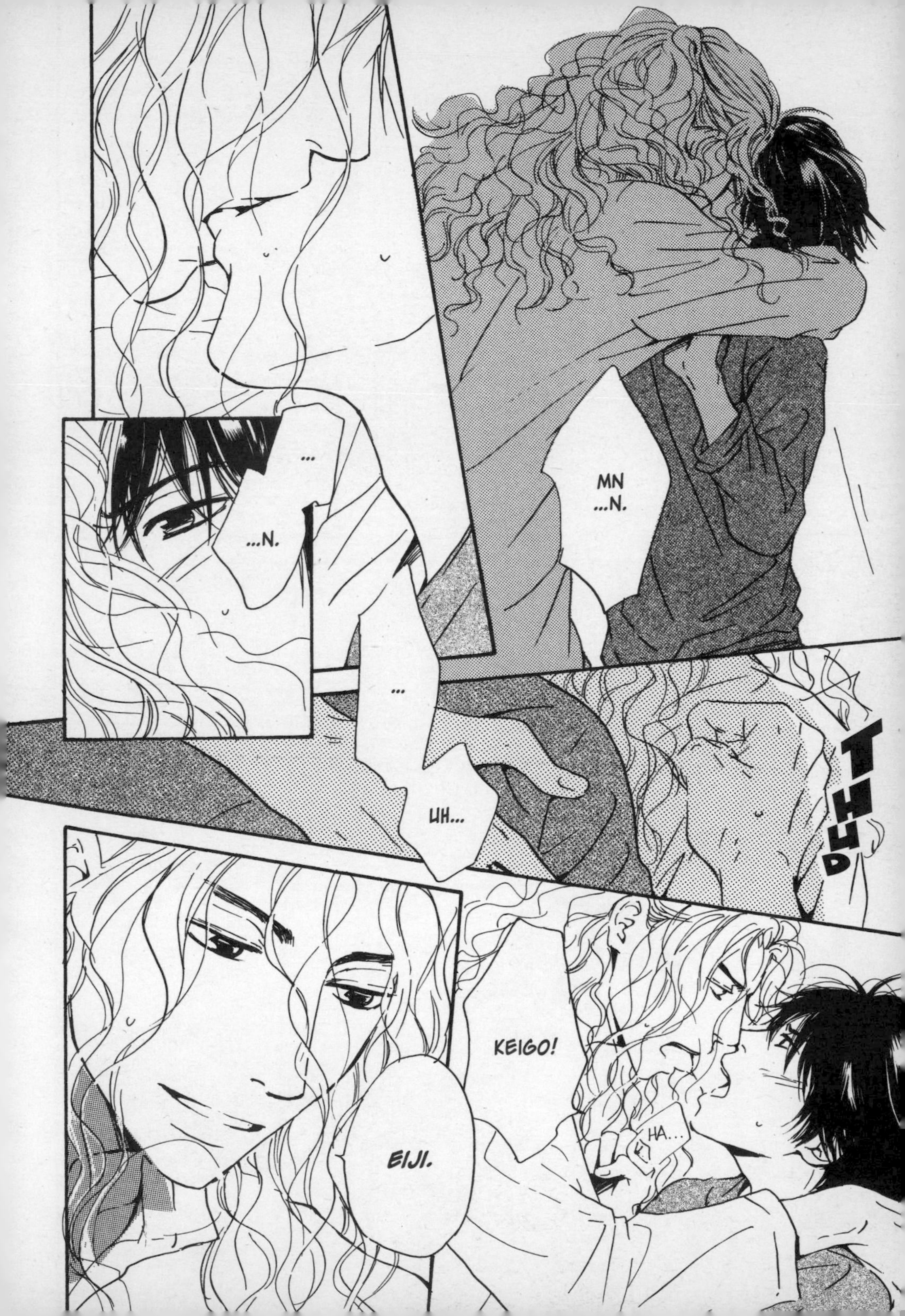
MN
...N.
...
...N.
...
UH...
THUD
KEIGO!
HA...
EIJI.

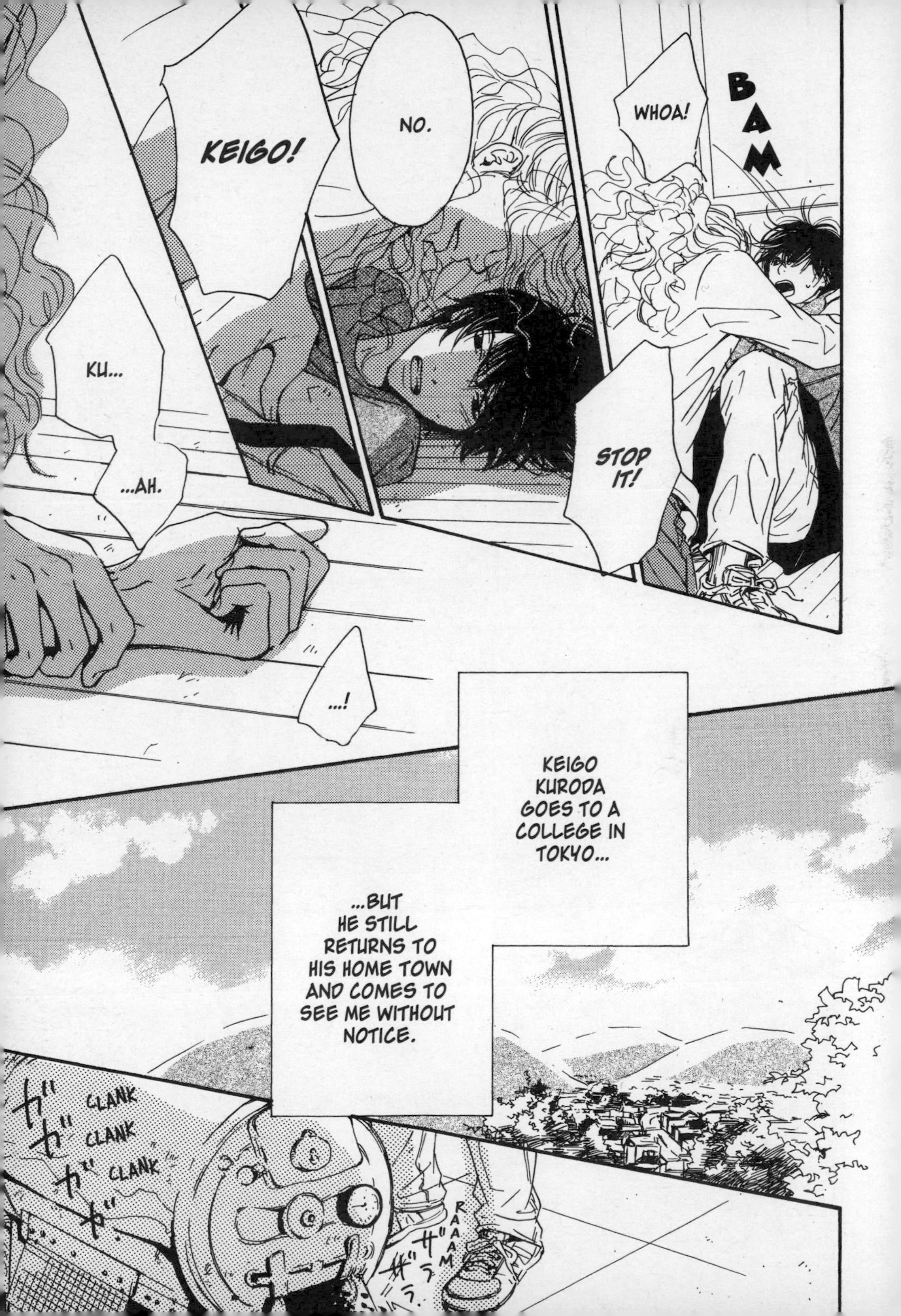

BAM
WHOA!
STOP IT!
NO.
KEIGO!
KU...
...AH.
...!
KEIGO KURODA GOES TO A COLLEGE IN TOKYO...
...BUT HE STILL RETURNS TO HIS HOME TOWN AND COMES TO SEE ME WITHOUT NOTICE.
RAAAM
CLANK
CLANK
CLANK

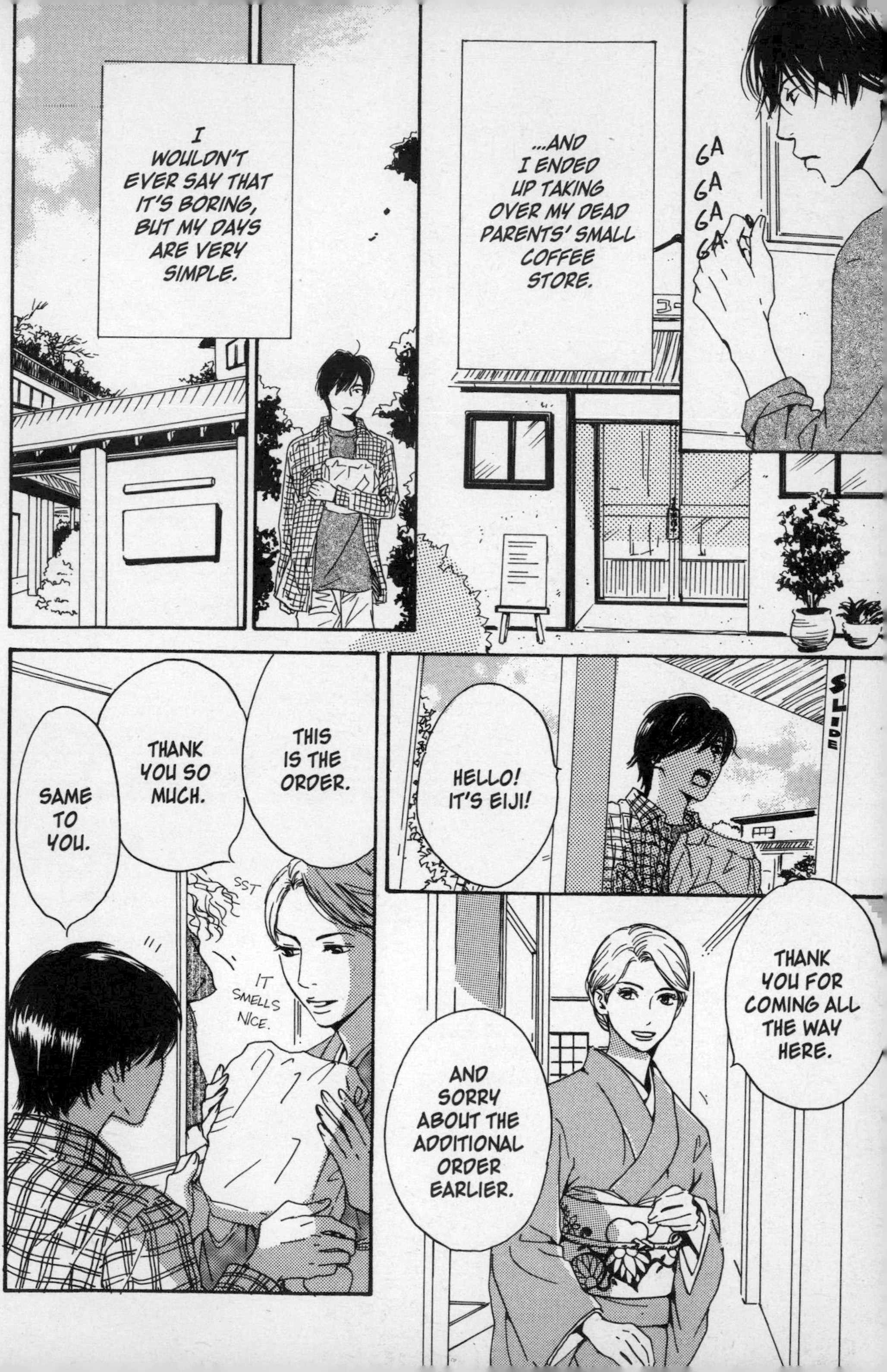
GA GA GA GA
...AND I ENDED UP TAKING OVER MY DEAD PARENTS' SMALL COFFEE STORE.
I WOULDN'T EVER SAY THAT IT'S BORING, BUT MY DAYS ARE VERY SIMPLE.
SLIDE
HELLO! IT'S EIJI!
THANK YOU FOR COMING ALL THE WAY HERE.
AND SORRY ABOUT THE ADDITIONAL ORDER EARLIER.
THIS IS THE ORDER.
THANK YOU SO MUCH.
SAME TO YOU.
SST
IT SMELLS NICE.

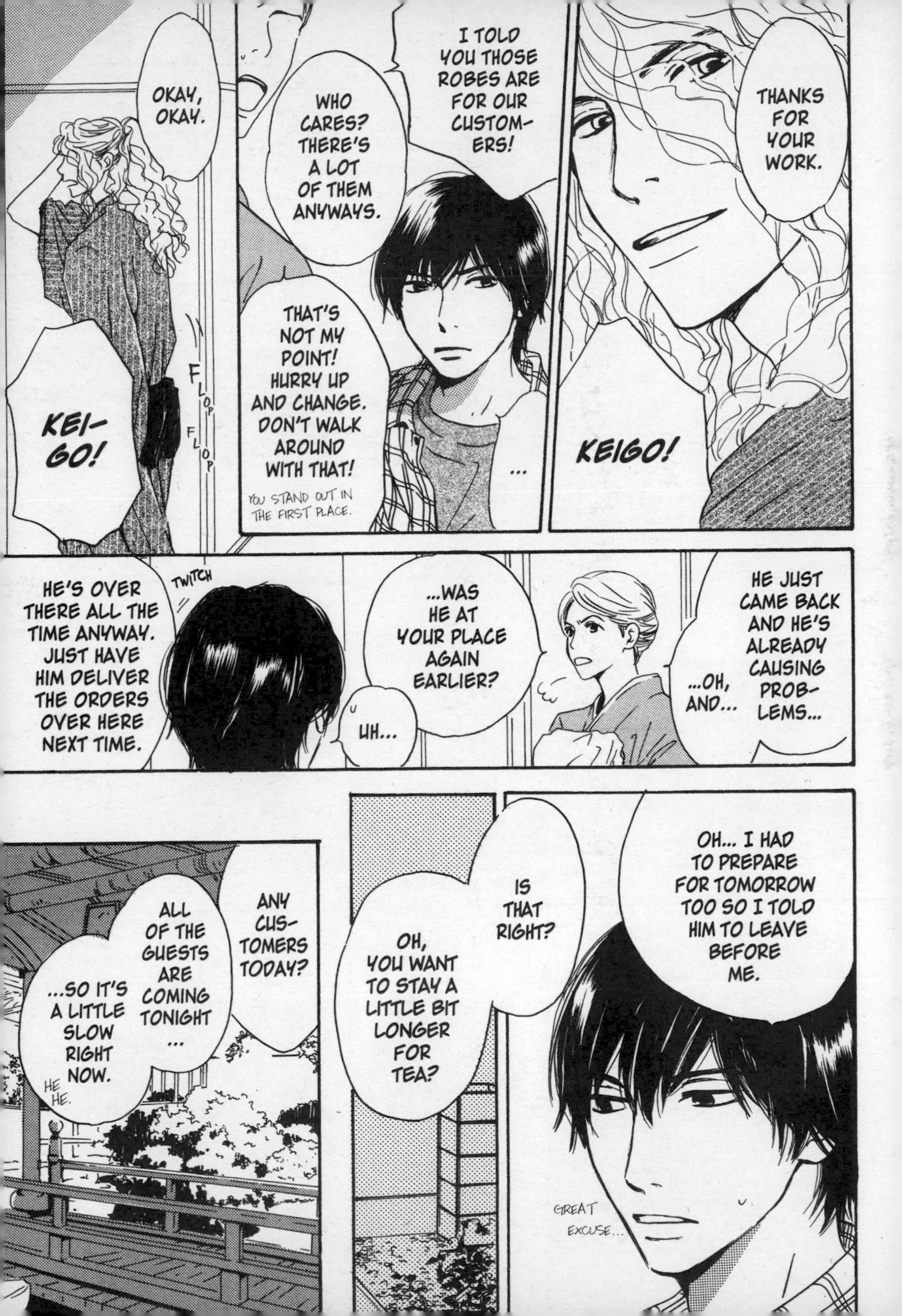
THANKS FOR YOUR WORK.
KEIGO!
I TOLD YOU THOSE ROBES ARE FOR OUR CUSTOMERS!
WHO CARES? THERE'S A LOT OF THEM ANYWAYS.
THAT'S NOT MY POINT! HURRY UP AND CHANGE. DON'T WALK AROUND WITH THAT!
...
YOU STAND OUT IN THE FIRST PLACE.
OKAY, OKAY.
KEI-GO!
FLOP FLOP
HE JUST CAME BACK AND HE'S ALREADY CAUSING PROB-LEMS...
...OH, AND...
...WAS HE AT YOUR PLACE AGAIN EARLIER?
UH...
TWITCH
HE'S OVER THERE ALL THE TIME ANYWAY. JUST HAVE HIM DELIVER THE ORDERS OVER HERE NEXT TIME.
OH... I HAD TO PREPARE FOR TOMORROW TOO SO I TOLD HIM TO LEAVE BEFORE ME.
IS THAT RIGHT?
OH, YOU WANT TO STAY A LITTLE BIT LONGER FOR TEA?
GREAT EXCUSE...
ANY CUS-TOMERS TODAY?
ALL OF THE GUESTS ARE COMING TONIGHT ...
...SO IT'S A LITTLE SLOW RIGHT NOW.
HE HE.

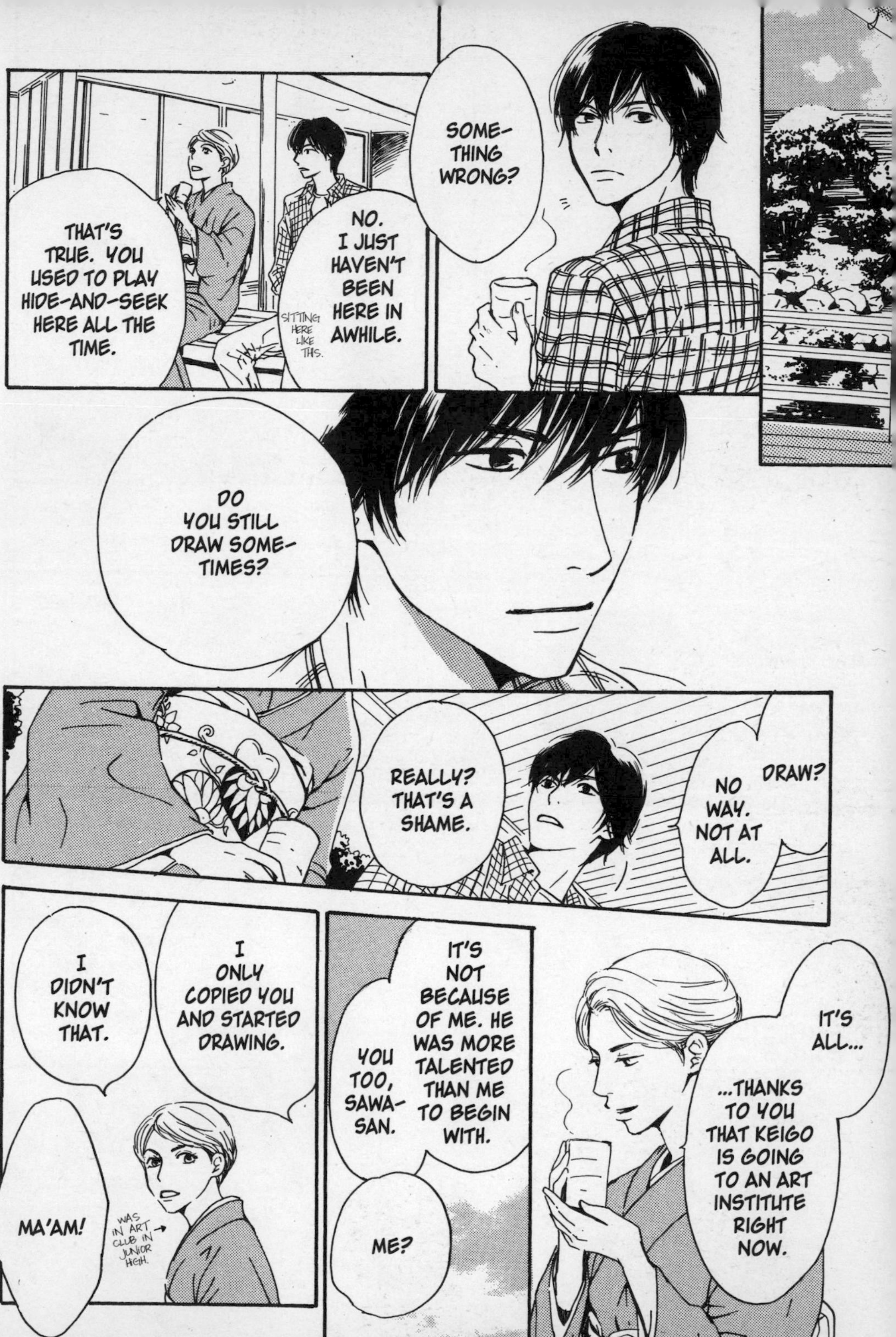
SOME-THING WRONG?
NO. I JUST HAVEN'T BEEN HERE IN AWHILE.
SITTING HERE LIKE THIS.
THAT'S TRUE. YOU USED TO PLAY HIDE-AND-SEEK HERE ALL THE TIME.
DO YOU STILL DRAW SOME-TIMES?
DRAW?
NO WAY. NOT AT ALL.
REALLY? THAT'S A SHAME.
IT'S ALL...
...THANKS TO YOU THAT KEIGO IS GOING TO AN ART INSTITUTE RIGHT NOW.
IT'S NOT BECAUSE OF ME. HE WAS MORE TALENTED THAN ME TO BEGIN WITH.
YOU TOO, SAWA-SAN.
ME?
I ONLY COPIED YOU AND STARTED DRAWING.
I DIDN'T KNOW THAT.
MA'AM!
WAS IN ART CLUB IN JUNIOR HIGH.

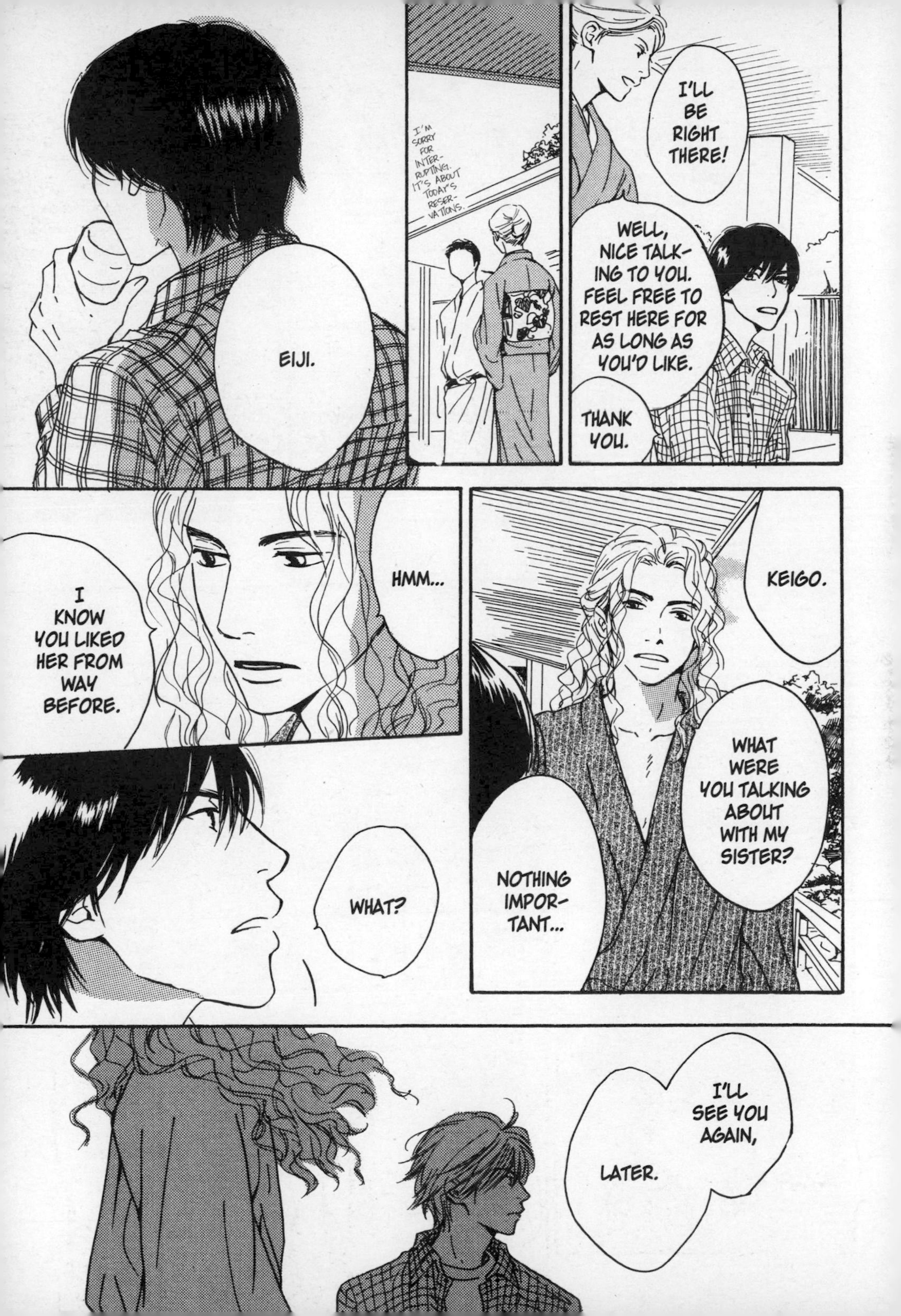
I'LL BE RIGHT THERE!
WELL, NICE TALKING TO YOU. FEEL FREE TO REST HERE FOR AS LONG AS YOU'D LIKE.
THANK YOU.
I'M SORRY FOR INTERRUPTING. IT'S ABOUT TODAY'S RESERVATIONS.
EIJI.
KEIGO.
WHAT WERE YOU TALKING ABOUT WITH MY SISTER?
NOTHING IMPORTANT...
HMM...
I KNOW YOU LIKED HER FROM WAY BEFORE.
WHAT?
I'LL SEE YOU AGAIN,
LATER.

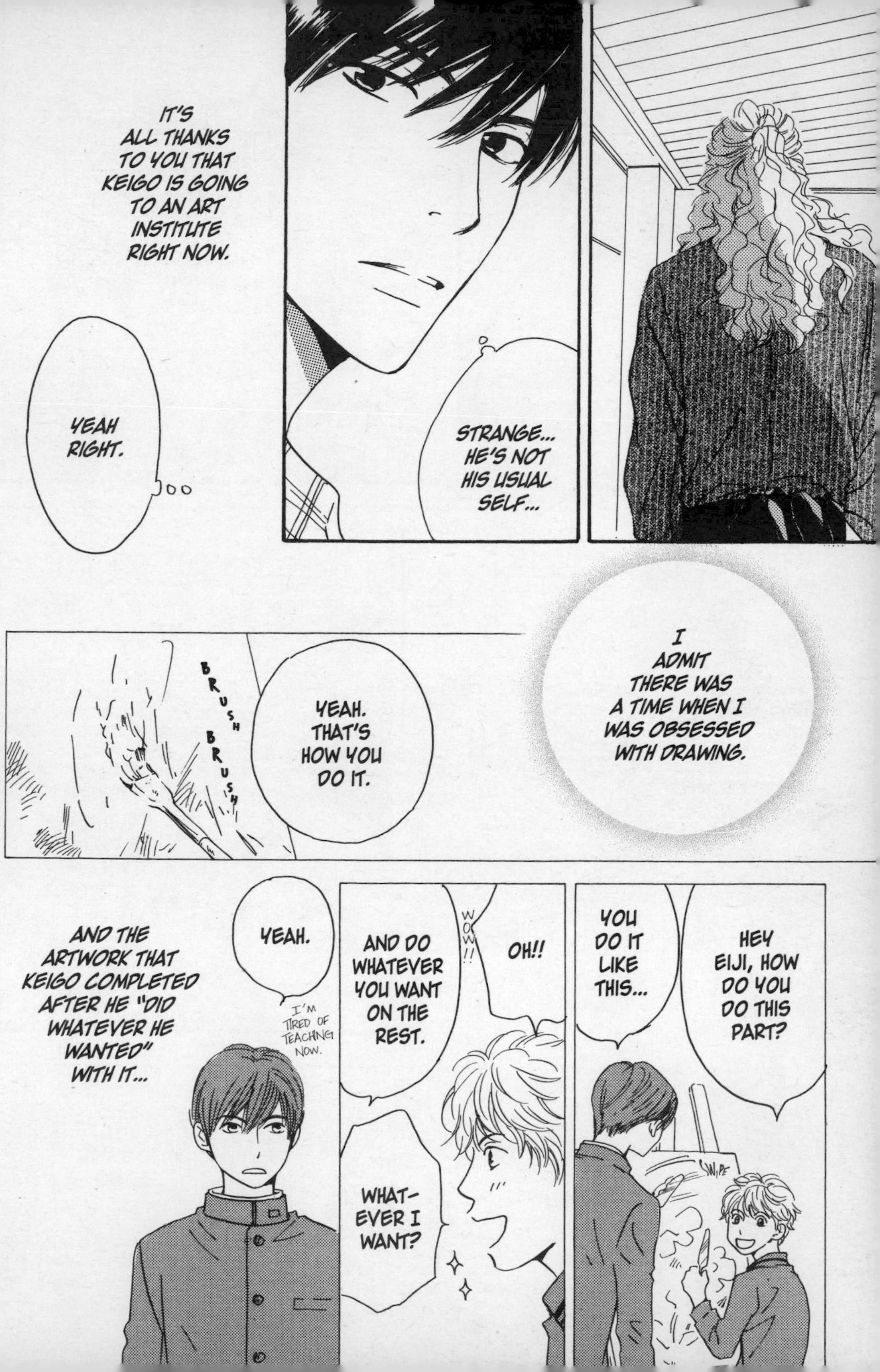
STRANGE... HE'S NOT HIS USUAL SELF...
IT'S ALL THANKS TO YOU THAT KEIGO IS GOING TO AN ART INSTITUTE RIGHT NOW.
YEAH RIGHT.
I ADMIT THERE WAS A TIME WHEN I WAS OBSESSED WITH DRAWING.
YEAH. THAT'S HOW YOU DO IT.
BRUSH BRUSH
HEY EIJI, HOW DO YOU DO THIS PART?
YOU DO IT LIKE THIS...
SWIPE
OH!!
WOW!!
AND DO WHATEVER YOU WANT ON THE REST.
WHAT-EVER I WANT?
YEAH.
I'M TIRED OF TEACHING NOW.
AND THE ARTWORK THAT KEIGO COMPLETED AFTER HE "DID WHATEVER HE WANTED" WITH IT...

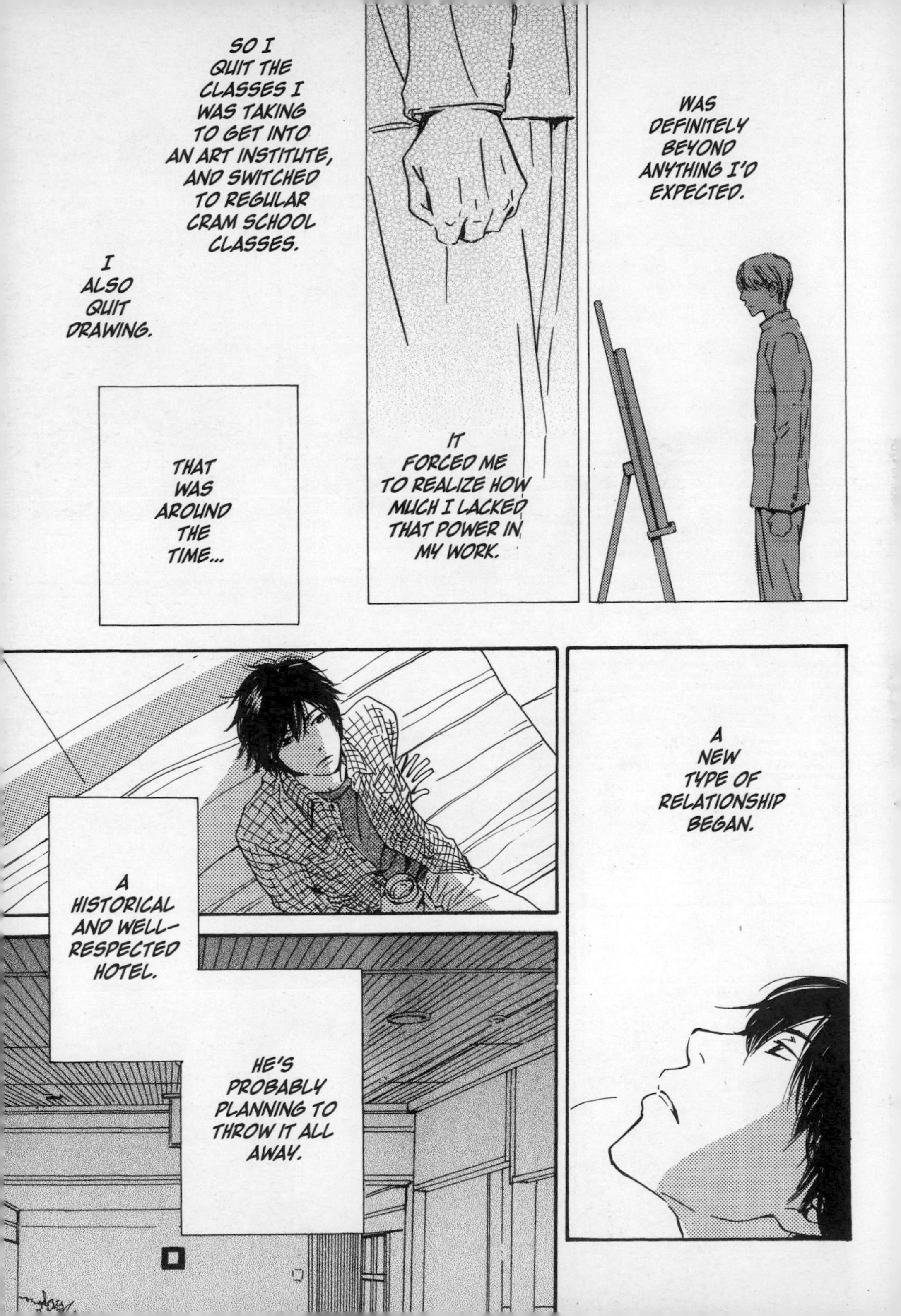
WAS DEFINITELY BEYOND ANYTHING I'D EXPECTED.
IT FORCED ME TO REALIZE HOW MUCH I LACKED THAT POWER IN MY WORK.
SO I QUIT THE CLASSES I WAS TAKING TO GET INTO AN ART INSTITUTE, AND SWITCHED TO REGULAR CRAM SCHOOL CLASSES.
I ALSO QUIT DRAWING.
THAT WAS AROUND THE TIME...
A NEW TYPE OF RELATIONSHIP BEGAN.
A HISTORICAL AND WELL-RESPECTED HOTEL.
HE'S PROBABLY PLANNING TO THROW IT ALL AWAY.

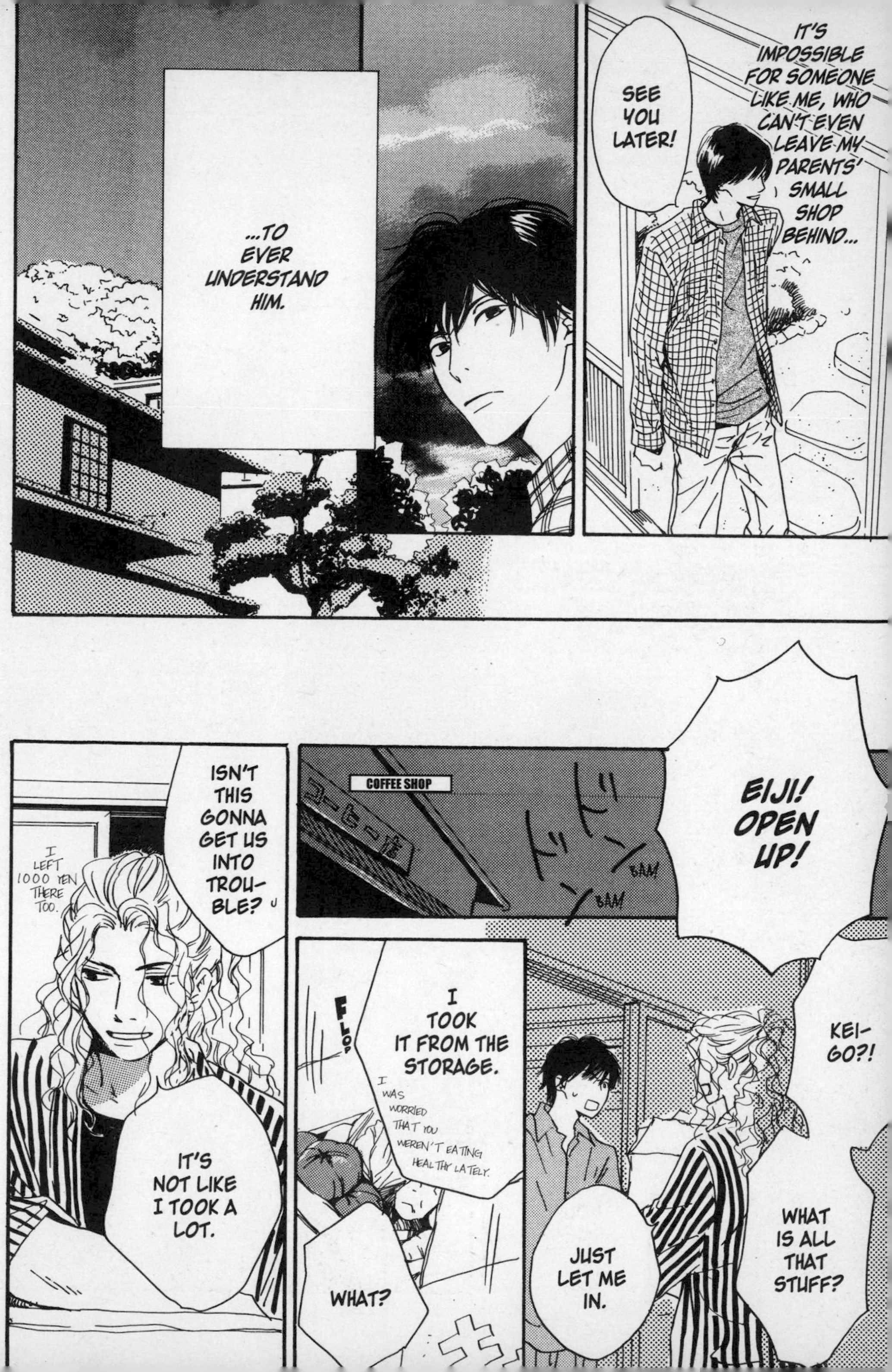
IT'S IMPOSSIBLE FOR SOMEONE LIKE ME, WHO CAN'T EVEN LEAVE MY PARENTS' SMALL SHOP BEHIND...
SEE YOU LATER!
...TO EVER UNDERSTAND HIM.
EIJI! OPEN UP!
COFFEE SHOP
BAM
BAM
KEI-GO?!
WHAT IS ALL THAT STUFF?
JUST LET ME IN.
I TOOK IT FROM THE STORAGE.
I WAS WORRIED THAT YOU WEREN'T EATING HEALTHY LATELY.
FLOP
WHAT?
ISN'T THIS GONNA GET US INTO TROUBLE?
I LEFT 1000 YEN THERE TOO.
IT'S NOT LIKE I TOOK A LOT.

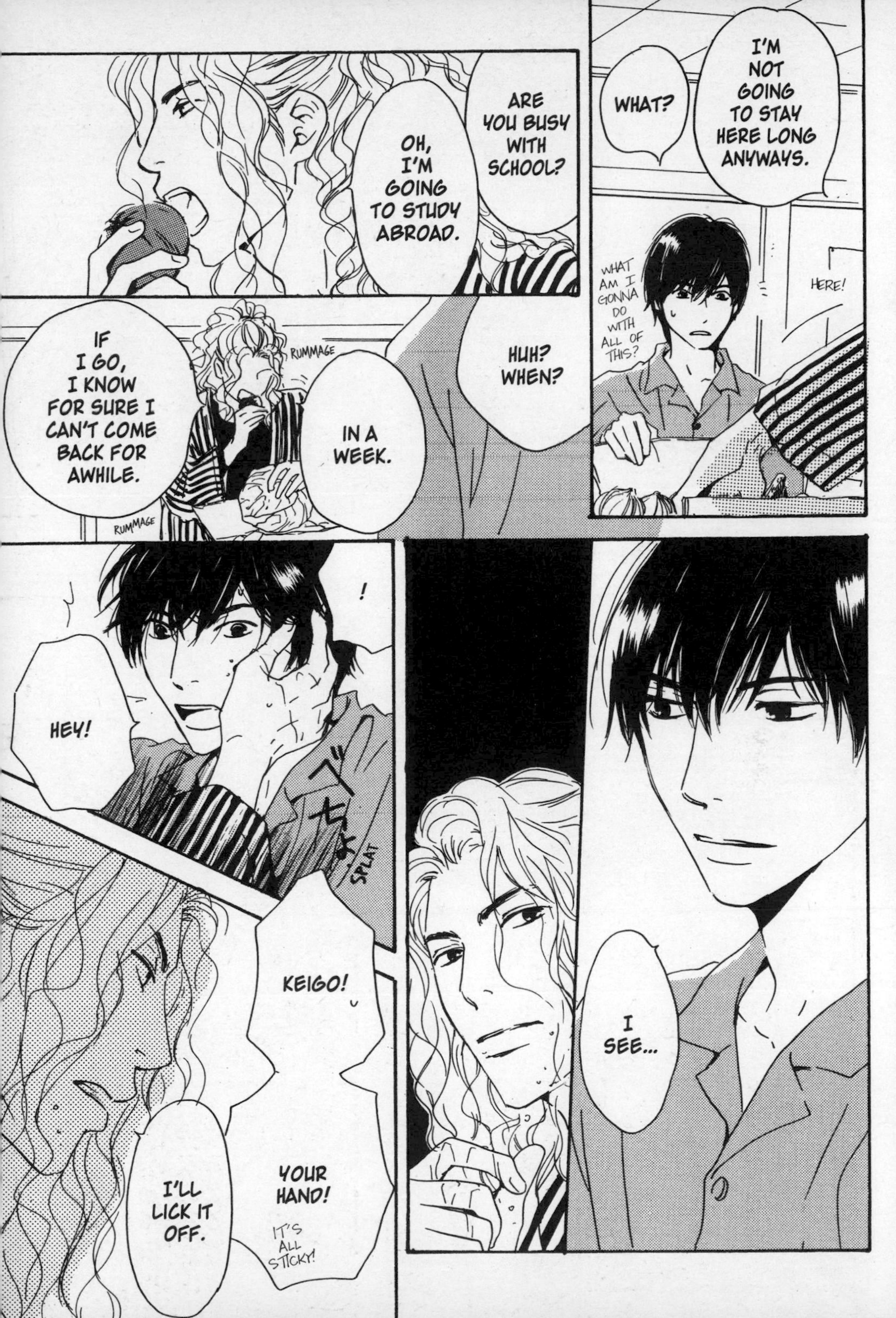
I'M NOT GOING TO STAY HERE LONG ANYWAYS.
WHAT?
HERE!
WHAT AM I GONNA DO WITH ALL OF THIS?
ARE YOU BUSY WITH SCHOOL?
OH, I'M GOING TO STUDY ABROAD.
HUH? WHEN?
IN A WEEK.
RUMMAGE
IF I GO, I KNOW FOR SURE I CAN'T COME BACK FOR AWHILE.
RUMMAGE
I SEE...
!
HEY!
SPLAT
KEIGO!
YOUR HAND!
IT'S ALL STICKY!
I'LL LICK IT OFF.

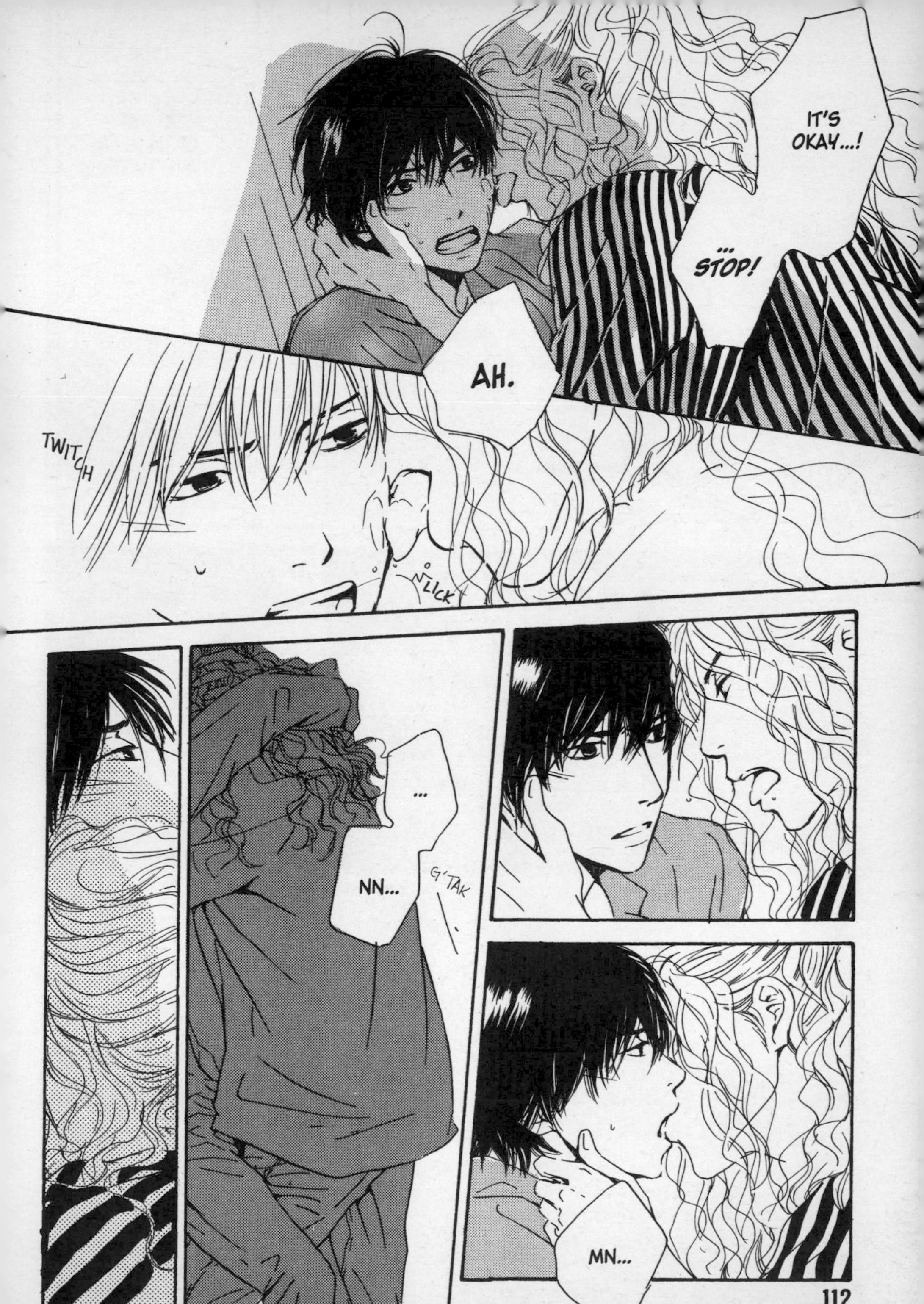
IT'S OKAY...!
...STOP!
AH.
TWITCH
LICK
MN...
...
NN...
G'TAK

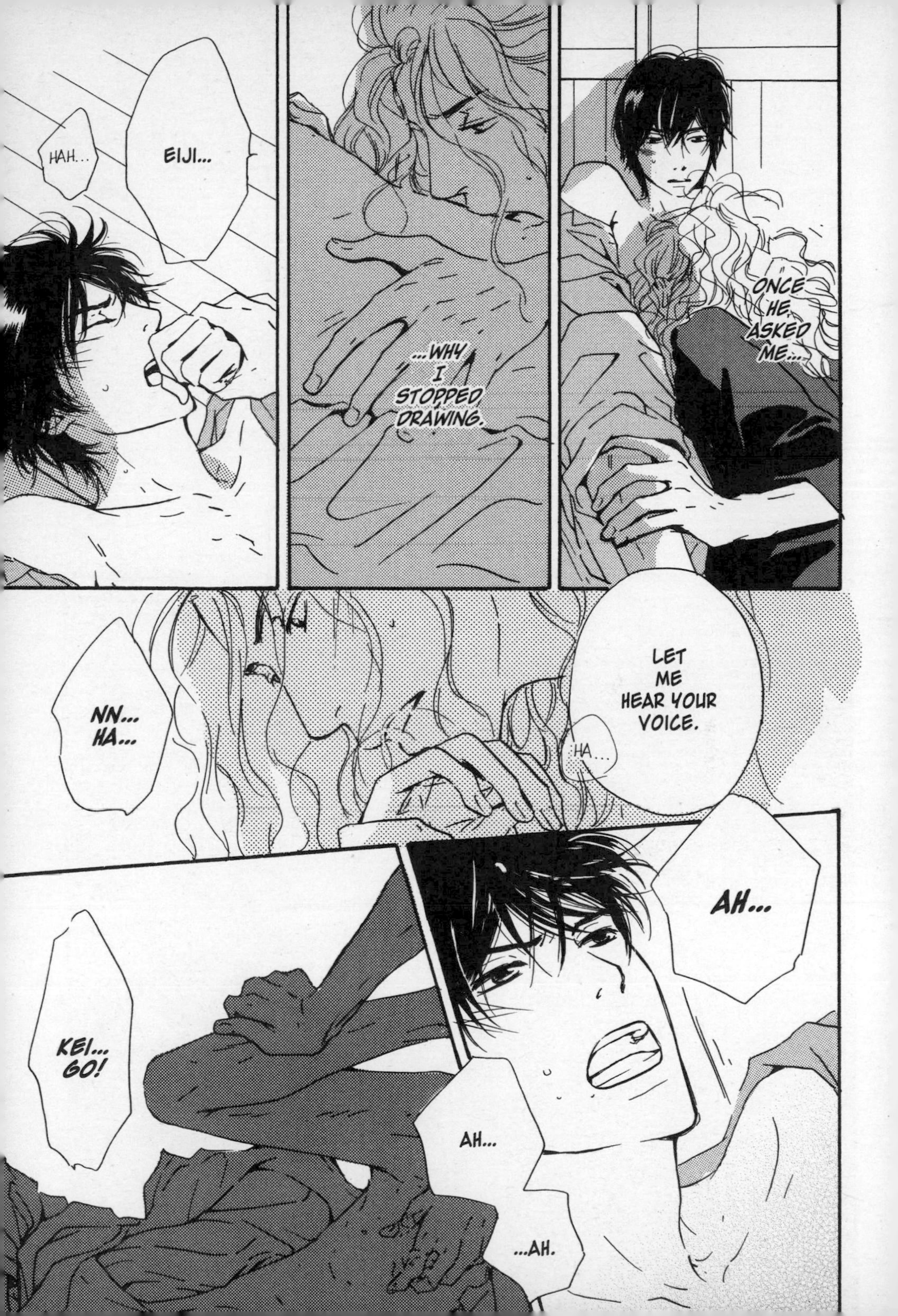

ONCE HE ASKED ME...
...WHY I STOPPED DRAWING.
EIJI...
HAH...
LET ME HEAR YOUR VOICE.
HA...
NN... HA...
AH...
KEI... GO!
AH...
...AH.

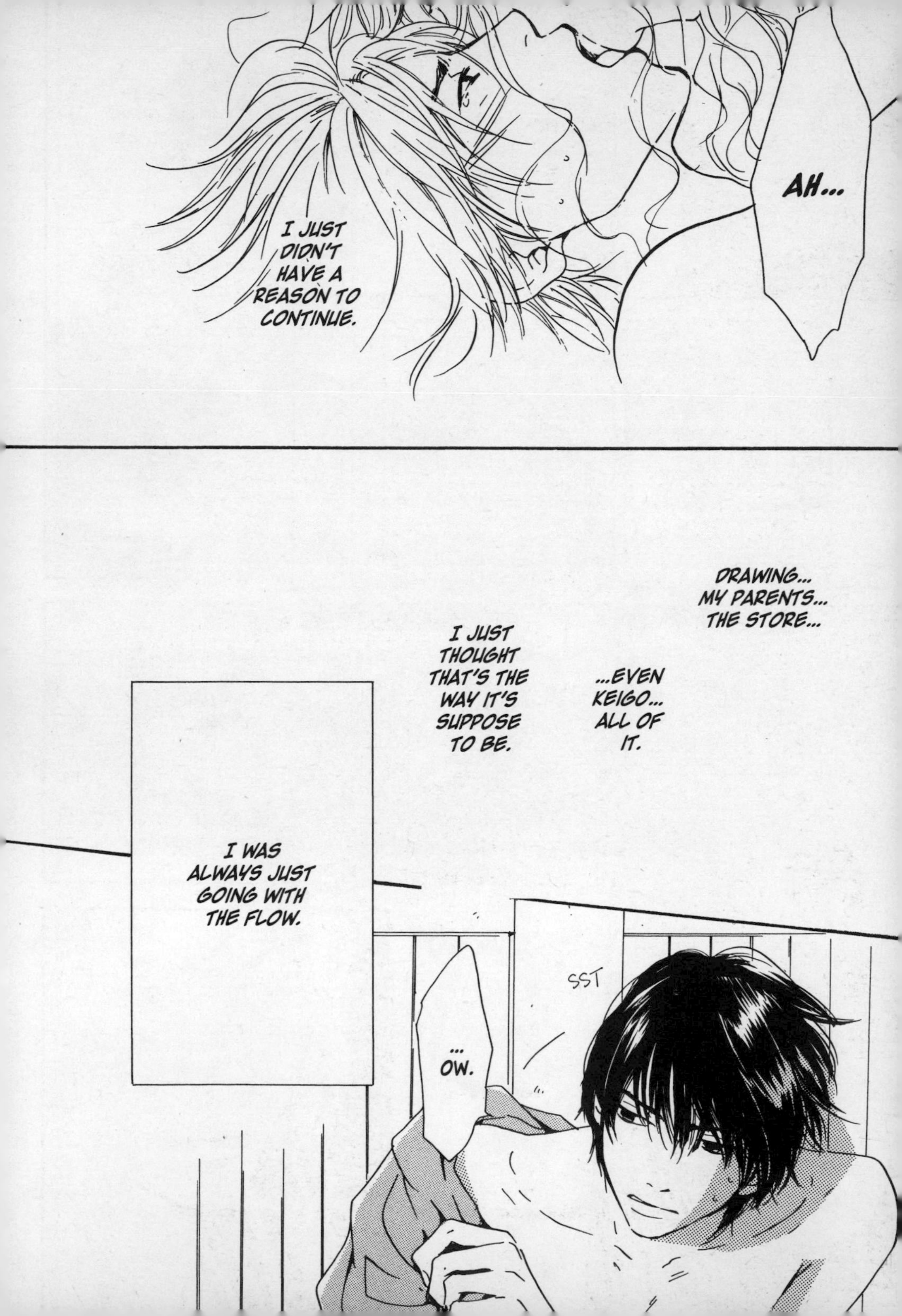
AH...
I JUST DIDN'T HAVE A REASON TO CONTINUE.
DRAWING... MY PARENTS... THE STORE...
...EVEN KEIGO... ALL OF IT.
I JUST THOUGHT THAT'S THE WAY IT'S SUPPOSE TO BE.
I WAS ALWAYS JUST GOING WITH THE FLOW.
SST
... OW.

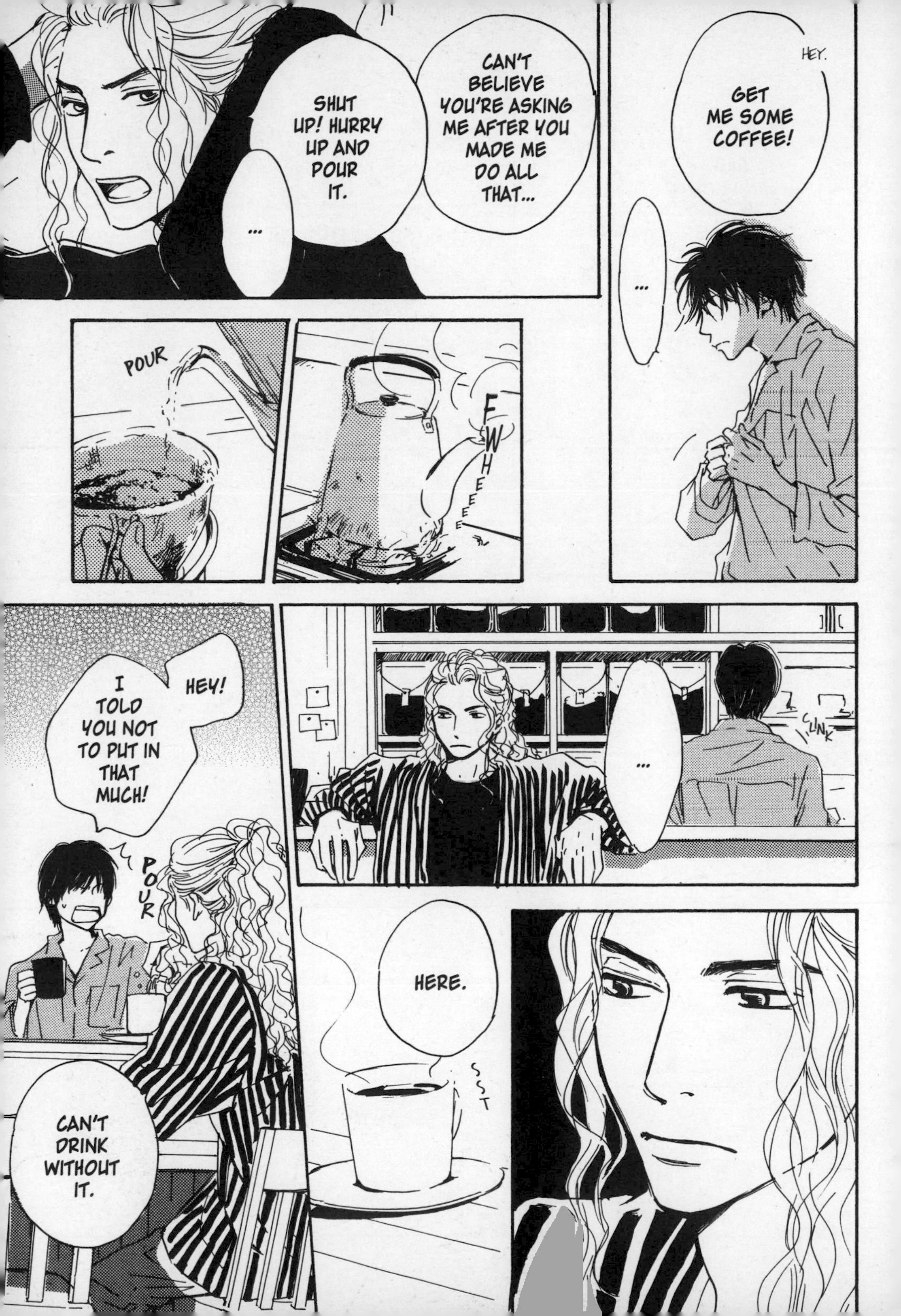
HEY.
GET ME SOME COFFEE!
...
CAN'T BELIEVE YOU'RE ASKING ME AFTER YOU MADE ME DO ALL THAT...
SHUT UP! HURRY UP AND POUR IT.
...
FWHEEEEE
POUR
CLINK
...
HERE.
SST
HEY! I TOLD YOU NOT TO PUT IN THAT MUCH!
POUR
CAN'T DRINK WITHOUT IT.

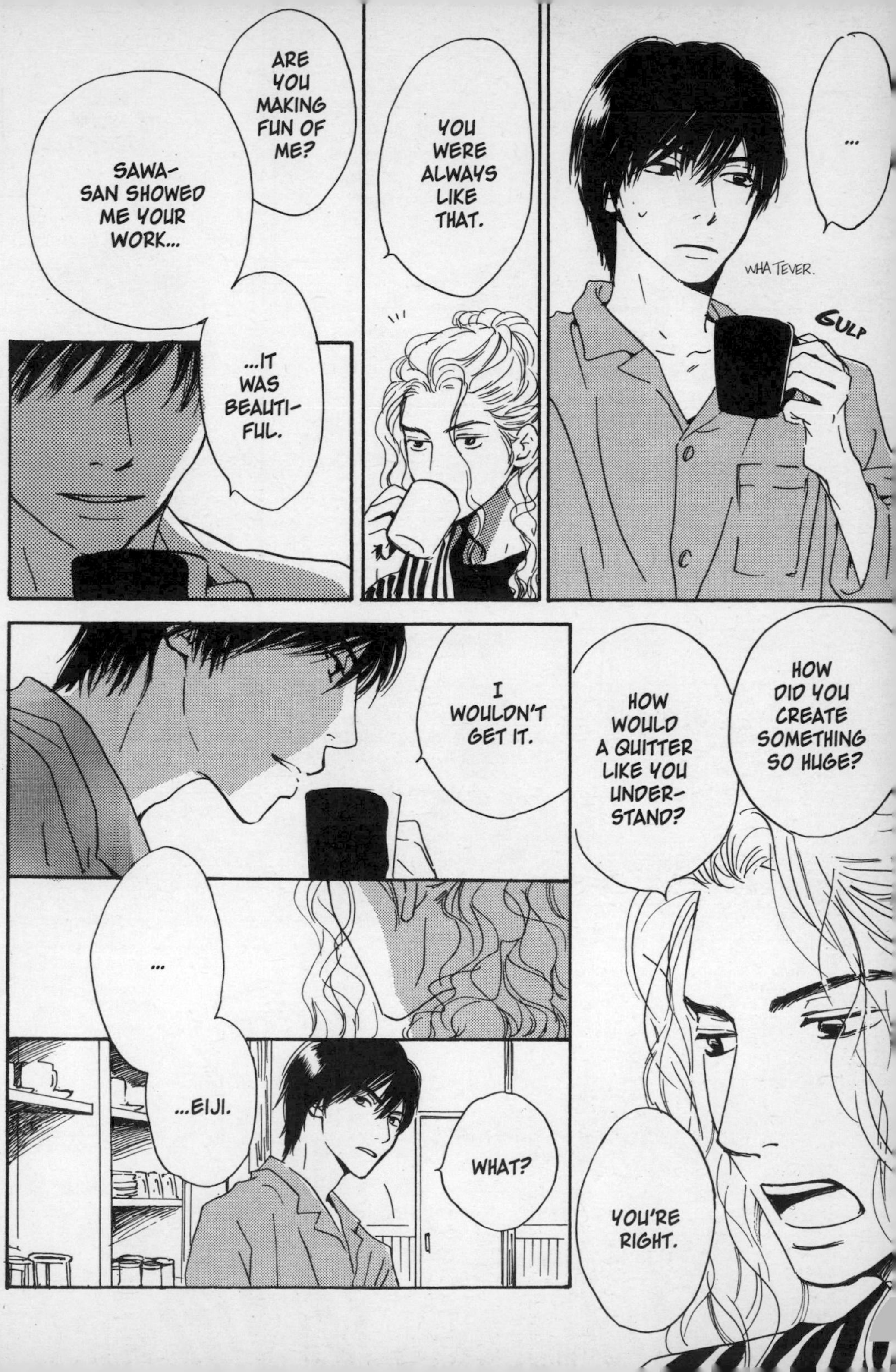
...
WHATEVER.
GULP
YOU WERE ALWAYS LIKE THAT.
ARE YOU MAKING FUN OF ME?
SAWA-SAN SHOWED ME YOUR WORK...
...IT WAS BEAUTIFUL.
HOW DID YOU CREATE SOMETHING SO HUGE?
HOW WOULD A QUITTER LIKE YOU UNDERSTAND?
YOU'RE RIGHT.
I WOULDN'T GET IT.
...
...EIJI.
WHAT?

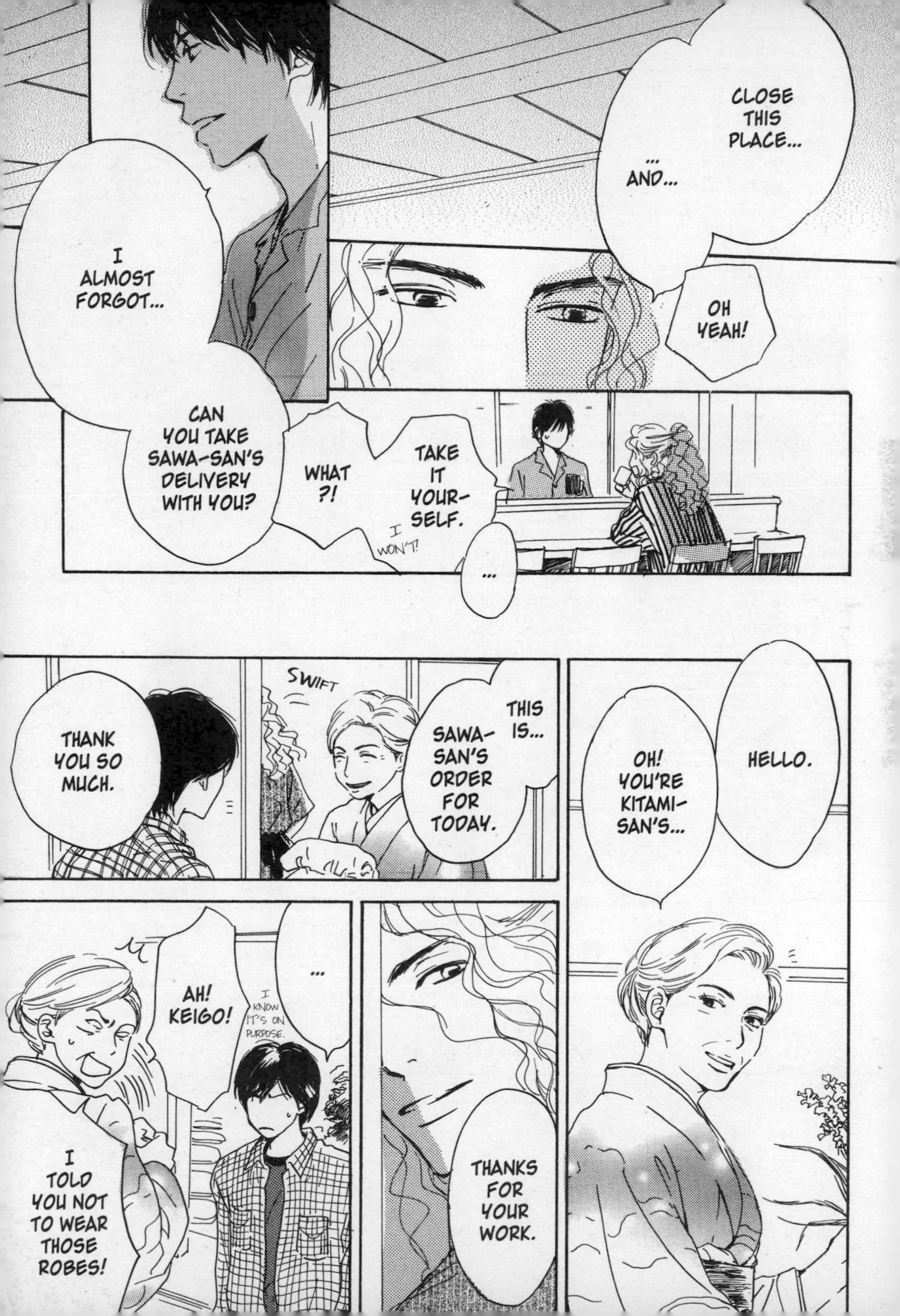

CLOSE THIS PLACE...
... AND...
OH YEAH!
I ALMOST FORGOT...
CAN YOU TAKE SAWA-SAN'S DELIVERY WITH YOU?
TAKE IT YOUR-SELF.
WHAT?!
I WON'T!
...
HELLO.
OH! YOU'RE KITAMI-SAN'S...
SWIFT
THIS IS...
SAWA-SAN'S ORDER FOR TODAY.
THANK YOU SO MUCH.
THANKS FOR YOUR WORK.
...
AH! KEIGO!
I KNOW IT'S ON PURPOSE.
I TOLD YOU NOT TO WEAR THOSE ROBES!

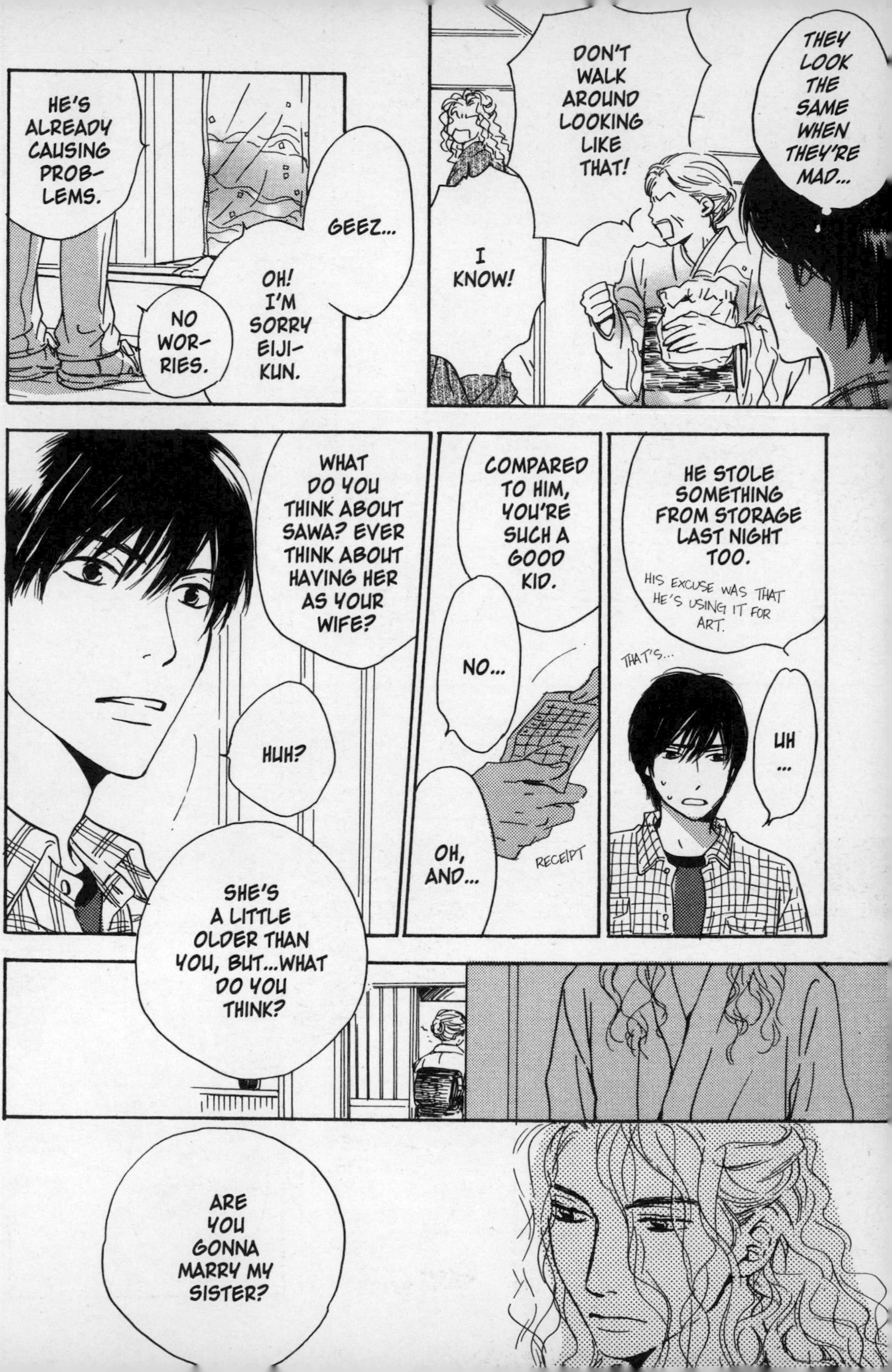
THEY LOOK THE SAME WHEN THEY'RE MAD...
DON'T WALK AROUND LOOKING LIKE THAT!
I KNOW!
GEEZ...
HE'S ALREADY CAUSING PROB-LEMS.
OH! I'M SORRY EIJI-KUN.
NO WOR-RIES.
HE STOLE SOMETHING FROM STORAGE LAST NIGHT TOO.
HIS EXCUSE WAS THAT HE'S USING IT FOR ART.
THAT'S...
UH ...
COMPARED TO HIM, YOU'RE SUCH A GOOD KID.
NO...
OH, AND...
RECEIPT
WHAT DO YOU THINK ABOUT SAWA? EVER THINK ABOUT HAVING HER AS YOUR WIFE?
HUH?
SHE'S A LITTLE OLDER THAN YOU, BUT...WHAT DO YOU THINK?
ARE YOU GONNA MARRY MY SISTER?

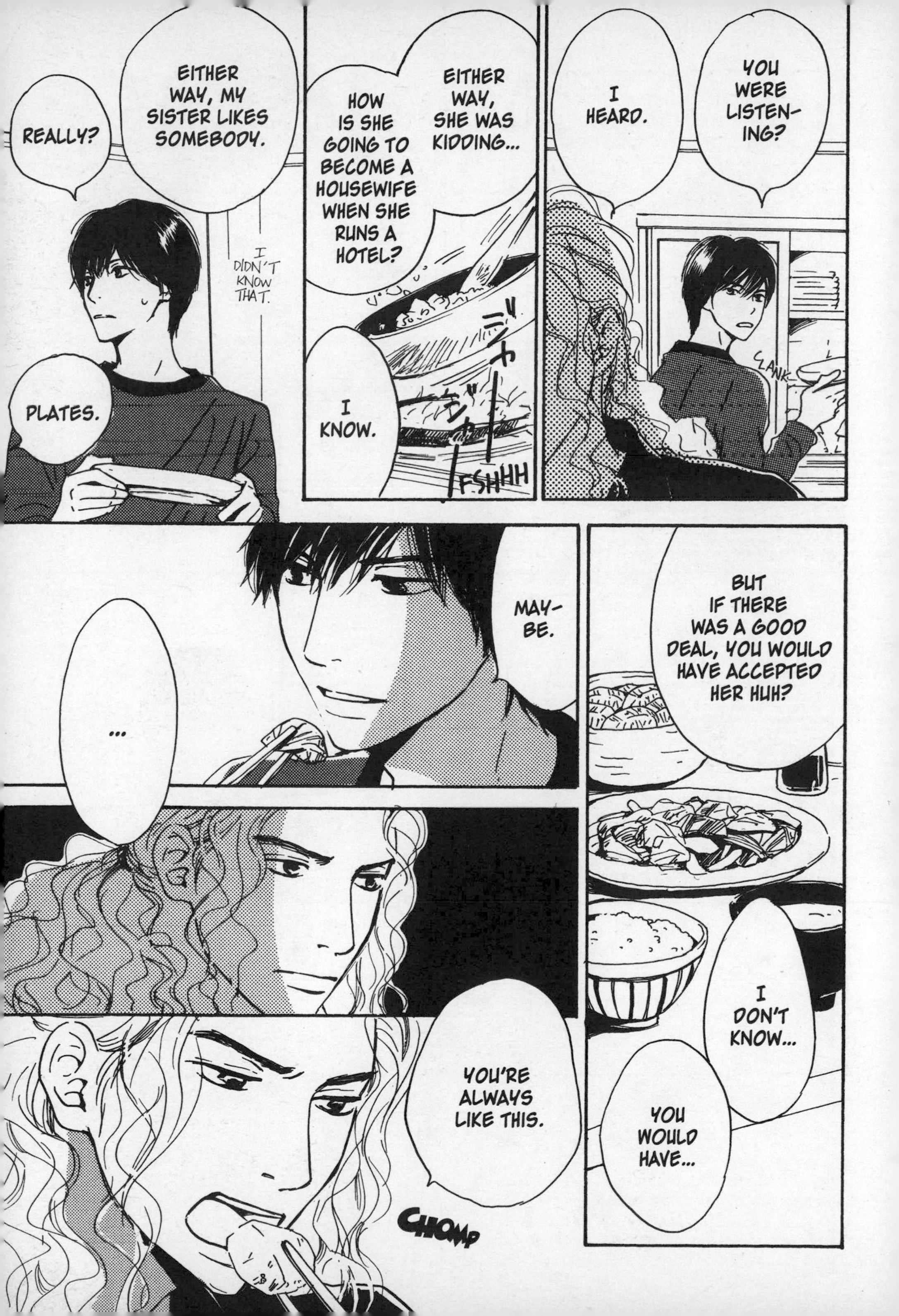
YOU WERE LISTENING?
I HEARD.
CLANK
EITHER WAY, SHE WAS KIDDING...
HOW IS SHE GOING TO BECOME A HOUSEWIFE WHEN SHE RUNS A HOTEL?
I KNOW.
FSHHH
EITHER WAY, MY SISTER LIKES SOMEBODY.
REALLY?
I DIDN'T KNOW THAT.
PLATES.
BUT IF THERE WAS A GOOD DEAL, YOU WOULD HAVE ACCEPTED HER HUH?
I DON'T KNOW...
YOU WOULD HAVE...
MAY-BE.
...
YOU'RE ALWAYS LIKE THIS.
CHOMP

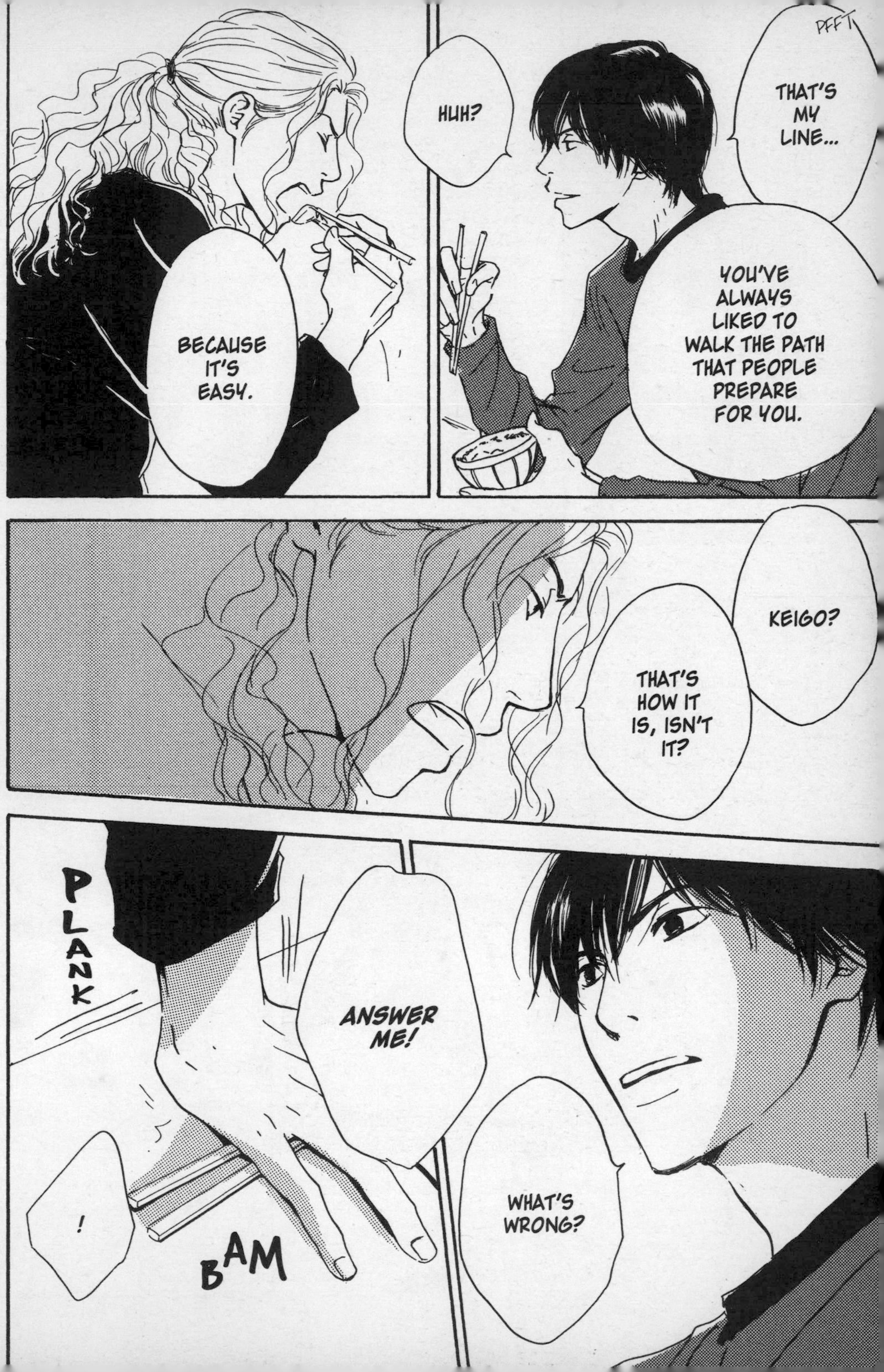
PFFT
THAT'S MY LINE...
HUH?
YOU'VE ALWAYS LIKED TO WALK THE PATH THAT PEOPLE PREPARE FOR YOU.
BECAUSE IT'S EASY.
KEIGO?
THAT'S HOW IT IS, ISN'T IT?
WHAT'S WRONG?
PLANK
ANSWER ME!
!
BAM

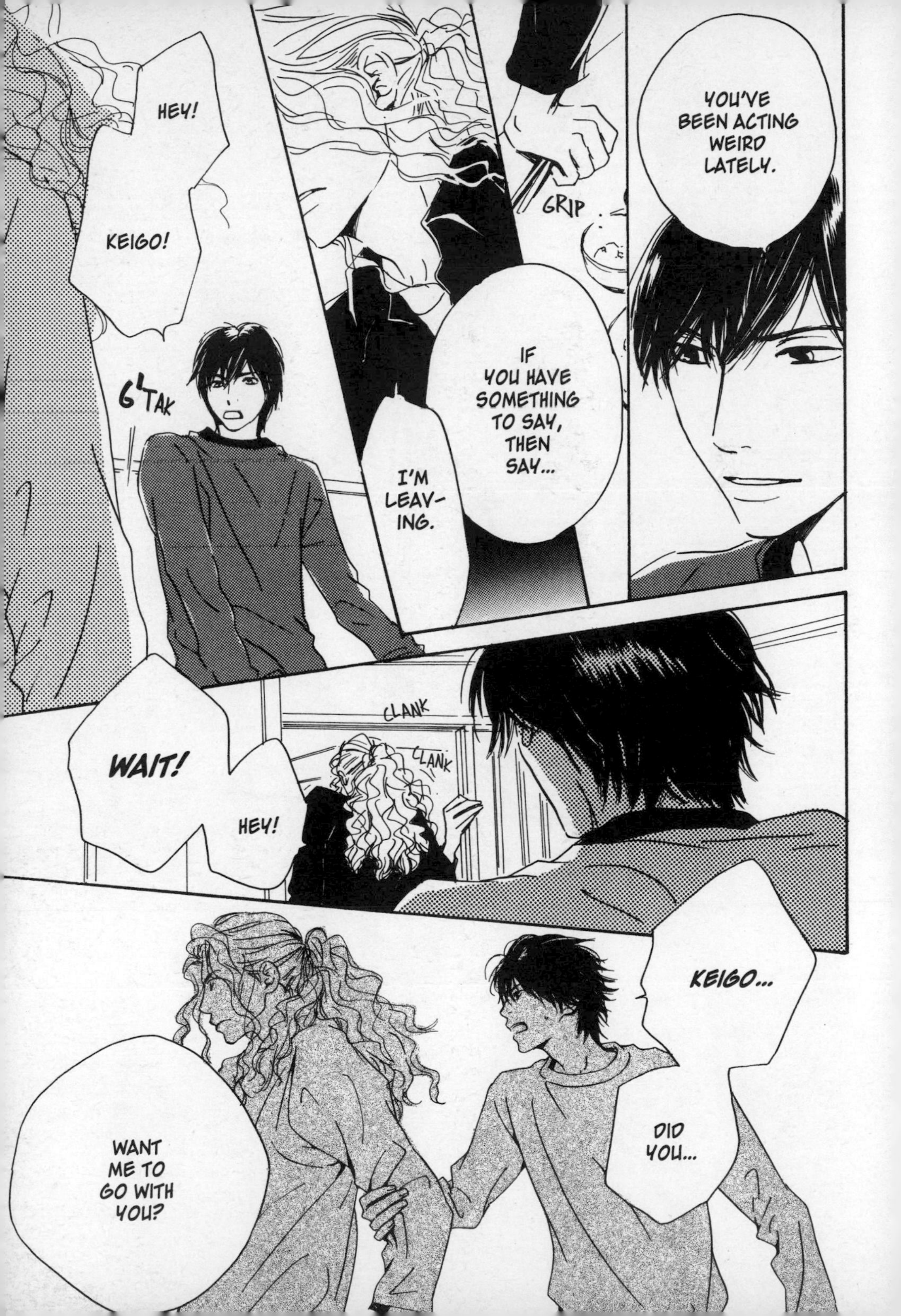
YOU'VE BEEN ACTING WEIRD LATELY.
GRIP
IF YOU HAVE SOMETHING TO SAY, THEN SAY...
I'M LEAV-ING.
HEY!
KEIGO!
G'TAK
CLANK
CLANK
WAIT!
HEY!
KEIGO...
DID YOU...
WANT ME TO GO WITH YOU?

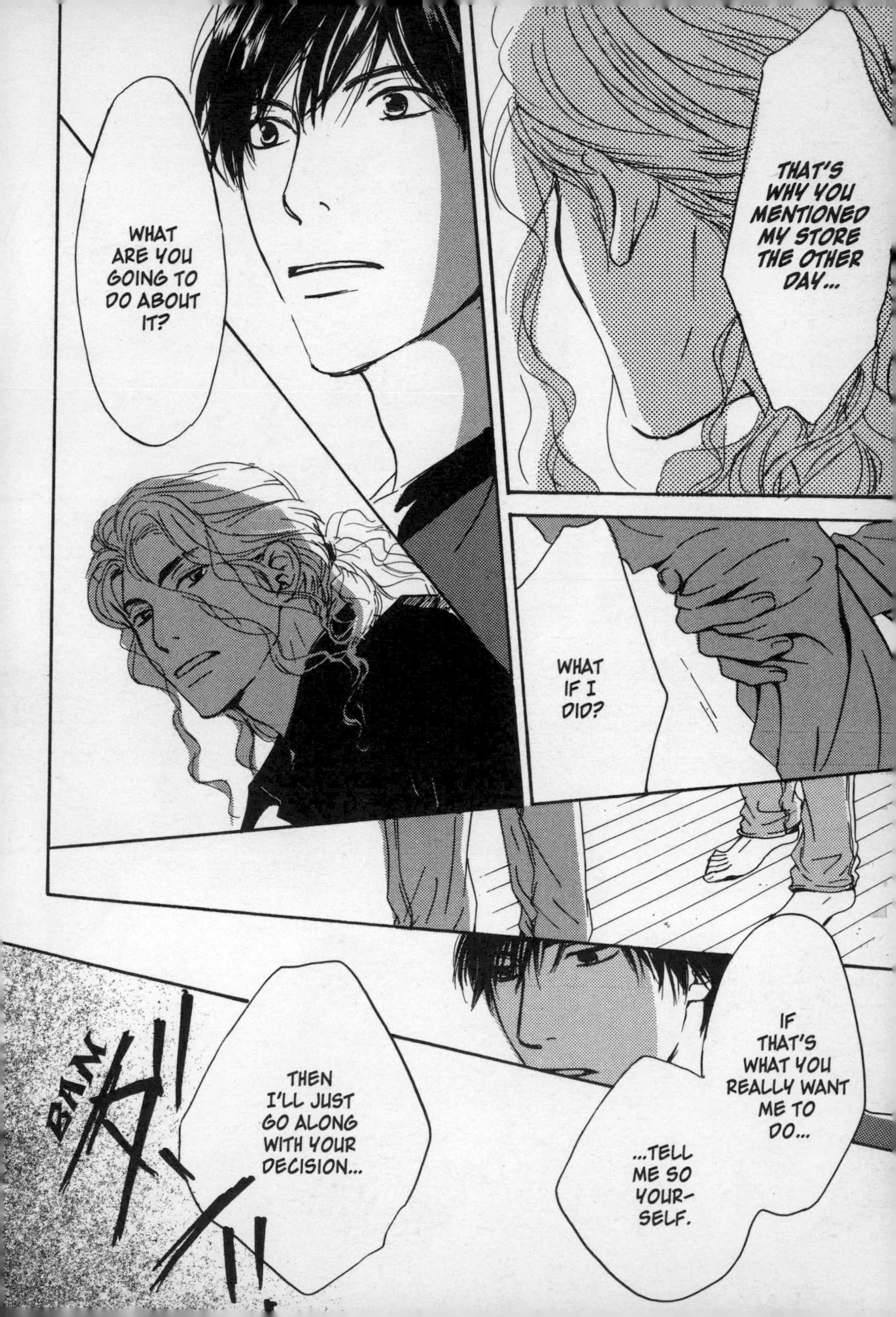
THAT'S WHY YOU MENTIONED MY STORE THE OTHER DAY...
WHAT IF I DID?
WHAT ARE YOU GOING TO DO ABOUT IT?
IF THAT'S WHAT YOU REALLY WANT ME TO DO...
...TELL ME SO YOUR-SELF.
THEN I'LL JUST GO ALONG WITH YOUR DECISION...
BAN

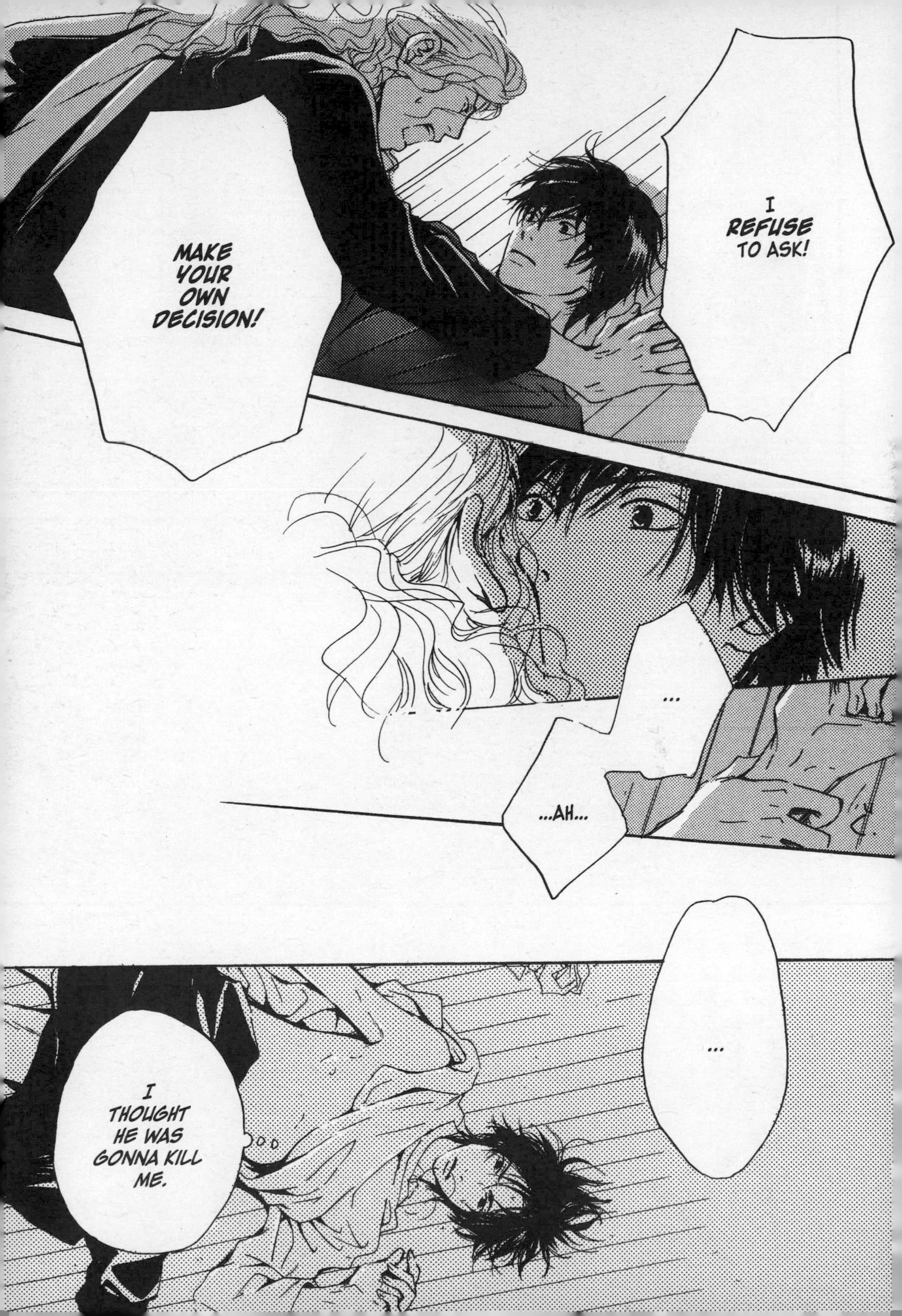
I REFUSE TO ASK!
MAKE YOUR OWN DECISION!
...
...AH...
...
I THOUGHT HE WAS GONNA KILL ME.

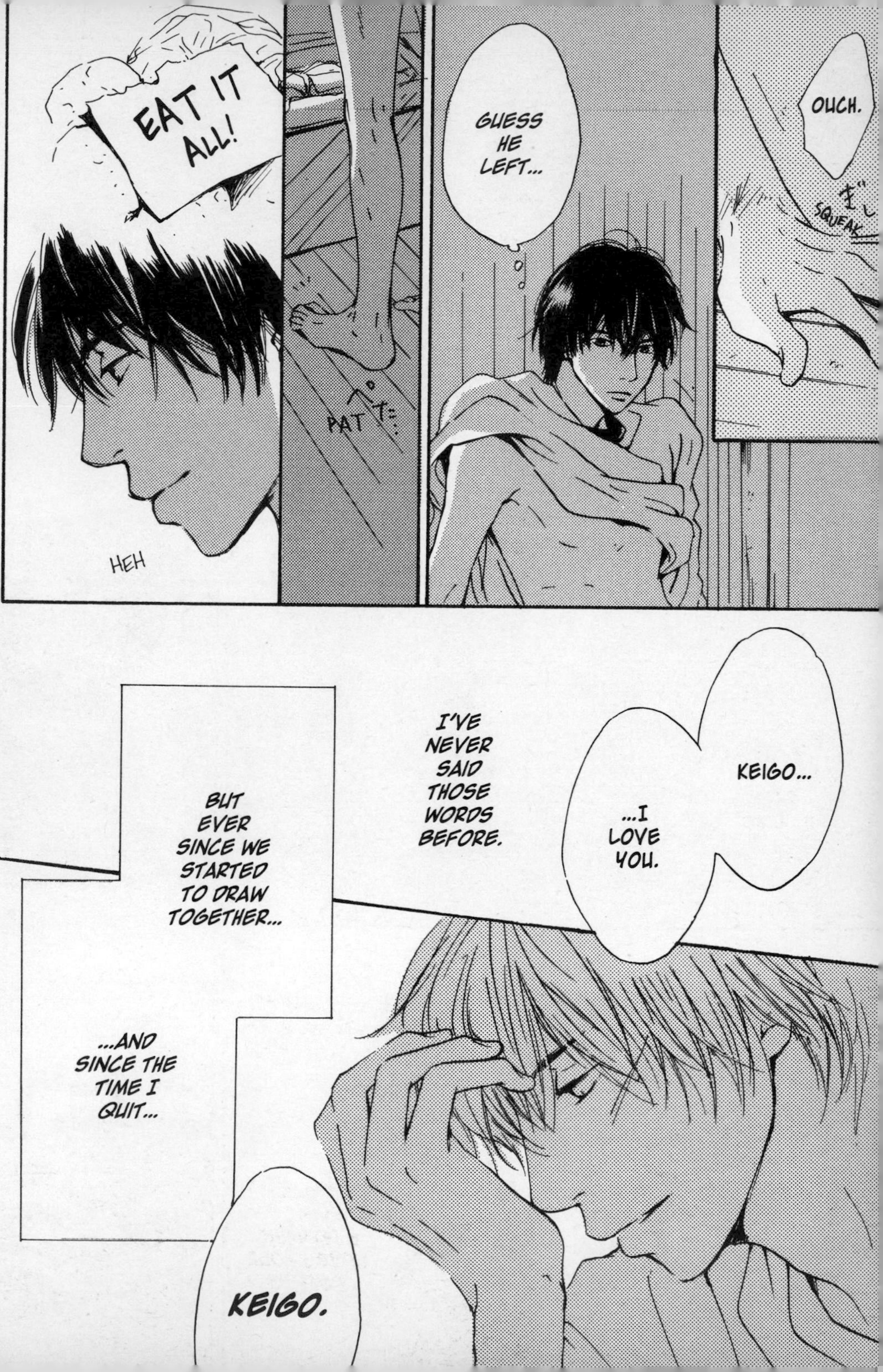
OUCH.
SQUEAK
GUESS HE LEFT...
PAT
EAT IT ALL!
HEH
KEIGO...
...I LOVE YOU.
I'VE NEVER SAID THOSE WORDS BEFORE.
BUT EVER SINCE WE STARTED TO DRAW TOGETHER...
...AND SINCE THE TIME I QUIT...
KEIGO.

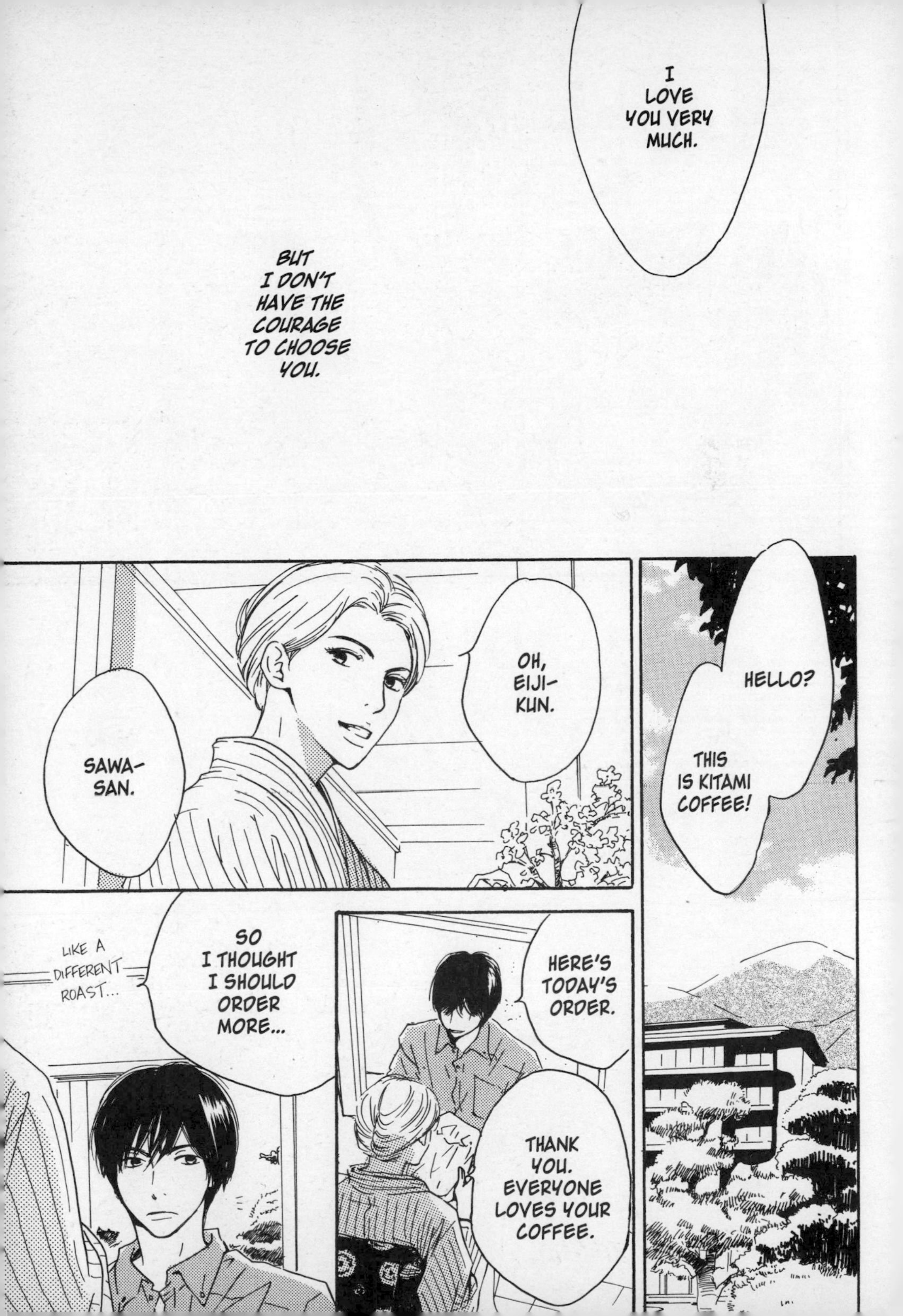
I LOVE YOU VERY MUCH.
BUT I DON'T HAVE THE COURAGE TO CHOOSE YOU.
HELLO?
THIS IS KITAMI COFFEE!
OH, EIJI-KUN.
SAWA-SAN.
HERE'S TODAY'S ORDER.
THANK YOU. EVERYONE LOVES YOUR COFFEE.
SO I THOUGHT I SHOULD ORDER MORE...
LIKE A DIFFERENT ROAST...

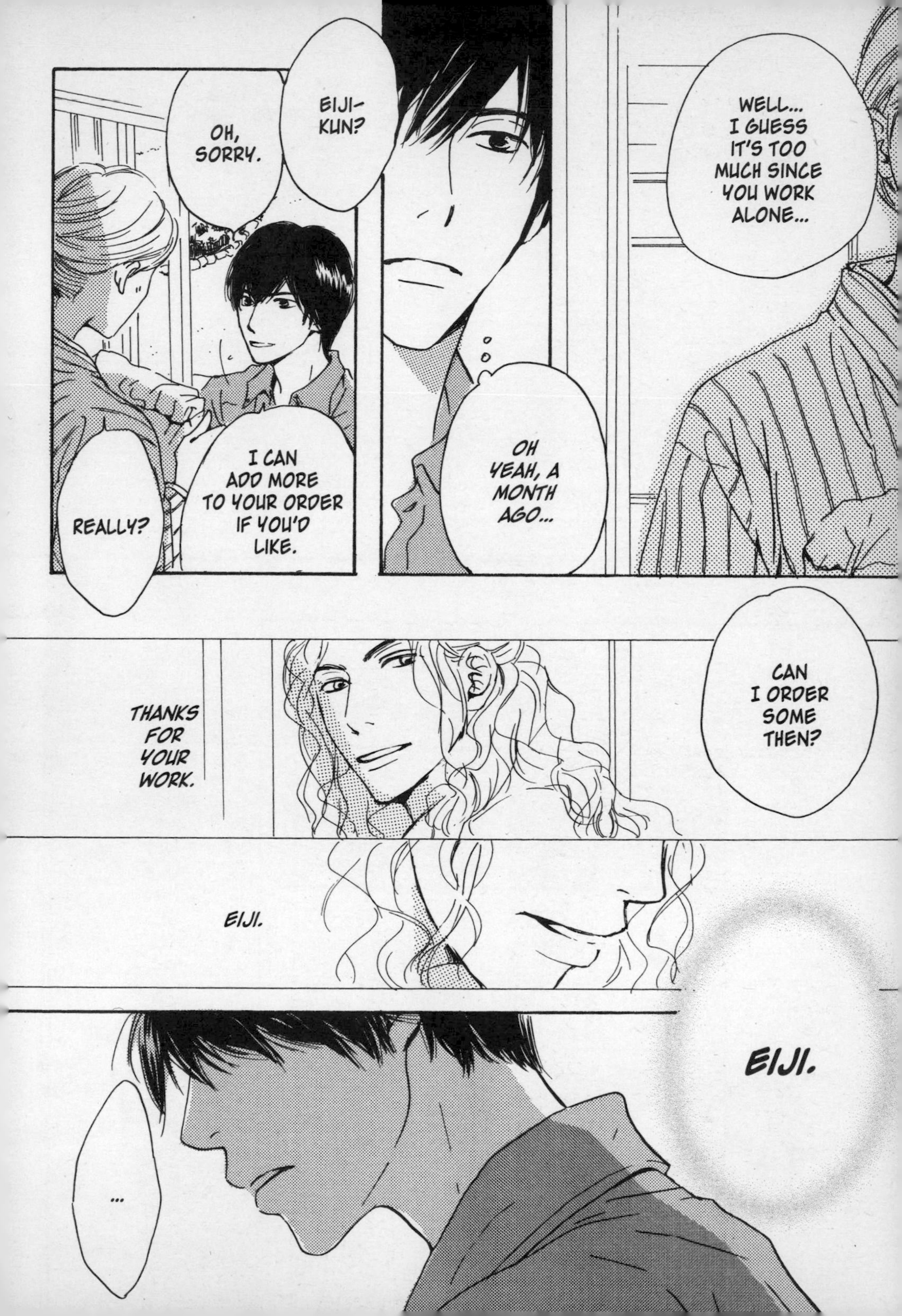
WELL... I GUESS IT'S TOO MUCH SINCE YOU WORK ALONE...
EIJI-KUN?
OH YEAH, A MONTH AGO...
OH, SORRY.
I CAN ADD MORE TO YOUR ORDER IF YOU'D LIKE.
REALLY?
CAN I ORDER SOME THEN?
THANKS FOR YOUR WORK.
EIJI.
EIJI.
...

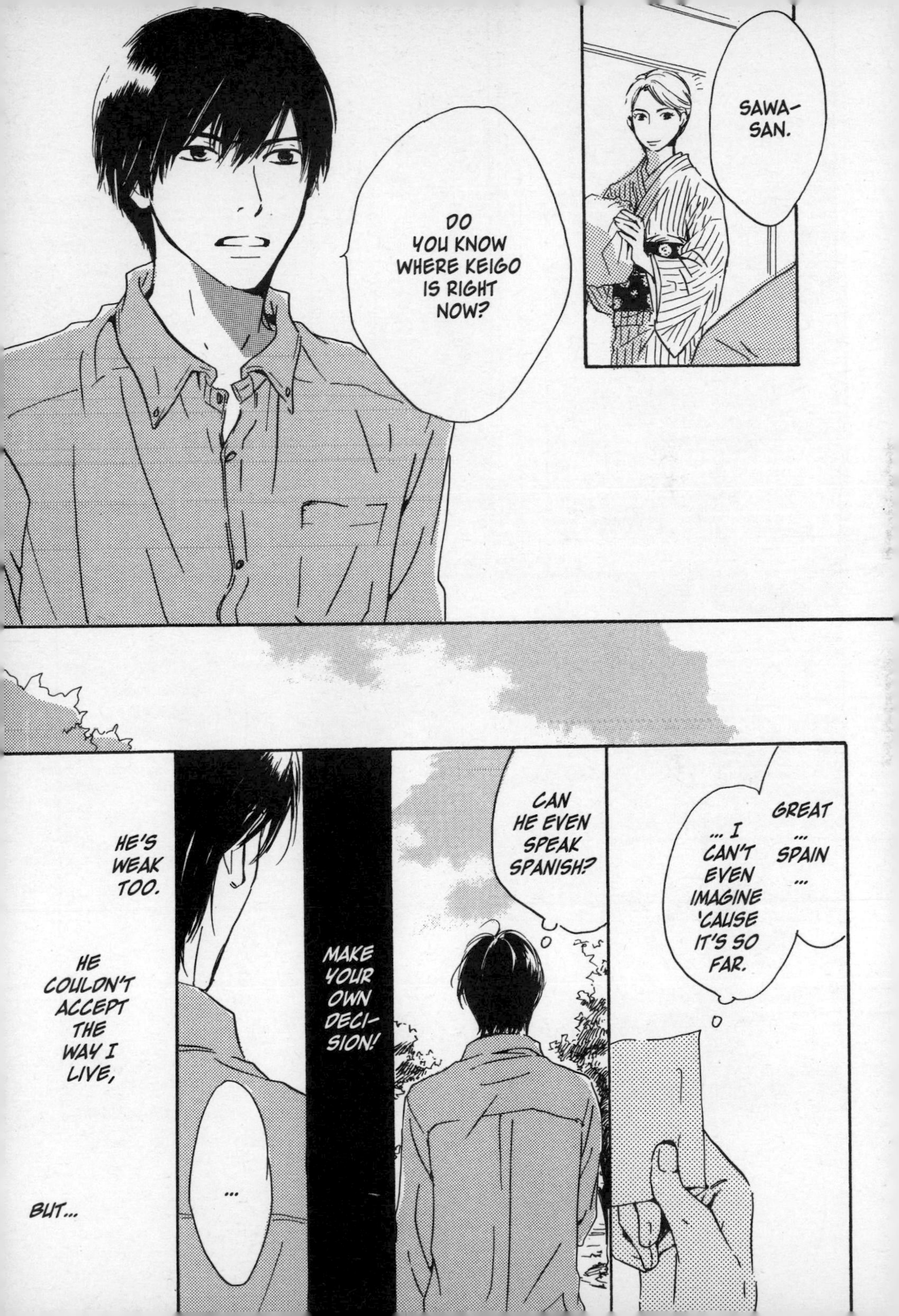
SAWA-SAN.
DO YOU KNOW WHERE KEIGO IS RIGHT NOW?
GREAT ... SPAIN ...
... I CAN'T EVEN IMAGINE 'CAUSE IT'S SO FAR.
CAN HE EVEN SPEAK SPANISH?
MAKE YOUR OWN DECI-SION!
...
HE'S WEAK TOO.
HE COULDN'T ACCEPT THE WAY I LIVE,
BUT...

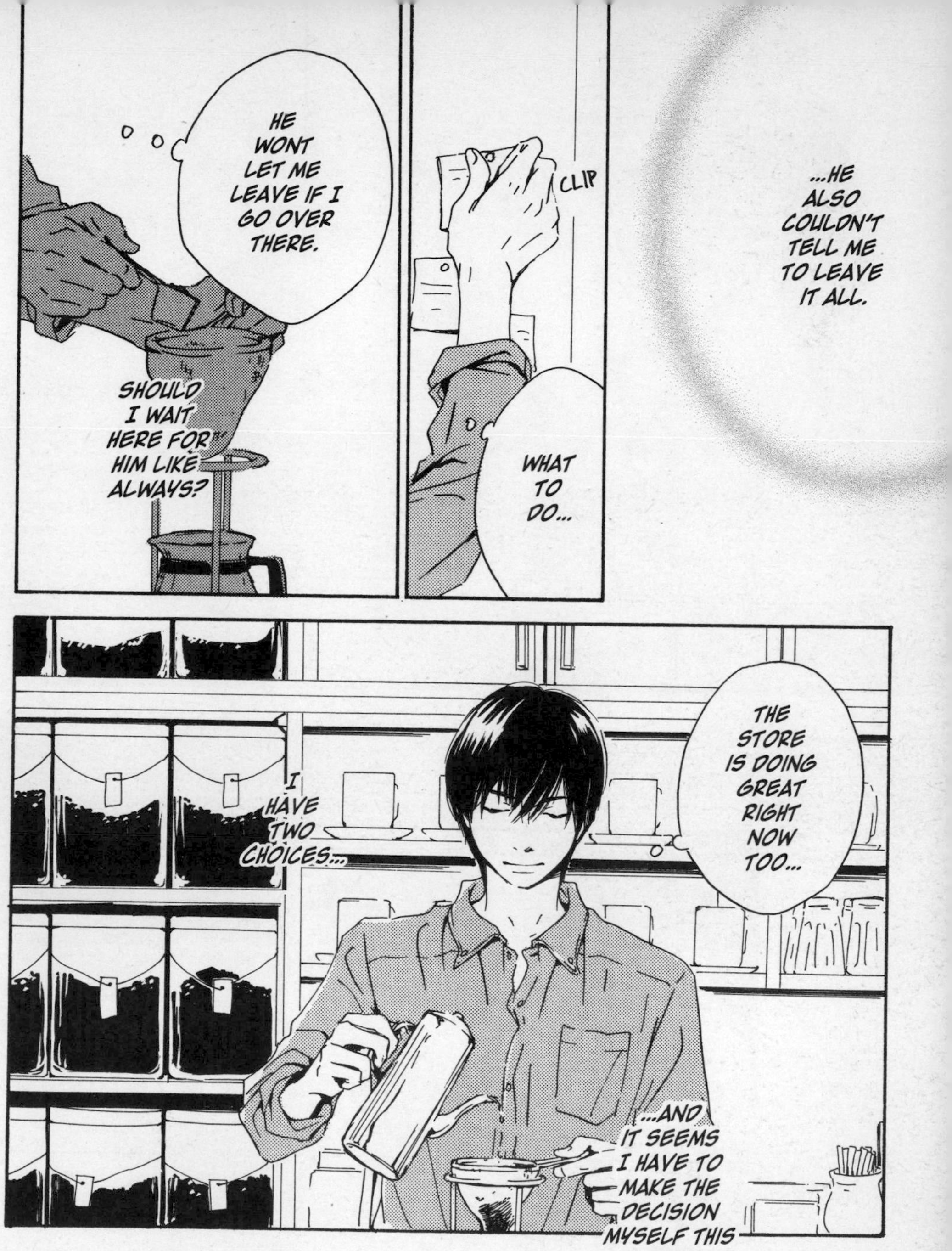
...HE ALSO COULDN'T TELL ME TO LEAVE IT ALL.
CLIP
WHAT TO DO...
HE WONT LET ME LEAVE IF I GO OVER THERE.
SHOULD I WAIT HERE FOR HIM LIKE ALWAYS?
THE STORE IS DOING GREAT RIGHT NOW TOO...
I HAVE TWO CHOICES...
...AND IT SEEMS I HAVE TO MAKE THE DECISION MYSELF THIS TIME.

END

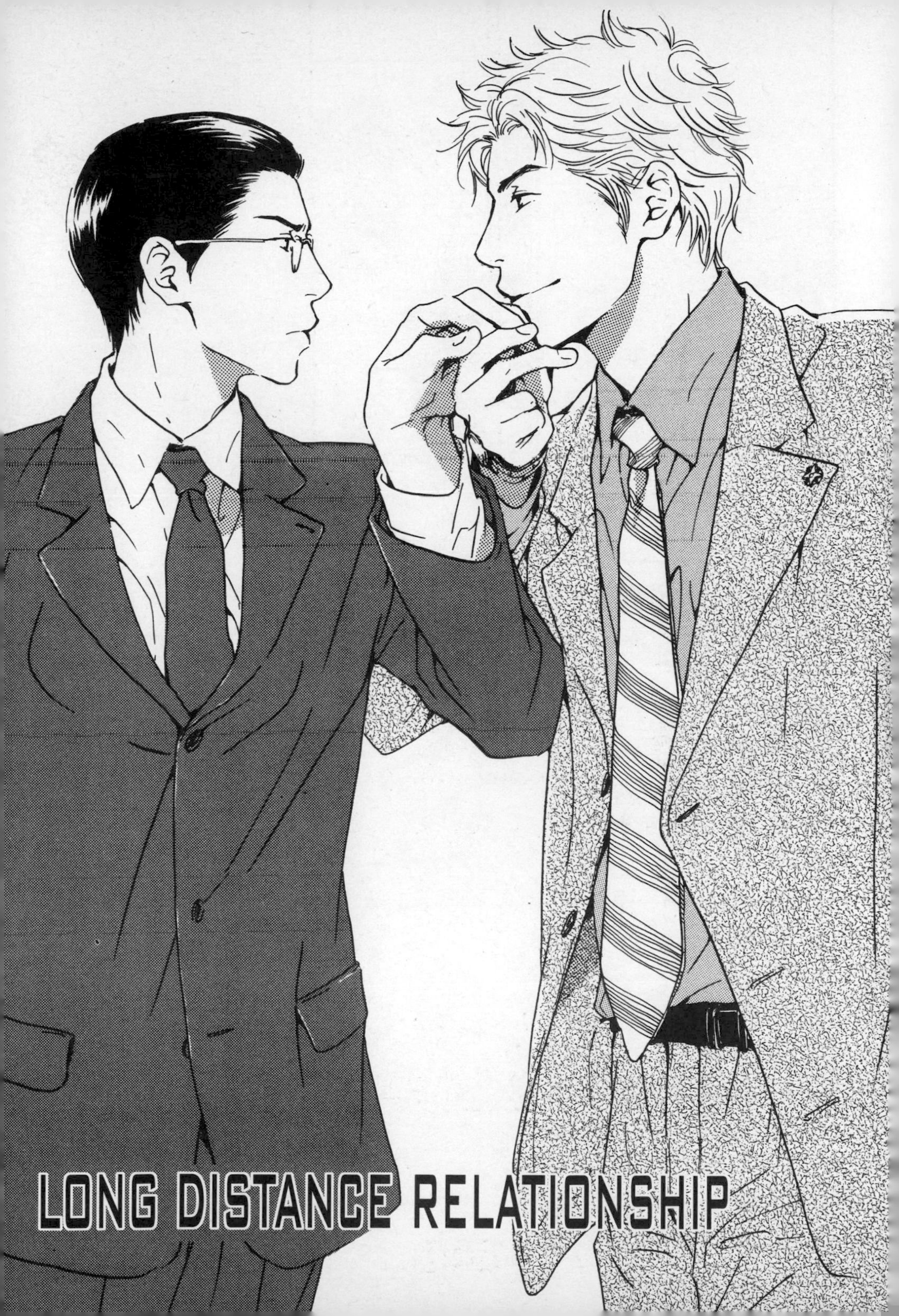
LONG DISTANCE RELATIONSHIP

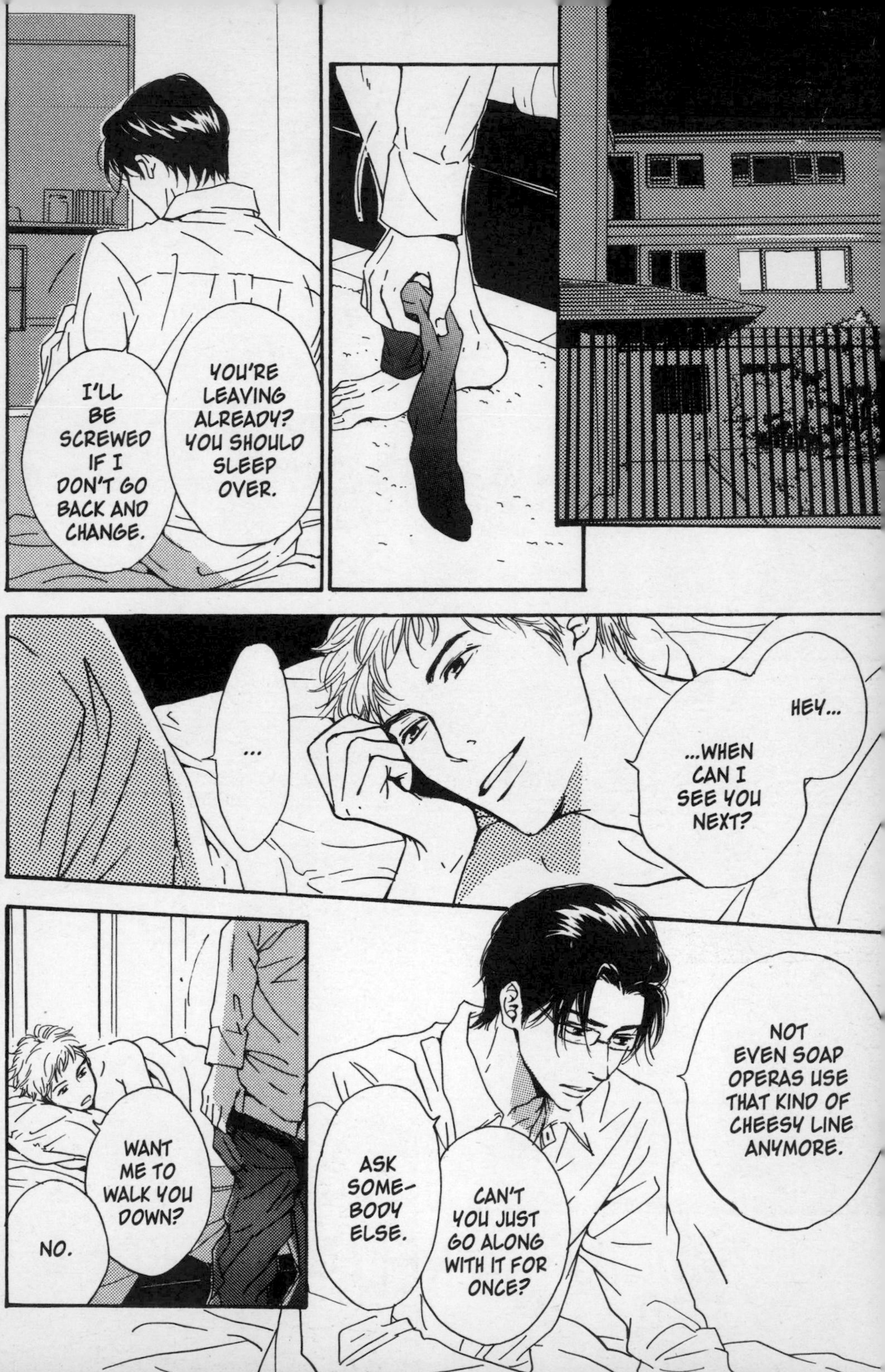
YOU'RE LEAVING ALREADY? YOU SHOULD SLEEP OVER.
I'LL BE SCREWED IF I DON'T GO BACK AND CHANGE.
HEY...
...WHEN CAN I SEE YOU NEXT?
...
NOT EVEN SOAP OPERAS USE THAT KIND OF CHEESY LINE ANYMORE.
CAN'T YOU JUST GO ALONG WITH IT FOR ONCE?
ASK SOME-BODY ELSE.
WANT ME TO WALK YOU DOWN?
NO.

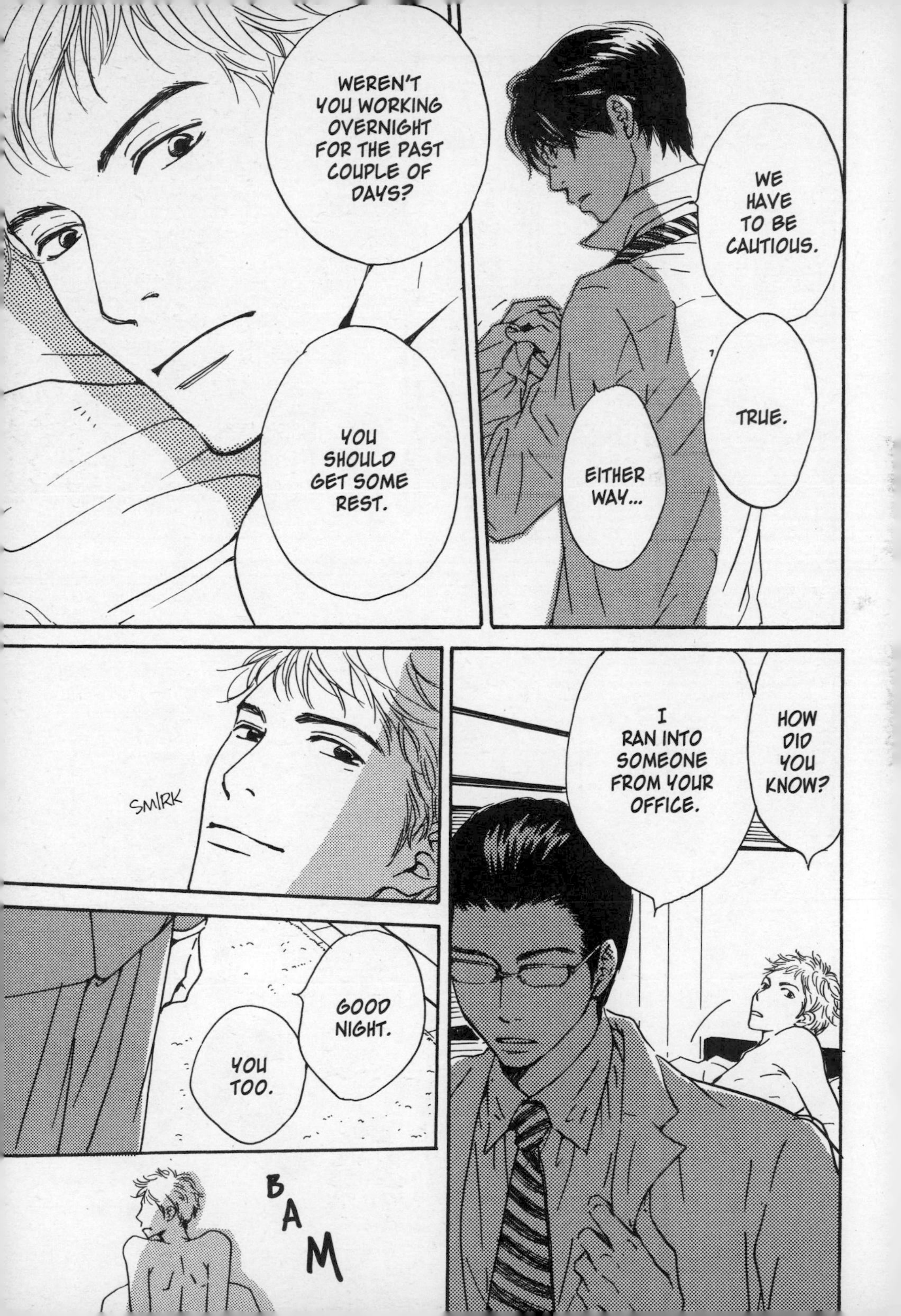
WE HAVE TO BE CAUTIOUS.
TRUE.
EITHER WAY...
WEREN'T YOU WORKING OVERNIGHT FOR THE PAST COUPLE OF DAYS?
YOU SHOULD GET SOME REST.
HOW DID YOU KNOW?
I RAN INTO SOMEONE FROM YOUR OFFICE.
SMIRK
GOOD NIGHT.
YOU TOO.
BAM

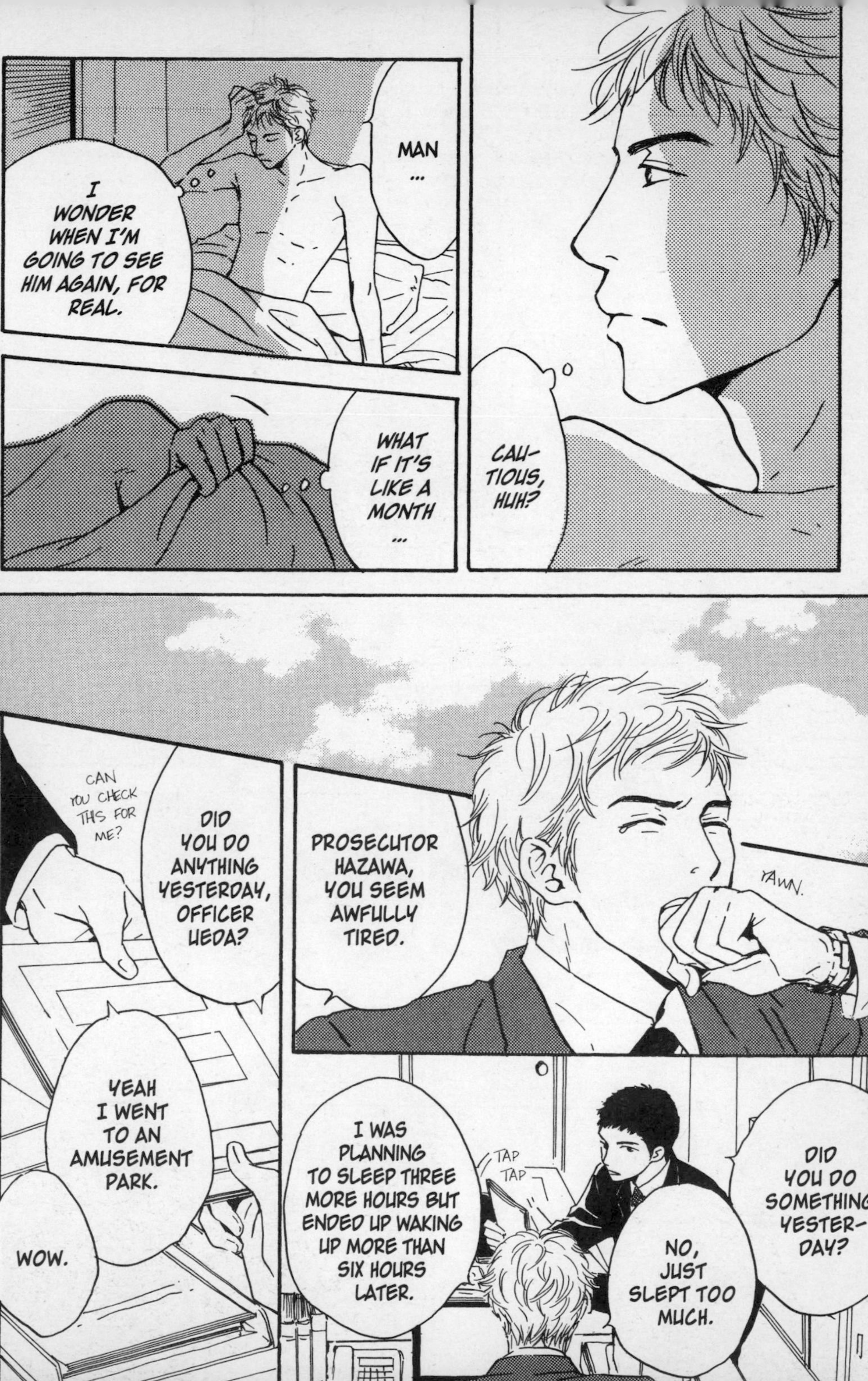
CAU-TIOUS, HUH?
MAN ...
I WONDER WHEN I'M GOING TO SEE HIM AGAIN, FOR REAL.
WHAT IF IT'S LIKE A MONTH ...
PROSECUTOR HAZAWA, YOU SEEM AWFULLY TIRED.
YAWN.
DID YOU DO ANYTHING YESTERDAY, OFFICER UEDA?
CAN YOU CHECK THS FOR ME?
DID YOU DO SOMETHING YESTER-DAY?
NO, JUST SLEPT TOO MUCH.
I WAS PLANNING TO SLEEP THREE MORE HOURS BUT ENDED UP WAKING UP MORE THAN SIX HOURS LATER.
TAP TAP
YEAH I WENT TO AN AMUSEMENT PARK.
WOW.

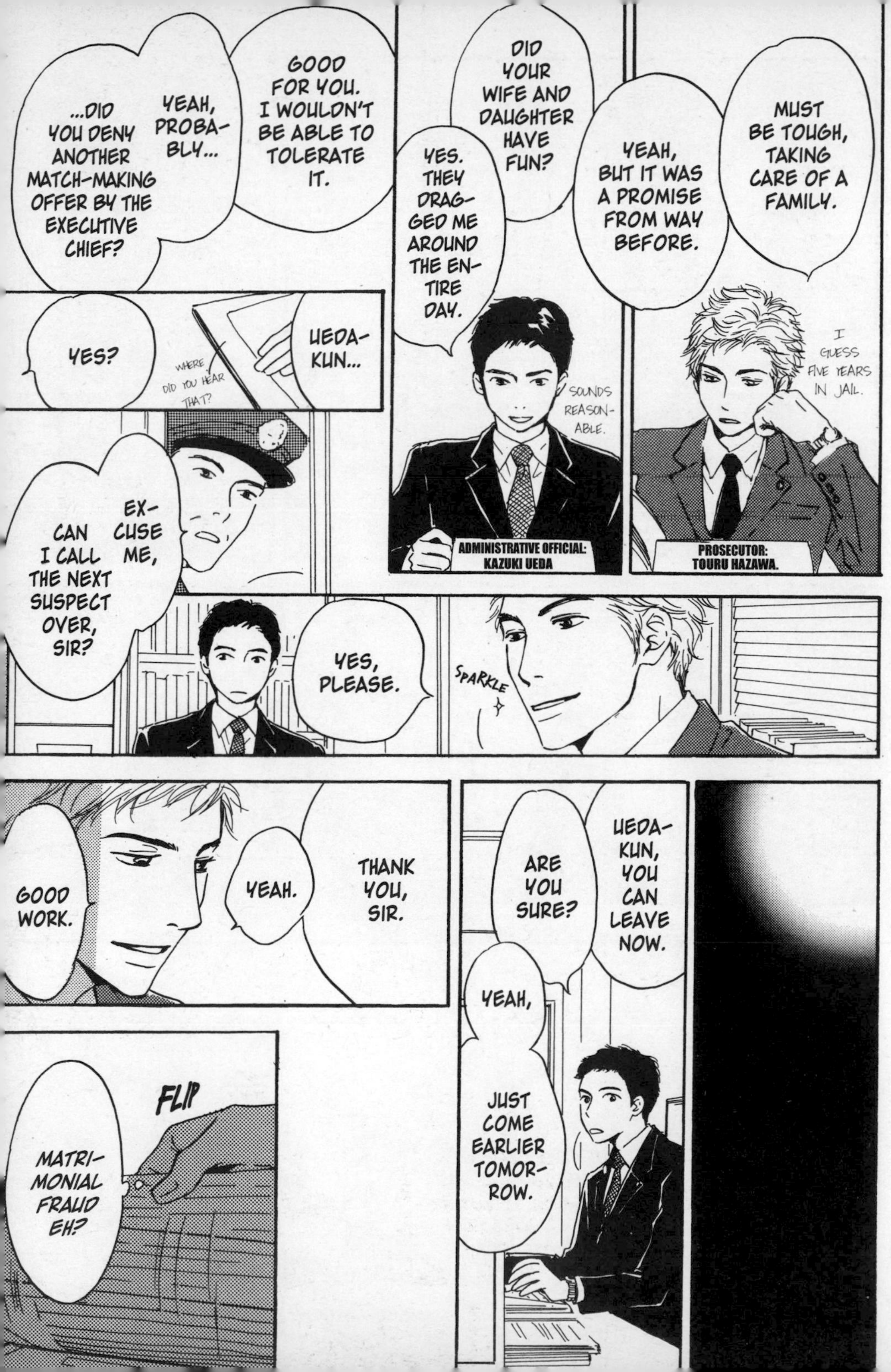
MUST BE TOUGH, TAKING CARE OF A FAMILY.
YEAH, BUT IT WAS A PROMISE FROM WAY BEFORE.
I GUESS FIVE YEARS IN JAIL.
PROSECUTOR: TOURU HAZAWA.
DID YOUR WIFE AND DAUGHTER HAVE FUN?
YES. THEY DRAG-GED ME AROUND THE EN-TIRE DAY.
SOUNDS REASON-ABLE.
ADMINISTRATIVE OFFICIAL: KAZUKI UEDA
GOOD FOR YOU. I WOULDN'T BE ABLE TO TOLERATE IT.
YEAH, PROBA-BLY...
...DID YOU DENY ANOTHER MATCH-MAKING OFFER BY THE EXECUTIVE CHIEF?
UEDA-KUN...
WHERE DID YOU HEAR THAT?
YES?
EX-CUSE ME,
CAN I CALL THE NEXT SUSPECT OVER, SIR?
SPARKLE
YES, PLEASE.
UEDA-KUN, YOU CAN LEAVE NOW.
ARE YOU SURE?
YEAH,
JUST COME EARLIER TOMOR-ROW.
THANK YOU, SIR.
YEAH.
GOOD WORK.
FLIP
MATRI-MONIAL FRAUD EH?

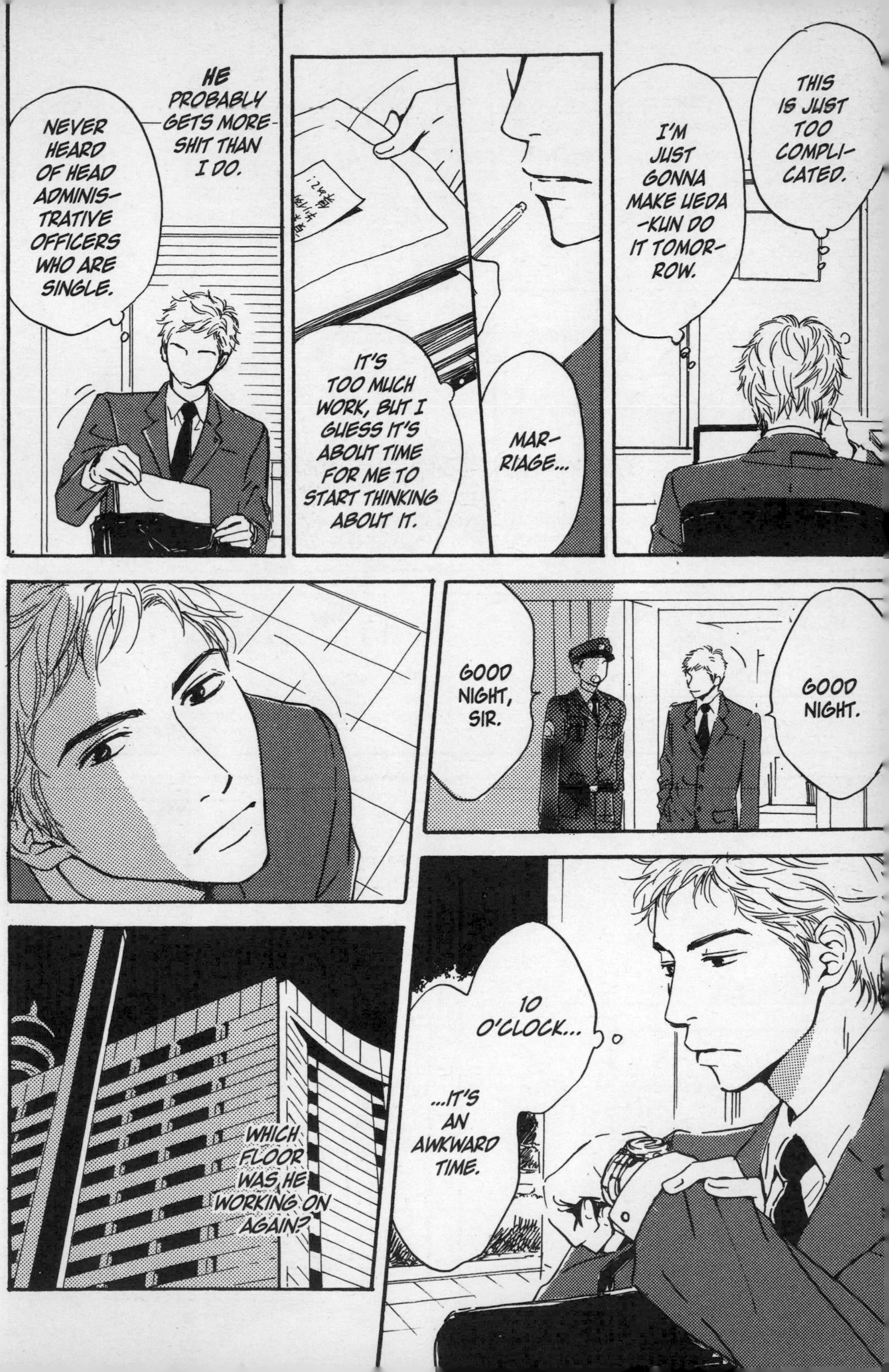
THIS IS JUST TOO COMPLICATED.
I'M JUST GONNA MAKE UEDA-KUN DO IT TOMORROW.
MARRIAGE...
IT'S TOO MUCH WORK, BUT I GUESS IT'S ABOUT TIME FOR ME TO START THINKING ABOUT IT.
HE PROBABLY GETS MORE SHIT THAN I DO.
NEVER HEARD OF HEAD ADMINISTRATIVE OFFICERS WHO ARE SINGLE.
GOOD NIGHT.
GOOD NIGHT, SIR.
10 O'CLOCK...
...IT'S AN AWKWARD TIME.
WHICH FLOOR WAS HE WORKING ON AGAIN?

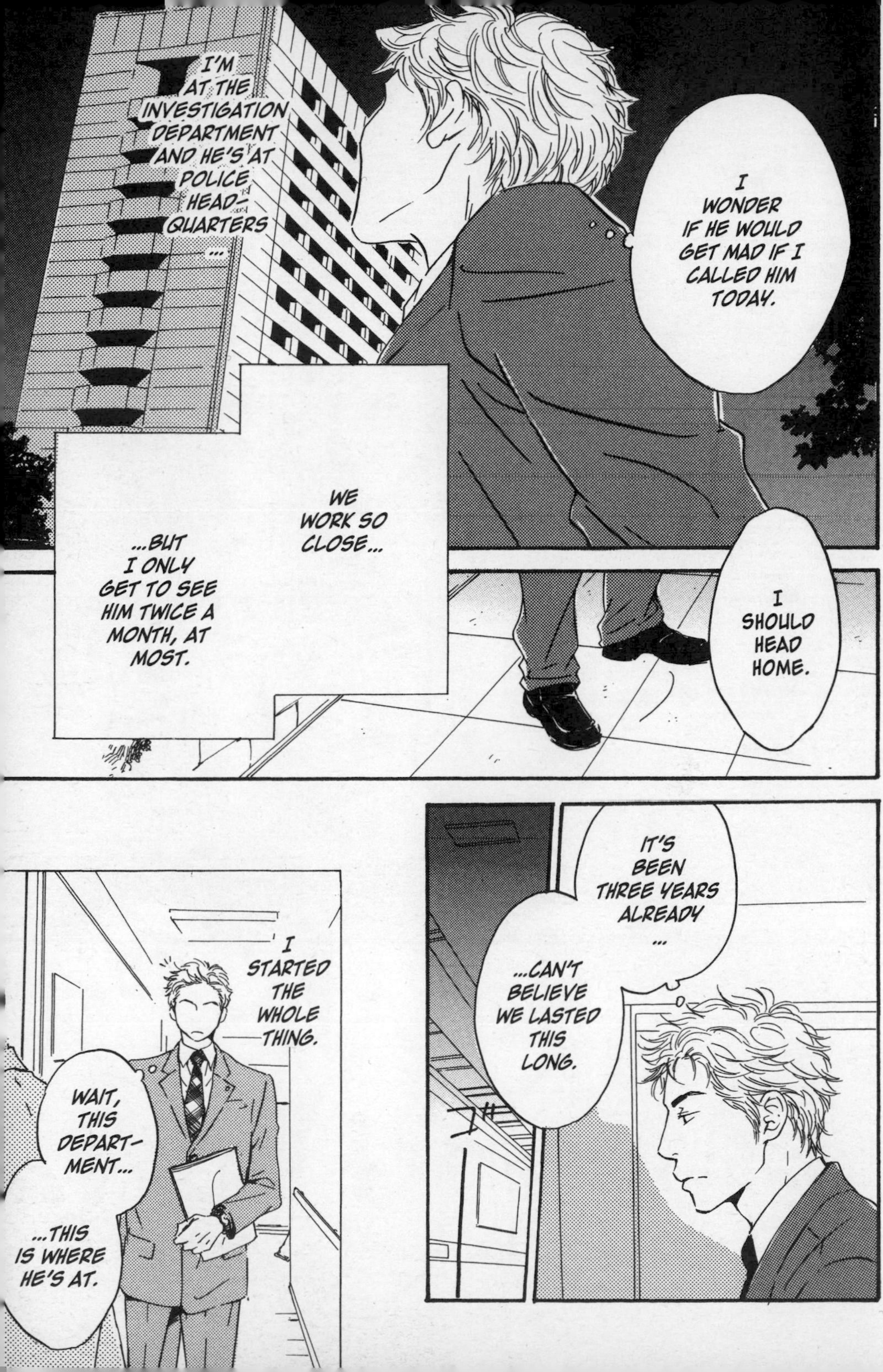
I WONDER IF HE WOULD GET MAD IF I CALLED HIM TODAY.
I'M AT THE INVESTIGATION DEPARTMENT AND HE'S AT POLICE HEAD-QUARTERS ...
WE WORK SO CLOSE...
...BUT I ONLY GET TO SEE HIM TWICE A MONTH, AT MOST.
I SHOULD HEAD HOME.
IT'S BEEN THREE YEARS ALREADY ...
...CAN'T BELIEVE WE LASTED THIS LONG.
I STARTED THE WHOLE THING.
WAIT, THIS DEPART-MENT...
...THIS IS WHERE HE'S AT.

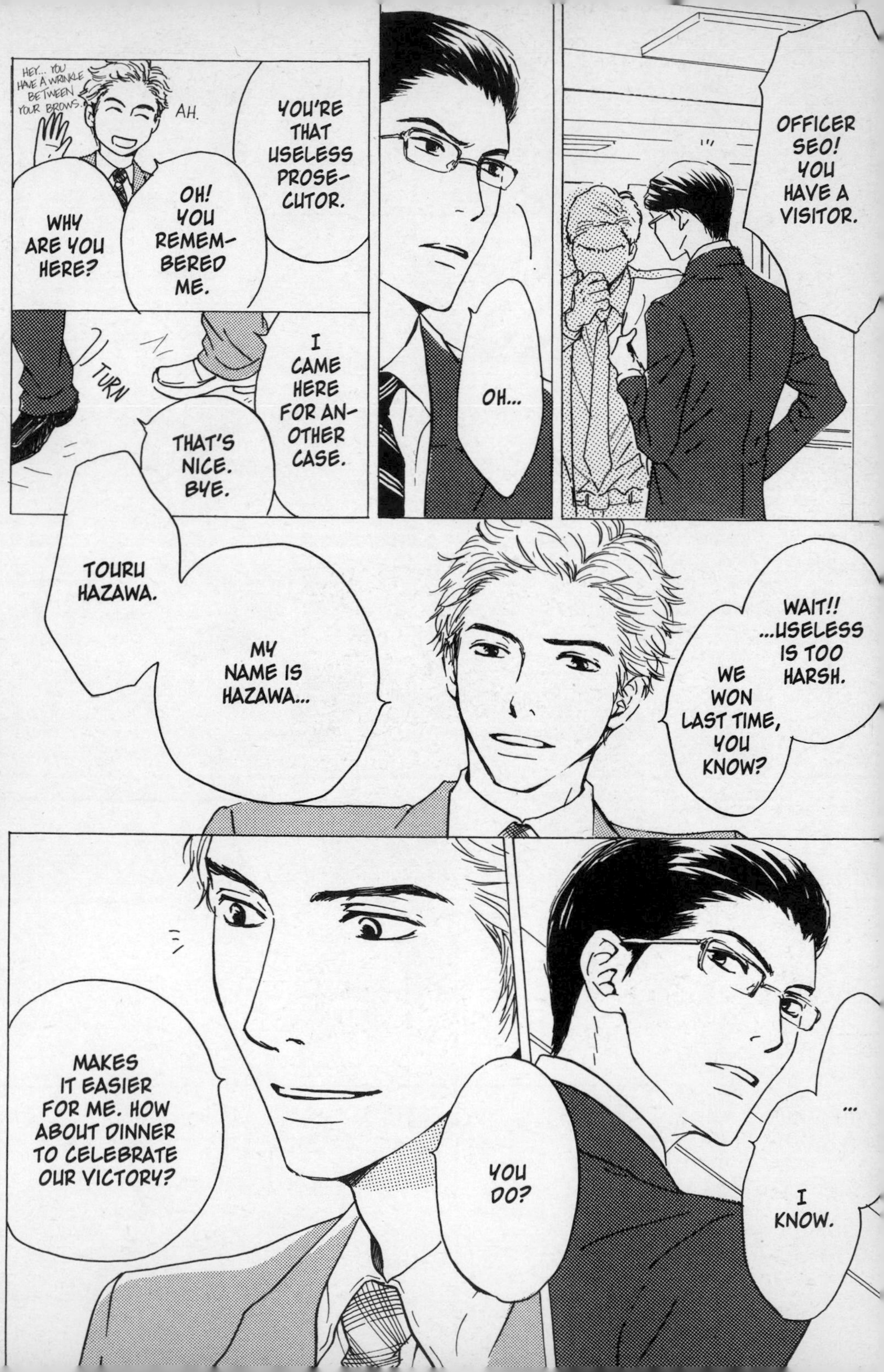
OFFICER SEO! YOU HAVE A VISITOR.
OH...
YOU'RE THAT USELESS PROSE-CUTOR.
OH! YOU REMEM-BERED ME.
WHY ARE YOU HERE?
AH.
HEY... YOU HAVE A WRINKLE BETWEEN YOUR BROWS...
I CAME HERE FOR AN-OTHER CASE.
THAT'S NICE. BYE.
TURN
WAIT!! ...USELESS IS TOO HARSH.
WE WON LAST TIME, YOU KNOW?
MY NAME IS HAZAWA...
TOURU HAZAWA.
...
I KNOW.
YOU DO?
MAKES IT EASIER FOR ME. HOW ABOUT DINNER TO CELEBRATE OUR VICTORY?

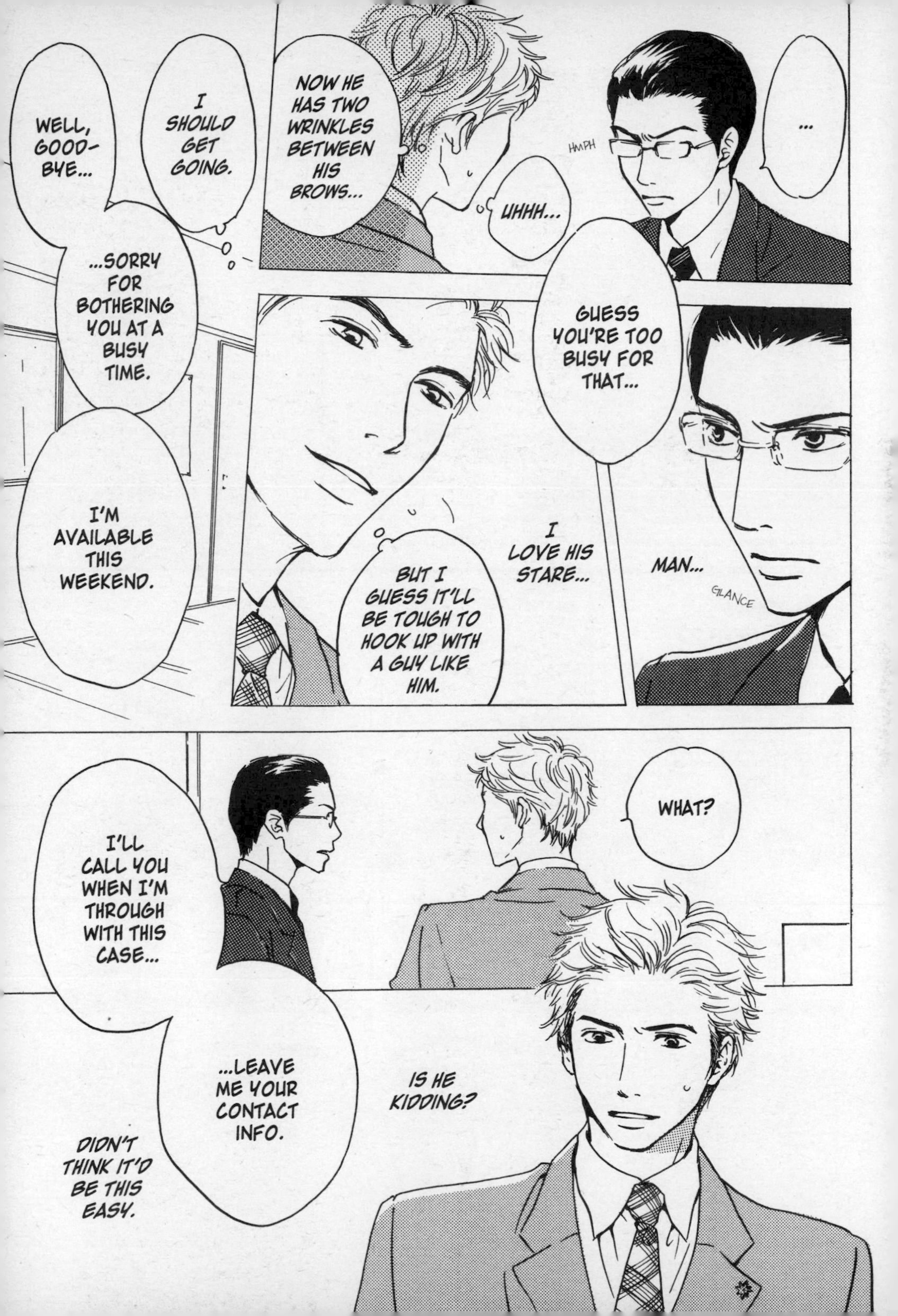
...
HMPH
UHHH...
NOW HE HAS TWO WRINKLES BETWEEN HIS BROWS...
GUESS YOU'RE TOO BUSY FOR THAT...
MAN...
GLANCE
I LOVE HIS STARE...
BUT I GUESS IT'LL BE TOUGH TO HOOK UP WITH A GUY LIKE HIM.
I SHOULD GET GOING.
WELL, GOOD-BYE...
...SORRY FOR BOTHERING YOU AT A BUSY TIME.
I'M AVAILABLE THIS WEEKEND.
WHAT?
I'LL CALL YOU WHEN I'M THROUGH WITH THIS CASE...
...LEAVE ME YOUR CONTACT INFO.
IS HE KIDDING?
DIDN'T THINK IT'D BE THIS EASY.

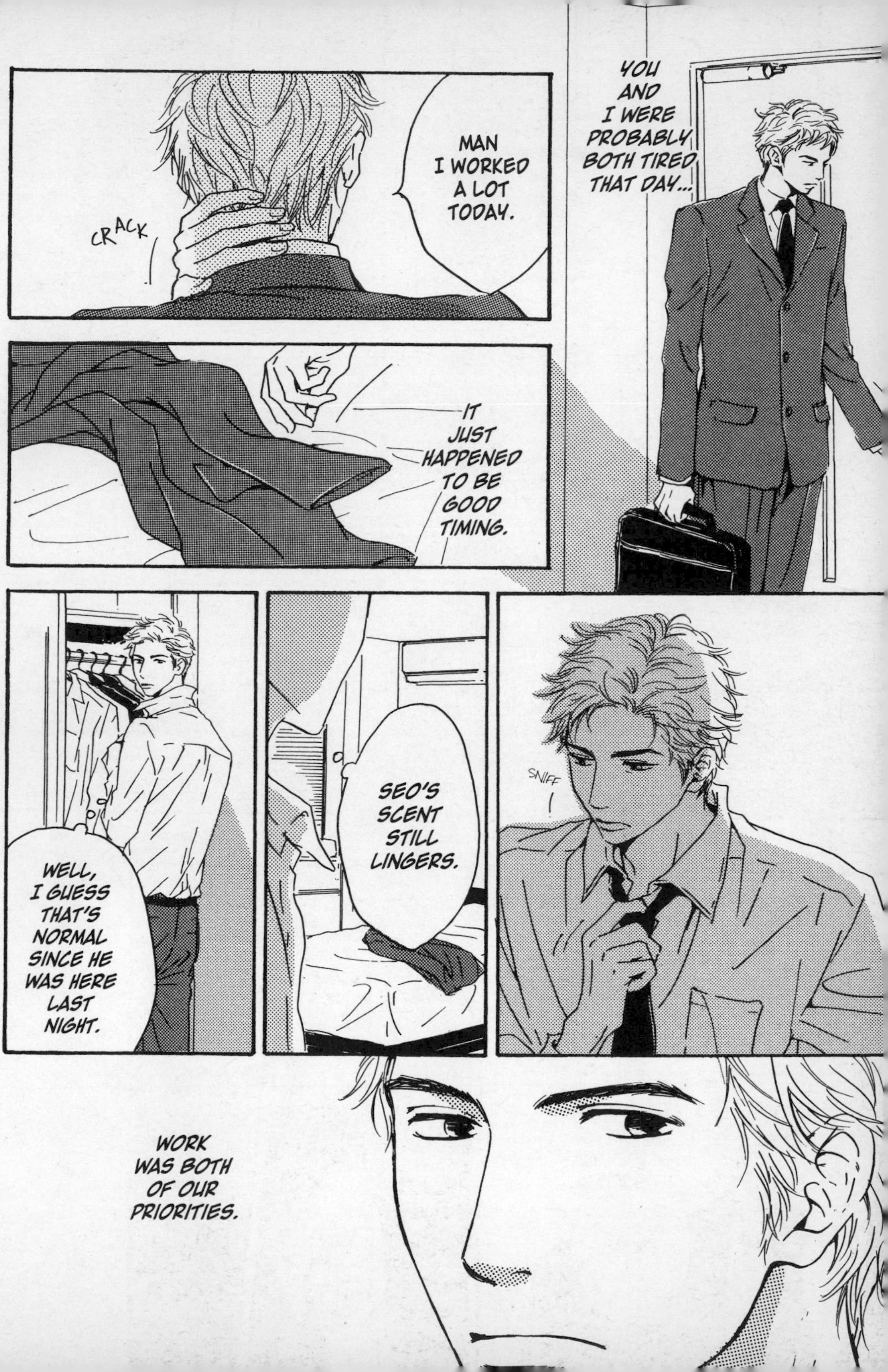
YOU AND I WERE PROBABLY BOTH TIRED THAT DAY...
MAN I WORKED A LOT TODAY.
CRACK
IT JUST HAPPENED TO BE GOOD TIMING.
SNIFF
SEO'S SCENT STILL LINGERS.
WELL, I GUESS THAT'S NORMAL SINCE HE WAS HERE LAST NIGHT.
WORK WAS BOTH OF OUR PRIORITIES.

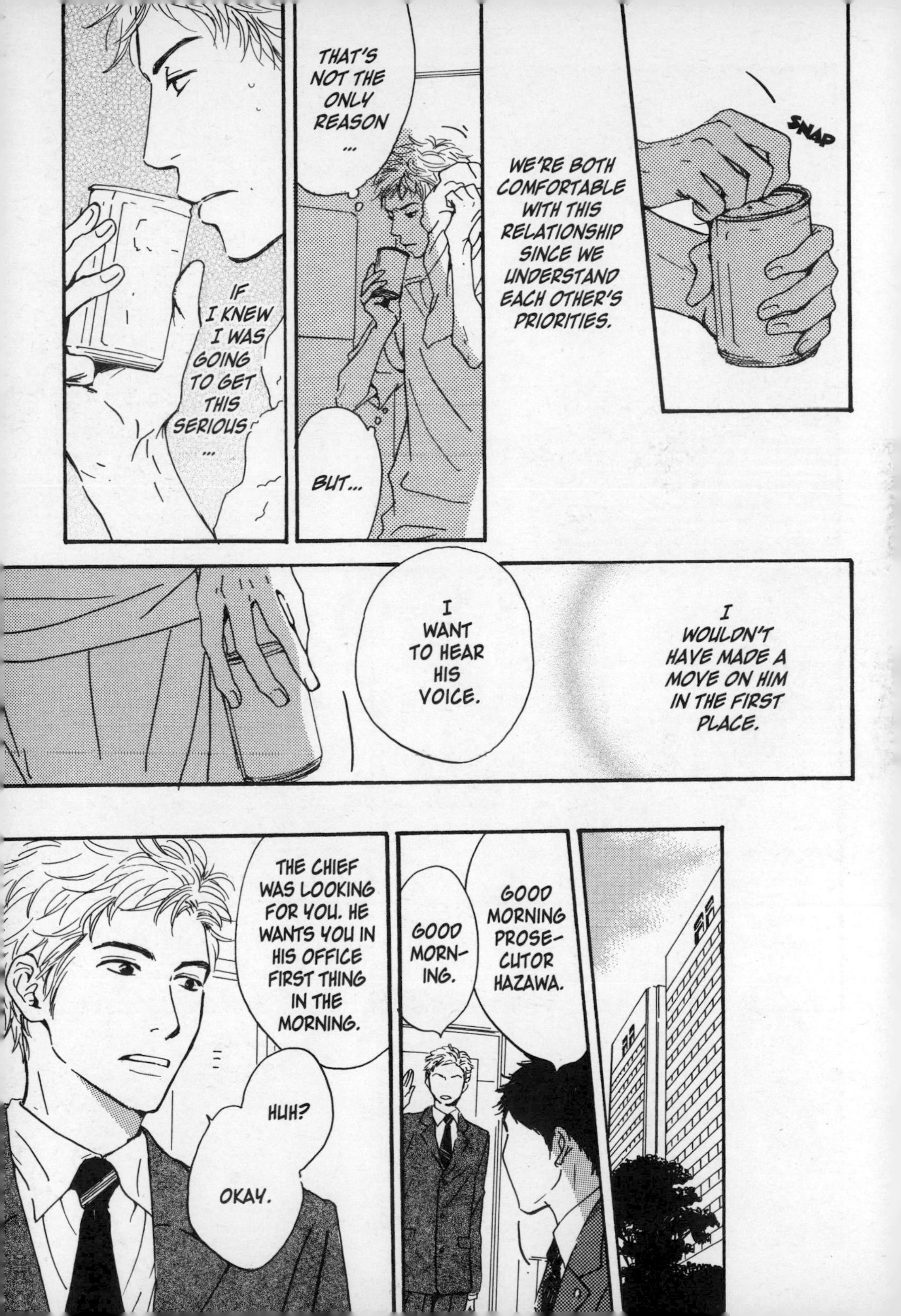
SNAP
WE'RE BOTH COMFORTABLE WITH THIS RELATIONSHIP SINCE WE UNDERSTAND EACH OTHER'S PRIORITIES.
THAT'S NOT THE ONLY REASON ...
BUT...
IF I KNEW I WAS GOING TO GET THIS SERIOUS ...
I WOULDN'T HAVE MADE A MOVE ON HIM IN THE FIRST PLACE.
I WANT TO HEAR HIS VOICE.
GOOD MORNING PROSE- CUTOR HAZAWA.
GOOD MORN- ING.
THE CHIEF WAS LOOKING FOR YOU. HE WANTS YOU IN HIS OFFICE FIRST THING IN THE MORNING.
HUH?
OKAY.

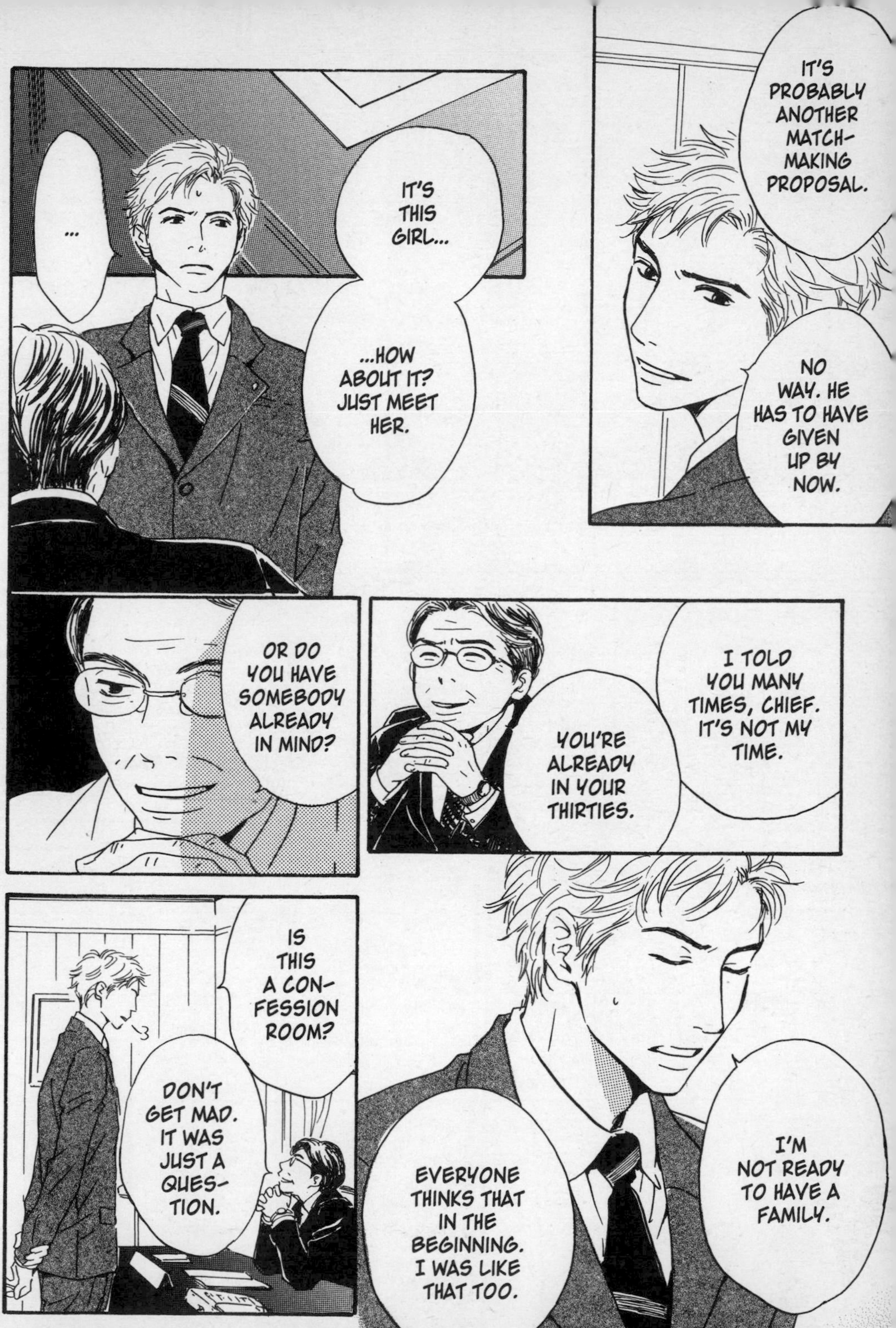
IT'S PROBABLY ANOTHER MATCH-MAKING PROPOSAL.
NO WAY. HE HAS TO HAVE GIVEN UP BY NOW.
IT'S THIS GIRL...
...
...HOW ABOUT IT? JUST MEET HER.
I TOLD YOU MANY TIMES, CHIEF. IT'S NOT MY TIME.
YOU'RE ALREADY IN YOUR THIRTIES.
OR DO YOU HAVE SOMEBODY ALREADY IN MIND?
I'M NOT READY TO HAVE A FAMILY.
EVERYONE THINKS THAT IN THE BEGINNING. I WAS LIKE THAT TOO.
IS THIS A CONFESSION ROOM?
DON'T GET MAD. IT WAS JUST A QUESTION.

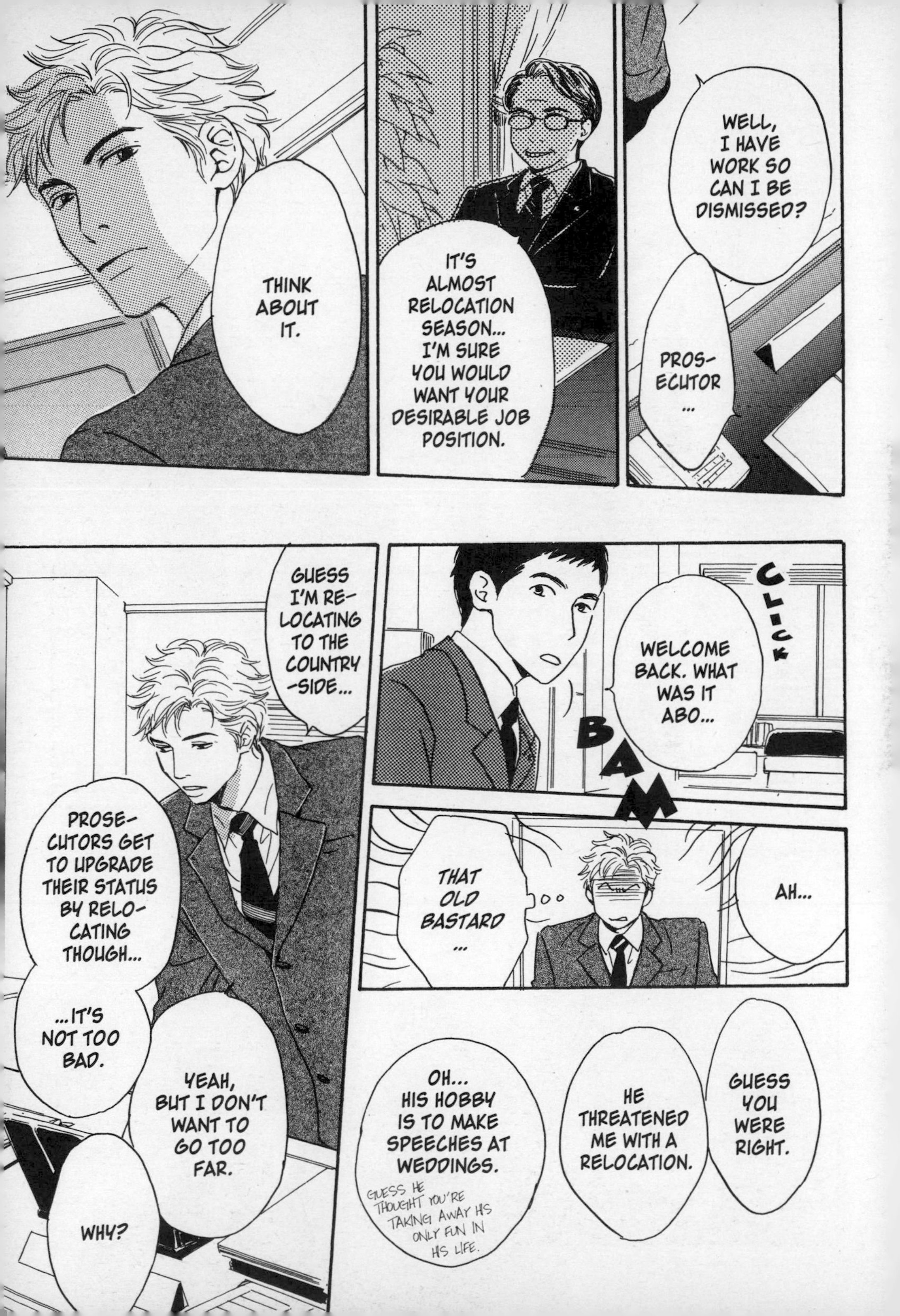
WELL, I HAVE WORK SO CAN I BE DISMISSED?
PROS-ECUTOR...
IT'S ALMOST RELOCATION SEASON... I'M SURE YOU WOULD WANT YOUR DESIRABLE JOB POSITION.
THINK ABOUT IT.
CLICK
WELCOME BACK. WHAT WAS IT ABO...
BAM
AH...
THAT OLD BASTARD...
GUESS YOU WERE RIGHT.
HE THREATENED ME WITH A RELOCATION.
OH... HIS HOBBY IS TO MAKE SPEECHES AT WEDDINGS.
GUESS HE THOUGHT YOU'RE TAKING AWAY HIS ONLY FUN IN HIS LIFE.
GUESS I'M RE-LOCATING TO THE COUNTRY-SIDE...
PROSE-CUTORS GET TO UPGRADE THEIR STATUS BY RELO-CATING THOUGH...
...IT'S NOT TOO BAD.
YEAH, BUT I DON'T WANT TO GO TOO FAR.
WHY?

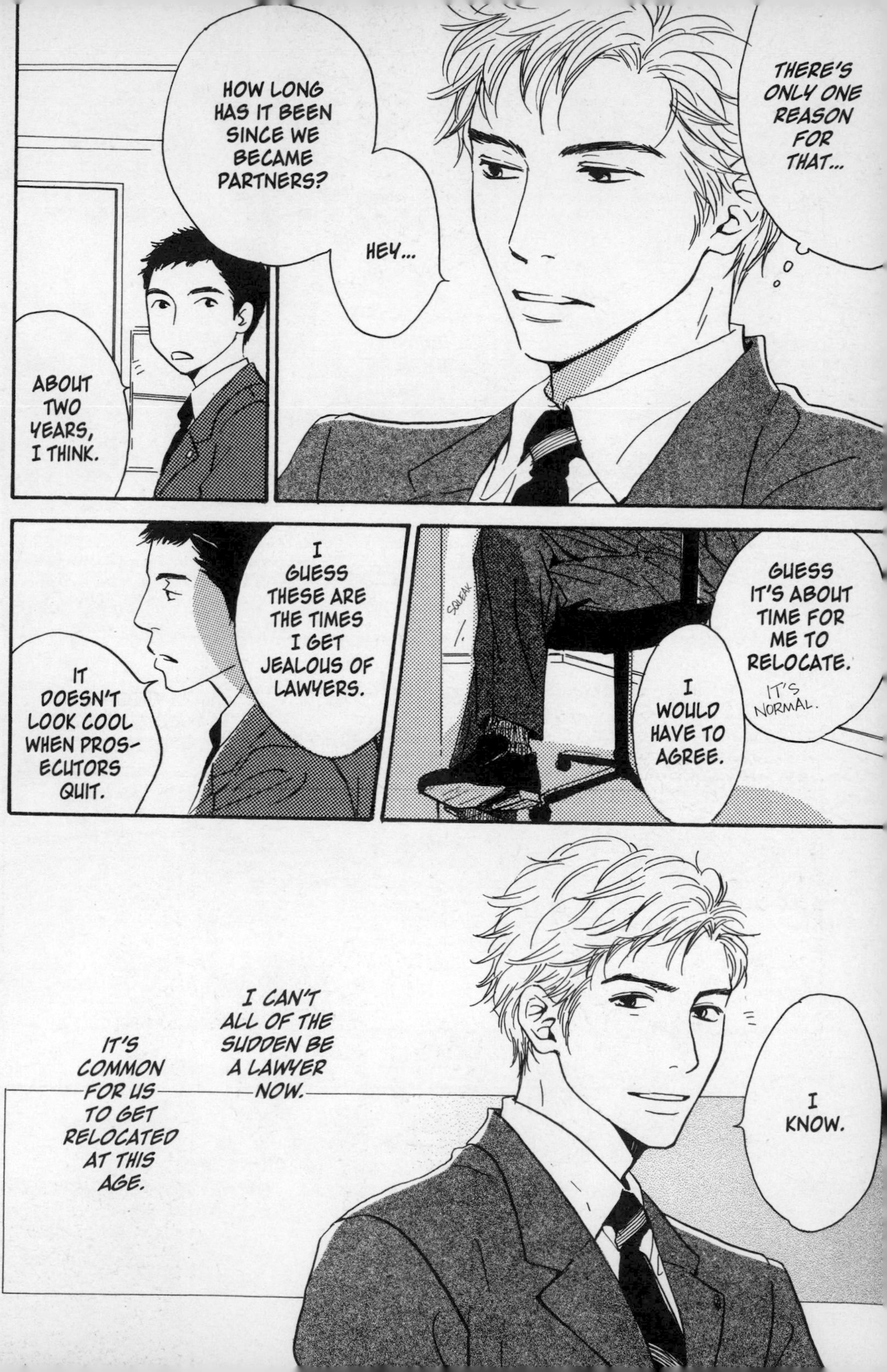
THERE'S ONLY ONE REASON FOR THAT...
HOW LONG HAS IT BEEN SINCE WE BECAME PARTNERS?
HEY...
ABOUT TWO YEARS, I THINK.
GUESS IT'S ABOUT TIME FOR ME TO RELOCATE.
IT'S NORMAL.
SQUEAK
I WOULD HAVE TO AGREE.
I GUESS THESE ARE THE TIMES I GET JEALOUS OF LAWYERS.
IT DOESN'T LOOK COOL WHEN PROS-ECUTORS QUIT.
I KNOW.
I CAN'T ALL OF THE SUDDEN BE A LAWYER NOW.
IT'S COMMON FOR US TO GET RELOCATED AT THIS AGE.

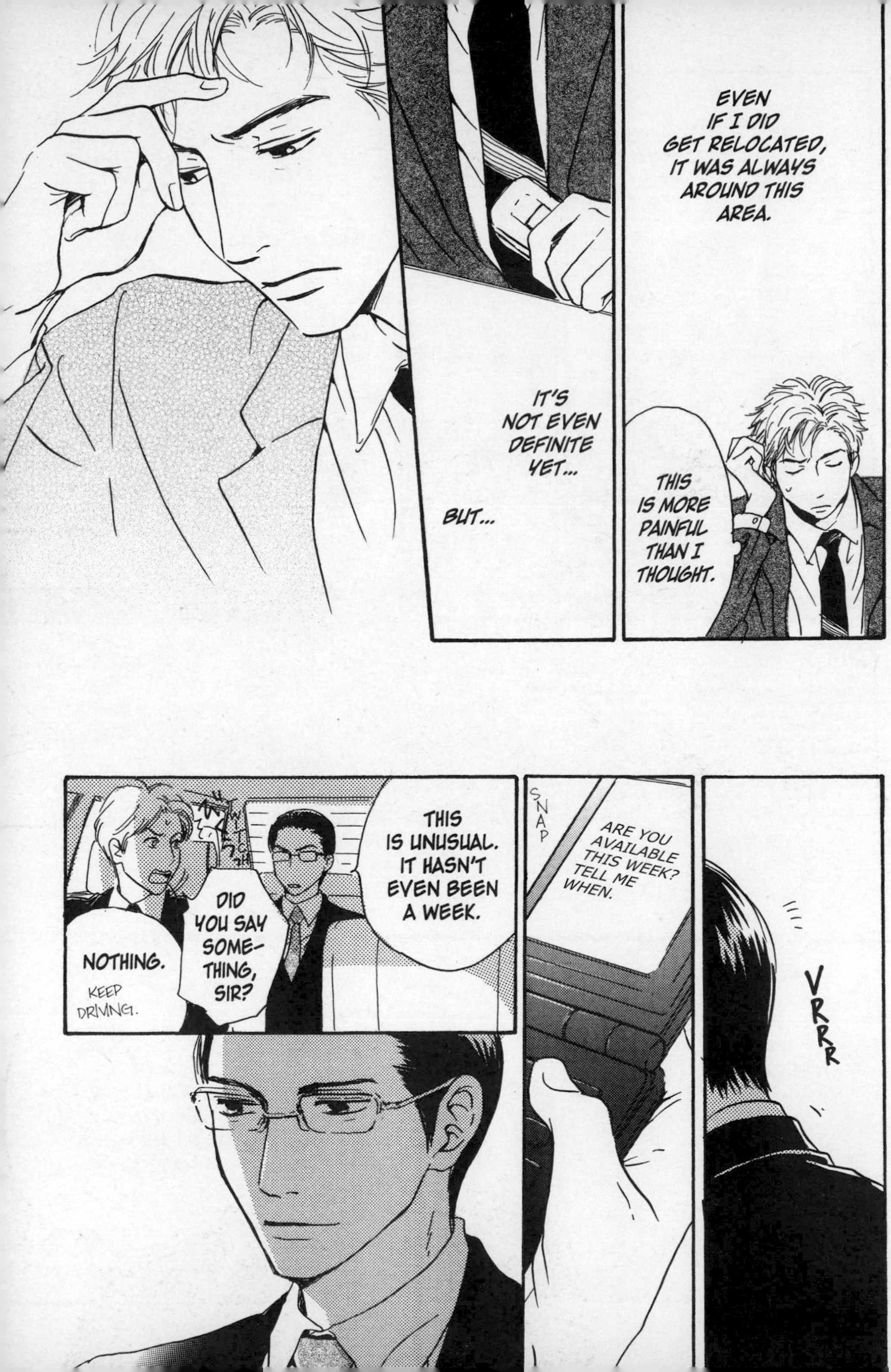
EVEN IF I DID GET RELOCATED, IT WAS ALWAYS AROUND THIS AREA.
THIS IS MORE PAINFUL THAN I THOUGHT.
IT'S NOT EVEN DEFINITE YET...
BUT...
VRRR
SNAP
ARE YOU AVAILABLE THIS WEEK? TELL ME WHEN.
THIS IS UNUSUAL. IT HASN'T EVEN BEEN A WEEK.
DID YOU SAY SOMETHING, SIR?
NOTHING.
KEEP DRIVING.

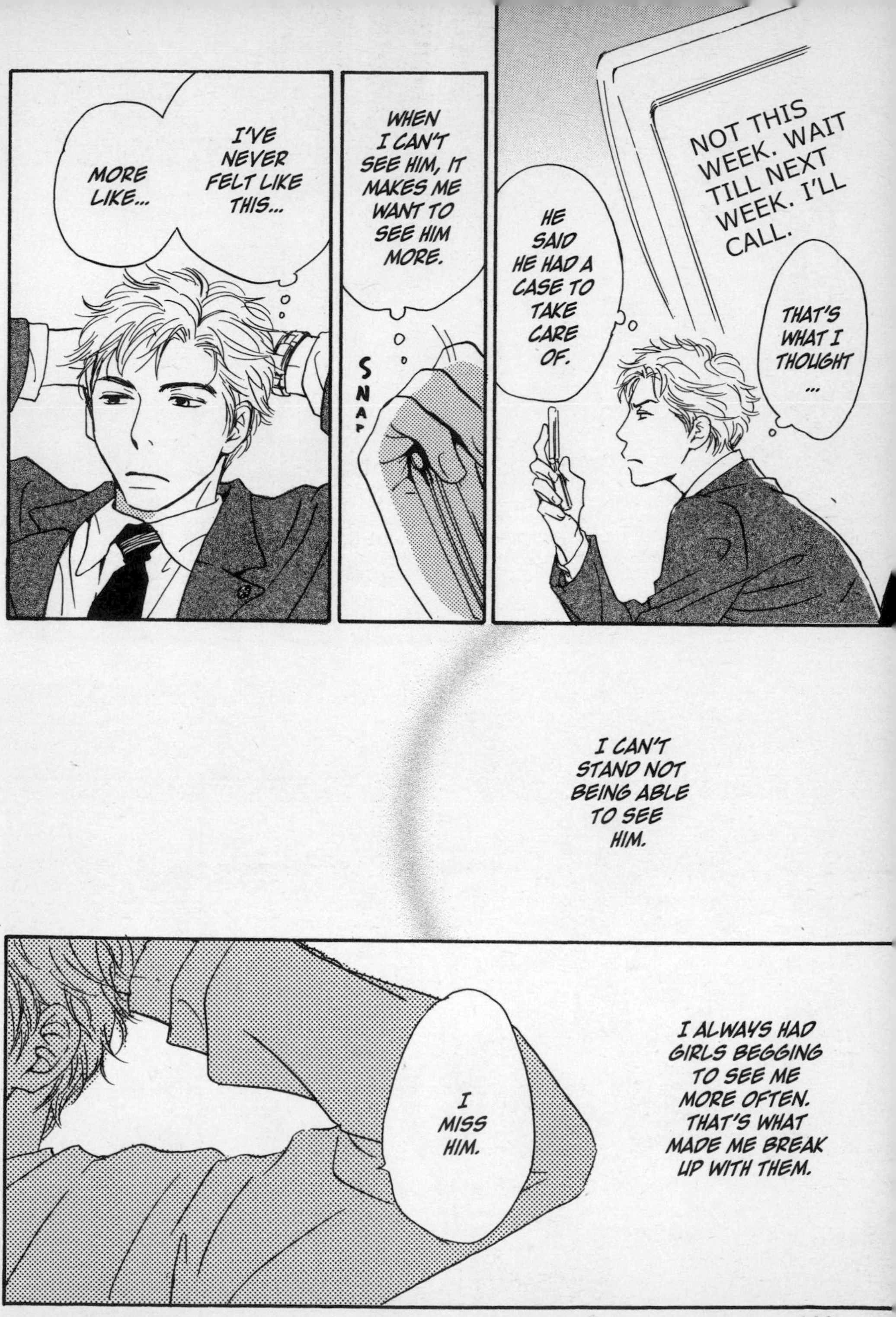
NOT THIS WEEK. WAIT TILL NEXT WEEK. I'LL CALL.
HE SAID HE HAD A CASE TO TAKE CARE OF.
THAT'S WHAT I THOUGHT ...
WHEN I CAN'T SEE HIM, IT MAKES ME WANT TO SEE HIM MORE.
SNAP
I'VE NEVER FELT LIKE THIS...
MORE LIKE...
I CAN'T STAND NOT BEING ABLE TO SEE HIM.
I ALWAYS HAD GIRLS BEGGING TO SEE ME MORE OFTEN. THAT'S WHAT MADE ME BREAK UP WITH THEM.
I MISS HIM.

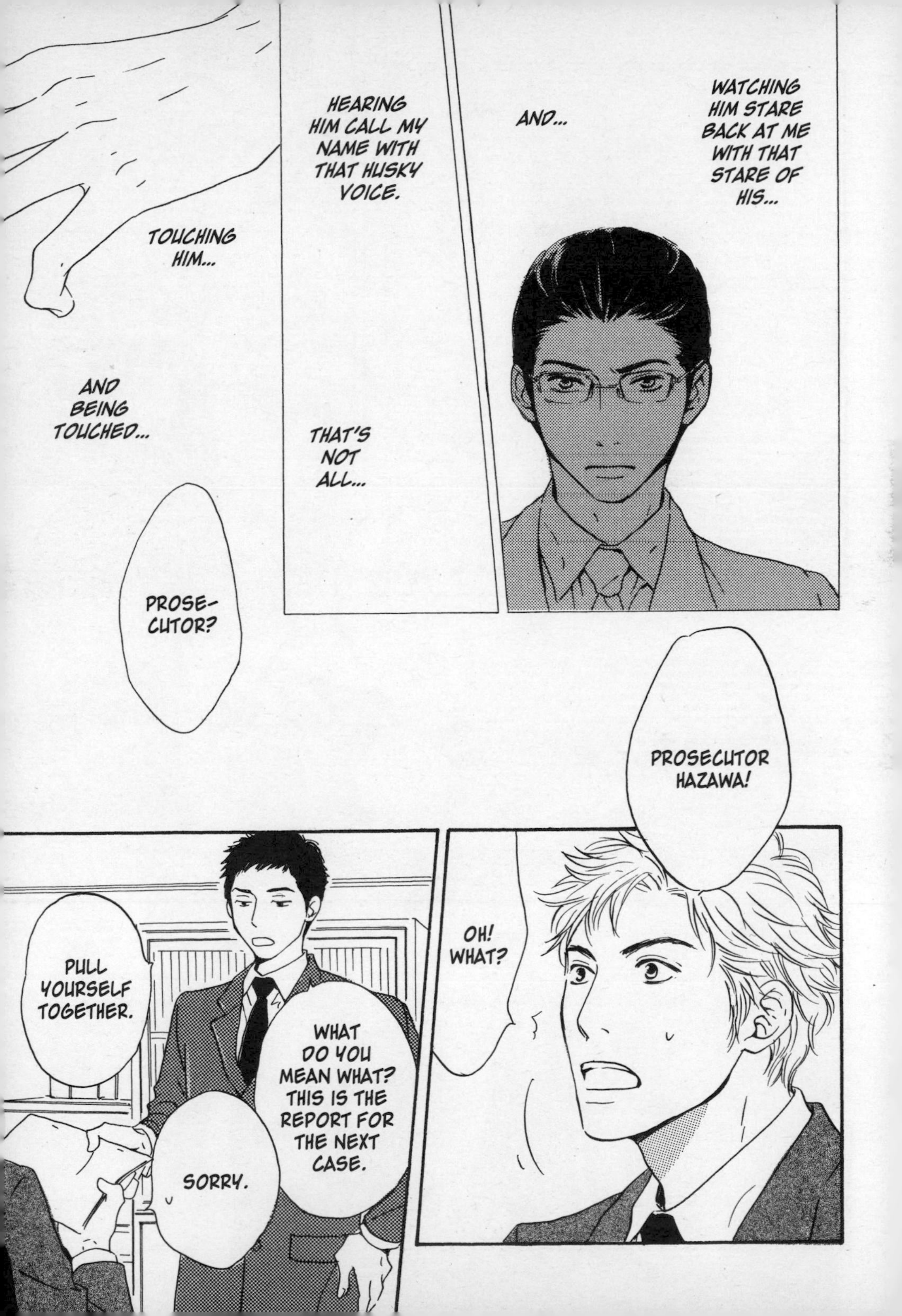
WATCHING HIM STARE BACK AT ME WITH THAT STARE OF HIS...
AND...
HEARING HIM CALL MY NAME WITH THAT HUSKY VOICE.
THAT'S NOT ALL...
TOUCHING HIM...
AND BEING TOUCHED...
PROSE-CUTOR?
PROSECUTOR HAZAWA!
OH! WHAT?
WHAT DO YOU MEAN WHAT? THIS IS THE REPORT FOR THE NEXT CASE.
SORRY.
PULL YOURSELF TOGETHER.

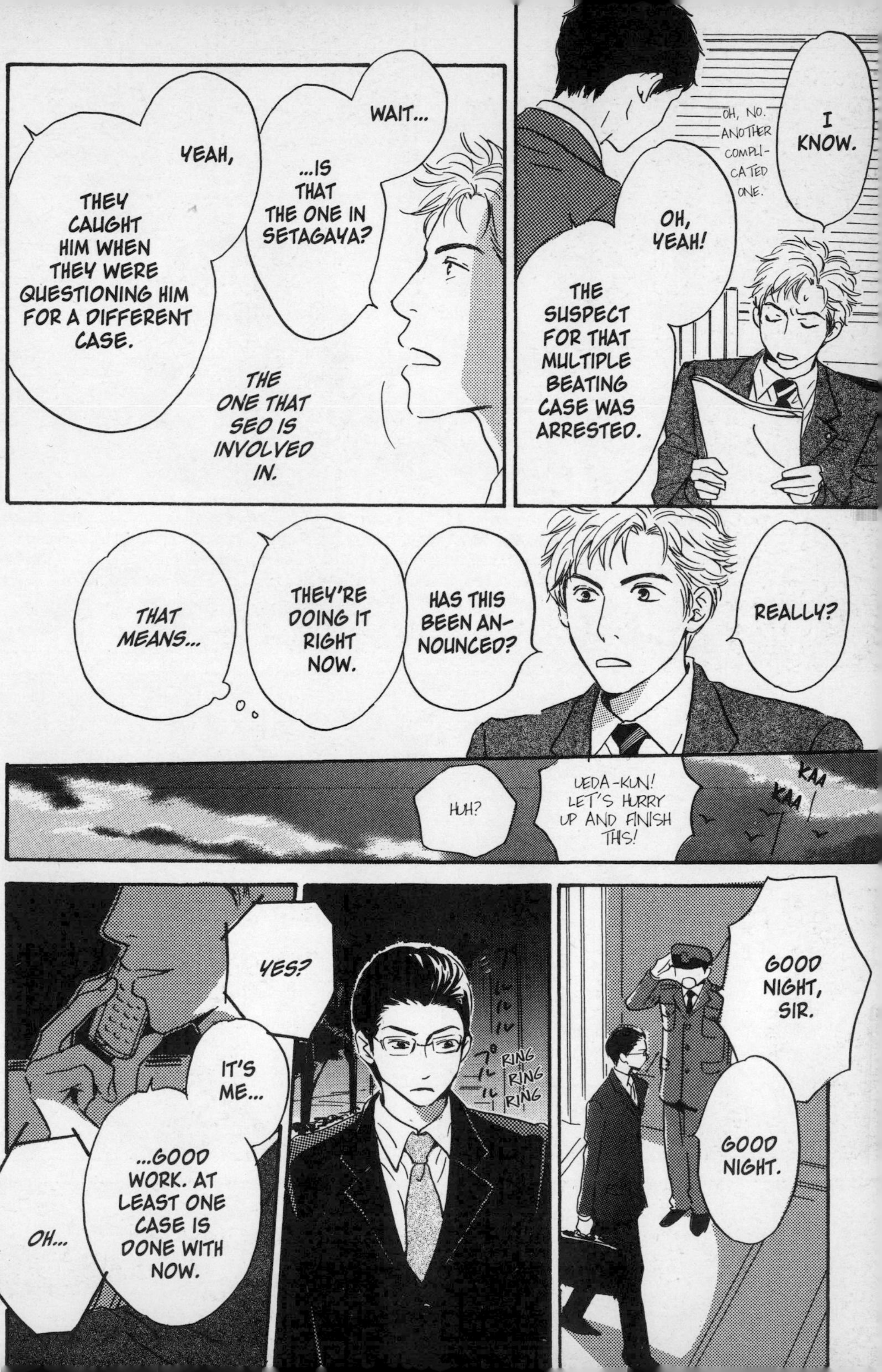
I KNOW.
OH, NO. ANOTHER COMPLI-CATED ONE.
OH, YEAH!
THE SUSPECT FOR THAT MULTIPLE BEATING CASE WAS ARRESTED.
WAIT...
...IS THAT THE ONE IN SETAGAYA?
YEAH,
THEY CAUGHT HIM WHEN THEY WERE QUESTIONING HIM FOR A DIFFERENT CASE.
THE ONE THAT SEO IS INVOLVED IN.
REALLY?
HAS THIS BEEN AN-NOUNCED?
THEY'RE DOING IT RIGHT NOW.
THAT MEANS...
KAA KAA
UEDA-KUN! LET'S HURRY UP AND FINISH THIS!
HUH?
GOOD NIGHT, SIR.
GOOD NIGHT.
RING RING RING
YES?
IT'S ME...
...GOOD WORK. AT LEAST ONE CASE IS DONE WITH NOW.
OH...

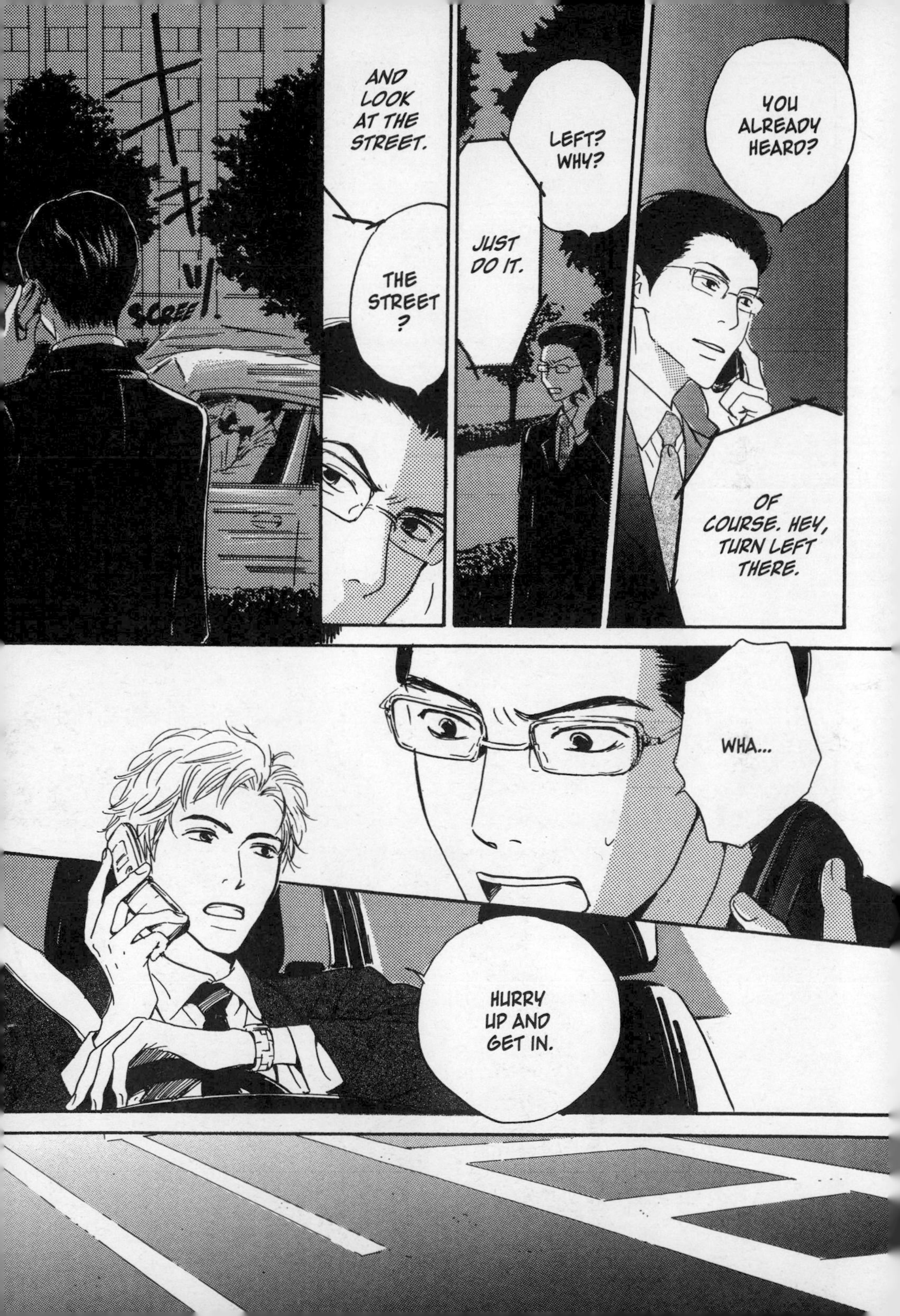
YOU ALREADY HEARD?
OF COURSE. HEY, TURN LEFT THERE.
LEFT? WHY?
JUST DO IT.
AND LOOK AT THE STREET.
THE STREET ?
SCREE
WHA...
HURRY UP AND GET IN.

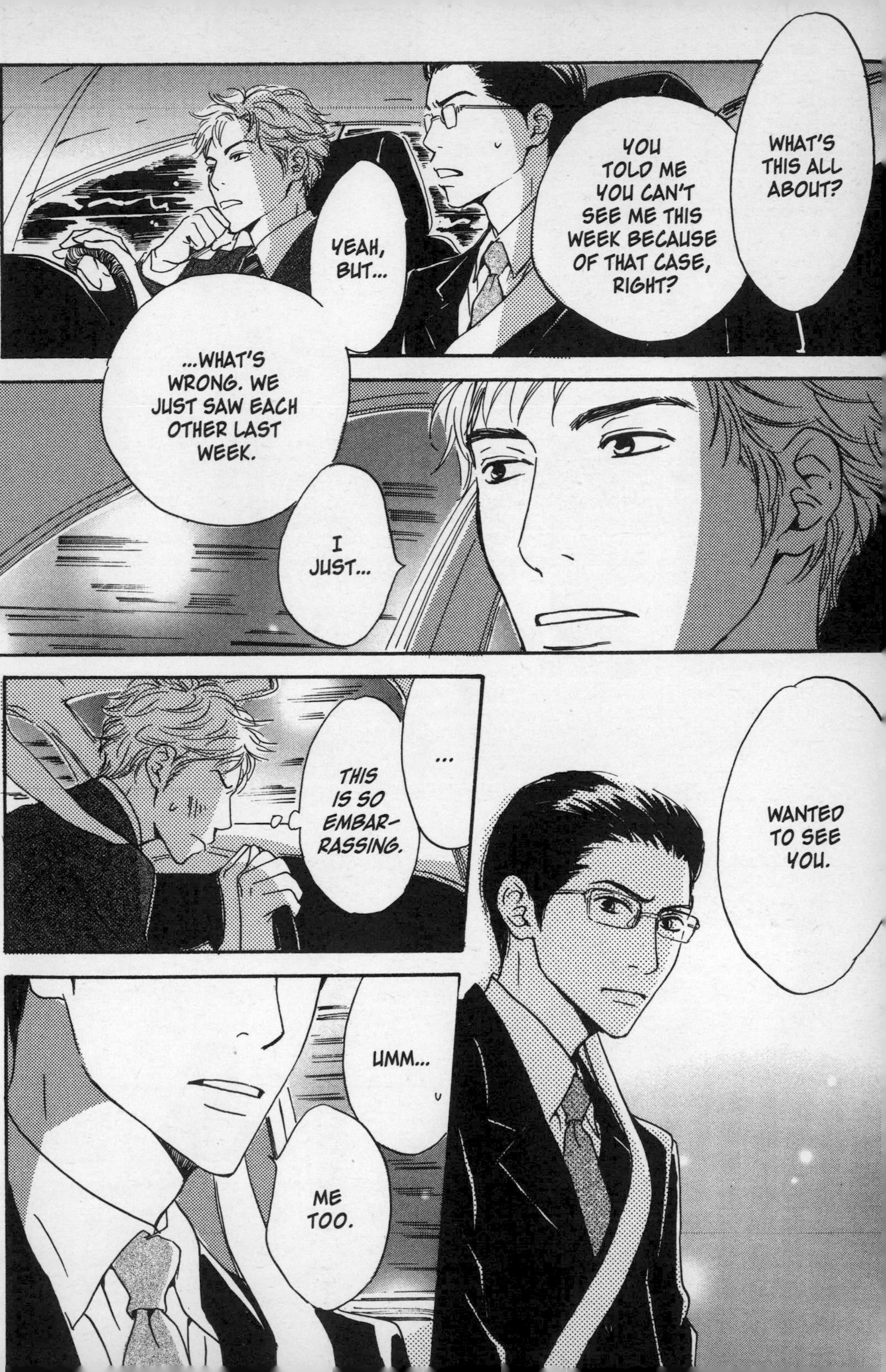
WHAT'S THIS ALL ABOUT?
YOU TOLD ME YOU CAN'T SEE ME THIS WEEK BECAUSE OF THAT CASE, RIGHT?
YEAH, BUT...
...WHAT'S WRONG. WE JUST SAW EACH OTHER LAST WEEK.
I JUST...
WANTED TO SEE YOU.
...
THIS IS SO EMBAR-RASSING.
UMM...
ME TOO.

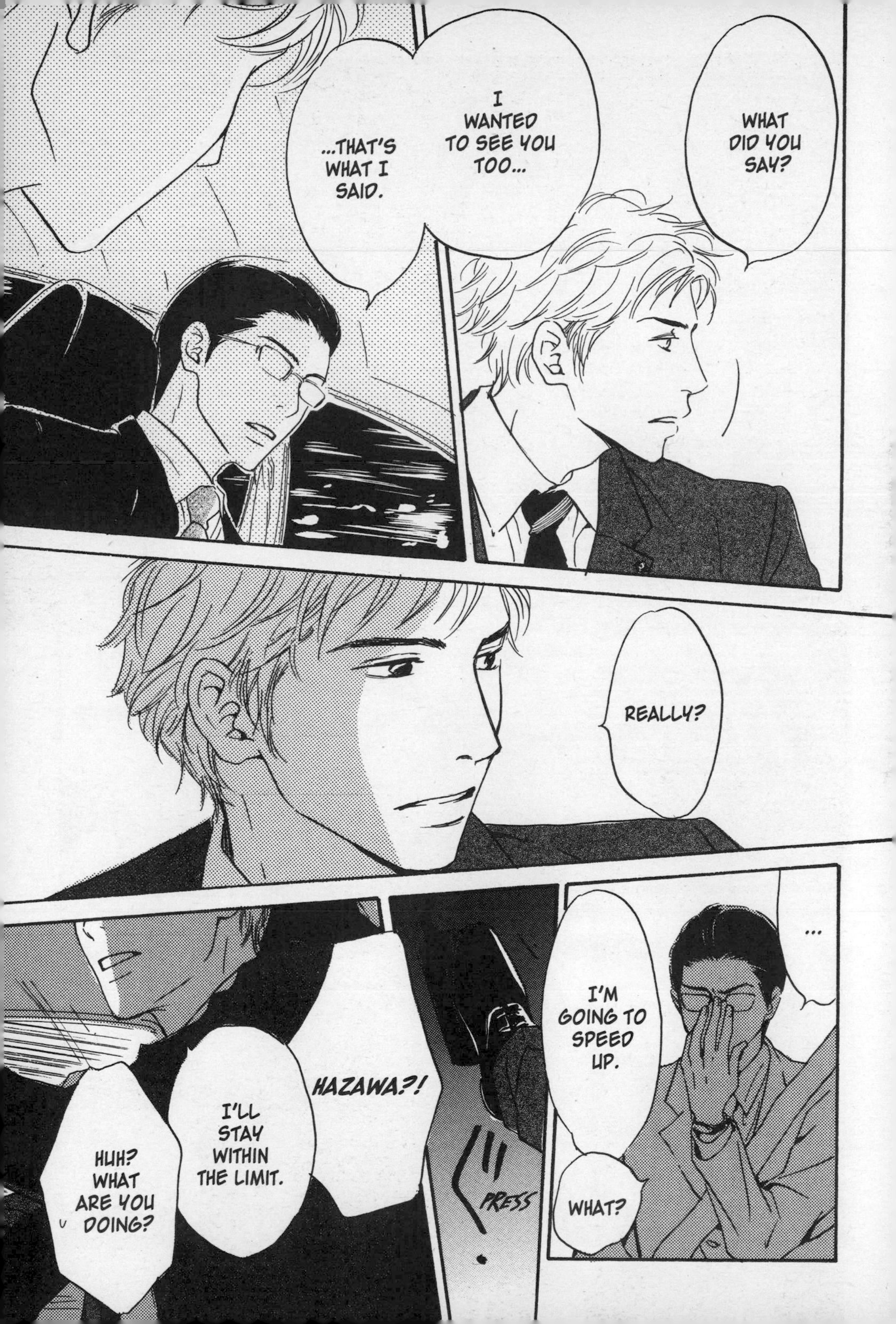
WHAT DID YOU SAY?
I WANTED TO SEE YOU TOO...
...THAT'S WHAT I SAID.
REALLY?
...
I'M GOING TO SPEED UP.
WHAT?
I'LL STAY WITHIN THE LIMIT.
PRESS
HAZAWA?!
HUH? WHAT ARE YOU DOING?

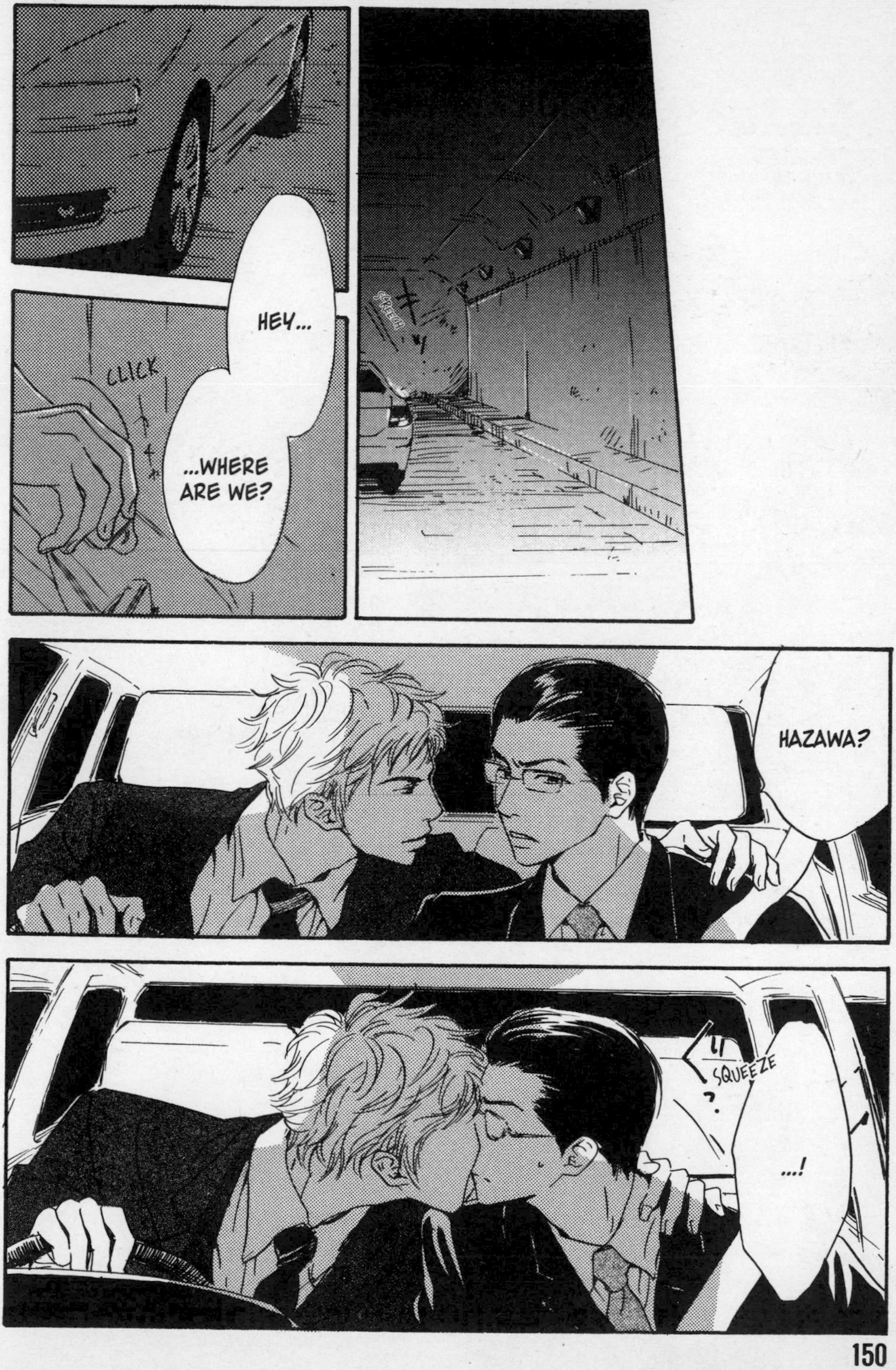
SCREECH
CLICK
HEY...
...WHERE ARE WE?
HAZAWA?
SQUEEZE
...!

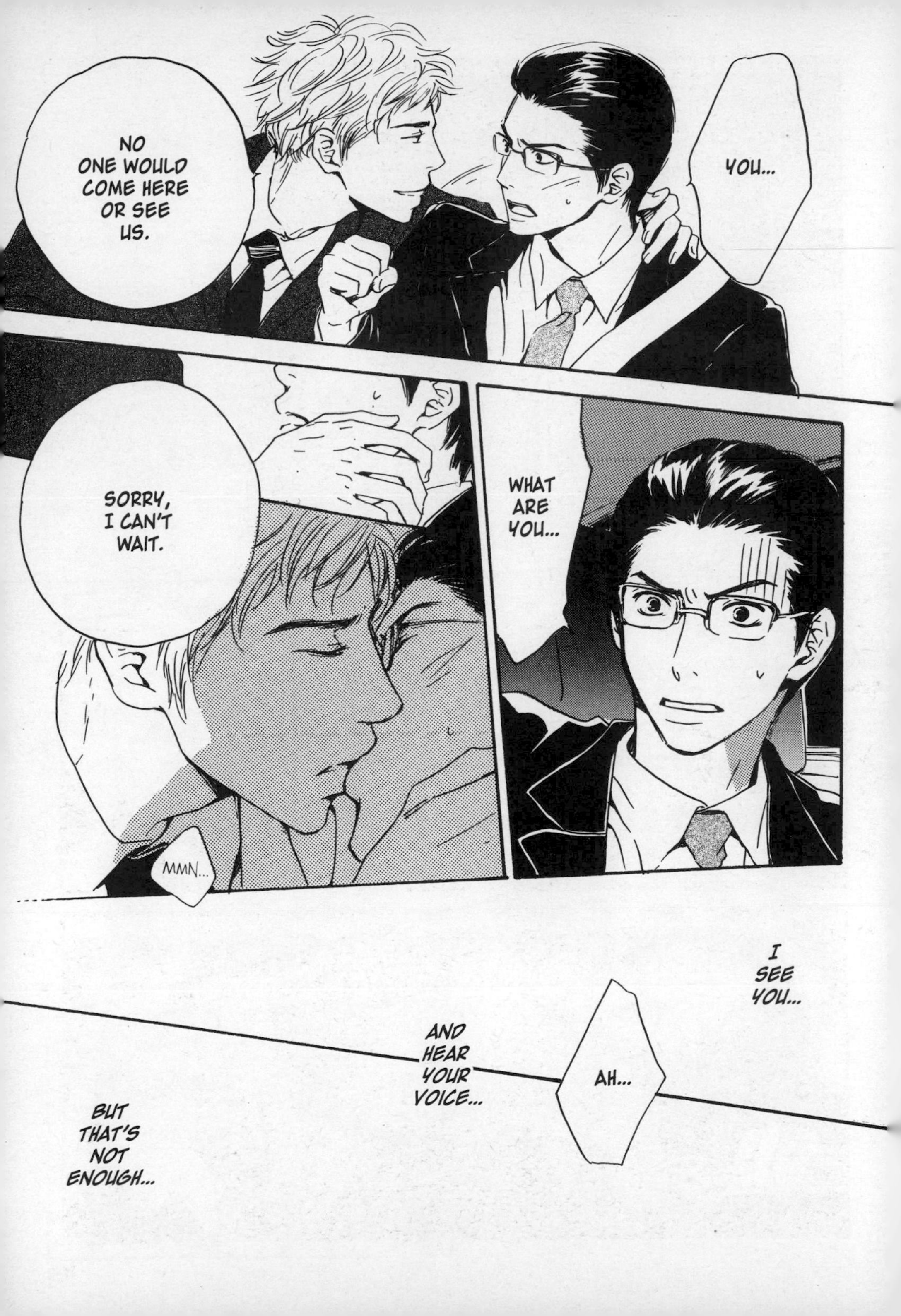
YOU...
NO ONE WOULD COME HERE OR SEE US.
WHAT ARE YOU...
SORRY, I CAN'T WAIT.
MMN...
I SEE YOU...
AH...
AND HEAR YOUR VOICE...
BUT THAT'S NOT ENOUGH...

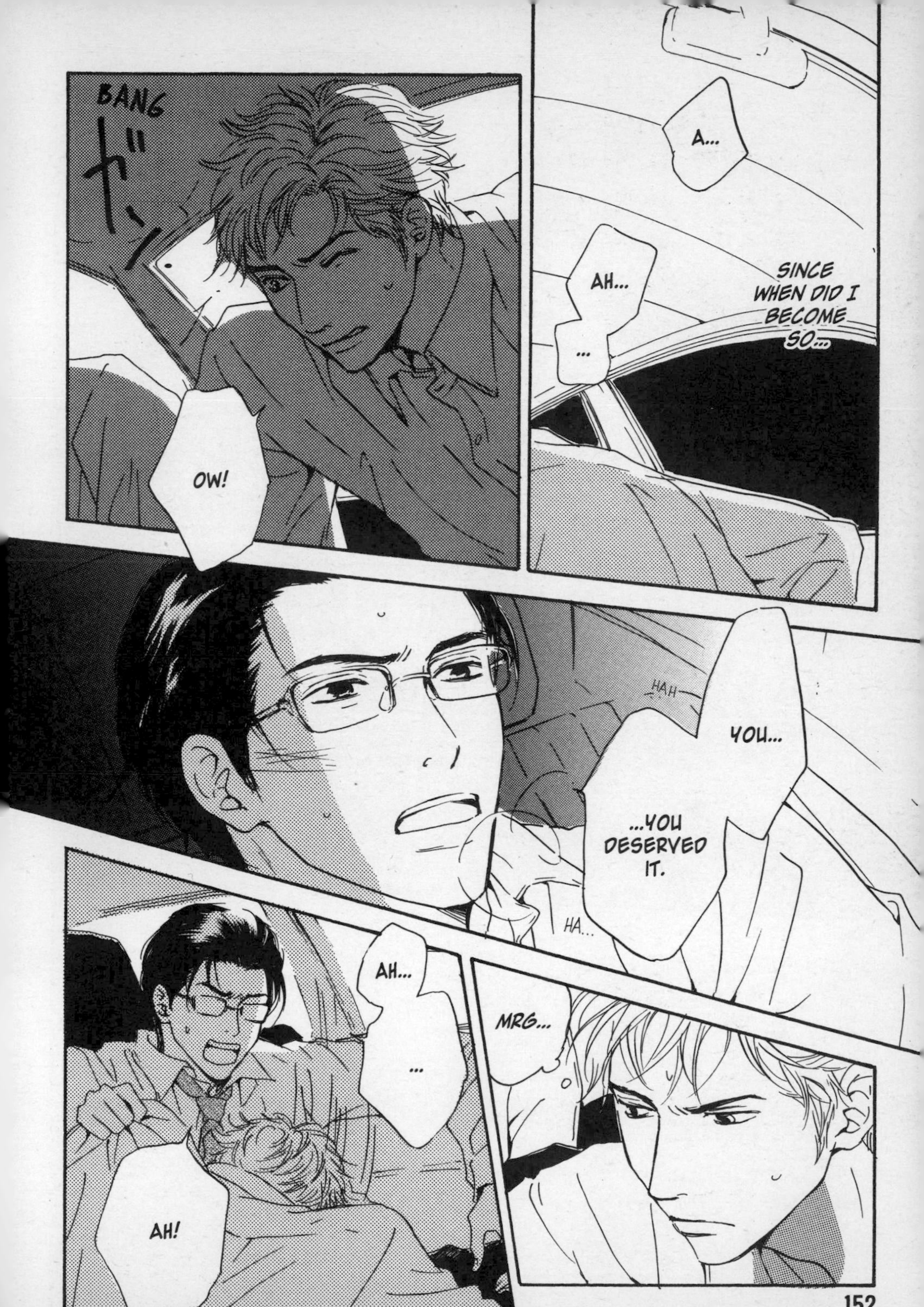
A...
AH...
...
SINCE WHEN DID I BECOME SO...
BANG
ガン
OW!
HAH
YOU...
...YOU DESERVED IT.
HA...
MRG...
AH...
...
AH!

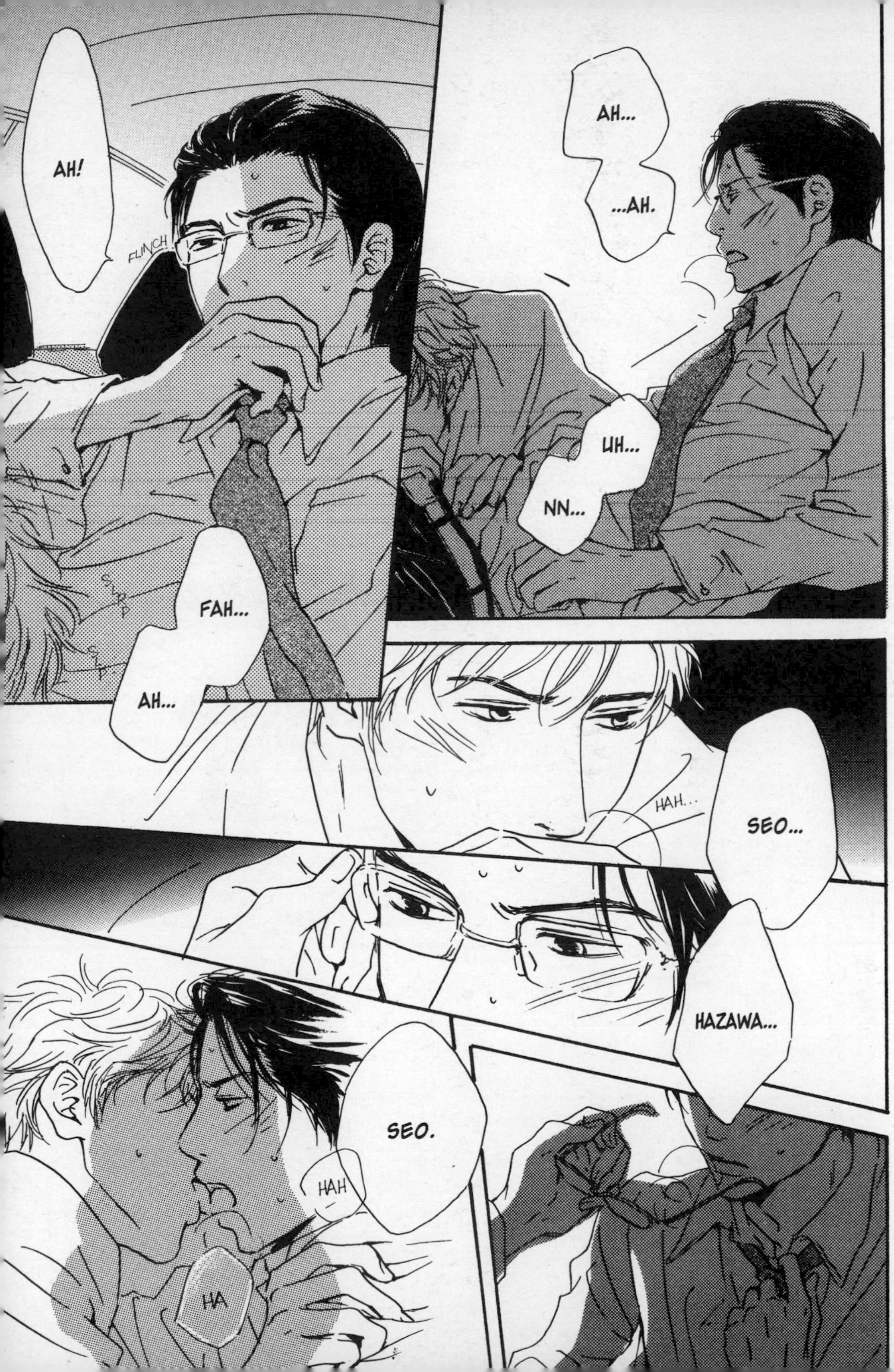
AH...
...AH.
UH...
NN...
AH!
FLINCH
FAH...
AH...
HAH...
SEO...
HAZAWA...
SEO.
HAH
HA

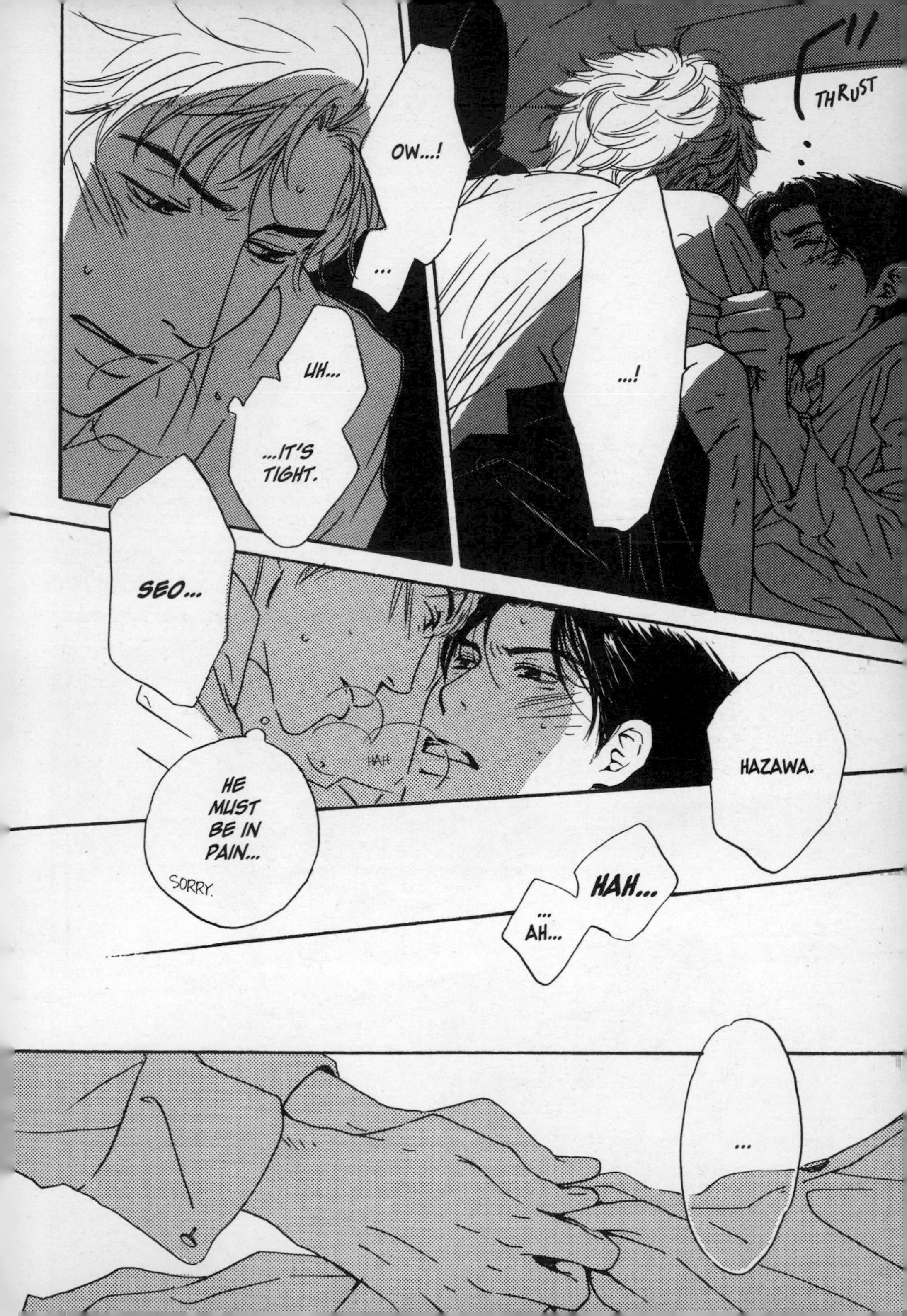
THRUST
OW...!
...
...!
UH...
...IT'S TIGHT.
HAZAWA.
SEO...
HAH
HAH...
... AH...
HE MUST BE IN PAIN...
SORRY.
...

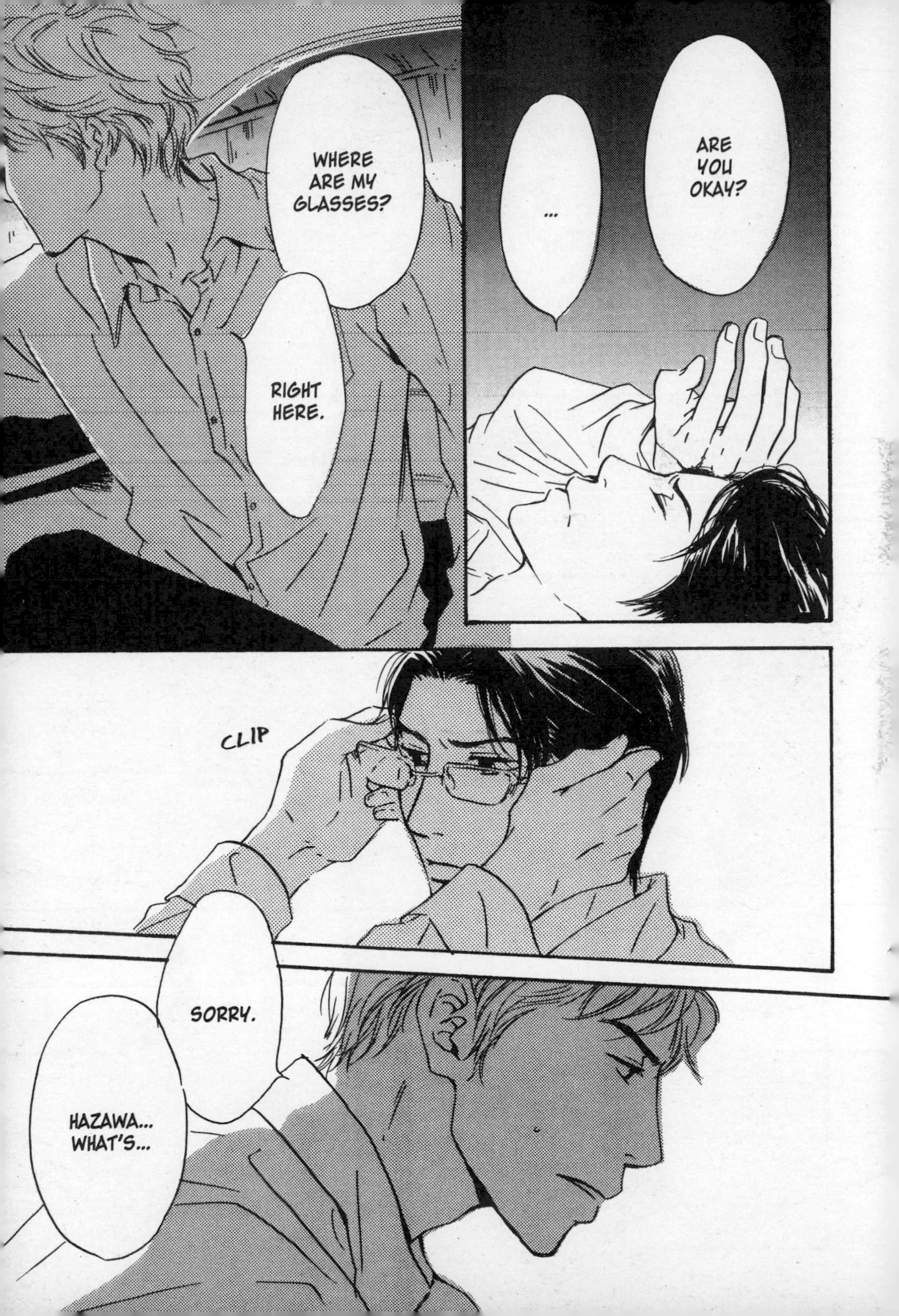
ARE YOU OKAY?
...
WHERE ARE MY GLASSES?
RIGHT HERE.
CLIP
SORRY.
HAZAWA... WHAT'S...

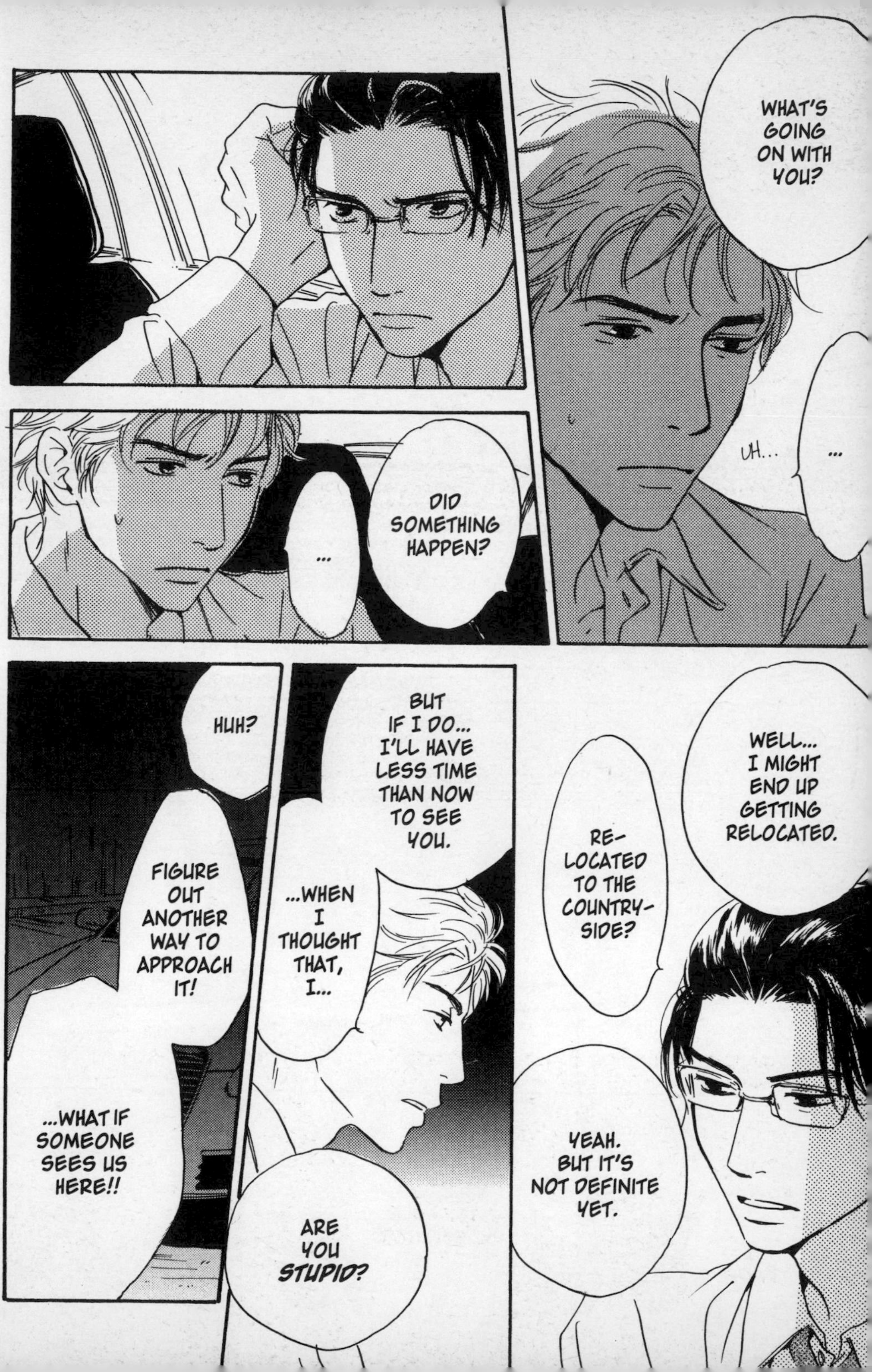
WHAT'S GOING ON WITH YOU?
...
UH...
DID SOMETHING HAPPEN?
...
WELL... I MIGHT END UP GETTING RELOCATED.
RE-LOCATED TO THE COUNTRY-SIDE?
YEAH. BUT IT'S NOT DEFINITE YET.
BUT IF I DO... I'LL HAVE LESS TIME THAN NOW TO SEE YOU.
...WHEN I THOUGHT THAT, I...
ARE YOU STUPID?
HUH?
FIGURE OUT ANOTHER WAY TO APPROACH IT!
...WHAT IF SOMEONE SEES US HERE!!

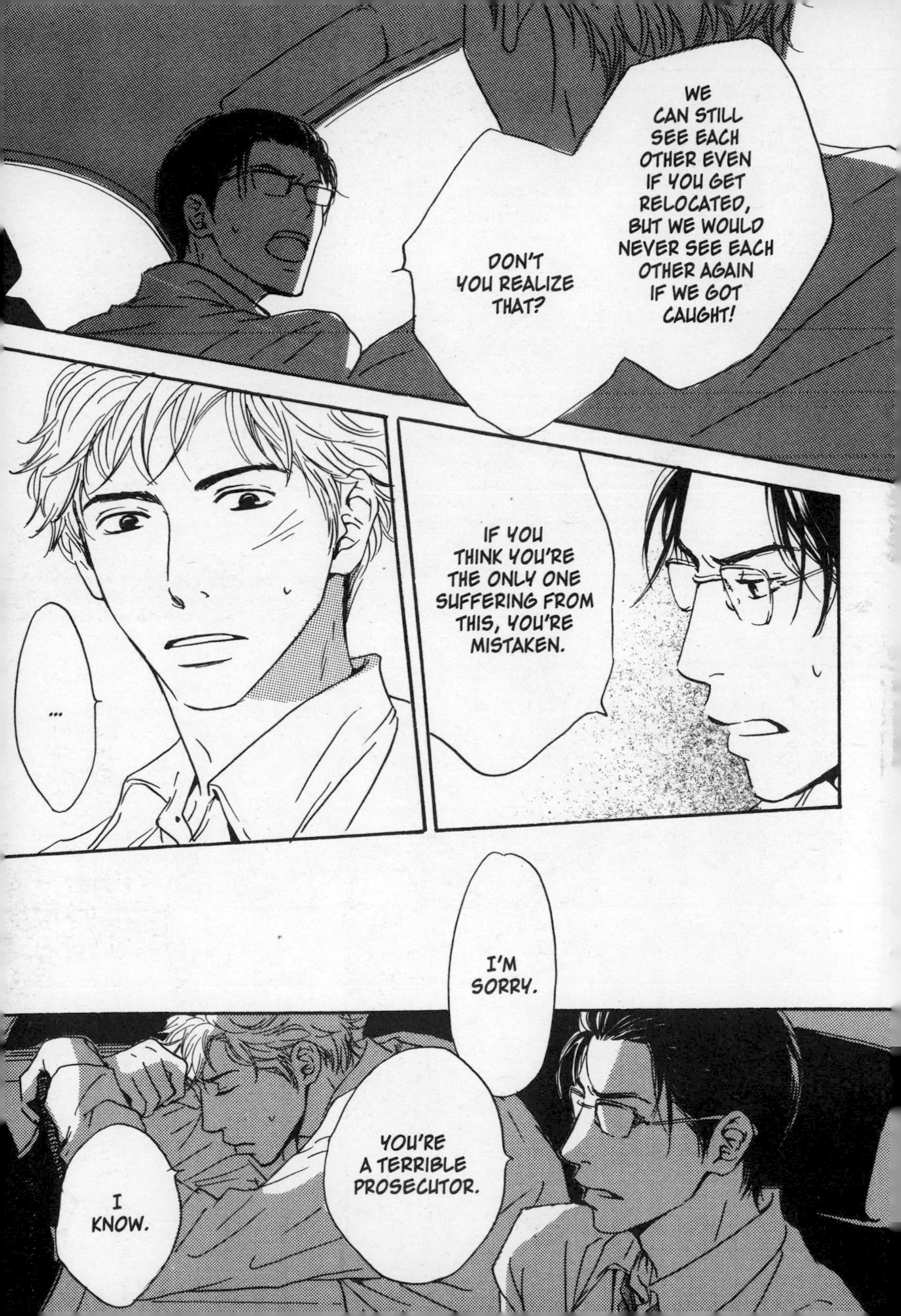
WE CAN STILL SEE EACH OTHER EVEN IF YOU GET RELOCATED, BUT WE WOULD NEVER SEE EACH OTHER AGAIN IF WE GOT CAUGHT!
DON'T YOU REALIZE THAT?
IF YOU THINK YOU'RE THE ONLY ONE SUFFERING FROM THIS, YOU'RE MISTAKEN.
...
I'M SORRY.
YOU'RE A TERRIBLE PROSECUTOR.
I KNOW.

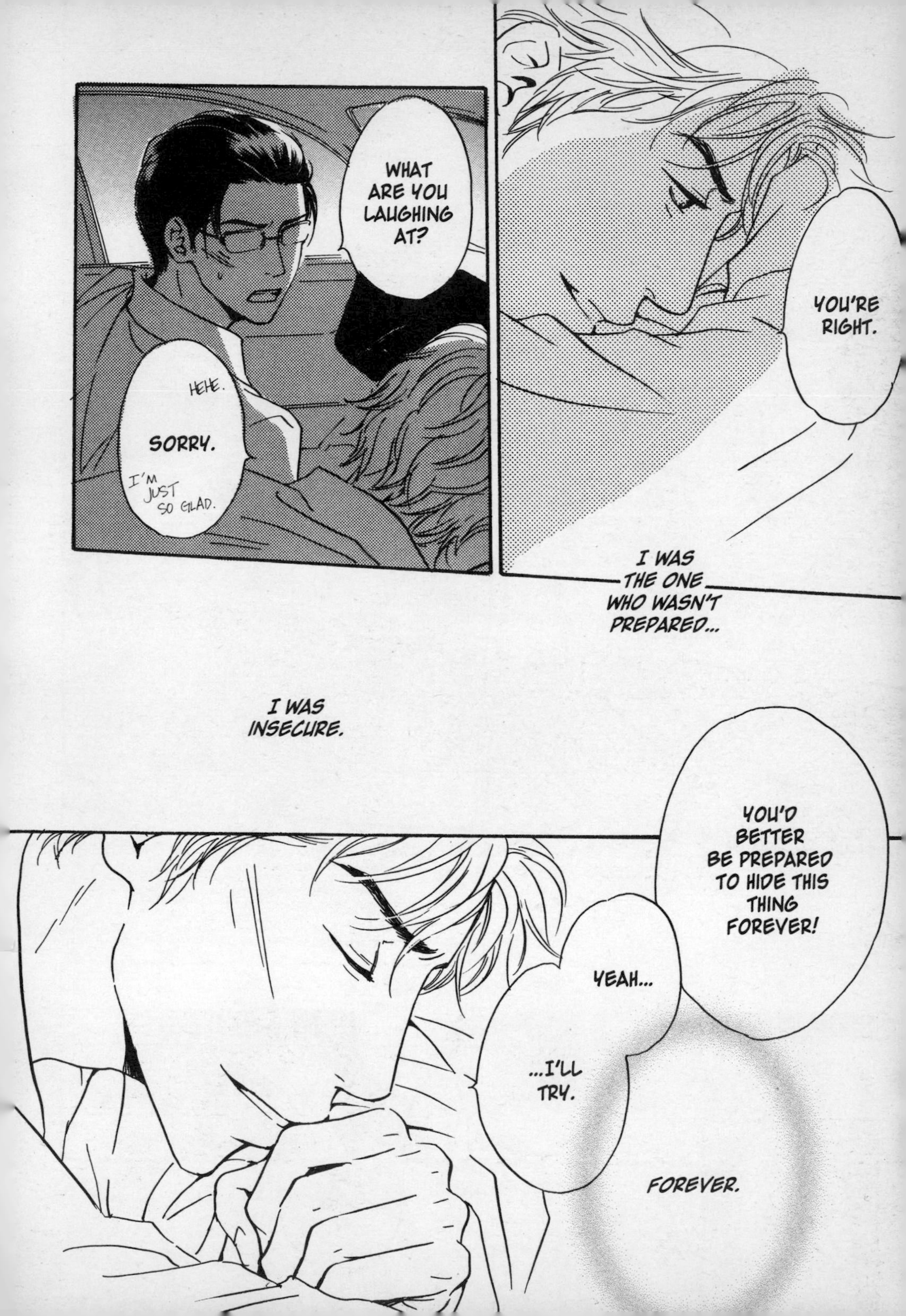
YOU'RE RIGHT.
WHAT ARE YOU LAUGHING AT?
HEHE.
SORRY.
I'M JUST SO GLAD.
I WAS THE ONE WHO WASN'T PREPARED...
I WAS INSECURE.
YOU'D BETTER BE PREPARED TO HIDE THIS THING FOREVER!
YEAH...
...I'LL TRY.
FOREVER.

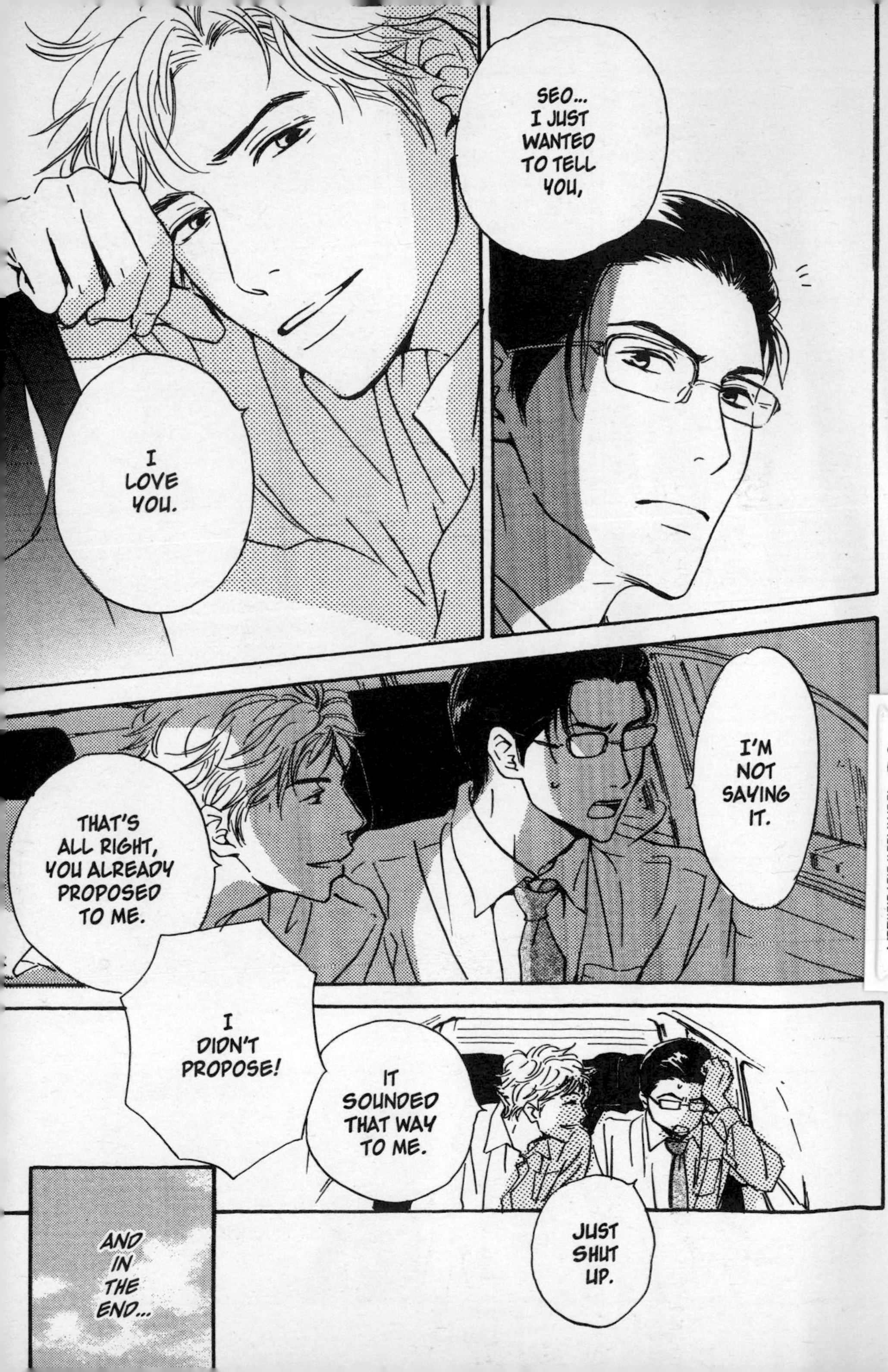
SEO... I JUST WANTED TO TELL YOU,
I LOVE YOU.
I'M NOT SAYING IT.
THAT'S ALL RIGHT, YOU ALREADY PROPOSED TO ME.
I DIDN'T PROPOSE!
IT SOUNDED THAT WAY TO ME.
JUST SHUT UP.
AND IN THE END...

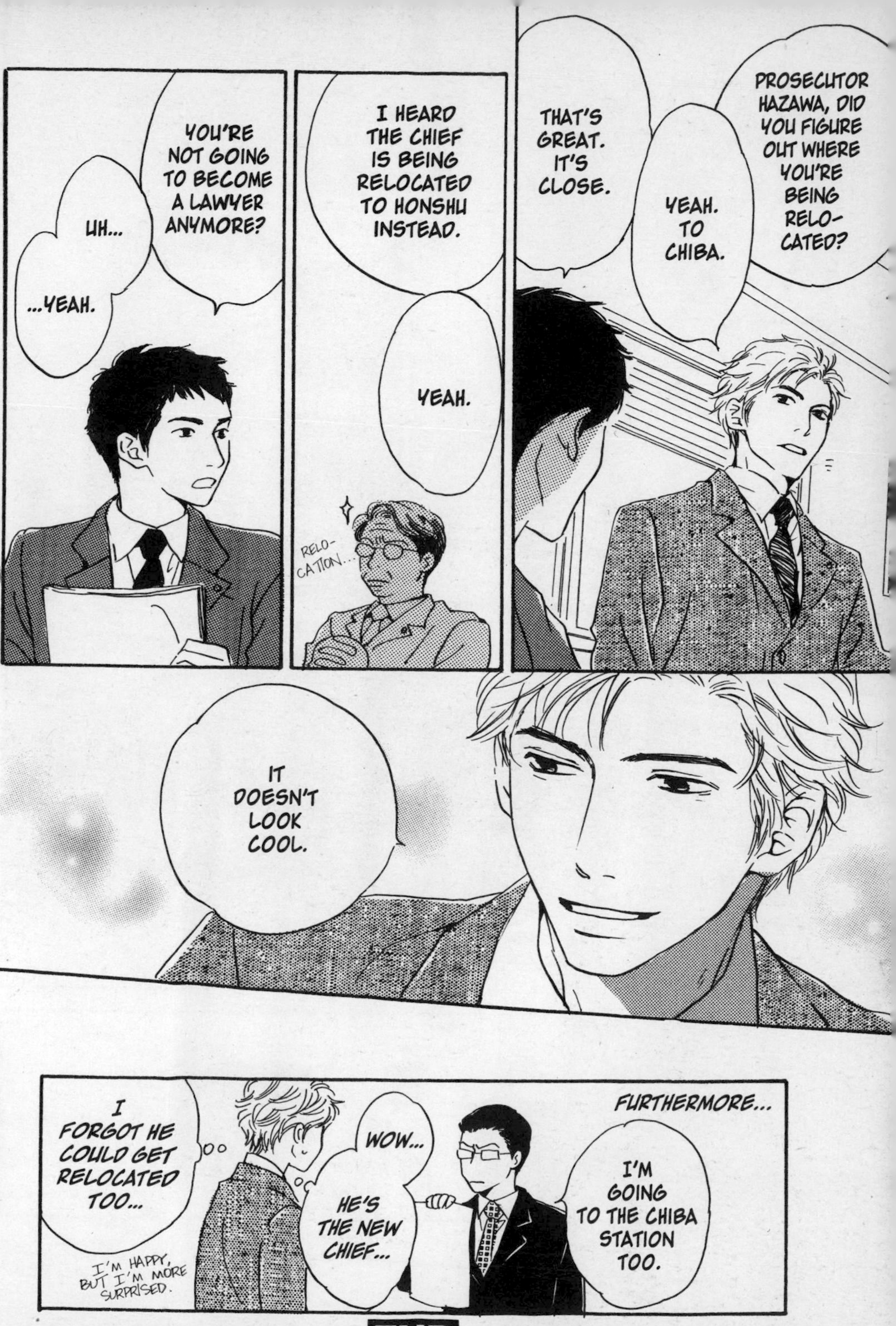
PROSECUTOR HAZAWA, DID YOU FIGURE OUT WHERE YOU'RE BEING RELOCATED?
YEAH. TO CHIBA.
THAT'S GREAT. IT'S CLOSE.
I HEARD THE CHIEF IS BEING RELOCATED TO HONSHU INSTEAD.
YEAH.
RELOCATION...
YOU'RE NOT GOING TO BECOME A LAWYER ANYMORE?
UH...
...YEAH.
IT DOESN'T LOOK COOL.
FURTHERMORE...
I'M GOING TO THE CHIBA STATION TOO.
WOW...
HE'S THE NEW CHIEF...
I FORGOT HE COULD GET RELOCATED TOO...
I'M HAPPY, BUT I'M MORE SURPRISED.

END

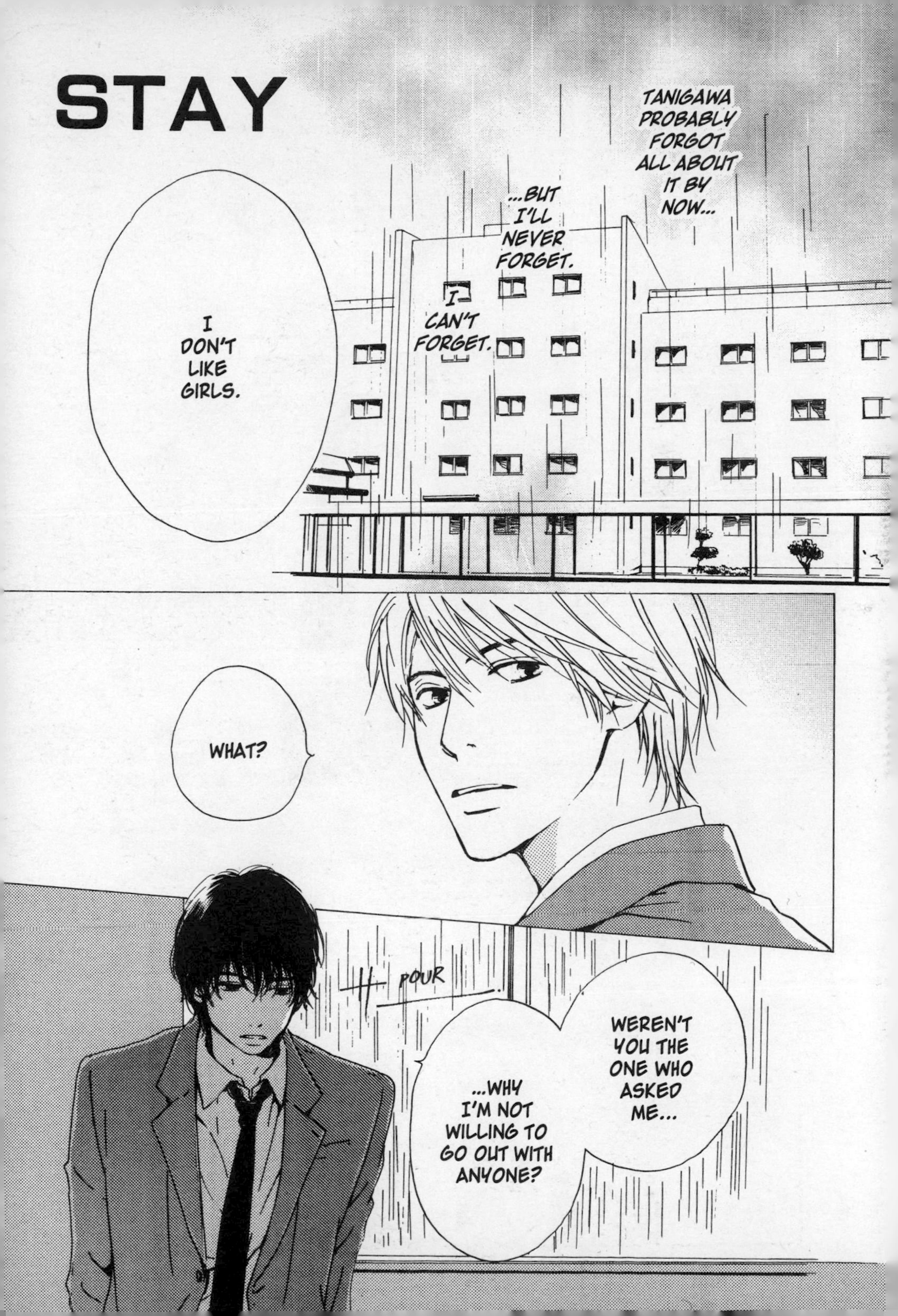
STAY
TANIGAWA PROBABLY FORGOT ALL ABOUT IT BY NOW...
...BUT I'LL NEVER FORGET.
I CAN'T FORGET.
I DON'T LIKE GIRLS.
WHAT?
POUR
WEREN'T YOU THE ONE WHO ASKED ME...
...WHY I'M NOT WILLING TO GO OUT WITH ANYONE?

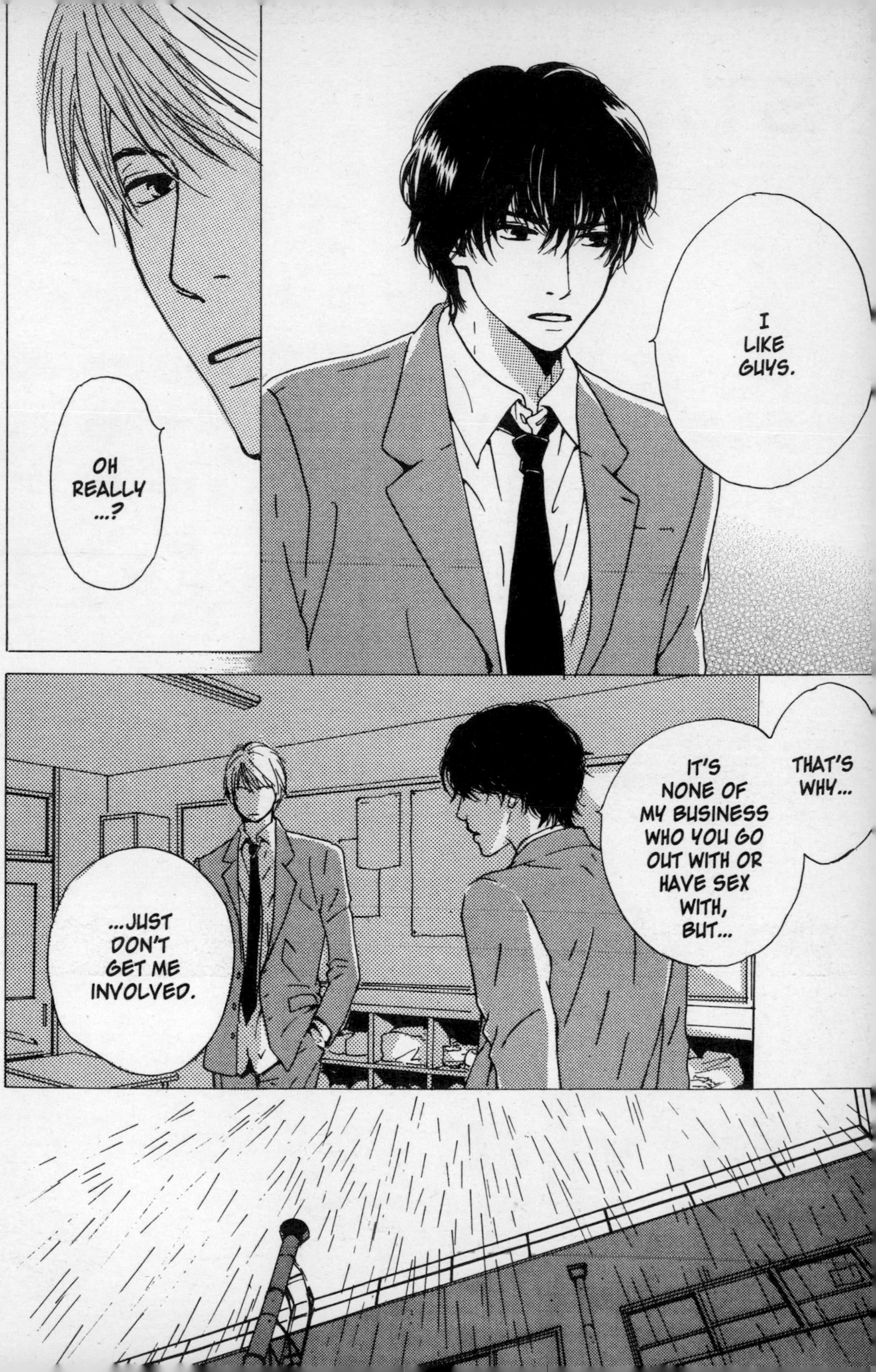
I LIKE GUYS.
OH REALLY ...?
THAT'S WHY...
IT'S NONE OF MY BUSINESS WHO YOU GO OUT WITH OR HAVE SEX WITH, BUT...
...JUST DON'T GET ME INVOLVED.

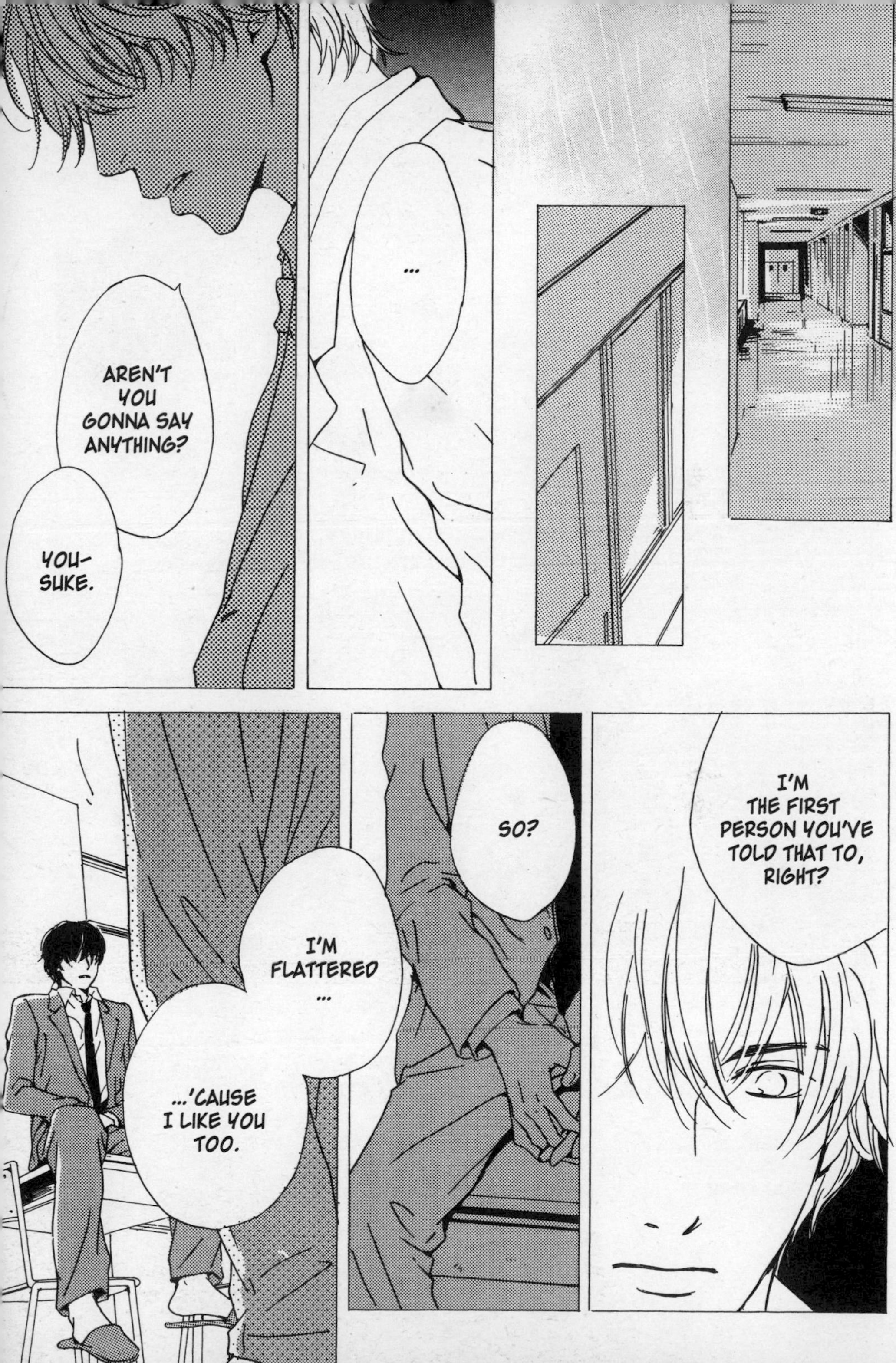
...
AREN'T YOU GONNA SAY ANYTHING?
YOU-SUKE.
I'M THE FIRST PERSON YOU'VE TOLD THAT TO, RIGHT?
SO?
I'M FLATTERED ...
...'CAUSE I LIKE YOU TOO.

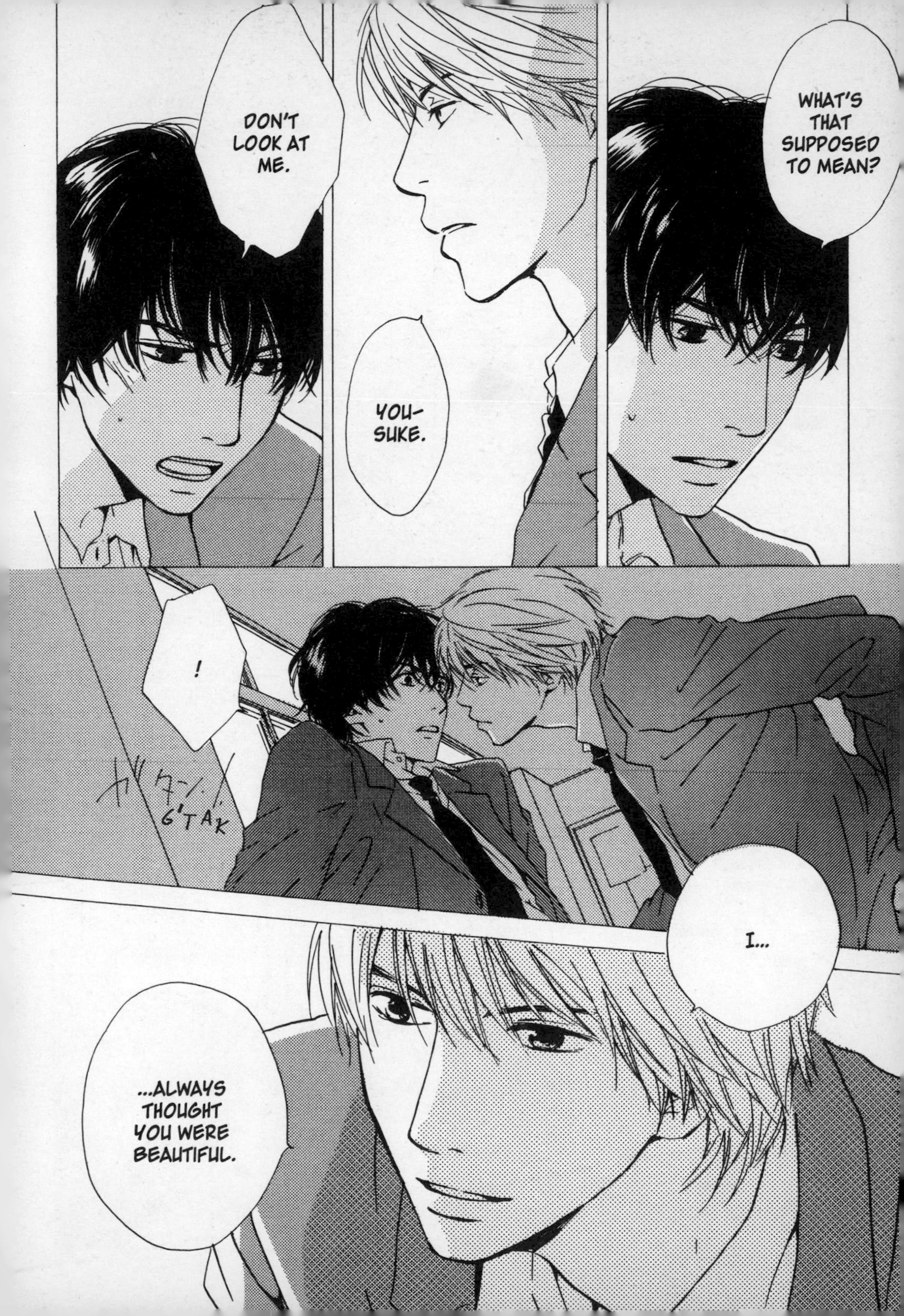
WHAT'S THAT SUPPOSED TO MEAN?
YOU-SUKE.
DON'T LOOK AT ME.
!
G'TAK
I...
...ALWAYS THOUGHT YOU WERE BEAUTIFUL.

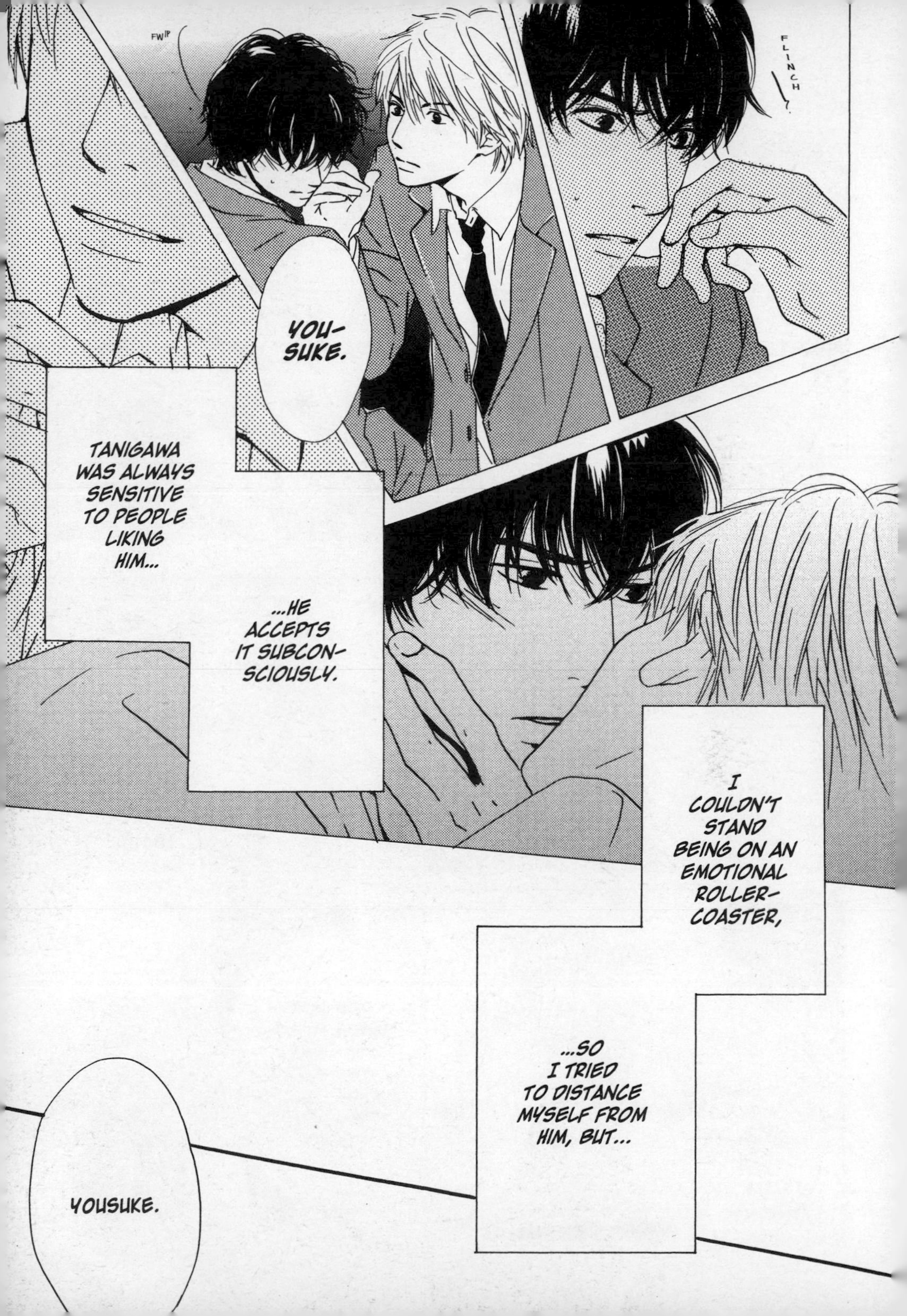
FLINCH
FWIP
YOU-SUKE.
TANIGAWA WAS ALWAYS SENSITIVE TO PEOPLE LIKING HIM...
...HE ACCEPTS IT SUBCONSCIOUSLY.
I COULDN'T STAND BEING ON AN EMOTIONAL ROLLER-COASTER,
...SO I TRIED TO DISTANCE MYSELF FROM HIM, BUT...
YOUSUKE.

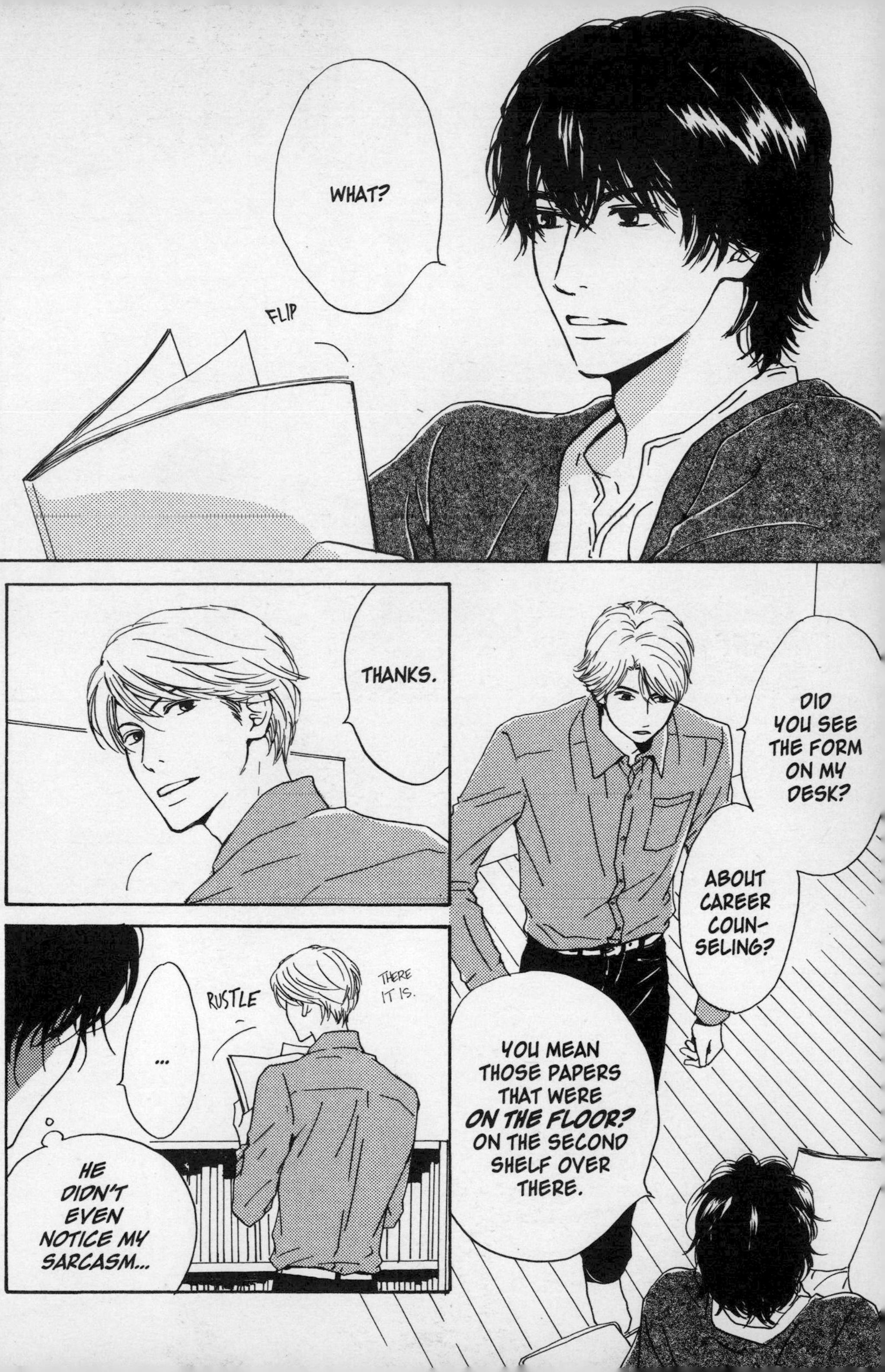
WHAT?
FLIP
DID YOU SEE THE FORM ON MY DESK?
ABOUT CAREER COUN-SELING?
YOU MEAN THOSE PAPERS THAT WERE *ON THE FLOOR?* ON THE SECOND SHELF OVER THERE.
THANKS.
THERE IT IS.
RUSTLE
...
HE DIDN'T EVEN NOTICE MY SARCASM...

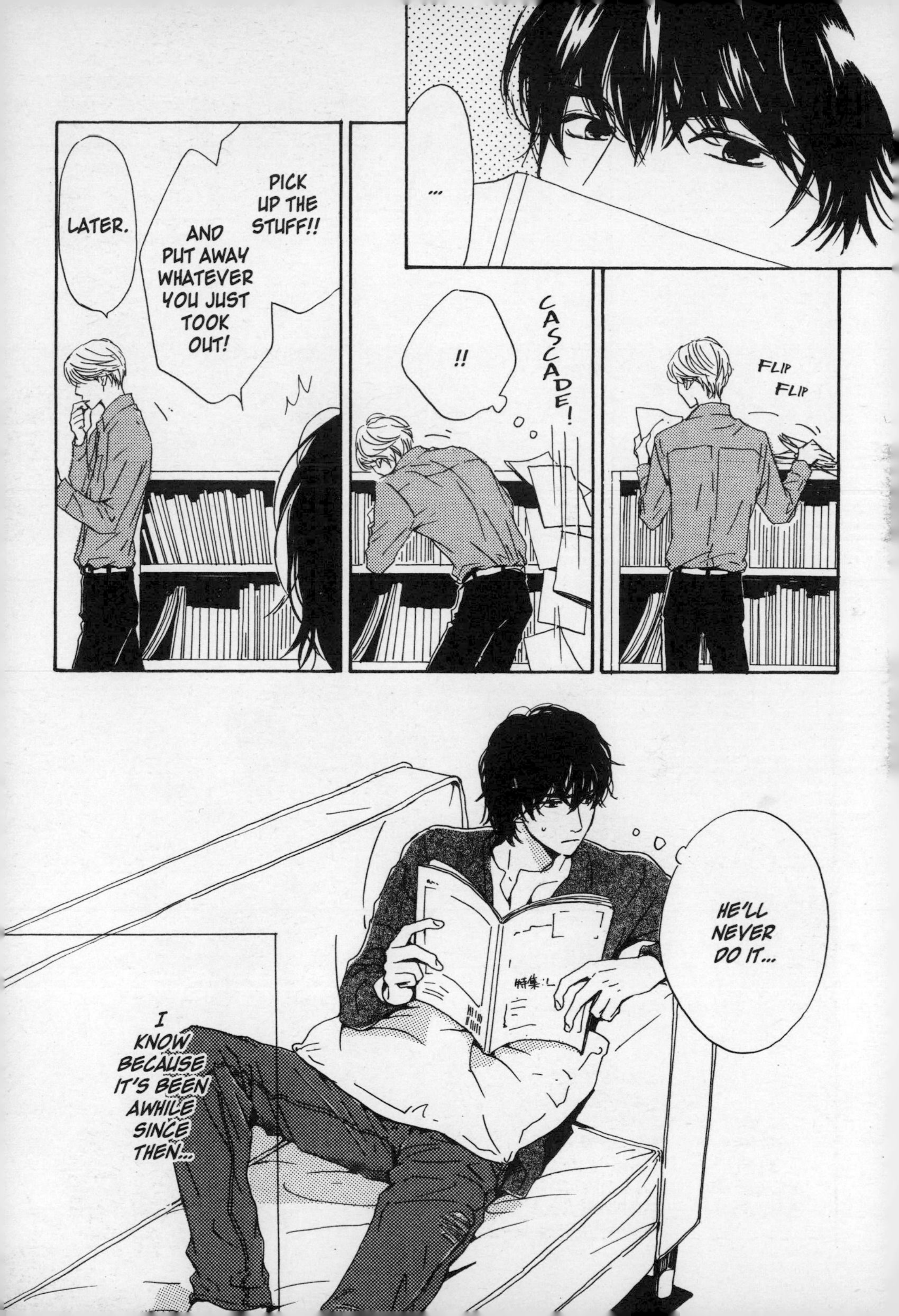
...
FLIP
FLIP
!!
CASCADE!
PICK UP THE STUFF!!
AND PUT AWAY WHATEVER YOU JUST TOOK OUT!
LATER.
HE'LL NEVER DO IT...
特集:L
I KNOW BECAUSE IT'S BEEN AWHILE SINCE THEN...

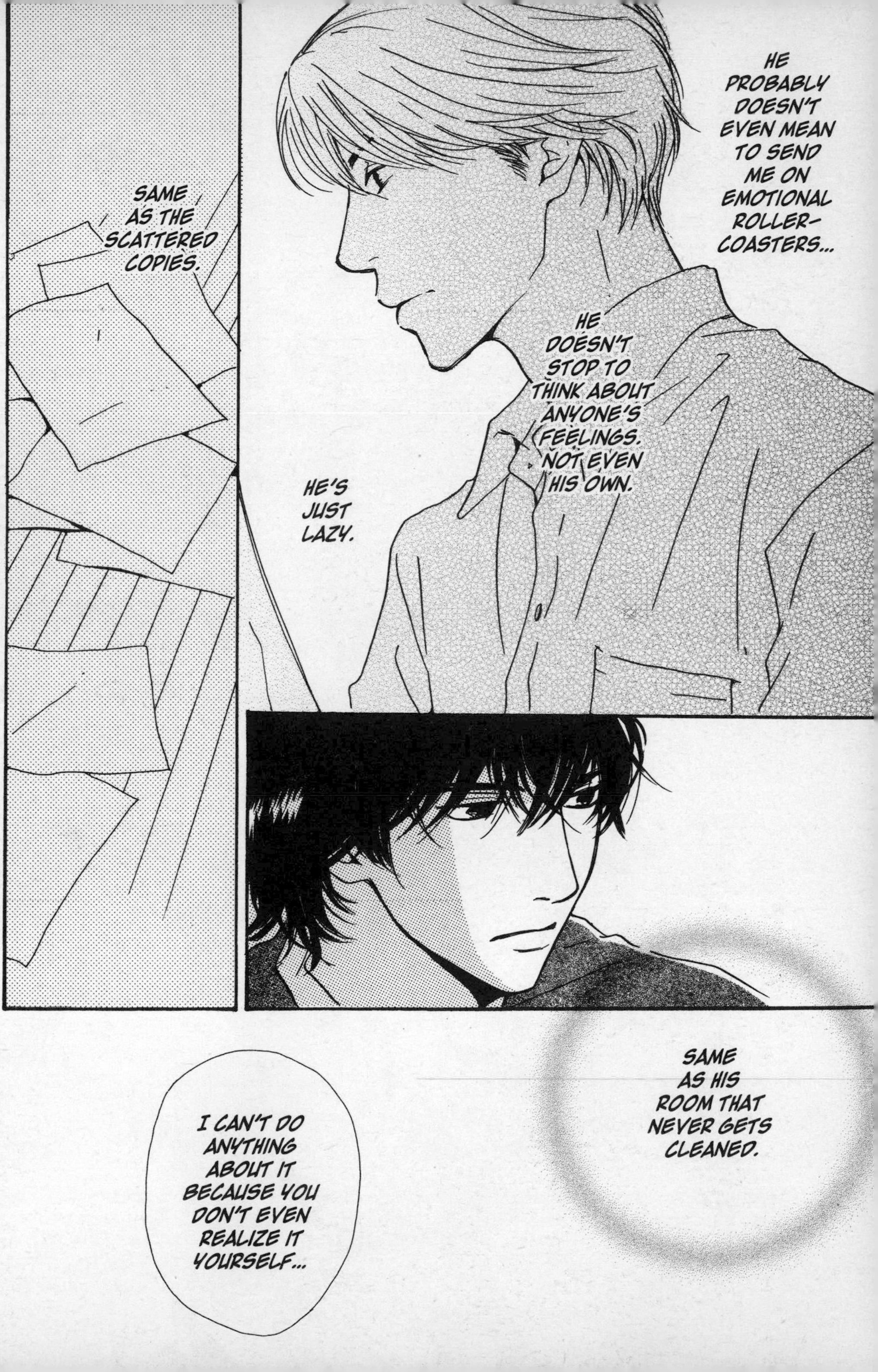
HE PROBABLY DOESN'T EVEN MEAN TO SEND ME ON EMOTIONAL ROLLER-COASTERS...
HE DOESN'T STOP TO THINK ABOUT ANYONE'S FEELINGS. NOT EVEN HIS OWN.
HE'S JUST LAZY.
SAME AS THE SCATTERED COPIES.
SAME AS HIS ROOM THAT NEVER GETS CLEANED.
I CAN'T DO ANYTHING ABOUT IT BECAUSE YOU DON'T EVEN REALIZE IT YOURSELF...

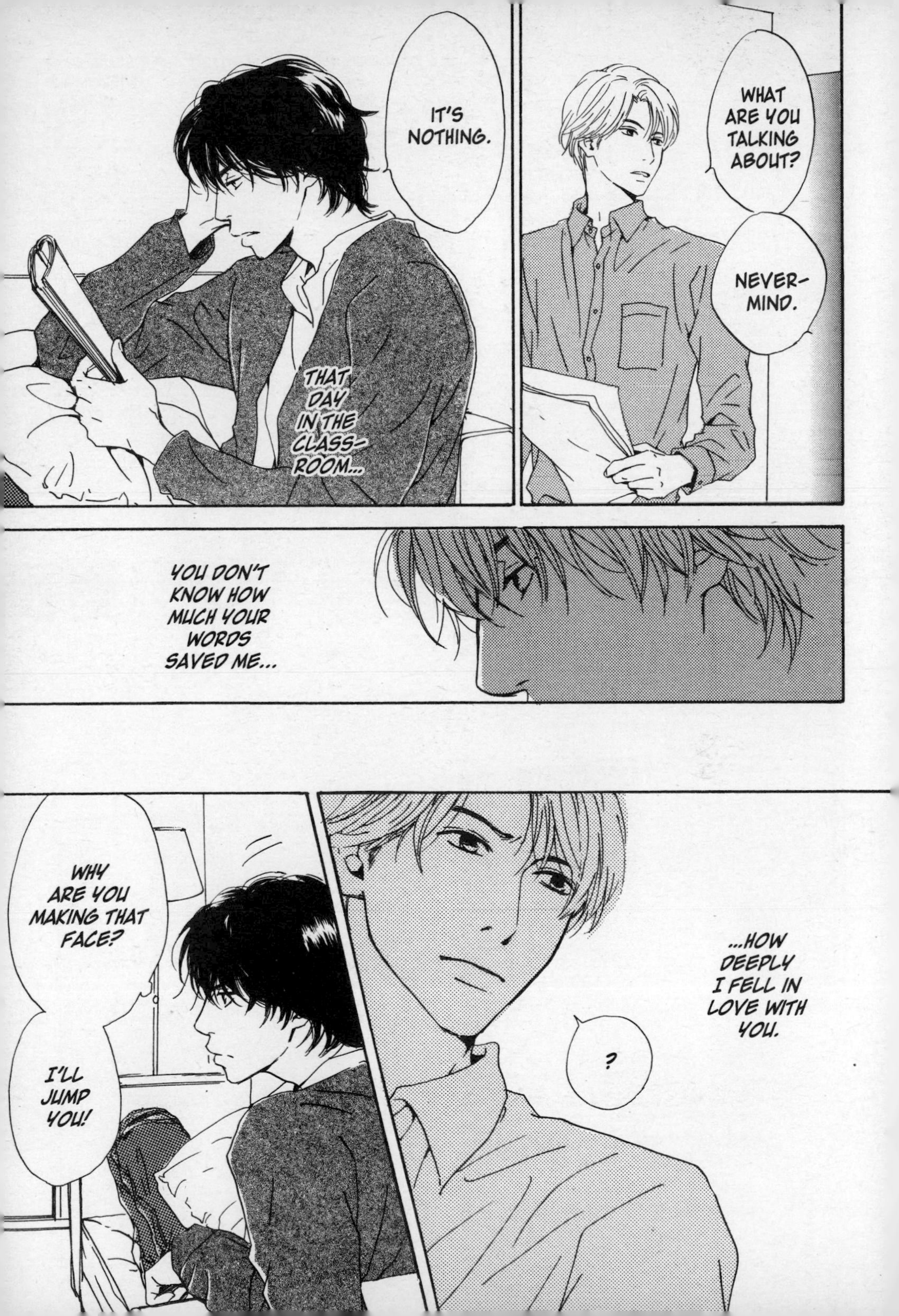
WHAT ARE YOU TALKING ABOUT?
NEVER-MIND.
IT'S NOTHING.
THAT DAY IN THE CLASS-ROOM...
YOU DON'T KNOW HOW MUCH YOUR WORDS SAVED ME...
...HOW DEEPLY I FELL IN LOVE WITH YOU.
?
WHY ARE YOU MAKING THAT FACE?
I'LL JUMP YOU!

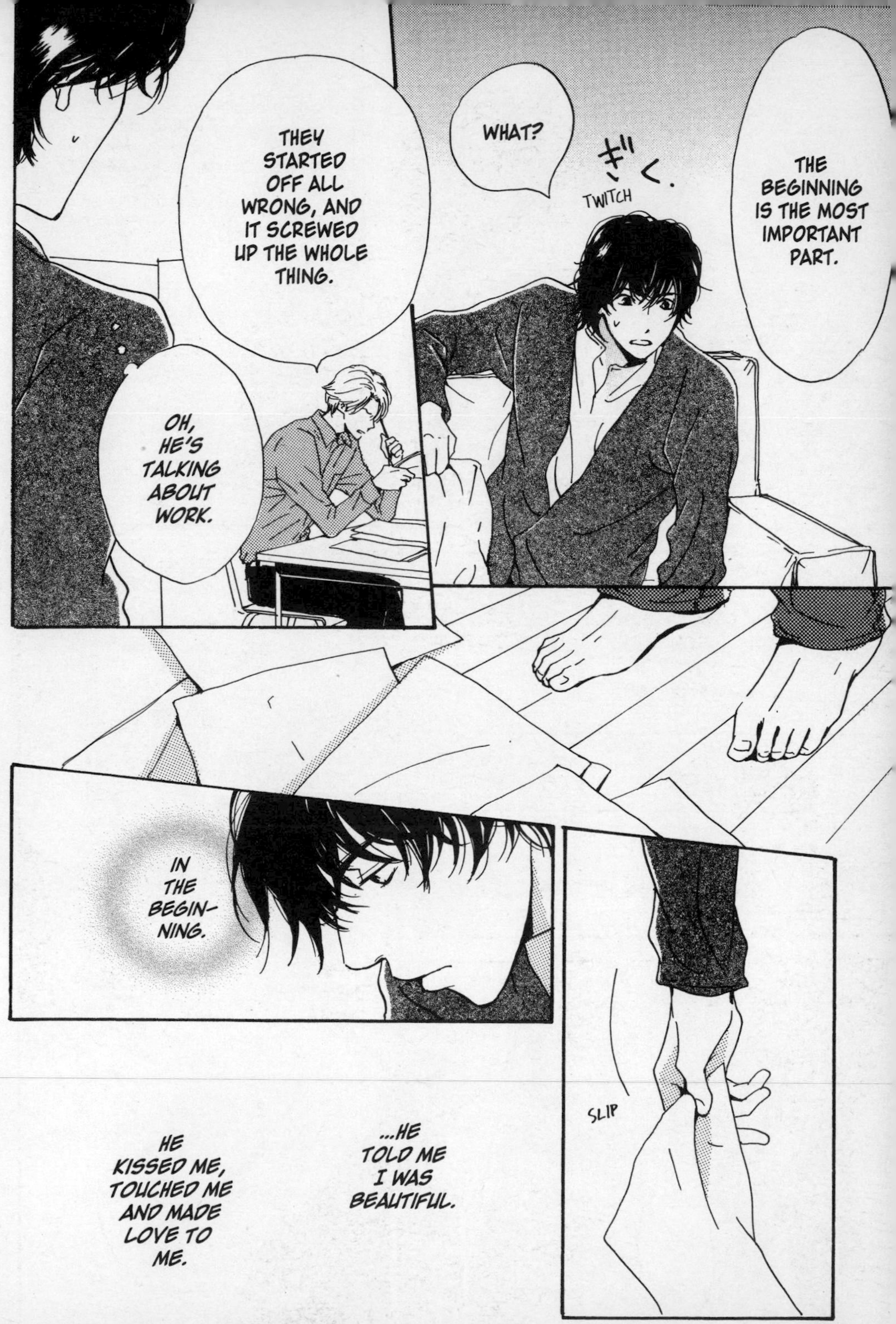
THE BEGINNING IS THE MOST IMPORTANT PART.
WHAT?
ぎく.
TWITCH
THEY STARTED OFF ALL WRONG, AND IT SCREWED UP THE WHOLE THING.
OH, HE'S TALKING ABOUT WORK.
SLIP
IN THE BEGIN-NING.
...HE TOLD ME I WAS BEAUTIFUL.
HE KISSED ME, TOUCHED ME AND MADE LOVE TO ME.

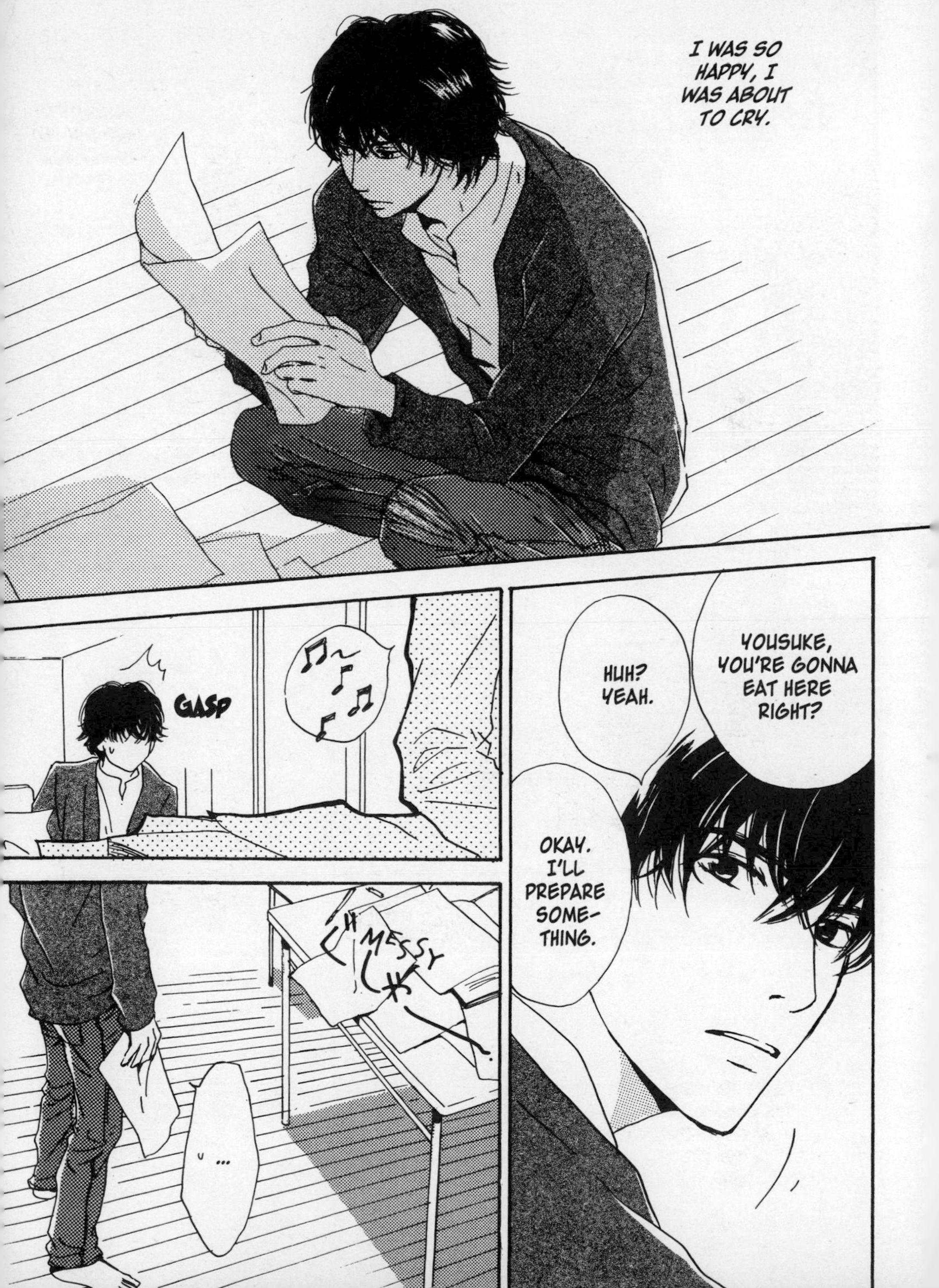
I WAS SO HAPPY, I WAS ABOUT TO CRY.
YOUSUKE, YOU'RE GONNA EAT HERE RIGHT?
HUH? YEAH.
OKAY. I'LL PREPARE SOMETHING.
GASP
MESSY
...

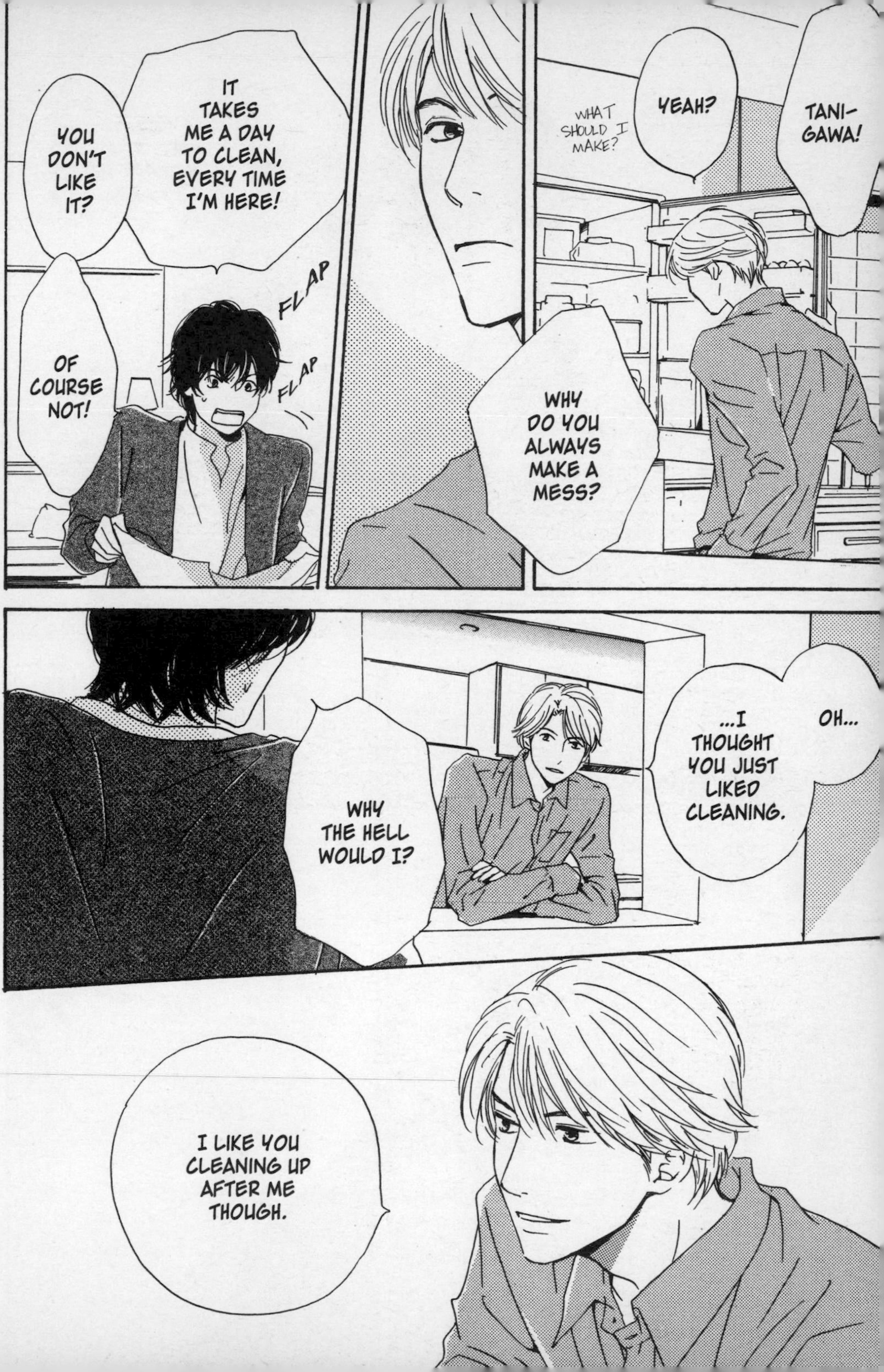
TANI-GAWA!
YEAH?
WHAT SHOULD I MAKE?
WHY DO YOU ALWAYS MAKE A MESS?
IT TAKES ME A DAY TO CLEAN, EVERY TIME I'M HERE!
YOU DON'T LIKE IT?
FLAP
FLAP
OF COURSE NOT!
OH...
...I THOUGHT YOU JUST LIKED CLEANING.
WHY THE HELL WOULD I?
I LIKE YOU CLEANING UP AFTER ME THOUGH.

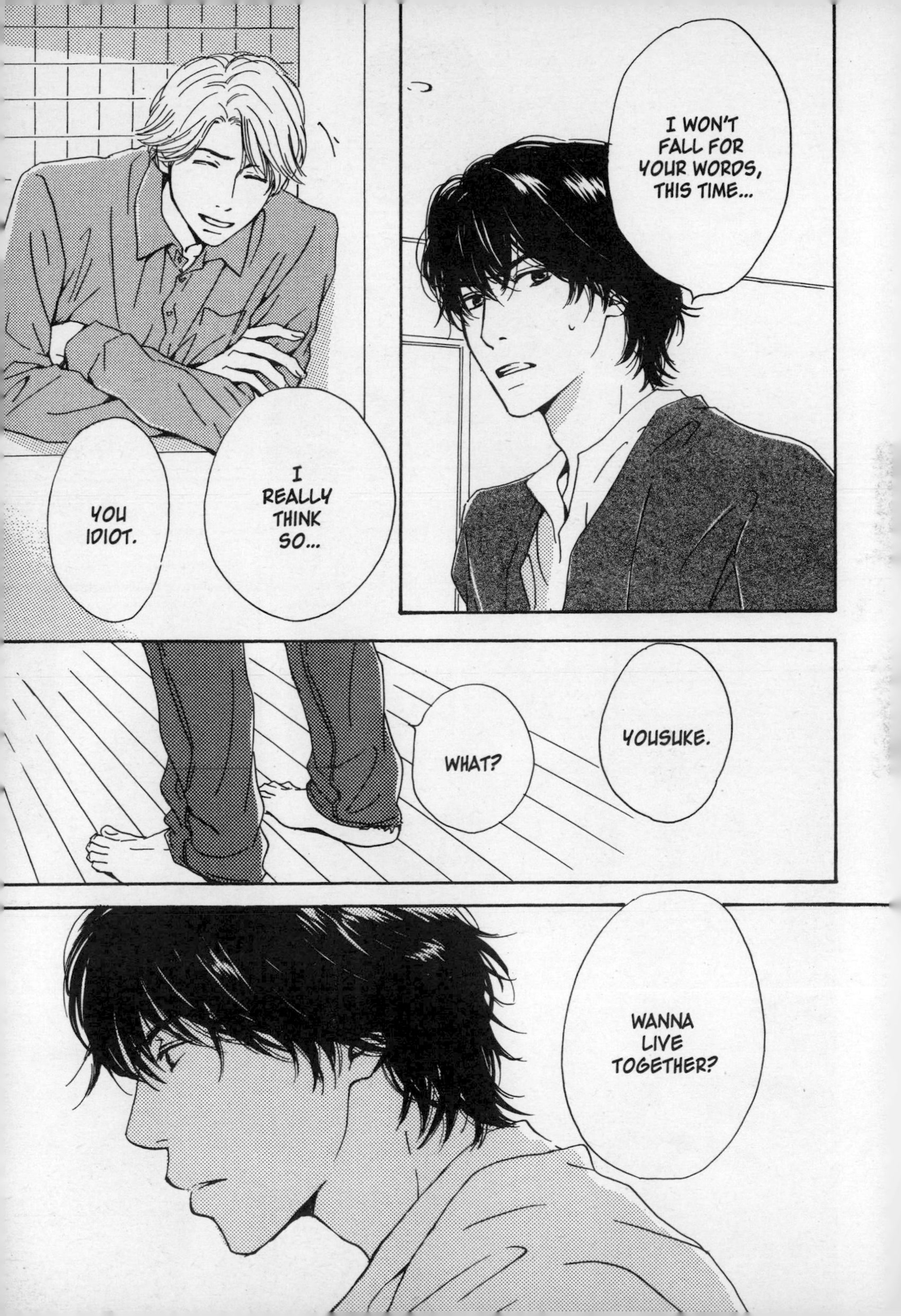
I WON'T FALL FOR YOUR WORDS, THIS TIME...
I REALLY THINK SO...
YOU IDIOT.
YOUSUKE.
WHAT?
WANNA LIVE TOGETHER?

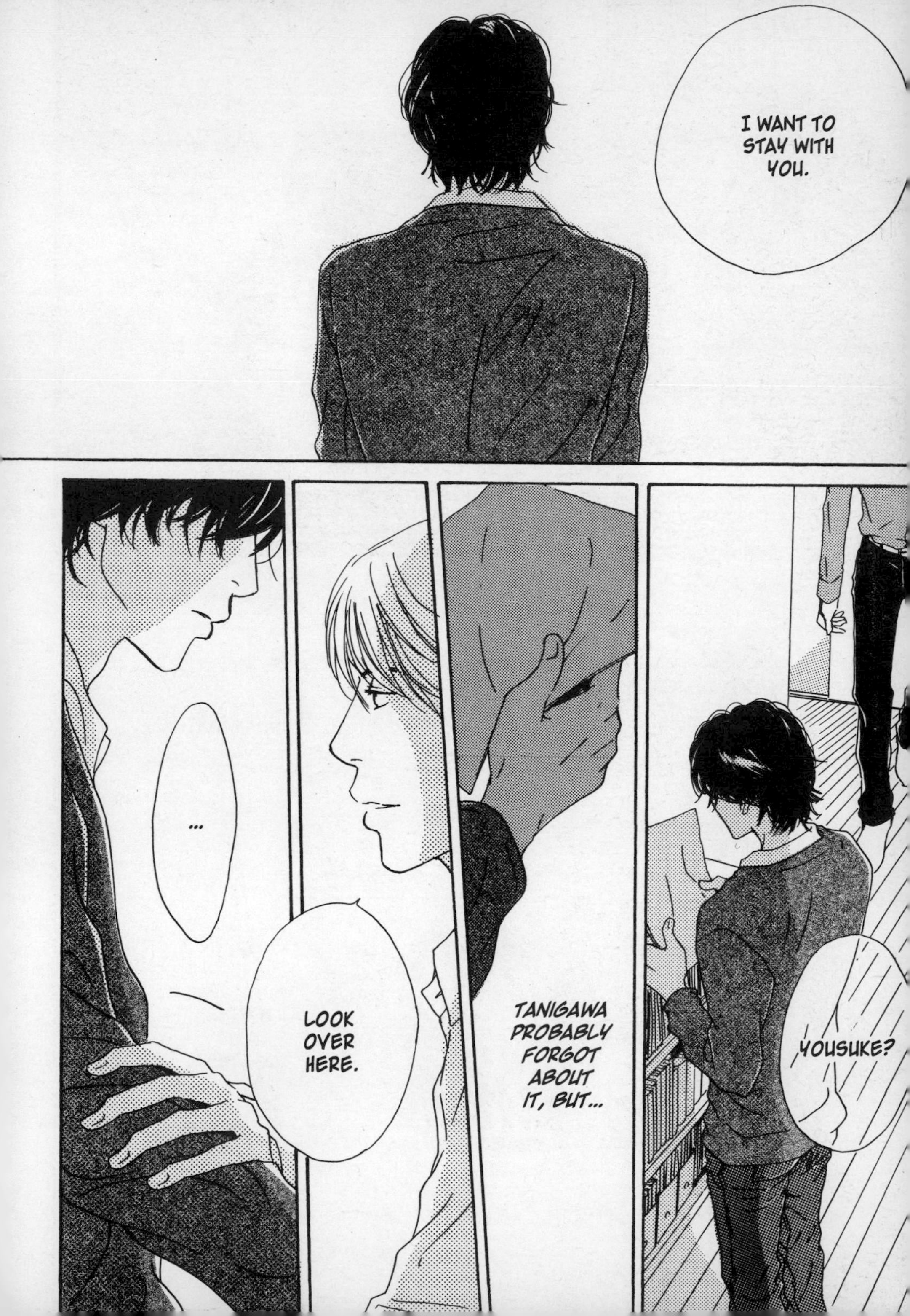
I WANT TO STAY WITH YOU.
YOUSUKE?
TANIGAWA PROBABLY FORGOT ABOUT IT, BUT...
LOOK OVER HERE.
...

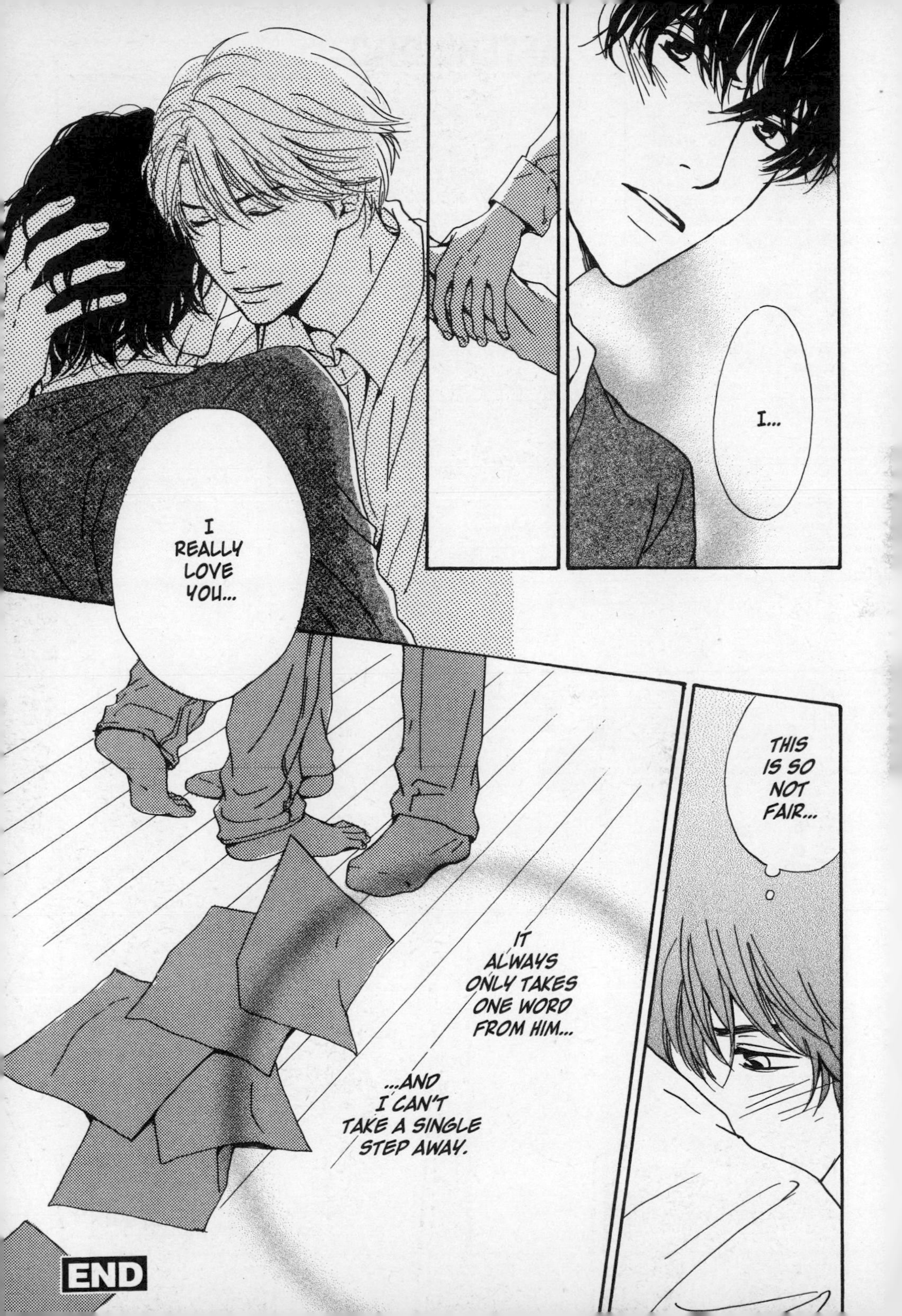
I...
I REALLY LOVE YOU...
THIS IS SO NOT FAIR...
IT ALWAYS ONLY TAKES ONE WORD FROM HIM...
...AND I CAN'T TAKE A SINGLE STEP AWAY.
END

AFTERWORD

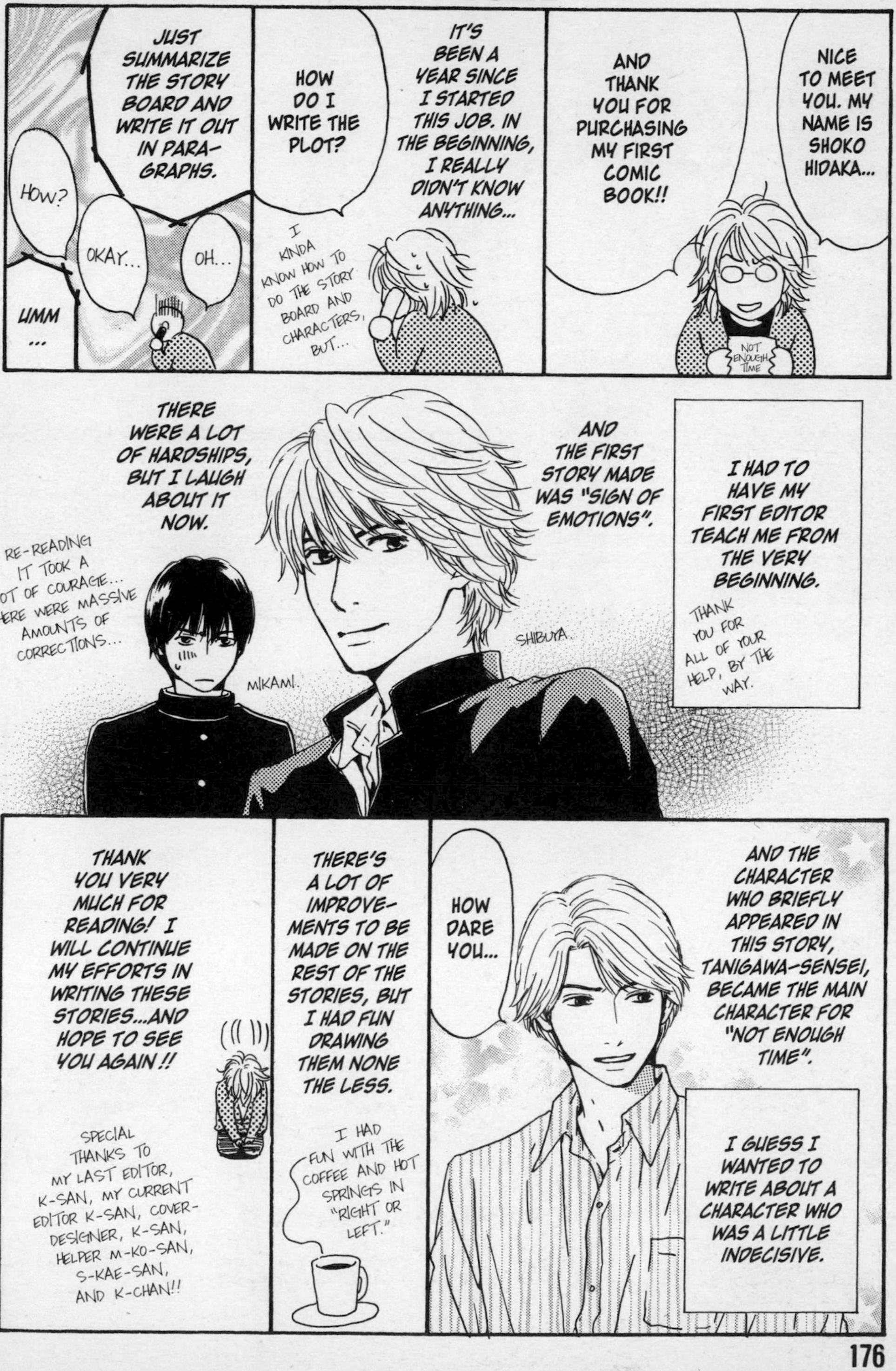

NICE TO MEET YOU. MY NAME IS SHOKO HIDAKA...
AND THANK YOU FOR PURCHASING MY FIRST COMIC BOOK!!
NOT ENOUGH TIME
IT'S BEEN A YEAR SINCE I STARTED THIS JOB. IN THE BEGINNING, I REALLY DIDN'T KNOW ANYTHING...
HOW DO I WRITE THE PLOT?
I KINDA KNOW HOW TO DO THE STORY BOARD AND CHARACTERS, BUT...
JUST SUMMARIZE THE STORY BOARD AND WRITE IT OUT IN PARA-GRAPHS.
OH...
OKAY...
HOW?
UMM ...
I HAD TO HAVE MY FIRST EDITOR TEACH ME FROM THE VERY BEGINNING.
THANK YOU FOR ALL OF YOUR HELP, BY THE WAY.
AND THE FIRST STORY MADE WAS "SIGN OF EMOTIONS".
SHIBUYA
THERE WERE A LOT OF HARDSHIPS, BUT I LAUGH ABOUT IT NOW.
RE-READING IT TOOK A LOT OF COURAGE... THERE WERE MASSIVE AMOUNTS OF CORRECTIONS...
MIKAMI
AND THE CHARACTER WHO BRIEFLY APPEARED IN THIS STORY, TANIGAWA-SENSEI, BECAME THE MAIN CHARACTER FOR "NOT ENOUGH TIME".
HOW DARE YOU...
I GUESS I WANTED TO WRITE ABOUT A CHARACTER WHO WAS A LITTLE INDECISIVE.
THERE'S A LOT OF IMPROVE-MENTS TO BE MADE ON THE REST OF THE STORIES, BUT I HAD FUN DRAWING THEM NONE THE LESS.
I HAD FUN WITH THE COFFEE AND HOT SPRINGS IN "RIGHT OR LEFT."
THANK YOU VERY MUCH FOR READING! I WILL CONTINUE MY EFFORTS IN WRITING THESE STORIES...AND HOPE TO SEE YOU AGAIN!!
SPECIAL THANKS TO MY LAST EDITOR, K-SAN, MY CURRENT EDITOR K-SAN, COVER-DESIGNER, K-SAN, HELPER M-KO-SAN, S-KAE-SAN, AND K-CHAN!!

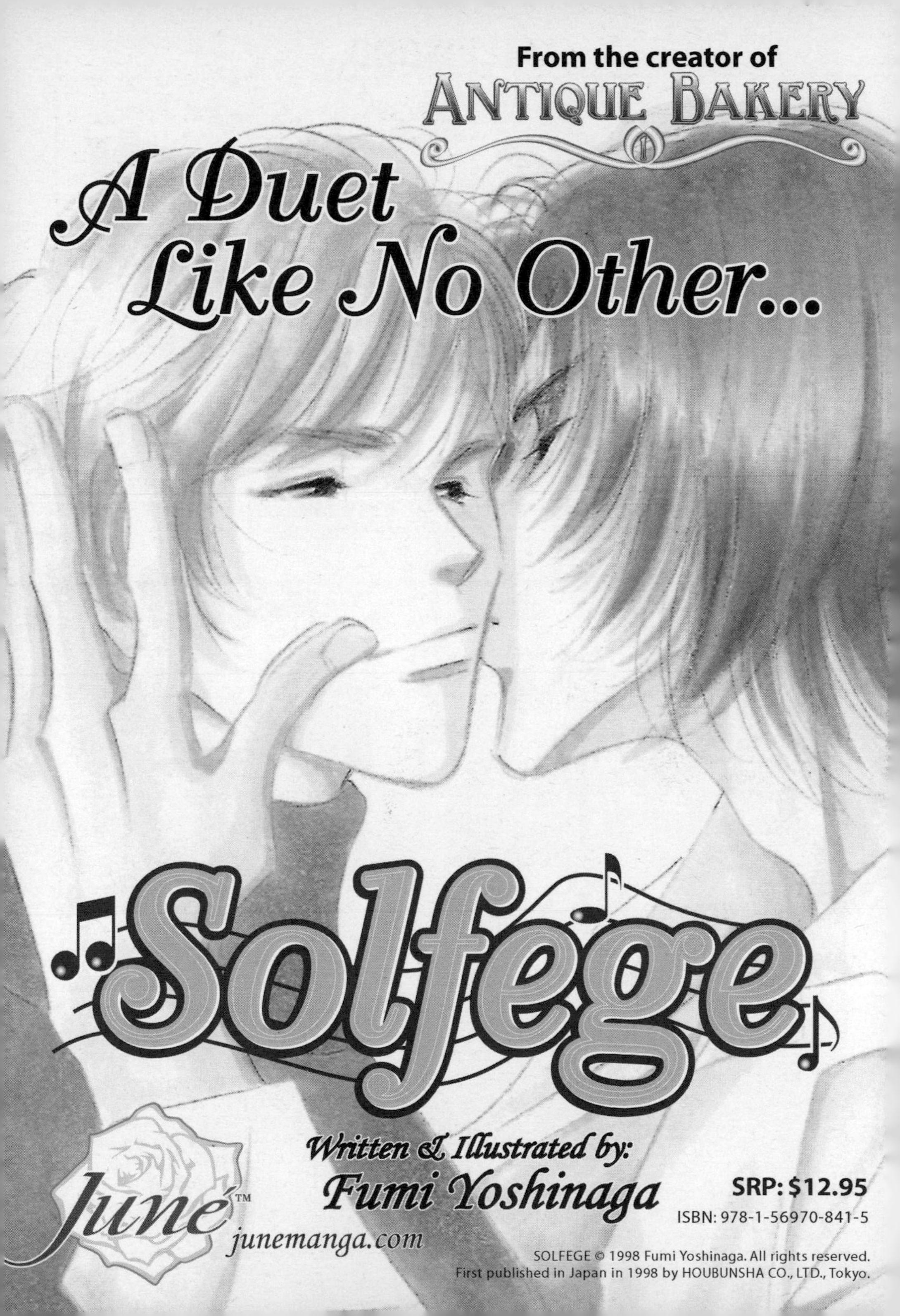
From the creator of
ANTIQUE BAKERY
A Duet Like No Other...
Solfege
Written & Illustrated by:
Fumi Yoshinaga
June™
junemanga.com
SRP: $12.95
ISBN: 978-1-56970-841-5
SOLFEGE © 1998 Fumi Yoshinaga. All rights reserved.
First published in Japan in 1998 by HOUBUNSHA CO., LTD., Tokyo.

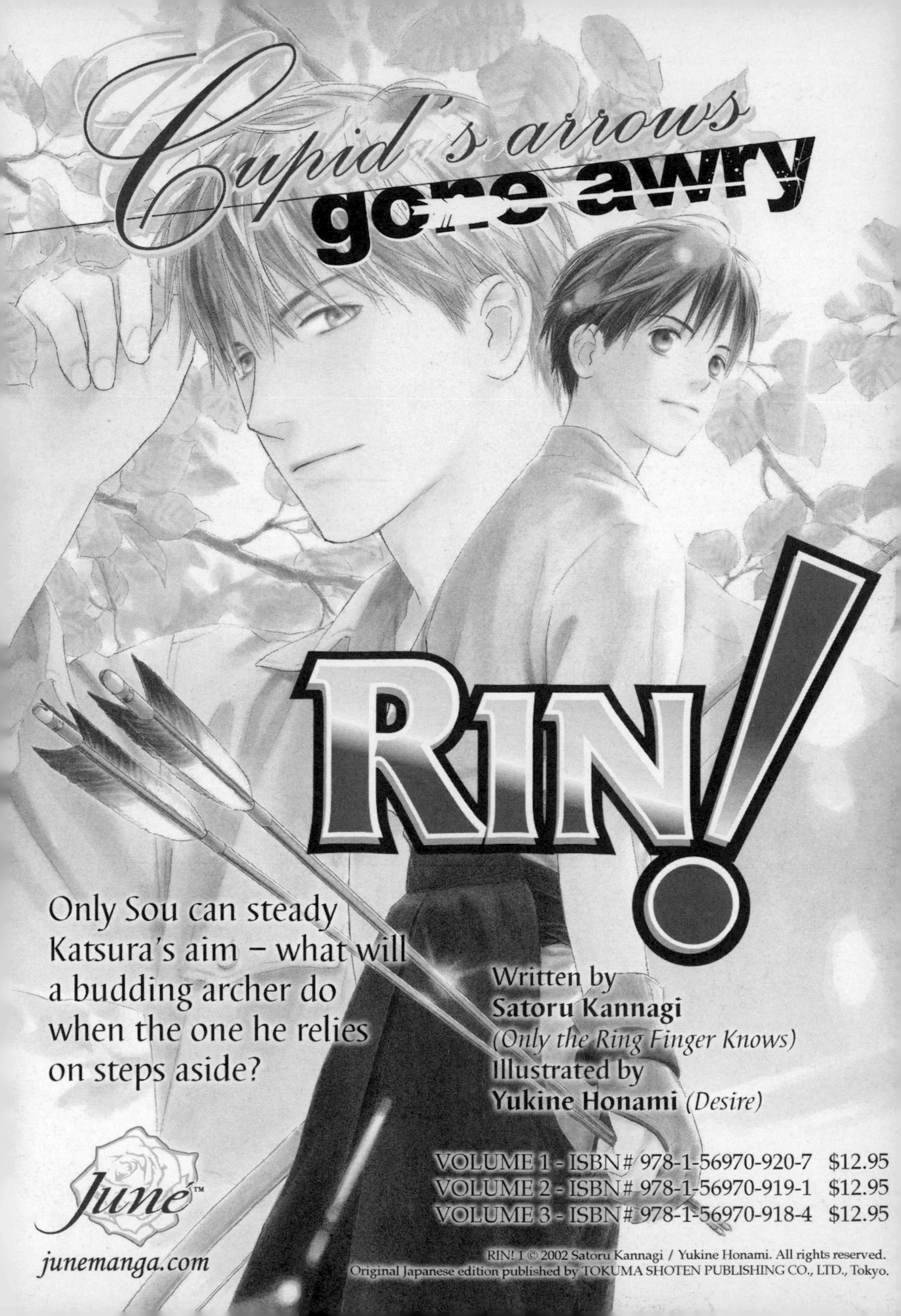
Cupid's arrows gone awry
RIN!
Only Sou can steady Katsura's aim – what will a budding archer do when the one he relies on steps aside?
Written by
Satoru Kannagi
(Only the Ring Finger Knows)
Illustrated by
Yukine Honami (Desire)
VOLUME 1 - ISBN# 978-1-56970-920-7 $12.95
VOLUME 2 - ISBN# 978-1-56970-919-1 $12.95
VOLUME 3 - ISBN# 978-1-56970-918-4 $12.95
June™
junemanga.com
RIN! 1 © 2002 Satoru Kannagi / Yukine Honami. All rights reserved.
Original Japanese edition published by TOKUMA SHOTEN PUBLISHING CO., LTD., Tokyo.

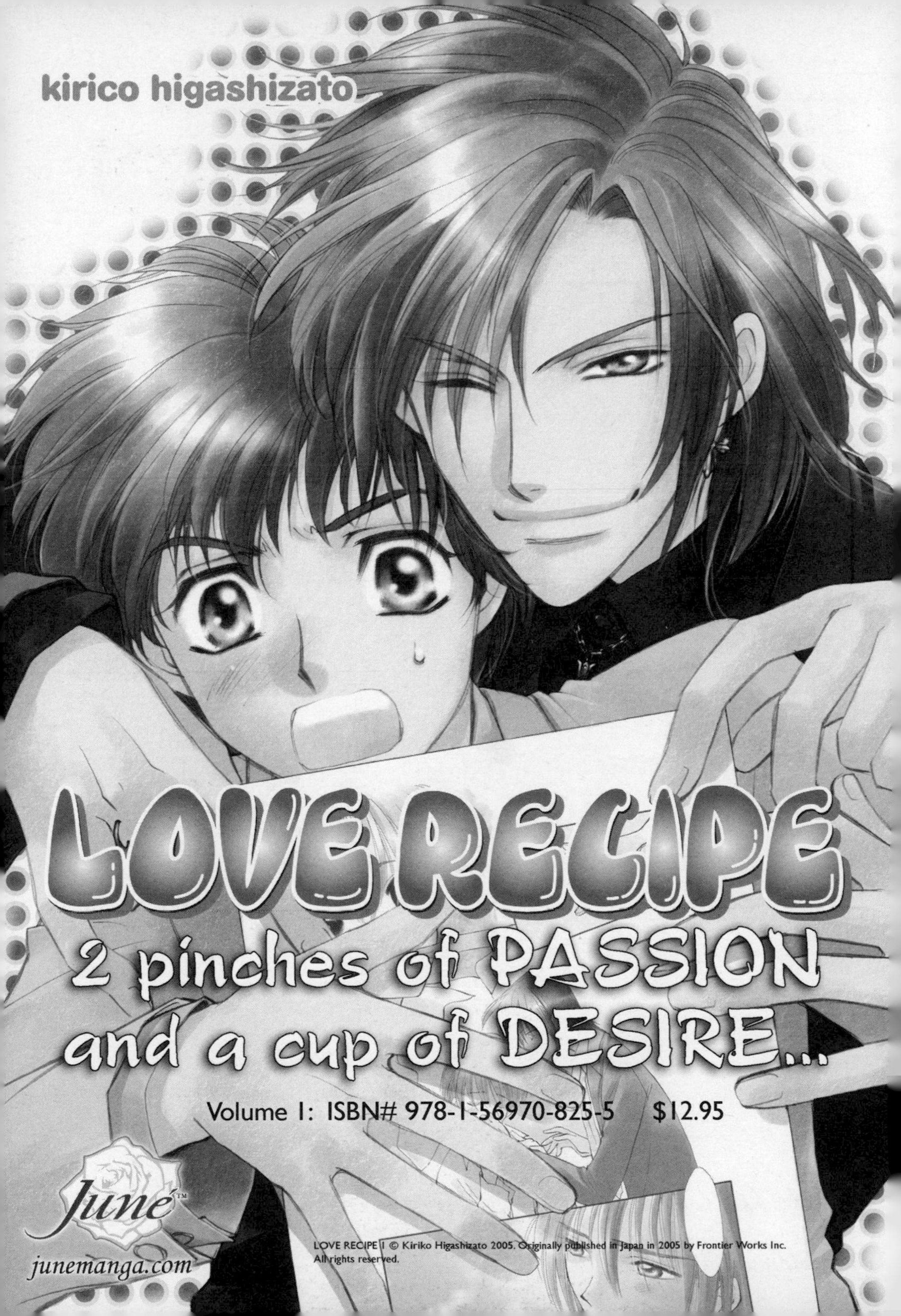
kirico higashizato
LOVE RECIPE
2 pinches of PASSION
and a cup of DESIRE...
Volume 1: ISBN# 978-1-56970-825-5 $12.95
June™
junemanga.com
LOVE RECIPE 1 © Kiriko Higashizato 2005. Originally published in Japan in 2005 by Frontier Works Inc.
All rights reserved.

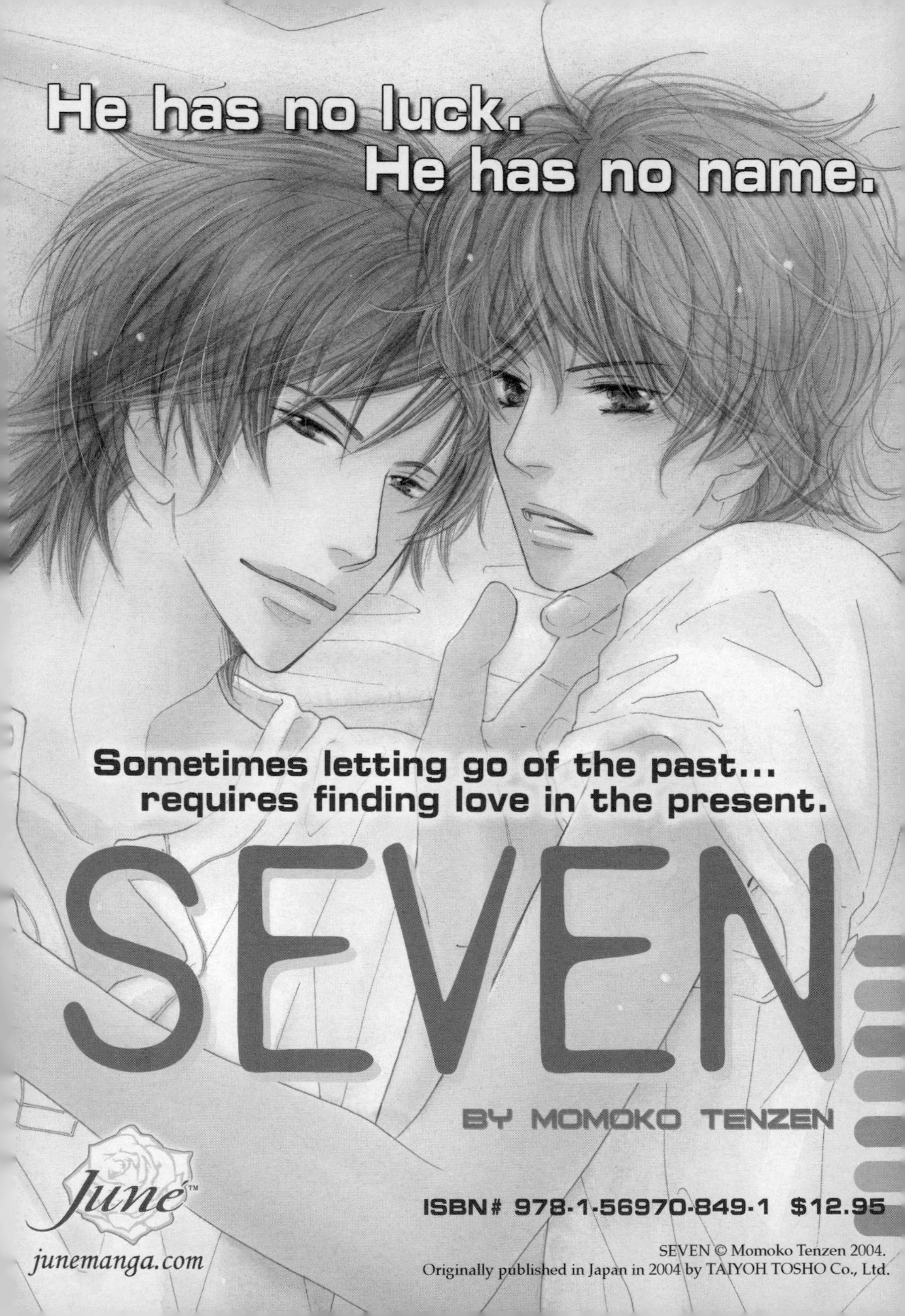
He has no luck.
He has no name.
Sometimes letting go of the past...
requires finding love in the present.
SEVEN
BY MOMOKO TENZEN
June™
junemanga.com
ISBN# 978-1-56970-849-1 $12.95
SEVEN © Momoko Tenzen 2004.
Originally published in Japan in 2004 by TAIYOH TOSHO Co., Ltd.

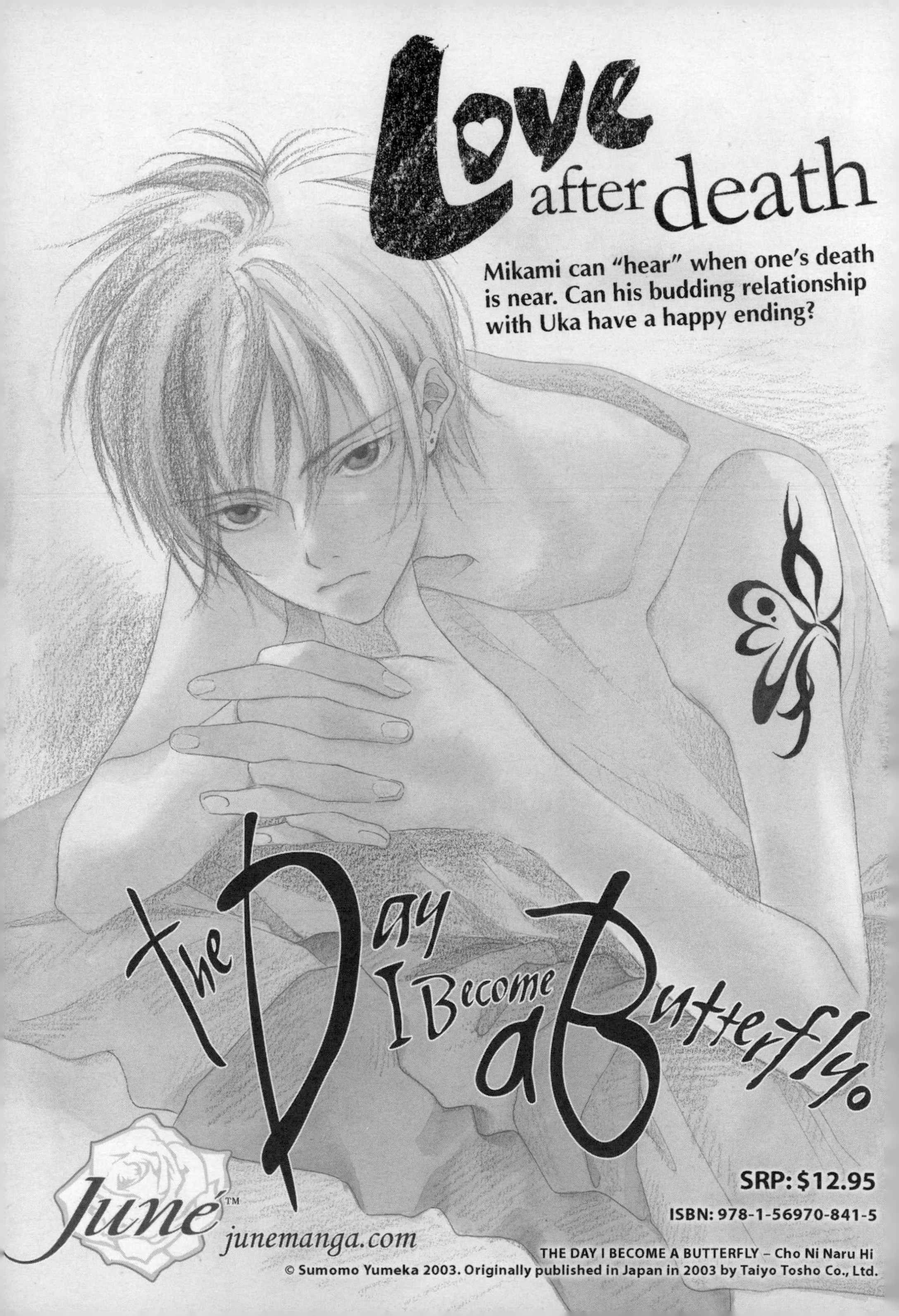
Love after death
Mikami can "hear" when one's death is near. Can his budding relationship with Uka have a happy ending?
The Day I Become a Butterfly
June™
junemanga.com
SRP: $12.95
ISBN: 978-1-56970-841-5
THE DAY I BECOME A BUTTERFLY – Cho Ni Naru Hi
© Sumomo Yumeka 2003. Originally published in Japan in 2003 by Taiyo Tosho Co., Ltd.

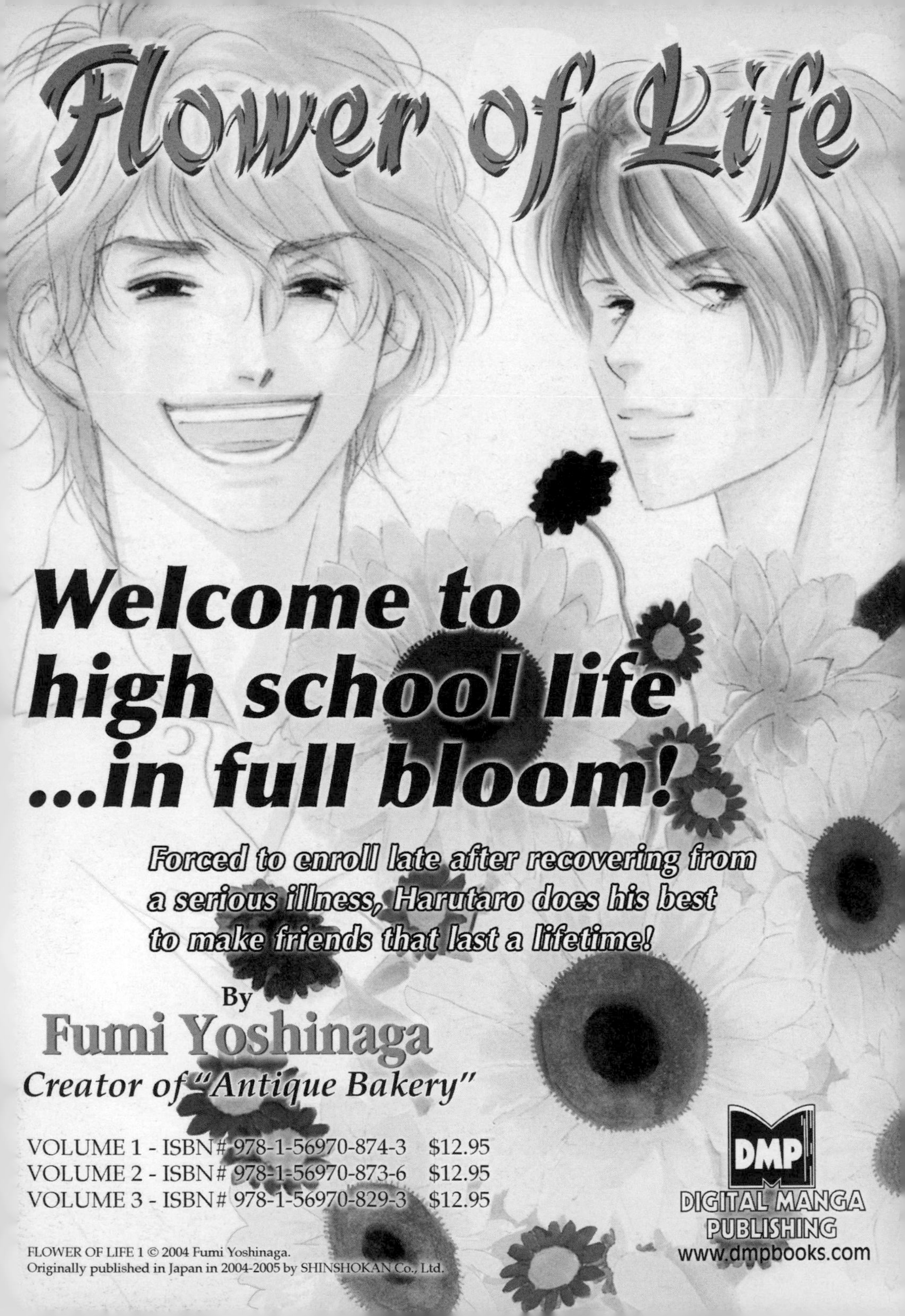
Flower of Life
Welcome to high school life ...in full bloom!
Forced to enroll late after recovering from a serious illness, Harutaro does his best to make friends that last a lifetime!
By
Fumi Yoshinaga
Creator of "Antique Bakery"
VOLUME 1 - ISBN# 978-1-56970-874-3 $12.95
VOLUME 2 - ISBN# 978-1-56970-873-6 $12.95
VOLUME 3 - ISBN# 978-1-56970-829-3 $12.95
DMP
DIGITAL MANGA PUBLISHING
www.dmpbooks.com
FLOWER OF LIFE 1 © 2004 Fumi Yoshinaga.
Originally published in Japan in 2004-2005 by SHINSHOKAN Co., Ltd.

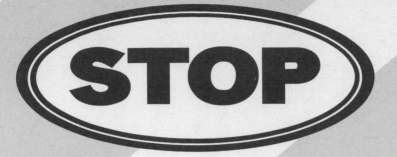

STOP

This is the back of the book! Start from the other side.

NATIVE MANGA readers read manga from *right to left*.

1
2
1
3
2
3
5
4
4
6
5
8
7
6

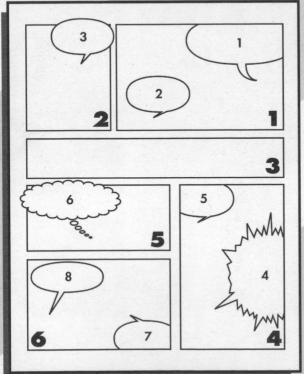

If you run into our ***Native Manga*** *logo on any of our books... you'll know that this manga is published in it's true original native Japanese right to left reading format, as it was intended. Turn to the other side of the book and start reading from right to left, top to bottom.*

Follow the diagram to see how its done.
Surf's Up!

NATIVE MANGA
READ RIGHT TO LEFT

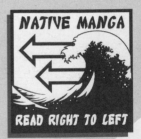